Myth and Authority

SUNY series in Contemporary Italian Philosophy

Silvia Benso and Brian Schroeder, editors

Myth and Authority

Giambattista Vico's Early Modern Critique
of Aristocratic Sovereignty

Alexander U. Bertland

Published by State University of New York Press, Albany

© 2022 State University of New York

All rights reserved

Printed in the United States of America

No part of this book may be used or reproduced in any manner whatsoever without written permission. No part of this book may be stored in a retrieval system or transmitted in any form or by any means including electronic, electrostatic, magnetic tape, mechanical, photocopying, recording, or otherwise without the prior permission in writing of the publisher.

For information, contact State University of New York Press, Albany, NY
www.sunypress.edu

Library of Congress Cataloging-in-Publication Data

Name: Bertland, Alexander U., author.
Title: Myth and authority : Giambattista Vico's early modern critique of aristocratic sovereignty / Alexander U. Bertland.
Description: Albany : State University of New York Press, [2022] | Series: SUNY series in Contemporary Italian Philosophy | Includes bibliographical references and index.
Identifiers: ISBN 9781438490199 (hardcover : alk. paper) | ISBN 9781438490212 (ebook) | ISBN 9781438490205 (pbk. : alk. paper)
Further information is available at the Library of Congress.

10 9 8 7 6 5 4 3 2 1

Ad Emanuela che ha sofferto molto mentre scrivevo

Contents

Acknowledgments	ix
Abbreviations and Use of Sources	xi
1. Approaching the *New Science*	1
2. Giambattista Vico: Early Modern Philosopher	41
3. Imaginative Universals	81
4. Feudalism	119
5. Secret Laws	153
6. The Roman Pantheon	193
7. Poetic Wisdom and Class Conflict	227
8. Is Vico Right?	273
Notes	293
Bibliography	319
Index	329

Acknowledgments

I would like to thank the Niagara University Research Council for their continued financial support for this project. I would also like to thank Richmond University for a grant to attend their Rome Fellows Symposium in 2019. I am deeply indebted to the staff of the Biblioteca Nazionale Centrale of Florence and of the Niagara University Library. I would especially like to thank Samantha Gust for her help with interlibrary loan. I also wish to express my gratitude to Giorgio A. Pinton, who gave me a large library of Vico texts to consult as I was writing.

My project could not have happened without the support of the Society for Italian Philosophy. This community has been a remarkable source of philosophical ideas as well as real fellowship. I would like to express my deep gratitude to Peter Carravetta, who helped me immeasurably with this project. I also would like to give special thanks to Silvia Benso, Brian Schroeder, Antonio Calcagno, Elvira Roncalli, Timothy Campbell, Pierre Lamarche, Steven DeCaroli, Robert T. Valgenti, Gaetano Chiurazzi, and Rita Šerpytytė. I have greatly benefited from my conversations with them and everyone in this group. In sadness, I would also thank Elena Pulcini and Remo Bodei, whom I met at the first SIP meeting but tragically could not be here to see the final product.

I have been thinking about Vico for quite some time, and I cannot thank everyone with whom I discussed his ideas. I would like to send special thanks to my teachers David Black and Donald Phillip Verene. The intense conversations I have had with Paolo Fabiani on Vico have been immensely valuable for me. I would like express special gratitude to Jennifer Murray, Arielle Saiber, Tanya Loughead, John Abromeit, George Trone, Harold Baillie, Ronald McKinney, John Schaeffer, Giulio Goria, Lee Rynski, Charlotte Thomas, Nancy duBois Marcus, and Thora Bayer for helping me think through Vico's ideas.

The process of writing is exceptionally difficult. I have had two guides who have given me the psychological and practical support I have needed to get through this project. Robert Babcock has helped me stay focused on what I want to accomplish with this project. Scott Campbell has talked me through many problems that have risen as I have worked through it. They have contributed more to this project that I could expect any friends to give. I would also like to send my gratitude to a variety of people who have helped me with the grueling process of learning Italian, especially Rita Bolzonella, Renata Vagaggini, Alberto Peruzzi, Jöelle Carota, Davide Salvo, Chiara Rosati, Stefano Monteleone, Ernesta McElvein, and Andrew Serio, everyone at the Centro Culturale Italiano di Buffalo, and anyone who had to hear my terrible American accent.

I thank my family for their help and endurance: Emanuela Pecchioli, Linda Bertland, John Bertland, and Aldo Pecchioli. I also appreciate the support of longtime friends who have given me inspiration throughout my academic development such as David Douglass, Cathy Toner, Harold Jenkins, Heather McEntarfer, Dan Potts, Camile Holmgren, Girish Shambu, Jacqueline DiFonzo, Eleanore Harrington, Jodi Hamann, Christine Galisdorfer, and Jared Reichman. I thank SomaFM for providing the soundtrack for this text. My Sugar gelateria in Florence provided much of the energy I needed for this project. Finally, I thank my two fencing clubs—Les Amis Fencing Club of Buffalo and Club Scherma Firenze—for allowing me to participate in a sport that dates back to Vico's time. They have taught me the importance of balance in so many different ways.

Abbreviations and Use of Sources

The focus of this work is the 1744 edition of the *New Science*. When I refer to the *New Science*, it will be to this edition. The 1725 and the 1730 editions are also worthy of study, and I will draw on them heavily at specific parts of this study. Since this particular study focuses on the account of poetic wisdom which Vico develops between the 1725 and 1730 editions, I am focusing on the final version published at his death. It is for purely stylistic reasons that I refer to the 1744 edition as the *New Science* so as not to repeat it each time.

When I cite the 1744 *New Science*, I will do it according to the standard paragraph numbers. These will appear in parentheses at the end of the reference or quotation. I used the Bergin and Fisch translation unless otherwise indicated. At times, Bergin and Fisch insert paragraph numbers into their translation for the purposes of cross-referencing. I have omitted those references. While I was working on this study, a new translation of the 1744 *New Science* by Jason Taylor and Robert Miner appeared from Yale University Press, but since I had already made substantial progress and was usually working with the Italian original, I did not consult it.

For these other works of Vico, the following abbreviations will be used.

AU *The Autobiography of Giambattista Vico*

AW *On the Most Ancient Wisdom of the Italians, Unearthed from the Origin of the Latin Language*

CJ *On the Constancy of the Jurisprudent*

NS25 The 1725 edition of the *New Science* by paragraph number

NS30   The 1730 edition of the *New Science* by page number
SM   *On the Study Methods of Our Time*

Other works of Vico will be referred to in the notes.

For the Italian and Latin editions of Vico's works, I mainly relied on Andrea Battistini's Mondadori edition.

Vico, Giambattista. *Opere.* 2 Volumes. Edited by Andrea Battistini. Milan: Arnoldo Mondadori Editore, 1990.

I also consulted the following editions of Vico's works.

Vico, Giambattista. "Allocuzione per le Nozze Regali di Carlo di Borbone." Translated and edited by Gian Galeazzo Visconti. *Bollettino del Centro di Studi Vichiani* 16 (1986): 243–292.
Vico, Giambattista. *Autobiografia.* Edited by Fausto Nicolini. Bologna: Società Editrice Il Mulino, 1992. This is a reprint by the Instituto Italiano per Gli Studi Storici. The original edition was published in 1947 by the Casa Editrice Valentino Bompiani, Milano.
Vico, Giambattista. *Opere.* Edited by Fausto Nicolini. Milan: Riccardo Ricciardi Editore, 1953.
Vico, Giambattista. *Opere giuridiche.* Edited by Paolo Cristofolini. Florence: C. Sansoni, 1974.
Vico, Giambattista. *La scienza nuova 1730.* Edited by Paolo Cristofolini and Manuela Sanna. Naples: Alfredo Guida Editore, 2004.

I used the following translations of Vico's works.

Vico, Giambattista. *The Autobiography of Giambattista Vico.* Translated by Max Harold Fisch and Thomas Goddard Bergin. Ithaca, NY: Cornell University Press, 1983.
Vico, Giambattista. *The Conspiracy of the Prince of Macchia and G. B. Vico.* Translated by Giorgio A. Pinton. Amsterdam: Rodopi, 2013.
Vico, Giambattista. "The Discovery of the True Dante." Translated by Christina M. Mazzoni. In *Critical Essays on Dante,* edited by Giuseppe Mazzotta, 258–260. Boston: G. K. Hall, 1991.
Vico, Giambattista. *The First New Science.* Edited and translated by Leon Pompa. Cambridge: Cambridge University Press, 2002.

Vico, Giambattista. "Giambattista Vico's 'Reprehension of the Metaphysics of René Descartes, Benedict Spinoza, and John Locke': An Addition to the *New Science*." Translated by Donald Phillip Verene. *New Vico Studies* 8 (1990): 2–18.

Vico, Giambattista. *The New Science of Giambattista Vico: Unabridged Translation of the Third Edition* (1744) *with the addition of the "Practice of the New Science."* Translated by Max Harold Fisch and Thomas Goddard Bergin. Ithaca, NY: Cornell University Press, 1986.

Vico, Giambattista. *On Humanistic Education (Six Inaugural Orations 1699–1707): From the Definitive Latin Text, Introduction and Notes of Gian Galeazzo Visconti*. Translated by Giorgio A. Pinton and Arthur W. Shippee. Ithaca, NY: Cornell University Press, 1993.

Vico, Giambattista. "On the Heroic Mind." Translated by Elizabeth Sewell and Anthony C. Sirignano. In *Vico and Contemporary Thought*, edited by Giorgio Tagliacozzo, Michael Mooney, and Donald Phillip Verene, 228–245. Atlantic Highlands, NJ: Humanities Press, 1976.

Vico, Giambattista. *On the Most Ancient Wisdom of the Italians Unearthed from the Origins of the Ancient Language Including the Disputation with the "Giornale de' letterati d'Italia."* Translated by L. M. Palmer. Ithaca, NY: Cornell University Press, 1988.

Vico, Giambattista. *On the Study Methods of Our Time*. Translated by Elio Gianturco. Ithaca, NY: Cornell University Press, 1990.

Vico, Giambattista. "Vico's Reply to the False Book Notice: The *Vici Vindiciae*." Translated by Donald Phillip Verene. *New Vico Studies* 24 (2006): 129–175.

In addition, I used Schaeffer's translation of Vico's *On Universal Law*. I used the version that appeared in the volumes of *New Vico Studies* before it was published as a collected volume.

Vico, Giambattista. "On the One Principle and One End of Universal Law." Translated by John D. Schaeffer. *New Vico Studies* 21 (2003).

Vico, Giambattista. "On the Constancy of the Jurisprudent (including *Notae*)." Translated by John D. Schaeffer. *New Vico Studies* 23 (2005).

Vico, Giambattista. "Dissertations [from the *Universal Law*]." Translated by John D. Schaeffer. *New Vico Studies* 24 (2006): 1–80.

I

Approaching the *New Science*

Giambattista Vico has been long regarded as a prominent figure in the history of Italian thought. His connection to Italian history, however, is a bit nebulous. He did not live during a particularly celebrated or especially infamous era in Italian history. He lived during the long period between the Renaissance and the Risorgimento when the Italian city states had lost their political influence and many had fallen under the direct control of foreign powers. While the peninsula produced notable works of art and science during this time, it does not capture the imagination as other periods in Italian history. Living in the province of Naples from 1668 to 1744, he was born into a Spanish colony, saw its ownership transfer to Austria after the War of Spanish Succession, and then saw it gain independence under Charles of Bourbon in 1734. More deeply and immediately, he witnessed the Neapolitan nobility entrench its power. While the central administrations of other regions were consolidating their power, the Neapolitan barons were solidifying their authority over their fiefs against the king. As a mercantile class grew in other parts of Europe, the Neapolitan middle class struggled to gain traction and evolve.[1] Politically and economically, Naples and Italy during Vico's lifetime were not at the forefront of what are now recognized as the major trends of European political and economic development. I wonder if this is part of the reason why he is often considered to be an outsider to the major trends in early modern thought. Had he written at the height of the Italian Renaissance like Machiavelli or during a turbulent period in the twentieth century like Antonio Gramsci, it might be easier to see how Vico's ideas connect to larger trends in Europe. As it is, Vico tends to be referred to as an innovator who thought about issues of anthropology, history, and interpretation long before others, but he is not studied as a voice among his contemporaries in the eighteenth century.

This study is an attempt to bring Vico into conversation with the more prominent early modern thinkers in Northern Europe. I use the term *early modern period* as it is used by historians of philosophy to describe the era between the end of the Thirty Years' War and the rise of Napoleon. It includes the Enlightenment and the Baroque period of Italian history. Philosophically, it runs from René Descartes and Thomas Hobbes to Immanuel Kant. I am not going to characterize Vico as an anti-Enlightenment outsider who critiqued mainstream ideas from afar. Instead, I will highlight his place within the prevailing European intellectual culture to show how he produced ingenious answers to the same problems that other authors were addressing. Throughout this study, I will identify philosophical problems addressed by prominent schools of thought during this period and show how Vico's ideas grow out of them. I hope that this will not only make the *New Science* more approachable to scholars of early modern thought but also will encourage them to consider Vico worthy of a place in conversations about the prominent issues of the period rather than a curious anachronism.

I will avoid pulling Vico out of his historical context. I will interpret his ideas though the lens of the distinct economic and political environment in which he lived. He had access to popular works of Northern Europe, since they generally circulated in Naples. My contention is that when one looks at the prevailing philosophical issues in Europe with the specific concerns of the Neapolitan community in mind, it is possible to develop a rich and full reading of his texts. This study will find in the *New Science* a possibility for an alternate pathway for considering the value of early modern philosophy. As commentators rethink what early modern philosophy means for our contemporary world, I hope that the voice of Vico and other thinkers of the Neapolitan Enlightenment can shed light on overlooked possibilities.

The starting point for this study is an insight proposed by Giuseppe Giarrizzo in his collection of essays entitled *Vico: la politica e la storia*. Vico's later works contain an extensive and detailed account of ancient Roman law and religion. One is tempted to wonder whether his systematic discussion accurately portrays Roman history. Giarrizzo avoids this question entirely. He argues that Vico's account has much more to say about the political situation in early modern Naples than ancient history.[2] Indeed, he is convinced that Vico's analysis of ancient Rome was motivated by a desire to understand contemporary political structures so that he could propose ideas for reform. He writes, "One should not forget, however, that the Vichian perspective is political and not social (concerned with anthropology [*primitivistica*]) and that his argument always moves from the present to the past and not vice versa."[3] This implies that Vico's interest in history was not primarily metaphysical or theoretical but was to find a way to improve Naples and Europe.

Vico tells the reader that he is thinking in these terms. He does not highlight this agenda as much as other ideas, but he does present it at the end of the *New Science*. As I will discuss, Vico's historical metaphysics proposes the existence of a cyclical ideal eternal history through which nations repeatedly pass. In accord with this, he suggests that after the fall of the Western Roman Empire, civilization fell into a barbaric state. When it rose again, the same laws that founded the original Roman civilization reappeared. Book 5 of the *New Science* is titled "The Recourse of Human Institutions which the Nations Take When They Rise Again," and it describes how the aristocratic institutions of early Rome appeared again in Europe (1056). He writes that, "in countless passages scattered throughout this work and dealing with countless matters, we have observed the marvelous correspondence between the first and the returned barbarism times" (1046). He is not just thinking about ancient civilizations as distant historical entities, but he is considering them in relationship to medieval and modern Europe. Importantly, he goes farther.

He actually tells the reader that it is easiest to understand the period after the fall of the Western Roman Empire, what he calls the second barbarism, by examining the birth of ancient Rome out of the first barbarism. He writes that by investigating the original rise of Roman civilization, "we shall bring more light to bear on the period of the second barbarism, which has remained darker than that of the first" (1046). He repeats this idea when he connects ideas of authority and ownership in early Rome to those in medieval Europe. He writes, "Upon this 'authority,' as upon numberless other institutions of the second barbarism, we throw light in this work from the antiquities of the first barbarism; so much more obscure have we found the times of the second than those of the first!" (1074). This may sound counterintuitive since one would expect events more chronologically proximate to be easier to grasp than more distant ones. Nevertheless, it was a common approach within the natural law tradition. Authors in that tradition were quite concerned that medieval laws were recorded in a corrupt way by scholars and church leaders who separated themselves from the cultures that produced them. The continued political influence of the church presented an obstacle for interpreting those records. To avoid contemporary bias, authors looked at ancient Roman law, since it was a clearer picture of feudal society.[4] Vico claims that because he lives in the civilization produced by the second barbarism, it is hard to see clearly how contemporary institutions grew out of it. By looking at the distant past, it becomes easier to conceive of the way civilizations manifest recurring trends.

Vico does not endorse Giarrizzo's point exactly. While he was very concerned about developing an objective method for his science, his Enlightenment perspective made him far more optimistic about his ability to understand Roman history than he had a right to be. Giarrizzo claims that the way to find value in Vico's ideas is to see them as depictions of his Naples rather than a description of Rome at all. Vico gives us no reason to think he would ever concede this much. Nevertheless, I am going to take his claim about his motivation for studying ancient Roman law as a cue to build an interpretation of the *New Science* as a discussion of modern Europe and, specifically, modern Naples.

Giarrizzo finds in Vico's works a valuable political agenda. He saw the possibility of evolving a just community in which people of all classes are treated fairly. He was also concerned, however, that a civilization would break apart if too much liberty were granted to any one class of people. So, he proposes that the goal of politics is to find a balance between the restrictive institutional bonds that hold civilizations together and the need to help a community evolve toward justice. Giarrizzo writes, "The work of the wise-prudent [*sapiente-prudente*] ruler is that of finding the equilibrium of justice between the rigid jurisprudence of the aristocratic regime and the looser jurisprudence of the monarchy."[5] The wise lawyer can grasp laws in their historical context and apply them in a way that serves justice at the expense of some of their traditional rigidity. In this light, Vico's writings become a critique of traditional laws in order to establish a just legislative system in Naples.

This study will try to give content to this political agenda. It will do so by examining a topic that Giarrizzo does not substantially address: poetic wisdom. Like a variety of twentieth-century commentators on Vico, Giarrizzo acknowledges that Vico's account of myth and language should fit into his political agenda, but he does not explore it. He writes, "the theories of language and heroic poetry, that ought to take on almost an autonomous level, are evidently developed to sustain a political argument and not vice versa, so also for his audacious proposals for a theory of myth."[6] He thus dismisses Vico's account of the Roman pantheon to focus specifically on Vico's account of universal law. My study will venture where Giarrizzo does not. It will establish the political significance of Vico's account of poetic wisdom by revealing it to contain a critique of the Neapolitan feudal aristocracy.

In my interpretation, Vico's account of poetic wisdom is an attempt to explain the history of Roman law and religion by exposing the underlying epistemological structure of the aristocratic minds that invented the pagan gods. Given Vico's stated objective, this mentality should have also produced the religion of the Middle Ages, and its rudiments should persist in the minds of the Neapolitan barons who continue to use those rituals to maintain their authority. Vico's discussion of the poetic wisdom critiques that mentality to help monarchs and lawyers better understand how aristocratic laws can be reformed. When a contemporary reader looks at Vico's fantastic and speculative account of the development of Roman religion, it certainly does not appear to be a discussion of the Neapolitan barons. Despite this, I argue that the better one understands the feudal institutions that dominated early modern Naples, the better one can see how his specific interpretations of myths fit those institutions.

For most of this chapter, I am going to outline some methodological concerns underlying this study. I will discuss what my approach to Vico's mythology will take seriously and what it will avoid. I will then discuss my strategy for developing a historically contextual reading of the *New Science* that still has philosophical value. In the third section, I will talk about Vico's own methodology to help think about how one should read his interpretation of the pagan gods. This will culminate in a discussion of the tension between Vico's metaphysical commitments and the idea that he is a political reformer. I hope that this will clear the way toward building a reading of the *New Science* as an examination of what is valuable about the ancient mentality and what calls for reform.

Before embarking on that, however, I would like to say some initial words about why this project might have philosophical value. I am portraying the *New Science* as an anti-baronial critique of the authoritarian structures of oligarchy. Is this a topic that contemporary political philosophy should be taking seriously as it considers the legacy of early modern thought? The current prevailing idea of early modern political philosophy centers on the development of social contract theory in thinkers such as Thomas Hobbes, John Locke, and Jean-Jacques Rousseau. In this framework, the primary concern is whether the people or a monarch or dictator should be the ultimate authority. Social contract theory argues that a government can only have legitimate power if it is granted by the people. A ruler must protect the rights of the people who grant that authority. This undercuts theories of divine right monarchy that hold that a central leader has an inherent right to decide how to rule. This tradition examines the history of institutions to identify when people's rights are adequately protected and when a monarch has become too powerful. In this context, political philosophy becomes an attempt to contrast the liberty given by democracy with the practical efficiency of a tyrant. In this paradigm, oligarchy is generally excluded. Vico makes one wonder whether the role of aristocracy is left too far outside of this discussion. Because the resistance to political evolution in Naples was coming from an aristocracy rather than a monarch, he developed an early modern philosophy that challenged the power of the aristocratic class.

A foundational argument in the *New Science* is that the first societies were neither democracies nor monarchies but oligarchies. I will examine this argument in detail later. Here, I draw attention to axiom LXXX, which states "Men come naturally to the feudal system [*ragione de' benefizi*] wherever they see a possibility of retaining in it or gaining from it a good and great share of utility, for such are the benefits [*benefizi*] which may be hoped for in social life" (260).[7] This axiom is central to this study. Vico's political philosophy holds that the real threat to modern civilization is the possibility of regression into feudalism and oligarchy. The threat may not literally be the possibility of a return to a system of fiefs and sharecroppers. It could mean that society regresses to the point that judicial and economic systems become an instrument for sustaining aristocratic privileges. If this is a concern that the contemporary world ought to take seriously, then perhaps the *New Science* may offer insight into it.

I want to point briefly to some examples that suggest democratic political systems in the West might be regressing to oligarchies. Particularly in the United States, Italy has a reputation for being a country that leans toward socialism. Yet, during his time as prime minister, Silvio Berlusconi oversaw the privatization of the Italian highway system, selling it to the private company Atlantia, which was a subsidiary of Benetton. In October of 2015, when Matteo Renzi served as prime minister, he privatized the Italian Post Office. Given that neither industry is particularly amenable to competition, this appears to be a case where the aristocrats have turned these services into revenue streams for their particular interests. It also extends the power of the aristocracy over the lower classes and removes their ability to have input. Once an industry is privatized, it is difficult for elected officials representing the people to supervise and restrain their activities.

In the United States, one can see a trend of business executives finding ways of removing consumer protections. During the late twentieth century, class action suits became popular as ways for consumers to force corporations to respond to their needs. In response to this, companies started including clauses in contracts that require parties to go to forced arbitration rather than civil court. Businesses have set up their own civil court system to adjudicate the complaints of consumers who have signed away their right to file claims in federal court. The United States Supreme Court ruled this to be constitutional in the case *American Express Co. v. Italian Colors Restaurant* (2013).[8] As a result, millions of citizens of the United States sign contracts waiving their right to civil lawsuits without realizing it. These are ways in which the aristocracy is not just building its wealth but is finding a way to get control over the decisions that affect the lives of common people.

These two examples do not in themselves demonstrate a general trend. Further, I do not mean to suggest that a collapse into oligarchy is the only thing that contemporary democracies need to be concerned about. Nevertheless, I wonder if it may be valuable to consider an alternate early modern paradigm that takes seriously the role feudalism has played in history and the possible danger of the return to oligarchy. I propose that Vico provided one such paradigm. As consumers in contemporary neoliberal economies come to worry more about the growing gap between the rich and poor, it may be productive to consider Vico's ideas within the legacy of early modern thought. Like Hobbes, Locke, and Rousseau, Vico was concerned about helping civilization advance to a point where everyone would be treated with justice and respect in a secure environment. Because he sought to understand the institutions and mentality of the aristocrats rather than monarchs, his answer may have insights the others have overlooked. I think this possibility invites us to take his *New Science* seriously. With this in mind, I turn to a discussion of how I will approach Vico's investigation of myth.

Ancient Pagan Religion and Problems of Interpretation

Giambattista Vico tells us that for most of his intellectual career he searched for the proper way to understand pagan mythology (34).[9] I will focus on the result of this journey as articulated in the 1744 *New Science*. His discussion of this topic is undoubtedly unusual to anyone coming to it for the first time. It does not read like other early modern texts that are now considered to be the bastions of this tradition. Despite its peculiar form, I maintain that his account is a serious philosophical investigation. In this section, I want to show how seriously Vico took this project as an initial justification for connecting it with his political philosophy.

Many authors who have examined Vico's account of poetic wisdom have provided great insights into it as an epistemological system and as a defense of the philosophical value of the imagination. Often, however, these commentators do not get into the details of Vico's seemingly incongruous portrayal of specific poetic characters. My study will not ignore the fine points of poetic wisdom. I argue that if one understands Neapolitan feudalism, it is possible to build a coherent reading of these poetic characters. Given how outlandish some of Vico's claims are to the contemporary reader, this may not seem possible. As one becomes aware of how strange feudal institutions were, one can see how his depiction of the Roman gods functions as a sensible response. Much of this study will be dedicated to connecting his depiction of the Roman pantheon with feudal institutions. Here, I want to show that Vico took his anthropological study of ancient Roman law seriously as a way to begin my justification for examining the specifics of Vico's depiction of poetic wisdom. I will not try to explain every detail Vico offers, and I will bracket certain aspects of his argument. Nevertheless, my goal is to enter the details of the poetic wisdom to see it not just as an explanation of mythical thought but as a political critique.

Like other early modern philosophers, Vico wanted to remove sources of error and bias from his science. His initial attempt to combine the study of ancient Roman law and religion was his largest work that was a set of three volumes collectively called *On Universal Law* that was published in 1721–1722. In the second volume, he claims that scholars have assumed that ancient poetic texts represent a special artistic style of writing that was used for special purposes. They thought that it was distinct from an ordinarily discursive language that people normally used. He claims this false assumption prevented them from realizing that early languages were entirely poetic and reflected typical means of communication in very ancient cultures (CJ 74). This meant that the search for the origin of language had to focus on onomatopoeia and singing rather than naming. This insight became very important in the 1730 *New Science*, where Vico argues that Homer's epics were not special works of art written by one person but were the product of a large oral tradition.

In the 1725 *New Science*, Vico explored the question of how the poetic epics became distorted over the centuries before calcifying into their current form. He identifies seven sources of textual corruption that separate them from their original cultural significance (NS25 23). For example, the reason why myths tend to include giant monsters is because people exaggerate when telling stories. So the giant monsters would have really been humans. Further, myths can change meanings as the significance of words in the myths evolve. Most importantly, as moral norms change, audiences expect different behaviors from heroes and their adversaries. Vico holds that as societies became more decadent, they would have wanted to see more licentious behavior from gods and heroes. Originally, however, they would have reflected a much more rigid morality (NS25 270–287). The specific examples he provides are often problematic. For example, he insists that the Latin word for gold originally signified wheat. This does not seem to be correct (NS25 280).[10] Nevertheless, his general concerns about textual corruption appear well founded.

In 1730, Vico published a substantially revised edition of the *New Science*. He spent the final years of his life revising this text, which was then republished in the year of his death. There, the major impediment for interpreting myths becomes psychological. Axiom II states, "It is another property of the human mind that whenever men can form no idea of distant and unknown things, they judge them by what is familiar and at hand" (122). This mental tendency leads to two problematic conceits. The conceit of nations causes one to assume that one's own nation was the first to invent all the institutions of civilization (125–126). This conceit blocks one of Vico's chief strategies for finding metaphysical truth in history. By using a cross-cultural analysis, he speculates that one can see how civilizations who have no contact with each other invent similar institutions such as religion and marriage. These independent but universal social inventions proves that they are an essential part of the course of history. If one focuses too much on showing that one civilization such as Greece or Rome created civilization first, one cannot see the universal course of history.[11] While this is important to Vico's thought, the other conceit is more significant for his theory of myth.

The conceit of scholars causes them to believe that "what they know is as old as the world" (127). This leads them to think that ancient authors sought the same erudite metaphysical or moral insights that contemporary philosophers seek. They suspect that because the earliest thinkers were unimpeded by modern culture and technology their minds could penetrate deeply into profound truths. This leads them to pore over ancient fables and stories in order to find philosophical insight. In the *New Science*, Vico rejects this approach to myth.

Vico identifies Plato and Francis Bacon as two of his most influential authors (AU 138–139). Nevertheless, he accuses them of falling victim to this conceit. It is not hard to find examples of these two authors interpreting ancient texts to find buried wisdom. In the *Symposium*, Plato has Socrates present his view of the metaphysical assent to love in the form of a myth related by the priestess Diotima. In 1609, Francis Bacon published *De sapientia veterum*, in which he found contemporary moral allegories in ancient myths. For example, he reads the story of Actaeon as a warning against prying, even accidentally, into a prince's secrets.[12] Actaeon's transformation into a stag represents the danger of being isolated from court life. The dogs killing and eating him represent the other servants of the prince taking advantage of the isolation. Both philosophers seem to think that the wisdom of ancient authors ought to be revered and studied. In response, Vico boldly asserts, "This discovery of the origins of poetry does away with the opinion of the matchless wisdom of the ancients, so ardently sought after from Plato to Bacon's *De sapientia veterum*." He announces that he will not excavate ancient texts to find ancient insights into philosophical truth or morality. Instead, in a manner consistent with what he said in the *Universal Law*, he will read these myths to understand the political institutions of ancient nations. He continues, "For the wisdom of the ancients was the vulgar wisdom of the lawgivers who founded the human race, not the esoteric wisdom of great and rare philosophers" (384). In his view, the ancients were indeed wise, but they were so because they could invent the rituals that were necessary to develop civilization and not because of their metaphysical insight. This establishes how and why Vico approaches ancient religion.

It is important to note that Vico himself had fallen prey to this conceit early in his career. In *On the Ancient Wisdom of the Italians*, Vico sought enduring metaphysical insights in the etymologies of ancient languages. His famous *verum-factum* principle was a product of this investigation.[13] He writes that because the words *verum* and *factum* were interchangeable in ancient Latin, it must be the case philosophically that one can know the truth only about what one makes (AW 45–47). Vico never abandons this idea entirely. By the time he starts writing the *Universal Law*, however, he emphasizes it much less and he stops using the ancient etymology as metaphysical evidence. He continues to do etymologies, but they are always to understand ancient Roman institutions and not philosophical truth. As Vico refined his approach, he became much more careful about his use of ancient texts.

As an example of how seriously Vico took the conceit of scholars, I turn to a passage where he discusses ancient symbolic writing. Before the discovery of the Rosetta Stone, it was tempting to look at Egyptian hieroglyphs as mystical inscriptions that lead to a magical truth. Vico realized that this was problematic. He specifically rejects the idea that Egyptian hieroglyphs had "the mystic meanings" (*i sensi mistici*) that the "learned" attributed to them (384).[14] He claims that this writing was suited to the audience to which they communicated. Since early languages communicated through signs and gestures, they developed a written language based on pictograms to communicate what was important to them. These were laws, descriptions of rituals, and records of heroic acts. Vico's hypothesis turned out to be basically correct with regard to the Egyptian language. Vico also foretells the discovery of the Mayan language. For most of the twentieth century, the investigation of the Mayan glyphs was stymied by the assumption that they were mystical objects for meditation. Only after much work and academic conflict was it revealed that they communicated religious fables, histories, and laws.[15] When Vico says something that anticipates later Western anthropological theories, I tend to attribute that to the fact that they write in the same tradition from the same set of assumptions. This particular anticipation shows that he recognized a tendency in modern scholars to seek mystical insights or ancient spirituality in ancient religions rather than see them in relation to political institutions. It also shows that he rejected the search for such spiritual meanings in mythic religions.

Despite these passages in Vico, the *New Science* cannot seem to shake its reputation for being a celebration of pagan spirituality. In chatting about Vico with others, I have encountered many who have assumed the *New Science* is a work of Renaissance astrology or romantic mysticism. As axiom II predicts, they have seen Vico's comments on the pagan gods and quickly associated him with familiar contemporary authors who sought spiritual metaphysical insights in ancient myths. This is understandable given both the pervasiveness of the twentieth-century desire to find common mythical traditions and the lack of research into the intellectual and political culture of the Neapolitan Enlightenment. Now that much more work has been done on early modern Naples, it is easier to see how Vico's discussion of poetic wisdom is a critique of the politics of ancient superstition similar to the projects of many other Enlightenment authors. To read the *New Science* in this way requires thinking about poetic wisdom as an analysis of the feudal politics of oligarchy rather than a work of spirituality.

The growth of Vico's search for interpretative errors contains a subtle but significant development. From the 1725 to the 1730 editions of the *New Science*, many details of Vico's account of myth do not change. Notably, his claim that thunder was the origin of language is present in the 1725 edition (NS25 104–105, 411). Nevertheless, the substance of his account changes. He now asserts that myths were produced by an alternate epistemological structure with a unique schema for conceptualization. In the first *New Science*, he had already seen the need for bracketing metaphysical reflection to understand ancient fables (NS25 314). In the 1730 edition, he sees that poetic wisdom is a completely separate mentality and emphasizes the need to avoid conceptual bias to enter into it. He used the term *imaginative universals* to identify the type of concept used by poetic wisdom. These universals are at the center of my study, and I dedicate chapter 3 to interpreting them. Before arriving there, I will continue to lay groundwork by further explaining my method and some of the limitations of my study.

There is good reason to think that Vico tried to use the best information available to build his position. It may not seem that way because the sources he uses are very unfamiliar to most contemporary readers. Nevertheless, he did use recent reports from the Americans and Asia.[16] His sources were limited, however, and despite a desire to do cross-cultural research, he did not have much evidence to work with and most of the *New Science* focuses solely on ancient Roman history. This makes his claims about his science's ability to find a truly universal pattern of history problematic.

It was common during the early modern period to search for universal patterns in history to explain the relationship between human nature, civil institutions, and natural law. Famously, social contract thinkers such as Thomas Hobbes, John Locke, and Jean-Jacques Rousseau speculated on the origin of civilization. David Hume wrote *The Natural History of Religion* to explain the origin of pagan religion.[17] Many other now less familiar authors like secular natural law theorist Samuel Pufendorf built theories based on speculative accounts of the first laws.[18] There was also an important tradition that debated the validity of feudal laws by speculating on the original political structures of ancient governments. François Hotman's work *Franco-Gallia* had a lasting impact on this tradition and other areas of early modern thought.[19] Vico's Neapolitan friend Gianvincenzo Gravina wrote *Del governo civile di Roma*, in which he traces the history of Rome from its origin to show that civilization functions better when the monarchy cooperates with the plebeians.[20] The fact that Vico centered his project on an account of the origin of civilization is indicative of his connection to larger trends in early modern thought.

From a postmodern perspective, however, this type of project is deeply problematic. It is apparent that any early modern attempt to understand the origin of civilization was merely a projection of their own interests and perspectives onto the past. This leads me to Giarrizzo's strategy of reading the account of Roman religion more as an account of the mentality of the Neapolitan barons than as an account of ancient Rome. I will then consider this as a critique of oligarchy that may have implications for understanding contemporary neoliberalism. I am not going to discuss whether Vico's account of myth or politics extends beyond early modern Europe and the contemporary situation in the West. Further, I will bracket any attempt to evaluate the universality of Vico's theory of myth as an account of cultural evolution. As I interpret the *New Science*, I will have to discuss it as an depiction of civilization's origin and the rise of ancient Rome, because that is the context in which Vico places it. This will be done in an effort to sort through and interpret the text. The philosophical question I want to raise will not be anthropological or archeological but will have to do with modern and contemporary manifestations of aristocratic authority.

Some may find this disappointing. Many come to the *New Science* out of a legitimate interest in pagan religion and ancient laws. Some may even come to the *New Science* to find metaphysical wisdom or even spirituality in very ancient religions. I wonder if this is a new manifestation of the conceit of scholars that could obscure the larger political message to be found in Vico's text. Contemporary Western thinkers have inherited a prevailing picture of mythical thought from twentieth-century academics and popular culture. This view probably has quite distant origins, but its immediate ancestors were the Romantic authors of the early nineteenth century. At the core of this pastoral view of mythical thought is the metaphysical idea that all things are unified into a type of world soul. Those living simple rural lives, unencumbered by technological or industrial responsibilities, can experience spiritual truth directly by working the land and engaging in pantheist rituals. This idea of pagan religion has probably always existed. Nevertheless, it became particularly prevalent in the twentieth century. It was popularly adopted by the countercultural movement of the 1960s. Psychoanalyst Carl Jung suggested that mythic symbols were evidence of archetypes in a collective unconscious. Authors such as Parker Tyler and Joseph Campbell found these archetypes in popular films.[21] Movies such as the highly popular *Avatar* have depicted inhabitants on another planet as defending this worldview against an invasion of humans bringing weapons and machinery to destroy the environment. There is much more that can be and has been said about the popular appeal of this view of myth. My concern is that this image of pagan religion could obscure the dimension of Vico's thought that I want to reveal.

I have no interest at all in making philosophical arguments against the pastoral view of mythical thought or pagan religion. I would encourage readers to remember, however, that Vico wrote well before the

Romantics brought their view of myth to prominence. More importantly, my reading of the *New Science* will portray it as a response to concerns that were much different from those that popularized the twentieth-century view of pagan religion. I do not want to impede anyone from using the *New Science* to inform a more contemporary view of pagan religion. Like Timothy Brennan, I do not think it is possible to produce authoritative readings of texts, and I certainly do not think my study will produce a definitive reading of the *New Science*.[22] Nevertheless, I want to open space for my reading by contrasting it with this prevailing twentieth-century idea of myth.

As the core of these philosophical theories of mythical thought was a desire to locate a communal connection that could bind people together in community and connect people to nature. An important place this was found was in the notion of *mana*.[23] This term is found everywhere in works on myth from the 1920s until the 1950s. It is a term taken from Polynesian religion that signified a magical force that animated and gave power to all substances. The existence of this term was reported by the Anglican priest Robert Henry Codrington. In the 1860s he had deeply immersed himself in the culture of the Melanesian people. He claimed mana was a substantive thing that rulers could acquire, have, and then use.[24] He described ways in which community leaders would tap into the energy of mana in some spiritual way to demonstrate their authority. When philosophers such as Mircea Eliade, Ernst Cassirer, and Lucien Lévy-Bruhl learned of this concept, they claimed that mana was at the core of a more basic distinction in pagan mentality between sacred and profane. At the earliest stages of mythical thought, mana represented the unified force that animates all things. Particularly for Cassirer, *mana* was the term that signified all experiences noticed by early mythical thinkers who were just beginning to formulate ideas and remember experiences.[25] Cassirer himself, of course, was quite concerned about possible negative uses of mythical thought. He expressed this in *The Myth of the State*, which was one of the first attempts to systematically demonstrate how the Nazis combined technology with mythical thought to launch their reign of terror.[26] Nevertheless, his epistemological account of mythical thought places mana at the center of a pantheist worldview that experiences the unity of thought.

Codrington's initial account of mana now appears highly problematic. His own desire to find magical unity in pagan mythology drove him to exaggerate the notion of mana. Recently, anthropologist Alexander Mawyer has shown that the term *mana* did not have any magical or ontological significance at all. It was simply a word that meant that something was strong or useful.[27] Twentieth-century philosophers and religious scholars jumped on this idea of mana because it seemed to give strength to the notion that the universe was connected through a magical force. Because of the impact this supposed discovery had in the intellectual community, the term appeared throughout popular culture and, especially, many video games. The anthropological evidence now, however, suggests that the term is not so mystical or so omnipresent as was once thought. Regardless of the debate over this term, my point is that there is no reason to go into the *New Science* looking for an early discovery of this notion of mana. Vico's culture had very different concerns from the ones that made this notion so appealing.

There are passages in the *New Science* that lend themselves to this magical and pantheistic view of mythical thought. The most prominent example of this is the repeated emphasis he places on a saying of Vergil: "Iovis omnia plena," or, as Bergin and Fisch translate it, "All things are full of Jove" (379, 490, 515). This reference to Jove connects it to his account of the birth of pagan religion. This phrase comes immediately from Vergil's *Eclogue* but, as Battistini points out, the passage in Vergil comes from the poet Aratus of Soli (315–240 BC).[28] His surviving work, the *Phenomena*, is an extended account of astronomy and the constellations. He opens it with a prayer to Zeus (using the Greek name), who is in all things. All of us are the offspring of Jove, who has put the heavens in motion so that plants can grow. He writes, "He [Zeus] tells what time the soil is best for the labour of the ox and for the mattock, and what time the seasons are favourable both for the planting of trees and for casting all manner of seeds."[29] Aratus's point is that it is possible to read natural signs to see when one ought to sow and reap. This presents an idea of Jove as a pantheistic mystical force that animated all things. One could quickly assume that Vico's use of the phrase indicates that this is his view of poetic thought.

A more careful reading of Vico's use reveals a different purpose. In the spirit of Aratus, he admits that the first people looked to natural phenomena to understand the commands of Jove. He writes, "The first men, who spoke by signs, naturally believed that lightning bolts and thunderclaps were signs made to them by Jove" (379). He makes two important caveats, however. First, he does not think that the first people responded to these commands in a philosophical or even spiritual way. He writes that only later did Plato understand this phrase of Vergil as signifying "the ether which penetrates and fills everything" (379). In his view, attributing a metaphysical reading of Vergil's saying to the first poets means falling into the conceit of scholars. The ability to have a metaphysical worldview would require a level of theoretical reasoning that the first poets could not have mustered (384). So, the first poets could not have experienced or understood Jove as a pantheistic world soul. Instead, they only responded to certain natural signs as if a person were communicating with them. In this view, poetic wisdom is not grounded in spiritual awareness or a mystical connection to a world soul but, instead, in responding to commands that they had unwittingly invented. The second caveat is that Vico tells us that directly that the primitive idea of Jove was false. He writes, "It is impossible that bodies should be minds, yet it was believed that the thundering sky was Jove" (383). Since the pagan religions lack a sound metaphysical basis, there is no reason to seek philosophical insight in these myths. Their significance, for Vico, is purely political.

Since the first poets thought of Jove as commanding like any other human would, it was possible for humans to imitate Jove and take on the role of the deity. Vico writes that Vergil's phrase "conferred human authority on those giants who had occupied the first vacant lands of the world, in the same sense of ownership" (490). Those poets who took possession of the first territories were able to command their followers as Jove did. Poetic wisdom is not about metaphysical truth but about systems of power and, ultimately, class dominance.

The pastoral view of myth obscures Vico's interest in the relationship of myth to class division. I speculate that the twentieth-century appeal of the collectivist view of myth was not so much that it was an alternative to technology but that it was a retreat from the growing wealth and power divide between the rich and poor. During this time, political systems such as communism and democracy were making bold claims about egalitarianism. Lived experience dictated, however, that the separation between the classes was not being overcome. While everyone could point to certain individuals who rose and fall in class status, class distinctions were not really going away. So certain individuals in the lower classes turned to a magical spirituality to escape their subordinate position while the upper class turned to it to deny the power they had over others. In this way, pagan religion became the egalitarian space from which one could deny social power structures. The *New Science* does the opposite. It uses myth to explain class division rather than find a time or place outside of it.

To speak directly, there are many religious and philosophical texts that discuss how it is possible to use myth to find spiritual wisdom. When one reads the whole *New Science*, one sees that very little if any of it is dedicated to the idea of a spiritual journey. It is primarily an attempt to find a metaphysical order in the history of class conflict. When commentators have focused on it as a discussion of mythical thought, they have largely overlooked what it has to say about class conflict. As a result, they have overlooked most of the content of Vico's presentation of poetic wisdom. This study will start from the idea that his account of poetic wisdom feeds into his anti-baronial political agenda. In this way, I will develop an interpretation that holds together the political and epistemological dimensions of his thought while finding value in his depiction of the Roman pantheon.

To end this section, I want to close with an alternate image of pagan religion that highlights what I find in Vico. I offer this as a counterpoint to the images offered by films like *Star Wars* or *Avatar* that emphasize a pantheist view of myth. Bong Joon-ho's 2019 film *Parasite* garnered much critical acclaim and many major awards. As contemporary society becomes more painfully aware of the deepening class divide, his film paints an intriguing microcosm of how class functions. The film upsets the common view of pagan ritual as the purview of the lower classes. Bong places mythical thought or at least astrology in the realm of the upper class, while the lower class concentrates on survival and pleasure. This matches my reading of Vico's account of poetic wisdom. In the *New Science*, the poets are able to found civilization because they can hear and respond to the commands of Jove. The late comers come under their command out of the desire for survival and to satisfy baser interests (18, 555). This is what plays out in the mansion depicted in *Parasite*.

The film opens in the basement apartment of the Kim family, who are quite poor. Two college age children, Ki Woo and Ki Jung, are searching the apartment for free wireless internet access. This is exemplary of the way poverty drives the family members to seek creative solutions to matters of survival. While the family is not necessarily good at restraining their own passions, they are able to find ingenious ways of manipulating the system in order to survive and fulfill their own desires. Their biggest project becomes faking their way into jobs to serve the upper-class Park family.

Bong does not reveal the father's profession, and the audience is left to assume that he has some high-paying corporate position. Instead, Bong emphasizes the way he dedicates himself to obeying the rules of propriety. He is particularly concerned that class boundaries are not violated. He focuses on obeying the rules of upper-class politeness and strictly prohibits himself from entering the world of the servants. He also punishes any of his servants who violate these rules. His worldview is constructed around self-discipline motivated by a desire to maintain his position in the upper class. The mother of the Park family obsesses over the social and educational development of her youngest son, Da Song. She turns to astrology and other unscientific methods in the hope that she can help him adjust. She channels her nervous energy into these rituals in a way that dominates her behavior despite their impracticality. The Kim family is able to exploit the superstitious tendencies of Mrs. Park and the rigidity of Mr. Park to scam their way into positions working for the family. The class conflict in the film depicts the adaptability of the Kim family against the self-discipline of the Park family.

Although this might not strike one as a movie about pagan religion, I suggest it depicts Vico's vision of poetic wisdom and class consciousness. As the film progresses, the Parks' inability to break out of their upper-class worldview becomes increasingly preposterous as it is revealed how detached their behaviors are from the world around them. Their worldview is constructed by a strict code of propriety and superstition that is fed by a desire to control themselves and distance themselves from others. While this code allows the rich family to have a sense of order and domination, it does not treat others with any sense of justice. It also turns out not to be a very practical way of organizing one's life and affairs. Vico's Naples was a city dominated by feudal lords who were also unable to adapt to changing situations. His account of poetic wisdom, in my reading, is an explanation of why this mentality was so strong and endured for so long. I think the Park family is a contemporary image of the barons that Vico hopes to critique.

The most famous work about myth in southern Italy is Carlo Levi's *Christ Stopped at Eboli*.[30] This work was based on the author's experiences while he was in exile in Basilicata in 1935–36. Besides showing the extreme poverty of the region, it suggests that the people in the region were following a pagan religion that was distinct from Christianity. This work reinforces the idea that pagan religion is for the lower classes. Vico, I will argue, can explain this manifestation of poetic wisdom. Even though it now seems counterintuitive, Vico depicts poetic wisdom as the mental structure of noble authority. This is at the core of my reading of the *New Science*.

Contextualizing Vico

Where did Vico sit chronologically? He was born in 1668, which was thirty-one years after the publication of René Descartes's *Discourse on*

*Method.*³¹ He died in 1744, the year the final version of the *New Science* was published. This was the same year that Jean-Jacques Rousseau served as secretary to the French ambassador to Venice, and it was just eleven years before the *Discourse on the Origin of Inequality* was published. Vico was twenty-two years younger than Gottfried Wilhelm Leibniz. He was seventeen years older than Bishop Berkeley, who published his *Three Dialogues between Hylas and Philonous* in 1713 and who outlived Vico by nine years. It is tempting to see all of these authors as living at the same time, but I think it is important to remember that Leibniz, Vico, and Rousseau really represent three different generations.

I have run across a few people who think of Vico as a Renaissance figure. There is, however, a substantial chronological gap between Vico and the Italian Renaissance. The 1744 *New Science* was published 232 years after Machiavelli wrote *The Prince* and 258 years after Pico della Mirandola wrote the *Oration on the Dignity of Man*. There was much intellectual activity in Naples in the interim. Giordano Bruno (1548–1600), Giambattista della Porta (d. 1615), and Tommaso Campanella (1568–1639) were all active during this time. Early modern thought arrived in Naples and the Accademia degli Investiganti was established in the middle of the seventeenth century by a group of intellectuals that included Tommaso Cornelio, Leonardo di Capua, and Francesco d'Andrea. Its goal was to promote the philosophy of Descartes and the new scientific method generally.³² The intellectual scene in Naples had evolved quite a bit since the Renaissance even if its political and economic system had not.

I have also run across people who think of Vico as a member of the Romantic movement. While his works influenced the Romantics, there was a substantial gap between his intellectual activity and that influence. It took a while for his works to be recognized outside of Naples and Venice. Martina Piperno's remarkable study, *Rebuilding Post-Revolutionary Italy: Leopardi and Vico's 'New Science,'* traces the influence Vico had on Italy at the end of the eighteenth century through the Risorgimento. She discusses the way his ideas were promoted by Vincenzo Cuoco (1770–1823), who made him a symbol of Italian thought. She then shows how Vico's theory of poetry influenced Giacomo Leopardi, Ugo Foscolo, and others working in Italy.³³ Outside of Italy, Melchiorre Cesarotti (1730–1808) was largely responsible for bringing attention to Vico's theory of poetry. In 1795, Frederick August Wolf published the *Prolegomena ad Homerum*, in which he argued that Homer was not one author but an oral tradition. Because Vico's texts were not heavily circulated, Wolf did not realize that the *New Science* had made this argument much earlier. It was not until 1807 that Cesarotti demonstrated to Wolf that Vico had first held this position.[34] It was at this point that Romantics like Samuel Taylor Coleridge were influenced by Vico's writings.[35]

I present this chronology to emphasize the chronological distance between Vico and the Renaissance and Romantic movements. This highlights his place in the early modern period, which thought of the Renaissance as a distant memory and had yet to anticipate substantially the Romantics. The next question is, where did Vico sit geographically?

In his *Autobiography*, he never mentions traveling outside the province of Naples. Nevertheless, the major works of seventeenth-century philosophy made it to Naples despite the inquisition.[36] More importantly, Naples was a center of Enlightenment thought. If there was an upside to the feudal control of Naples and the absence of commerce, it was that the study of law became the main road to the middle class. A large number of law students became interested in philosophy and science. While the Neapolitan Enlightenment is not nearly as famous as the Scottish Enlightenment, it did not lack for intellectual talent. The poetic theory of Gianvincenzo Gravina (1664–1718) actually had more influence in Europe in the eighteenth century than Vico. Pietro Giannone (1676–1748) wrote an important history of Naples that was highly critical of church influence.

While Vico did not gain the European attention he had hoped for, he was considered a prominent thinker in Naples, as demonstrated by the interest his works generated. In 1744, Damiano Romano published *L'origine della giurisprudenza romana contro alla moderna opinione del Signor D. Gio. Battista Vico* in which he took issue with Vico's claim, among other things, that Roman law developed independently of the Twelve Tables of Athens.[37] Koen Stapelboeck discusses how Vico had an influence on the Neapolitan debate about the value of commerce through the writings of Carlantonio Broggia, who defended his traditional view. Ferdinando Galiani published his early work *Della moneta* in 1751 as a response to Broggia.[38] In 1768, G. F. Finetti published a work defending the Roman Catholic view of the origin of humanity against Vico's account of the state of nature and the pagan origin of religion.[39] Vico was ingrained in the intellectual culture of Naples in the eighteenth century.

The Neapolitan Enlightenment also produced a number of important thinkers in the generation after Vico. Antonio Genovesi (1713–1769) taught the first ever university course in political economics at the University of Naples in 1754.[40] In 1780, Gaetano Filangieri (1753–1788) started publishing *The Science of Legislation*, which included an extended critique of the feudal rule that was hampering Naples. His work acquired a good deal of international attention. Before his early death, Filangieri entered into a correspondence with Benjamin Franklin.[41] G. M. Galanti was a pioneer in geographical research who did important economic surveys of the rural areas of the province of Naples.[42] One could add to this the advancements in archeology that were being made in conjunction with the research being done at Pompeii.[43] Despite the political and economic problems in the province, the eighteenth century was a period of profound intellectual activity in Naples. Fortunately, more scholarly attention is being paid to this period.

My study will try to read the *New Science* as a product of this time and place. A recent essay by Christina Mercer helps to explain my approach.[44] She argues that during the 1960s and '70s the study of early modern philosophy was dominated by the method of radical reconstruction. This approach held that the best way to find philosophical value in a text is to appropriate the ideas of early modern philosophers regardless of the context in which they were written. Commentators during this time would not necessarily ignore all historical evidence, but their objective was to find relevant ideas regardless of whether the philosopher could have recognized their meaning. Recent writers on Vico have shown that this approach was particularly damaging to understanding his works.[45]

Mercer argues that in the 1980s a silent revolution moved the study of early modern thought toward a contextualist approach. She characterizes this in terms of the "Getting Things Right Constraint." She defines this as that "historians of philosophy should not attribute claims or ideas to historical figures without concern for whether or not they are ones the figures would recognize as their own."[46] This criterion does not call for the discovery of definitive readings based on clear authorial intentions. Nevertheless, one does have to study the context enough to know whether or not the philosopher could have actually held a position. One needs to look at the arguments that were circulating and the political situation to see if a view was something the philosopher could have recognized. This means I am going to bracket a number of topics that are often associated with Vico that I do not think he would have recognized. I am not interested in impeding others from using Vico's ideas in discussions about these topics. Nevertheless, in an effort to build a reading of the entire *New Science*, I will follow Mercer's methodology by trying to hold onto topics I think Vico could have seen. I want to underline three contemporary debates into which Vico is often drawn that I do not think he would have considered.

First, I am going to bracket the twentieth-century debate about the necessity of foundational myths for developing or preserving community.[47]

While Vico sees myth as essential to the founding of nations, he does not appear concerned with the question of whether those myths need to be maintained to sustain a nation in the human age. He is certainly concerned that political institutions maintain their influence to keep a civilization from falling into selfish decadence, and he holds that rhetoric has a role in preventing this. I do not find him to be concerned with whether specific mythical images or historical narratives are essential to this process. At least, he does not address it as it was debated by twentieth-century authors who argued about the need to defend or undermine national symbols.

Second, I am also not going to explore Vico's works to find an anti-Cartesian or anti-Enlightenment agenda. While he certainly makes arguments against Descartes, I will not use them in the context of the twentieth-century debate between scientific positivism and the philosophical value of art and the imagination. Instead, I will think of Vico as part of a general movement away from theoretical approaches to natural science and toward more empirical ones. The group of theoretical authors who are commonly labeled by us as rationalists worked primarily in the seventeenth century. They emphasized the importance of innate ideas as a foundation for knowing truth. By the end of that century, a counter-movement including John Locke questioned their reliance on purely abstract mathematics. By the middle of the eighteenth century, science had become primarily an experimental endeavor. The French encyclopedists, among others, emphasized the importance of physical evidence, observation, and experimentation. I will portray Vico as part of this trend from one type of science to another. I do not think his early attacks on Descartes made him anti-Enlightenment. Rather, they were a sign of the way the development of his thought flowed with the major intellectual trend of the eighteenth century.

Finally, I am also not going to consider Vico as the first historicist. Many authors have thought of Vico in this way. In *Between Past and Future*, Hannah Arendt describes him as "the father of modern history."[48] She praises him for recognizing that there is a coherence to the realm of human making that is both separate from nature and also philosophically valuable. For her, this is a positive development. Cardinal Joseph Ratzinger identifies Vico as representative of the turning point where Western thought shifted from the search for metaphysical truth to placing humanity at the center of the universe.[49] He recognizes that Vico himself had limited influence but claims he represented a greater trend toward a more humanist idea of truth. He laments the way that this leads to skepticism. Ratzinger draws this image from the *verum-factum* principle. This historicist portrayal of Vico is highly prevalent. When one takes this approach to Vico, however, one obscures his Platonic and Enlightenment commitment to truth.

When the *verum-factum* principle is examined in the *Ancient Wisdom*, one sees that it is actually an argument opposing skepticism rather than defending it. He maintains that it is always possible for a human to know substantial truth about human making. He always thought of this truth as metaphysical and universal (AW 53–56). It is part of the emphasis Vico places on the universal structure of history. Whether or not Vico was the turning point at which Western thought moved toward humanist historicism, his dedication to metaphysics indicates to me that he would not have recognized his science as historicist.

In bracketing these three approaches to Vico and focusing on what would have interested him, I believe I am opening the possibility for a new and contemporary reading of his work. I do not deny that my own context is influencing this reading. One could say that I am turning Vico's account of poetic wisdom into a critique of institutional authority that is framed by some of the same methodological assumptions as contemporary accounts of biopower. This is probably correct. Nevertheless, I do not claim, nor do I think Mercer claims, that the "getting things right" approach leads to hermeneutic objectivity. I have no doubt that the future will bring other readings of Vico. I do think it provides a way to develop a rich interpretation of his work that does justice to its complexity. It is easy to praise Vico for his defense of myth or condemn him for his support of radical historicism if one does not get into the substance of his ideas. By taking his context seriously, I believe one can find deeper and more challenging ideas in the details of his science.

One of the most intriguing aspects of Mercer's essay is that she calls for plurality within the contextual approach. She acknowledges that commentators bring different skills to early modern texts such as careful philological analysis, philosophical critique and aesthetic interpretation.[50] She encourages authors to be aware of their particular skills. She writes, "In order to maximize our understanding of early modern philosophical materials, proper care needs to be taken to identify and navigate the contextualist materials relevant to our projects. The trick is to match the project to our skills."[51] She comments, though, that the contextual approach means that most projects require a range of skills. Most authors are not versed in all of them. Nevertheless, if they are aware of their limitations, the greater philosophical conversation can move forward in enriching ways.

My training is in the history of philosophy, but much more from the perspective of philosophy rather than history. I am deeply appreciative of historians who have helped me understand the intellectual and political culture in which Vico worked. My contextualist approach to the *New Science* is going to prioritize philosophical ideas and head toward the goal of bringing Vico into further contemporary conversations about political philosophy. As mentioned above, I do not present this as the only way of reading the *New Science*. One of the most inspiring aspects of Mercer's essay, however, is that she takes seriously the need to work to get things right while still acknowledging that different authors can develop different valuable perspectives. I sincerely hope this study can contribute to a growing conversation about Vico rather than close off other possible ways of reading the work.

The idea of looking deeper into Vico's intellectual context is obviously not new. Despite the prevailing twentieth-century trend to portray him as isolated, a number of scholars worked to explicate his context. Here I will point to some important examples. In his seminal *Introduzione a G. B. Vico* published in 1961, Nicola Badaloni painted a careful portrait of the intellectual culture of Vico's Naples. He traced how the members of the Accademia degli Investiganti, such as Tommaso Cornelio and Leonardo di Capua, transmitted scientific ideas from Northern Europe into Naples and set the agenda for debates about science in Neapolitan culture.[52] He also discusses how the *luminosi* or philosophers of light such as Gianvincenzo Gravina influenced debates in that community.[53] In the essay "Chi sono i contemporanei di Vico?" Paolo Rossi identifies a variety of sources about ancient religion and the origin of society that Vico may or may not have had at his disposal. He identifies the few eighteenth-century authors Vico does discuss. This provides important context for Vico's understanding of ancient Roman religion, among other issues.[54] Further, Andrea Battistini traced the way early modern debates about rhetoric, poetry, and the imagination influenced Vico's ideas. He opens his work *Vico tra antichi e moderni* with a chapter discussing how early eighteenth-century Naples was concerned about the possibility of finding universal and historical truth and the way it felt attacked by libertines who denied the value of cultural institutions. Battistini highlights how Vico's works defend the search for universal truth against these influences.[55] These are some examples of important scholarly work that has been done to put Vico into context.

My project will draw on these sources, but I am not going to spend much time tracing specific historical connections between Vico and his predecessors. I am more interested in situating Vico in his general intellectual and cultural context. Two recent works have been quite influential to my work in this regard.

In *La filosofia dell'immaginazione in Vico e Malebranche*, Paolo Fabiani reconsiders the Cartesian thought of Malebranche and then shows how Vico's works may be read as a development of his thought. Particularly in the United States, Malebranche has been regarded as a secondary figure in the rationalist movement who is known primarily for his occasionalist explanation of the relationship of God to the universe. Fabiani highlights Malebranche's concern with the origin of falsehood and superstition.

Like other early modern thinkers, Malebranche wanted to find ways to reduce sources of error, but he took this concern to the point where he developed an account of pagan civilization. Making a distinction similar to Vico's between pagan and Christian society, Malebranche claims that without the insight of God, the pagans needed to build a community based on corporeal needs. This means that pagan society was always in conflict because its people will always fight over those goods which cannot be divided.[56] It also means that social bonds for them always depend on the relationship of the mind and body as understood through the imagination. Pagan communities are built as the imagination forms connections between bodily needs and relations to other people. Specifically, the imagination learns how to fulfill individual wants by imitating others in the community. As Fabiani explains, this dependence on imitation limits the ability of people to form connections based on truth because they can only imitate physical activity without seeing the motivation behind it.[57] As a result, pagan society can only be based upon the falsehoods of *amour propre* (*amor proprio*).[58] From there, Malebranche developed a theory of rhetoric and social communication based on his theory of the mimetic imagination.[59]

Fabiani then shows how Vico's account of pagan mythology echoes Malbranche's ideas. He discusses the way in which Vico's account of poetic wisdom uses a similar account of mimesis and bodily imagination to develop an account of ancient Roman politics. I find Fabiani's work valuable because it connects Vico to a larger Enlightenment trend that sought to critique pagan epistemology. Because Vico holds that poetic wisdom was necessary for the establishment of early civilizations, he had to defend its historical value as well as the importance of studying it. From there, it is easy for the contemporary reader to assume his overall view of poetic wisdom was positive. When Vico is put into conversation with Malebranche, however, his critical attitude to ancient myth becomes clearer. Vico tells the reader directly that poetic wisdom was harsh and cruel, and he often reminds the reader that it would be problematic for contemporary nations to live under those laws. Fabiani's work invites the reader to look at the *New Science* more as a critique of mythical thought than as a mentality to politically engage.

Another recent work that has rethought Vico's intellectual and cultural context is Barbara Ann Naddeo's *Vico and Naples: The Urban Origins of Modern Social Theory*. She acknowledges that Vico buried his political theory within his text. Undaunted, she enters into his early works on history and jurisprudence to find it. She develops her interpretation around the fact that new forms of urbanization had developed. Her thesis is that "Vico therewith employed old concepts to the novel ends of diagnosing and accounting for the atypical behavior of new metropolitan groups, whose innate desires and goals he would grant the quality of finality, or teleology in his subsequent work."[60] Naddeo recognizes that urbanization had created new theoretical problems that were of great interest to the authors in Naples. While recent work has been done on urbanization in early modern thought in general and specifically in Naples, Naddeo is the first commentator to find this concern driving Vico's thought. Her work is an example of how deepening our understanding of the context of early modern thought can open up new dimensions on Vico's works.

Naddeo carefully analyzes the way Vico's historical account of the *Conspiracy of the Prince of Macchia* portrays social unrest as evidence that the old orders of Naples and the old idea of the Popolo was being replaced by class divisions drawn along economic lines.[61] Not only were institutions changing but so were ideas of class and rights. She connects this development to Vico's discussion of universal law. She reads his Roman legal history such that it does not just document the way political institutions had changed, as past authors had done, but instead shows how ideas about rights evolved over the course of Roman history. Unlike Livy's history, she writes, "for Vico, each legal regime inflected and institutionalized the new nature of the relationship among the patrons and clients of Rome."[62] Each new manifestation of this relationship brought with it new laws and rights. In *On Universal Law*, Roman history serves as a prescriptive account as to how the judiciary in modern Naples can work to improve the rights of the citizens and the stability of the city.[63] By looking at Vico's account of social theory based on urbanization, Naddeo reveals this practical dimension to Vico's thought.

In Naddeo's account, the 1725 *New Science* loses some of this prescriptive dimension. Vico gets so enamored with using the history of Rome as a basis for a universal history that the political agenda of his work fades. She writes, "the exemplarity of Rome in the *Scienza Nuova* invoked a brand of cosmopolitanism that curiously wanted a vocation:

it was a call to legal theory without praxis."⁶⁴ She then ends her study without moving forward to the 1744 *New Science*.⁶⁵ Her study is quite an accomplishment. It shows how Vico's apparently non-political stance does come out of a prescriptive political agenda even if it is hard to find. I will build on this political agenda that Naddeo finds in Vico, but my focus will be on his account of poetic wisdom in the later *New Science*.

My study will draw on the work of Fabiani and Naddeo as it builds a political interpretation of Vico's account of poetic wisdom. From Fabiani's work, I will take seriously the idea that the account of poetic wisdom is an epistemological and political critique of the superstitions of oligarchs. From Naddeo's work, I will take seriously the idea that there is a prescriptive level to Vico's account of social theory that encourages the judiciary to develop better laws for maintaining human rights. In a sense I will combine the two by reading the poetic wisdom as a source of obstacles for the development of justice so that it gives legislators and lawyers a better idea of how to develop a just system without damaging the stability of the community.

The Method of the *New Science*

Vico's account of Roman religion is both extensive and daunting. He expends much effort explaining specific stories and images of the gods and heroes. He does not explain directly how he organizes all of these analyses. If one wanted to be charitable, one could say the section on poetic wisdom has a baroque sensibility in which themes spiral and weave around a variety of detailed images drawn from ancient texts. If one did not want to be charitable, one could say it is a disorganized and contradictory list of peculiar observations. I suggest that if one takes Vico's method seriously, one can at least make sense of why this section is so serpentine.

Vico modeled his approach on Francis Bacon's inductive method of *cogitare videre* or "think and see" (163, 359).⁶⁶ He appreciates the way Bacon's method dictates that one should develop theories while the evidence is being gathered. Rather than simply testing discrete hypotheses, the scientist ought to cycle back and forth between evidence and theory while developing an account. The objective is to create unifying accounts that seamlessly unite the evidence with the theory. Even further, in a manner completely the opposite of Descartes, Bacon holds that the scientist should draw on evidence and ideas from different disciplines while formulating accounts. Rather than simply drilling down on a particular problem, the scientist should work to make connections between areas of study to present a comprehensive picture rather than remain focused on one discipline or one problem at a time. This echoes his discussion of the art of topics in the *Study Methods* in which he emphasized the importance of making connections (SM 12–20).

In his section on method, he identifies three sets of proofs: theological, philosophical, and philological. The first two call on the scientist to look for a metaphysical order to history and see how it manifests itself in particular ways (345–348). The philological proofs refer not just to the study of language but to the proper use of historic and linguistic evidence in general in a way that refers back to use of ancient texts that he had proposed in the first *New Science* (352–358). The important point is that these three proofs are supposed to work together rather than be used discretely. The theological proofs are the most important since they reveal that history does not unfold mechanically but through a complex relationship of divine influence and human agency, as I will discuss later. The other two types of proofs intertwine. He writes, "with the help of the preceding philosophical proofs, the philological proofs both confirm their own authority by reason and at the same time confirm reason by their authority" (359). If the science succeeds, then the evidence drawn from these proofs fit together perfectly.

To evaluate whether his interpretations of myths are sound, Vico will question whether his philosophical theory and philological evidence harmonize in a way that does not seem particularly forced or convoluted. In one of his philological proofs, he writes, "Our mythologies agree with the institutions under consideration, not by force and distortion, but directly, easily and naturally" (352). Entailed in this is a commitment to not simply pick and choose his evidence. He commits himself to drawing from the entire range of poems available to build his descriptions. He especially takes seriously the harsh brutality that is depicted in many of these myths. As I mentioned earlier, I am not particularly concerned about whether Vico successfully depicts ancient Roman religion. I think it is important to recognize that his painstaking attempt to account for all of the myths he could find is not a sign of eccentricity but stems from a sincere desire to avoid error by being as comprehensive as possible. This extends an invitation to enter into the depth of his account to see how he fits these stories together.

The idea that an account needs to be complete to be correct is not at all unusual. In fact, in the *Discourse on Method*, Descartes himself claims that one of the criteria of his method is to provide accounts so complete that nothing is overlooked.⁶⁷ I think the structure of the *New Science* takes the method to such an extreme that Vico's strategy becomes obscured. In book 1, he completely separates the philosophical evidence from the philosophical. He offers a chronological table where he lists much of the historical data on which he relies. He then proposes a list of philosophical axioms in the next section. This book concludes with his statement of his method, which calls the reader to bring those facts and theories together. Once book 2 commences, he fully commits to his method, and he always presents his philosophical ideas and philological evidence in a way that is merged together as completely as possible. This makes sense given that the goal of his science is to do just that. The section on poetic wisdom is difficult to read because it is not presented in a systematic way. Nevertheless, there is no reason to think that it is an attempt to be fanciful or mystical. Instead, it is a function of how he is trying to do his philosophy.

The challenge of reading the *New Science* is compounded by the fact that it works across different disciplines. Book 2 has two different agendas that do not compete with each other but create further structural tensions. On the one hand, he wants to explain how Roman law developed and use this as a model for a universal idea of history. This calls for a chronological account of the development of law. On the other hand, he wants to demonstrate that poetic thought is an independent form of thought. To show that, he demonstrates that poetic wisdom has a variation for all of the disciplines that modern thought does. This, rather than chronology, provides the structure of the second book. The invention of Jove represented the first crude metaphysics. He then claims, "From this, as from a trunk, there branch out from one limb logic, morals, economics and politics, all poetic; and from another, physics, the mother of cosmography and astronomy, the latter of which gives their certainty to its two daughters, chronology and geography—all likewise poetic" (367). He then embeds the chronological development of ancient Roman law into this disciplinary format. This causes some redundancy. For example, he describes the invention of the first imaginative universal Jove in the "Poetic Metaphysics" and then again in the "Poetic Morals" (379, 504). The "Poetic Logic" falls between the two. I do not think the two accounts of Jove are contradictory, but they do require the reader to see it from different angles and then piece them together. Of course, that may make it easier to understand, at least in some regards, or it may provide connections to help the reader see how the whole narrative fits together.

If any readers come to my study confounded by the *New Science*, I hope this discussion of his method helps provide a path of entry. It also provides a guide for the way I will approach the poetic wisdom. I will try to fit his images together to tease out the underlying themes of the imaginative universals he describes. I will try to understand the core impulses behind particular poetic characters and then trace it through the different associations Vico makes. Unlike him, however, I will then try to make explicit the connections between these characters and the behavior of Neapolitan aristocrats. This will develop an interpretation of the *New Science* that Vico could at least recognize. While I am not going to attend to the metaphysical breadth of his work, I think that I can respect his critique of aristocratic authority.

Freedom and Universal History in the *New Science*

In this last section of this introductory chapter, I will discuss a particular philosophical point that has troubled commentators on Vico. He posits that there is an ideal eternal history through which all nations pass. At the same time, he tells the reader that he seeks political reform. It is not immediately clear how he can hold both positions. In order to read the *New Science* primarily as a call to improve the situation in Naples, it is important to resolve this tension. In other words, it is necessary to explain how human agency is possible given a universal path of history.

There is a strong temptation to read Vico in Hegelian terms. Vico does claim that divine providence works through human action in hidden ways. This looks much like Hegel's idea of the cunning of reason.[68] Rather than approaching Vico though Hegel, however, I want to try to put this controversy in the context of a debate in early modern philosophy that Vico would have recognized. I will try to stick to the getting things right approach by putting Vico into conversation with other early modern thinkers who tried to reconcile human agency with God's design. When one approaches Vico through this lens, it is possible to read the *New Science* as strongly committed to the importance of free choice and moral responsibility.

To begin, I will summarize the ideal eternal history. If Vico has a famous idea, it is that history is circular. Humanity falls into a barbaric state. This was described in the Bible by Noah's flood but also happened more recently with the collapse of the Roman Empire. Once humanity rediscovers religion, it passes through three ages. In the *Universal Law*, he attributes these designations to Varro (CJ 35). He changes this in the *New Science*, though, because Varro focused on just Roman law. As a result, he succumbed to the conceit of nations and argued that ancient laws and institutions all had Latin origins. Vico turns to the Egyptians, as related by Herodotus, who identified the three ages of civilization: the age of gods, the age of heroes, and the age of humans (52). Book 4 is dedicated to showing how institutions such as governments and languages appear differently in the three ages. Eventually, civilization loses its moral cohesion and collapses into a barbarism of reflection (1106). Divine providence helps humanity rise again out of this fall. Axiom LXVI describes this course of history most vividly: "Men first feel necessity, then look for utility, next attend to comfort, still later amuse themselves with pleasure, thence grow dissolute in luxury, and finally go mad and waste their substance" (241). One can see here Vico's serious attitude and a distaste for extravagance.

The three ages may be characterized this way. The age of gods commences when giants invent the imaginative universal Jove and thus found pagan religion. Only certain giants become theological poets. Other giants, who did not recognize the call of the gods, eventually wander into the altars of the poets and submit to their authority. They become the *famuli* of the theological poets. They live in the asylums of the theological poets and their offspring. They also receive the protection of the poets. They are, however, a distinct social class who do not participate in the religion of the poets. This is the initial class distinction. The heroic age begins when the tension between the two classes produces actual conflict. At this point, the poets and the *famuli* evolve into heroes and plebeians. In axiom LXXXVI, Vico quotes Aristotle's claim in the *Politics* that "the nobles swore to be the eternal enemies of the plebs" (271). Governments at this time were not monarchies but groups of aristocrats who defended their traditions from the plebs who demanded political and legal recognition (666). The age of humans develops as governments, either democratic or monarchial, develop systems that rule justly and treat everyone fairly.

The borders between these ages are not distinct. For Vico, history shows that not all institutions advance at the exact same rate. It is possible to separate theoretically the poets from the heroes. The poets live in separate asylums and protect their *famuli*. The heroes have banded together to pool their resources and resist the attacks of the plebeians. At times in the *New Science*, however, Vico does not appear particularly interested if the nobles are more like theological poets or heroes. Along with him, I am not going to be concerned about whether a particular poetic character is a result of the divine or heroic age. Nevertheless, there is an important point about the heroic age that needs to be emphasized.

Giarrizzo rightly highlights the fact that Vico dedicated most of the *New Science* to the age of the heroes.[69] He spends almost no time on the age of humans outside of the passages where he describes institutions across the ages and a very brief passage in the conclusion (1101–1108). The age of gods often gets the most attention by commentators because of its dramatic story of the creation of Jove, the birth of pagan religion, and early poetic language (385–399, 404–412). Most of the book on poetic wisdom, however, deals with the class conflict that occurred during the heroic age. Even his discussion on poetic language treats the way in which the heroes communicated their power to the plebeians (412–427). Book 3 highlights the harsh actions of Achilles and Agamemnon and other heroes in Homer's epics (786). This came from an oral tradition that depicted the heroic age (808). While the birth of civilization with the thunder and the collapse of civilization into the barbarism of reflection raise some of the most immediate questions that come out of the *New Science*, Vico's interest was held by the heroic age. This is what I will later connect to his account of feudalism.

To understand the role of human agency in this metaphysical pattern, it is necessary to look at the mechanism that drives it. Divine providence guides civilization through the three ages by orchestrating events in such a way that humans produce the opposite of what they desired. In an important section of book 2, he summarizes moments when divine providence produces more advanced human institutions out of the human desire to keep things the same. He opens this passage by writing, "Herein is divine providence to be supremely admired, for when men's intentions were quite otherwise, it brought them in the first place to fear the divinity, the cult of which is the first fundamental basis of commonwealths" (629). The prime example of this is that the pre-civilized giants wanted to act solely on their animalistic passions, but they ended up checking those desires by creating a god to worship. Divine providence does not work through some mechanism of direct spiritual intervention. It works through human responses to events that are either natural or spring from the evolution of human institutions.

Vico actually gives a metaphysical argument to explain why divine providence does not rely on miraculous phenomena. While Vico does not emphasize it as much as other early modern philosophers do, he does hold that God is perfect. So divine providence must act in the most perfect way possible. This means that it must direct humanity in the most efficient manner possible. He writes, "Since divine providence has omnipotence as minister, it must unfold its institutions by means as easy as the natural customs of men" (343). His point is that divine providence is so potent and efficient that it does not need to use supernatural miracles to achieve its purpose. If one knows where to look, divine providence may thus be found in the ordinary course of human events.

The term *divine* in "divine providence" does refer to the existence of a higher power or, at least, a higher ordering principle for reality. This is shown in the frontispiece where it is symbolized by the ray coming from the triangle in the sky (5). He also uses the term *divine* in the sense of hidden (342). It is up to the Vichian scientist to divine—in the sense of divination—and to recognize how providence has orchestrated human events to help humanity along. This is an occasion where he does play up the similarity between the first poets, who used divination to understand the commands of the pagan gods, and the philosopher, who looks for signs in human history. The key point, however, is that providence is hidden in plain sight. To see it, a philosopher has to break out of a particular perspective to see history from a metaphysical perspective.

If one were to ask Vico what evidence he has for the existence of divine providence, he could say, at least initially, two things. First, he would emphasize that the bestial passions lying within humans are too strong for them to control on their own. They would need some sort of divine consultation or motivation to invent the pagan religions that inspired self-restraint (178). This will be a major focus in the next chapter when I explain his account of the creation of Jove. Vico is committed to the idea that no human civilization has ever come into being without the moralizing force that comes with religion (179). The key point here is that even the false first religions could not develop without divine guidance. Second, he could say that without a divine order, there is no way that many different cultures would develop the same institutions separately. The conceit of nations has tricked people into thinking their civilization created all institutions first and gave it to others. From a more objective view, Vico claims, one can see that different civilizations created the institutions independently, thereby demonstrating the influence of providence (146). Every nation, in Vico's view, had its own unique independently created thunder god (193). While his application of this idea to history is unusual, in general this is not an unusual line of reasoning to attack skepticism and defend metaphysical truth.

Despite finding this universal pattern in history, Vico tells us that science and philosophy ought to have practical value. He tells us in axiom V that, "to be useful to the human race, philosophy must raise and direct weak and fallen man, not rend his nature or abandon him in his corruption" (129). This claim may surprise those who see Vico as an apolitical thinker.[70] Nevertheless, it confirms Naddeo's claim that he was interested in promoting justice in politics. He underlines this in axiom VI, where he says, "Philosophy considers man as he should be and so can be of service to but very few, those who wish to live in the Republic of Plato and not to fall back into the dregs of Romulus" (131). While this may confirm that Vico has a fairly low opinion of humanity, he does think leaders can come forward and govern well in popular commonwealths or monarchies in the third age of humanity. He describes human judgments in the third age in this way: "In these the governing consideration is the truth of the facts, to which, according to the dictates of conscience, the laws benignly give aid when needed in everything demanded by the equal utility of causes" (974). Just human rulers should look carefully at the facts and the needs of people. They should then consult their conscience and the divine order of the universe to rule fairly. As Fabiani discusses, the leaders need to avoid error and see the greater metaphysical processes of the universe to make sound judgments. Studying the *New Science* can aid this process. This is what Vico thinks philosophy ought to do. Yet, how can this conform to his idea of an ideal eternal history?

To answer this question, I think it is helpful to relate it to the way seventeenth-century French philosophers debated the relationship of God's will, human civility, and human virtue. Given that Vico is interested in defending a metaphysical order of history and civil behavior, this debate would have been particularly relevant for him. While contemporary philosophers working on the early modern period may not be familiar with this debate, it had a major impact at the time. In *Putting on Virtue: The Legacy of the Splendid Vices*, Jennifer A. Herdt presents a deep and thorough historical analysis of the question of whether acting in a civil manner would help one achieve virtue and, more importantly, grace.[71] The question could be expressed as whether worldly virtue had any relationship to divine goodness. More directly and broadly, the question was whether human society was corrupt and should be avoided or whether it was an arena for positive action. Vico, of course, took the later option.

What is particularly relevant for Vico is Herdt's account of the anatomists, who included Baltasar Gracián, Blaise Pascal, and Pierre Nicole.[72] These thinkers were interested in moral anatomy which looked at the way human desires were shaped by political and social context. Gracián, a Jesuit, argued that if approached the right way civil life could lead to proper virtue. For Gracián, nature was incomplete and required human art and civility to complete it. If one builds on nature properly and follows those aspects of courtly life that allow for human stability and tranquility, then one can achieve virtue.[73] Herdt writes that Gracián's view goes so far as to suggest that "heroic human virtue acquires a certain likeness to divine greatness, a likeness capable of winning God's love and grace."[74] The Jansenists went the other way. Nicole argued that courtly life and pagan philosophy can create the appearance of virtue but do not produce actual virtue. When the pagan strives for a happy and tranquil life they do it out of self-love, but true charity does not come from love of oneself at all.[75] For writers in Nicole's tradition, God has already created the best universe and it is hubristic to think that the universe could be improved or that one can find grace on one's own. In Nicole's view, pagans have the potential to act with general grace absent of God's blessing. One can only be truly virtuous, however, if one receives efficacious grace from God.[76] This was a key debate in a long discussion of the relationship of grace to human agency.

In *Tra religione e prudenza: la 'filosofia practica' di Giambattista Vico*, Enrico Nuzzo discusses how this debate came to Naples.[77] He describes the way that the works identified as *saggezza moderna* appeared in Naples in the middle of the seventeenth century, and he focuses on the works of the disciple of Montaigne, Pierre Charron (1541–1603). This movement, which was in line with the Jansenists, separated the true self from civil institutions and social development.[78] Nuzzo discusses the way Neapolitan intellectuals opposed *saggezza moderna*. They connected a Cartesian theory of the passions to the natural law of Grotius in order to show the importance of the connection between psychological states and civil engagement.[79] Further, they rejected the ideas of Nicole and other Jansenists because they saw their inward turn as opposed to classical humanism.[80] This represented a general movement toward finding universal truth in the civil world and promoting the ethical value of political activity. Nuzzo goes into great depth into Vico's response. He particularly emphasizes the way Vico presents an intersubjective view of human nature to justify the philosophical importance of civil society.[81] This point becomes important in the next chapter. Here I want to return to the question of divine providence and human agency.

The intellectual culture of Naples wondered whether the study of civilization could lead to metaphysical knowledge of God. Given that God is perfect how could historical investigation not lead to metaphysical truth? Yet, given the fallen and corrupt nature of human beings, how could human history reveal anything about God? Even further, how could human virtue be connected to human civility? When one reads the *New Science* in this context, it becomes easier to see how it envisions moral action. It does not want to deny the importance of God's influence, but it also wants to defend the study of human institutions and the value of human behavior.

I think Vico reveals his position in the commentary on axiom CIV. The axiom itself states, "The remark of Dio Cassius is worthy of consideration, that custom is like a king and law like a tyrant; which we must understand as referring to reasonable custom and to law not animated by natural reason" (308). Dio Cassius suggests that people enjoy obeying custom because it conforms to what they do anyway, while the law is an external imposition. Vico accepts this point but with a major caveat. He clarifies that laws can only exist over the long term if they conform to custom. So ultimately, law and custom must merge. When Vico qualifies the statement, however, he adds "reasonable custom," which suggests that some customs are not reasonable, and "law not animated by natural reason," to confirm that some laws are unjust. This implies that there is the possibility for civilizations to err not only in the way they make legislation but also in the way they develop customs. Vico acknowledges that civilizations do have the potential to stray from the proper metaphysical path. Moreover, it suggests that Vico does not defend the moral value of all law and all custom but only of those that conform to the divine order. This already connects both the discovery of truth and advancement of moral virtue to both God's order and civil activity. He then explains how this is possible.

The bestial state of barbaric giants living outside of civilization does not reveal their inherent nature. I will explain this more fully in the next chapter. The point here is that they are in a state of privation from community and from their own physical and mental capacities for living in civilization. In this state, they cannot do good works. Humans have "a potentiality for them [good works] which is ineffectual" (310). This has the form of Nicole's claim about the difference between general grace and efficacious grace. There is a major difference, however. For both Nicole and Vico, God's will is needed to give humans efficacious grace. For Nicole, this happens through God's act of charity. Vico grounds this in civil action. For Vico, providence naturally provides humans with the opportunity to actualize their natural civil potencies. By guiding humanity back into civilization, providence allows humans to do real good works. In this way, Vico connects God's divine will to doing good works in society. By valuing civil activity in this way, Vico is more on the side of the Jesuits than Nicole in this debate.

More significantly, in Vico's model free choice and human agency become quite important. If one views grace as Nicole does or, more strongly, as the Calvinists do, then it is God's decision to grant grace or not. Human agency may have a role to play in the decision, but God's act directly bestows grace whether a person desires it or not.

In Vico's model, divine providence creates an opportunity for humans. Providence can only bestow grace once humans have freely chosen to follow its advice. Free civil action is actually a necessity for receiving grace. He writes, "it [grace] therefore cannot act without the principle of free choice, which God aids naturally by His providence" (310). This is not exactly humans forcing God to give grace, since it is up to God to bestow God's providence initially. Nevertheless, humans do have the freedom to accept or decline the advice and so can choose to accept the gifts of providence or not. If they perform the civil actions counseled by providence, they can accept grace and advance along the course of the ideal eternal history.

Axiom VIII states that "things do not settle or endure out of their natural state" (134). In Vico's chronology, humans have spent far more time in civilization than outside of it. So the civil state is natural to them. He writes that "man has free choice, however weak, to make virtues of his passions; but that he is aided by God naturally by divine providence and supernaturally by divine grace" (136). He adds here "divine grace," but that is beside the point. Divine providence is not the cunning of reason in that it does not force humans along a dialectical path. Instead, it uses natural circumstances to advise humans. Its mechanism can only spiritually and practically function if humans make decisions to follow the direction in which one leads. Vico emphasizes that divine providence does not force humans to act. The natural signs it gives encourage humans to follow the path, but they can choose not to listen.

When one understands this view of providence, one can understand an exceptionally important point in Vico that is often overlooked: he really does think that the Roman civilization was the best one. He writes, "Thus the very care for piety and attachment to religion brought the people to civil sovereignty. In this respect the Roman people went beyond all others in the world, and for that reason it became master of the world" (1101). Vico does not try to defend this claim by comparing Rome with other global civilizations, and it is pretty clear this is a Eurocentric statement one would expect from an eighteenth-century European writer. Nonetheless, it tells the reader that one should regard the history of Rome not as the product of an inevitable course of history. Ancient Rome achieved what it did because its people chose to follow the advice of providence. Whereas other civilizations regressed back into feudalism or were conquered, the Romans actually made it to the final stage. It is easy to lose sight of this point in the *New Science* because Vico rarely speaks in this way directly. Regardless, it is an essential point for his political philosophy. Ancient Rome is the goal that Naples or some other European power ought to achieve. The human age will not come automatically. Civilization must work for it.

Norberto Bobbio's discussion of Vico's political philosophy helps explain why this point about Rome is so hard to see in the *New Science*. He points out that the text does not spend time discussing corrupt forms of government like many other works of political theory. This is because Vico's focus is on explaining how different types of government are appropriate in different eras. Since laws and customs conform to the people governed, if a system of power works for people at a certain stage of the ideal eternal history, then it is the appropriate form of government. Systems of power change, Bobbio argues, because the lower classes force that change on the rulers. So Vico is not interested in describing what it would mean to rule poorly.[82] I would add, however, that while Vico does not describe what it would mean for a system of government to become corrupt, I think he gives reason to think about why a form of government, heroic aristocracies, could last too long. Rome avoided this problem, and Vico is hoping that Naples also could avoid it.

I think this reading of the ideal eternal history also changes how one might think of the barbarism of reflection. It would be easy to read that barbarism as a tragedy that civilization should do anything in its power to avoid. After all, he describes it as a horrible time of civil conflict that brings civilizations like Rome to destruction. If one were to read that too strongly, then a civilization would try never to leave the age of gods or the age of heroes if it could avoid it. Why move closer to the precipice if one does not have to? Riccardo Caporali, however, makes the important point that Vico did not really develop a full theory of the barbarism of reflection or the recourse of nations until the 1730 *New Science*.[83] This is when I suggest Vico fully formed his position against feudalism. Caporali argues that the barbarism of reflection, rather than being a warning, demonstrates that providence will keep humanity from completely collapsing. Rather than being a disaster to avoid at all costs, it is a safety net that providence uses when humanity can no longer sustain the balance it needs to keep society together.[84] In this view, Vico may actually be suggesting that risking the fall into barbarism might be superior to remaining in a state of feudal authority once it is has outlived its usefulness. The barbarism is providence's way of protecting humanity's survival.

In this introduction, I have discussed my approach to the *New Science* and to some of the traditional issues that authors have found in Vico. My goal, ultimately, is to get to an explanation of his poetic wisdom and to show how it presents a picture of aristocratic power in

Naples. To do this and to adhere to the "getting things right" approach, I want to find a key point of connection between the *New Science* and its contemporaries. I have laid a groundwork for reading him as an early modern thinker rather than a renaissance or proto-contemporary one. Nevertheless, I want to pin down one key debate in early modern philosophy to which he responded. That debate will be the problem of human socialization. I propose that by seeing poetic wisdom as a response to this philosophical problem, it will be possible to understand both the picture of power that the *New Science* gives and the practical political ideas that fall from it.

2

Giambattista Vico:
Early Modern Philosopher

The goal of this chapter is to find a pathway to Vico's account of poetic wisdom—and, specifically, his account of Jove—as an epistemological structure. I do not want to come at the poetic wisdom either from a discussion of ancient traditions of rhetoric or from contemporary conceptions of mythical thought. I also do not want to consider it separately from its historical context. In the next chapter, I will focus on defining the imaginative universal, but I do not want frame it simply from within Vico's text. My goal here is to find debates and discussions within early modern thought to consider how the discovery of Jove could represent a solution to a problem in early modern philosophy. Of course, I do not have access to Vico's own thought process outside of what he tells us in the *Autobiography*. Nevertheless, in accord with the "getting things right" approach, I think this will lead to a fruitful way of interpreting his text. Further, it makes sense to travel from what is familiar to what appears strange. Readers who come at the *New Science* from the contemporary conception of early modern thought often find it a peculiar work. By shining light on the way the early modern paradigm actually leads to Vico's discovery, I think it will be easier to find value in his account.

As a starting point, I want to contest the popular image of Vico as a socially and intellectually isolated thinker whose writings were separate from the prevailing trends of early modern thought. I do this in part because this image of him has become so prevalent, at least in the United States, that I need to present an alternate image to move my project forward. While most who work on him directly have already spurned the image of him as isolated, I have had many encounters with people who still hold onto it. Further, I should address some significant textual passages in which Vico presents himself as isolated that have fed this image. Ultimately, I will sketch a picture of Vico as engaged in the Neapolitan intellectual community and interested in greater European trends. This will serve as a launching point toward finding a connection between early modern thought and the discovery of poetic wisdom.

The reclusive image of Vico is not recent. After the publication of the 1725 *New Science*, an announcement for it was published in Leipzig that gravely misrepresented not only the ideas of the work but also basic facts about the text and its author. It claimed that Vico was an abbè. In his response, Vico points out that he has been married for thirty years and has five living children.[1] He speculates that such a misrepresentation is either an indication of the critic's complete ignorance or that it is an intentional attack by a fellow Neapolitan.[2] Either way, it is intriguing that Vico, one of the few early modern philosophers with a family, would be labeled a solitary abbot. This image would stick with Vico and would be promoted most heavily by Isaiah Berlin.

Berlin does not deny that Vico was influenced by a range of scholarly works, and he devotes much of his influential essay on him to examining his sources. Nevertheless, Berlin paints a dramatic and exceptionally bleak view of his personal and intellectual life. He writes, "He lived in embittered poverty; he had little contact with the life around him; he was a cripple all his life as a result of a fall in childhood." For Berlin, his isolation ends up being a positive thing—for us if not for Vico—because it encouraged him to forge on ahead on his own path. He claims, "When Vico said that he was a solitary traveller in territory hitherto traversed by no one, this often repeated classical cliché for once expressed the literal truth."[3] This prepares the ground for his presentation of Vico's thought as anti-Enlightenment.

The facts suggest that Vico's life could not have been quite so dire. He never made much money, which did make his life uncomfortable. Nevertheless, in 1735 newly arrived King Charles of Bourbon made him the court historiographer (AU 204). It is hard to imagine him getting this position if he was out of contact with the larger Neapolitan community.

Another story speaks to Vico's connections. Ferdinando Vincenzo Spinelli, Prince of Tarsia (1691–1753), belonged to one of the wealthiest families in Naples. In 1735, he commissioned the famous architect Domenico Antonio Vaccaro to design the Palazzo Tarsia, which would hold the Biblioteca Spinelli, a collection of books, art, mathematical instruments, and other museum pieces. The part of the palazzo that housed the Biblioteca was called the Temple of Minerva in the spirit of the archeological dig that was started at Herculaneum. He commissioned Vico to write the epigram that was carved above the entrance. It read, "Born in heaven from Jupiter's brain, Minerva / Dwells here on earth in golden shelters worthy of Jupiter."[4] This is an example of the thriving intellectual culture that was growing in Naples. It also provides more evidence that Vico was neither isolated nor forgotten. Spinelli's decision to commission Vico shows that he had achieved important status in the community.[5]

I do not have a clear picture of Vico's personality. He expresses bitterness about losing the competition for becoming the professor of law (AU 160–161). This response seems appropriate given his belief that he had a good chance and then being told that he ought to withdraw from the competition (AU 162–163). Croce found evidence that Vico would show great affection but also that he struggled to restrain a harsh temper. Evidently Vico was quite angry when he learned that Damiano Romano published a critique of his view of the law of the twelve tables.[6] Of course, such anger might also be understandable. He certainly had the capacity to ridicule others, as one can see in his response to the false book notice. It is hard to find other authors who describe Vico's personality, so it is hard to know what it would have been like to socialize with him.

Berlin's claim about him being a cripple comes the opening of the *Autobiography*. He recounts that he fell from a ladder in his father's bookstore and seriously injured his head. He survived, but it gave him a serious disposition. He writes, "as a result of this mischance he grew up with a melancholy and irritable temperament such as belongs to men of ingenuity and depth." He then claims that because of the fall he is "quick as lightning in perception" and that he is among the type that "take no pleasure in verbal cleverness or falsehood" (AU 111). This opens his story up to interpretation. Is he apologizing for having a negative disposition or has he found a backhanded way to praise his own abilities? His writing style rarely breaks from a disciplined tone. When he does tell the occasional joke, it is usually to make fun of another author.[7] It is unclear whether this should lead us to accept the idea that he had "little contact with the world around him" as Berlin writes.

The main issue to address, however, is Vico's own comments about his isolation. From 1686 to 1695, Vico left his law studies at the University of Naples to work as a tutor in Vatolla, which was about 120 kilometers south of Naples. He claims he did this in part because his health was threatened by consumption, and he wanted to recover in the countryside. This worked, and he writes that "The good air would restore his health" (AU 119). He must have returned to the city periodically, since he managed to finish his law degree during this time.

Yet in the *Autobiography* he dramatizes his stay in Vatolla as if it were a time of exile. When he returned, he described himself as "a stranger in his own land," because the physics of Descartes was so popular (AU 132). As a result, he "lived in his native city not only a stranger but quite unknown" (AU 134). This lends credence to the idea that he was driven by an anti-Cartesian agenda and that he was intellectually alone. It is important, however, to look at his context more closely.

Vico laments that in choosing to take the position at Vatolla he sacrificed the opportunity to build relationships with the older generation of Neapolitan thinkers. This is understandable. Many of us have experienced being away from an institution and then discovering upon return that they had become excluded from its social network. Even if he returned to Naples periodically, he would not have been able to maintain associations with others as easily as those who stayed. He tells the reader he had not only seen his connections with the professors at the university weaken, but he also grew envious of the other young students who had been able to build connections in his absence (AU 134). What is often overlooked is that Vico does not present this separation as a permanent setback. It was merely an obstacle. Vico takes pride in the fact that he had the determination, intellectual ability and, evidently, social skills to overcome it.

A year later, he started to make contacts, notably with leading Neapolitan intellectual Gregorio Caloprese. He writes, "From then on he [Vico] began to rise in fame as a man of letters" (AU 136). He would soon earn his position as a professor of rhetoric at the University of Naples, and he would gain entry into major academies, including the Accademia dell'Arcadia. He describes many other friendships he had with Neapolitan intellectuals. Domenico d'Ausilio, the teacher of Piero Giannone, had highly praised the *Universal Law* and, Vico writes, "from that day they contracted a very close friendship which lasted as long as that great man of letters lived" (AU 148). He writes of Paolo Mattia Doria that "in Doria's discourse he perceived a mind that often gave forth lighting-like flashes of Platonic divinity, so that thenceforth they remained linked in a noble and faithful friendship" (AU 138). He criticizes Doria for praising Descartes too highly without recognizing the Platonic ideas lying underneath, but Vico did dedicate the *Ancient Wisdom* to him. Gianvincenzo Gravina had read and admired Vico's *Life of Antonio Carafa* and "thenceforth he carried on an intimate correspondence as long as Gravina lived" (AU 154). These passages indicate that Vico was engaged with the scholars around him. We are only getting his perspective on this, and perhaps Vico has an inflated view of these relationships. Nevertheless, it would be very odd for him to make these claims and be as isolated as Berlin thought. There is no question that Vico was an independent thinker. He describes himself by saying, "Vico blessed his good fortune in having no teacher whose words he had sworn by" (AU 133). He would certainly need some separation to develop the original ideas that he did. I am not sure this gives one reason to think of him as antisocial or completely isolated from his community.

The more serious textual concern is found in his *New Science*. He boldly announces that "for purposes of this inquiry, we must reckon as if there were no books in the world" (330). He backs this up by rarely referencing his contemporaries. Northern European philosophers are referred to sparingly if at all in the 1744 *New Science*. Descartes is mentioned only once in reference to his *Optics* (706). Hobbes and Spinoza are mentioned briefly in his attacks on Stoics and Epicureans (179, 335, 338, 1109). John Locke and Nicolas Malebranche do not appear at all. In the *New Science*, he also never mentions his Neapolitan contemporaries like Mattia Doria, Gravina, D'Andrea, Caloprese, and Giannone. He names these authors quite frequently in the *Autobiography*, but their absence from the *New Science* encourages one to read it as a work outside of its intellectual time.

In response to this, it is important to discuss the genesis of the 1725 *New Science*. He relates an important story in his *Autobiography* that is well known in the Vico community. When he first embarked on the idea of writing a *New Science*, he wanted to write an account of the history of natural law as a critique of "the improbabilities, absurdities and impossibilities which his predecessors had rather imagined than thought out." He wrote this version but decided not to publish it. He gives two reasons. Methodologically, it was because with this negative approach "the human mind is not enlarged." Presumably a series of critiques would focus the reader on errors of others and not lead them to his positive metaphysical account of history. So, he decided to present his ideas directly. Practically, it had too many pages so he could not afford to back the project (AU 166). Instead, he wrote what became the 1725 *New Science*, which was, one would assume, smaller. In that text, Descartes and Locke are just mentioned one time and Spinoza is not mentioned at all. He kept avoiding such references in the 1730 and 1744 *New Science*.

It is quite possible that he invented the story that he could not afford to publish the *New Science in Negative Form*. This could be a falsehood he signals when he misreports his birth year. It is possible that the climate of censorship in Naples actually caused him to hold back that version because he feared it would be condemned by the church.[8]

Regardless of whether that was the true motive, I find the important takeaway from this story is that Vico tells us that he is thinking about other authors as he is writing. His *Autobiography* does not discuss his *Conspiracy of the Macchia*, which was never published because it apparently did not serve the interests of the Spanish government.[9] If Vico were really concerned about negative repercussions of his *New Science in Negative Form*, he could have simply not mentioned it. By bringing it to the reader's attention, he indicates that we should not think of the published *New Science* as existing outside of the larger conversation. He alerts us to his stylistic choice not to address other positions at length, but he wants us to know he considered them.

It is worth mentioning that other Neapolitan authors did not refer extensively to their colleagues. For example, in 1709 Vico's friend Paolo Mattia Doria published the first edition of *La vita civile* with the *educazione del principe*. He also revised this over the next few years. He does not refer to his contemporaries. He often refers to Tacitus, Machiavelli, and also Hobbes, who are primary targets of his treatise. He does refer to the essays of Pierre Nicole.[10] Given the fact that Doria was primarily a mathematician, it is not surprising that he refers extensively to Descartes and the early seventeenth-century mathematician Bonaventura Cavalieri.[11] Doria does not refer, however, to other authors working in Naples. In his *Della ragion poetica*, Gianvincenzo Gravina refers to a multitude of ancient authors and many poets and commentators from the sixteenth century. He does not address other seventeenth-century authors, however.[12] There were cases, obviously, where authors would write treatises against other authors, as Damiano Romano did against Vico. Nevertheless, Vico's decision not to talk about his contemporaries and minimally reference other early modern philosophers was not an unusual one.

Of course, since the *New Science in Negative Form* no longer exists, it is impossible to know what is in it. It is tempting to think it was a response to the issues in early modern philosophy that have since become prominent, but it could have responded to many other trends. After the 1730 edition of the *New Science*, Vico wrote the "Reprehension of the Metaphysics of René Descartes, Benedict Spinoza, and John Locke," which he thought about adding to the *New Science* but did not.[13] This brief passage emphasizes the claim that one cannot do science or understand virtue without an idea of divine providence. It then expands on the critique of these authors as Stoics and Epicureans, which one already finds in the *New Science*. These are not the topics that one would hope for if one were looking for a connection between Vico and the current picture of early modern thought.

It is quite possible that the work responded to another tradition entirely. Vico laments the inability of philosophers and historians to understand ancient history. He boldly asserts that "all that has so far been written is a tissue of confused memories" (330). This suggests that he may have been more concerned with historical issues than metaphysical ones. I wonder if it was a response to the natural law tradition of Grotius that debated the value of feudalism. An important member of this tradition was François Hotman (1524–1590). He defended the French feudal tradition and used the works of Tacitus to argue that the very early Gauls and Germans lived under an aristocratic rule that assured the liberty of all. Contrary to Vico, he argues that the Romans destroyed that system and imposed an imperial and tyrannical rule. Hotman appears briefly in the *New Science* (437, 600, 1057). He was also the topic of the discourse Vico gave in his abortive attempt to win the chair of law (AU 161–163). Because this tradition endeavored to build its arguments through the use of historical research, Vico may have had much more to say about these authors than some of the more currently recognized figures in early modern thought. As my study continues, I will draw this philosophical conversation about feudalism into the discussion.

These details from the *Autobiography* and elsewhere give reason to think of Vico as an active professor of rhetoric who circulated among the intellectual community of the university. The bigger question is whether he fully rejected the intellectual trends of his day, as Berlin argues. I think Berlin has built his argument on a misunderstanding of Vico's position that will be useful to expose.

Beckett contra Berlin

Berlin portrays Vico as a lone defender of the ancients against an overwhelming tide of scientific thought. The initial problem with this is that Vico was hardly alone.[14] In *The Shock of the Ancient*, Larry F. Norman presents an extended account of the debate in seventeenth-century France over the value of ancient knowledge. Norman specifically criticizes Berlin, who perpetuated the idea that Vico was the first modern author to try to defend the value of ancient systems of learning.[15] Norman shows that Vico did not come up with the idea of defending ancient systems of learning out of nothing but that this was already a complex topic of discussion. He shows that the debate in France was not a simple matter of conservative thinkers versus innovators, but that subtle and nuanced positions developed around the issue of how modern and ancient views could be used and integrated. The mere fact that Vico entertained the possibility that ancient methods could be redeployed in modern ways does not give reason to paint him as an anti-modern or a solitary voice. This is an example of how expanding one's idea of early modern philosophy makes it easier to see how Vico fits into it.

Further, Vico, who drew inspiration from both Plato and Francis Bacon, does not defend ancient thought at the expense of modern science. Instead, he tries to derive the best ideas from both. In the *Study Methods*, he claims, "To avoid both defects [in ancient and modern study methods], young men should be taught the totality of sciences and arts, and their intellectual powers should be drawn to the full" (SM 19). In other words, to get the most out of their education, students ought to draw from all study methods available. This raises an intriguing point. Much of his reputation as an anti-modern developed during the 1970s and '80s, when postmodern theorists were struggling to move beyond positivism. It developed while there was a growing trend to promote pluralism and the value of the imagination against the edifice of unified scientific thought. Since then, the climate has dramatically changed. In academia, if not in popular culture, the importance of science is continuing to grow. Nevertheless, both scientists and humanities scholars are wondering if there is profit in working together rather than standing in opposition. Many scholars in the humanities are now working to defend science and contribute to its growth.[16] Vico may have much more to contribute to this approach than he ever did as an opponent of Descartes's critical method.

I maintain that Berlin overlooks a key point in Vico that is foundational for my project. Specifically, he overlooks the way poetic wisdom functions as a means of political communication. To understand how he misses this, it is necessary to step back and talk about his general approach to Vico.

Berlin was a paradigmatic example of the radical reconstruction approach that Christina Mercer identified. He writes, "In reading Vico it is constantly necessary to sift the chaff from the grain."[17] He justifies this by pointing to "Vico's lack of literary talent." Further, he claims that "they [his ideas] fly apart and pursue their own paths through the mass of superfluous and, at times, wildly irrelevant matter with which their author's digressive and intuitive mind is at all times clogged; nevertheless their intrinsic force and uniqueness somehow break through."[18] He uses this as justification to pass over his metaphysical commitments and his account of Roman mythology in order to portray him as a radical historicist.[19]

In *The Legacy of Vico in Modern Cultural History*, Joseph Mali looks carefully at Berlin's use of Vico and contextualizes it in Berlin's overall philosophy. He traces the way Berlin finds in Vico a new and imaginative hermeneutic method for the practice of history.[20] From there, Berlin finds a proto-pluralist position of human nature and civilization.[21] At the core of Berlin's reading is the *verum-factum* principle.[22] As I have already mentioned, Vico did not present this as a historicist principle. Nevertheless, Berlin finds in Vico's principle a problem that leads him to attribute a unique historicist view to him.

Berlin recognizes an ambiguity in the *verum-factum* principle. Does it apply to individual making or collective making? Using the reasoning of the principle, it seems as if an individual could know only what that one person made. If this were the case, however, then the *verum-factum* principle would not allow anyone to understand the larger course of history. Berlin finds a way to expand the application of the principle in one particular passage. Vico writes, "the world of civil society has certainly been made by men, and that its principles are therefore to be found within the modifications of our own human mind" (331). Because all humans share cognitive characteristics, it is possible to remake mentally what was made by others in the past. This gives one access to any act of making in the course of civil history. For Berlin, this insight contains the brilliance of the *verum-factum* principle. Berlin writes, "Vico transformed this notion and gave it immensely greater scope and depth (and increased its dangerously speculative character) by extending it to the growth in time of the collective or social consciousness of mankind."[23] In Berlin's reading, the *verum-factum* principle draws its validity from a link that binds humanity together across different historical eras. Thereby, he finds in Vico a historicist conception of truth which still allows an investigator to comprehend radically distant worldviews.

To help solidify this interpretation, Berlin then connects Vico to the Renaissance idea of the human as microcosm. As a paradigm example, Pico della Mirandola claimed that the dignity of man is found in the human ability to become every other type of creature.[24] A human could descend to the level of plants and animals by focusing on nutritive or bestial activities. A human could also ascend to the level of the angels through reason. In this way, the human is a microcosm of everything in the universe. While Vico restricts his position to human history, it is an analogous move. Berlin writes, "The ancient analogy between the individual and society, microcosm and macrocosm, ontogenesis and phylogenesis, dominates Vico's thought as much as that of the Renaissance."[25] Berlin's *New Science* depends on the mind's ability to recognize itself as a microcosm and then transform into other human cultures.

From there, Berlin moves to other Renaissance ideas, especially magic. He defines this Renaissance belief by writing, "the belief in magic as the acquisition of power by the subject over the object by re-entering it, immersing oneself in it, and so re-assimilating it to oneself, a notion which is at the heart of much Renaissance natural philosophy."[26] He reads Vico as probing ancient religion by imaginatively engaging it in thought and action. He writes, "Vico (influenced perhaps by 'magical' theories of becoming one with the object, widespread in the Renaissance) is one of the true fathers of the doctrine of the unity of theory and practice."[27] From there, it is not hard to read his account of Jove as an entrance into a spiritual.

The problem with Berlin's reading is that Vico spends remarkably little time discussing these issues. He does not use the term *microcosm*. He also does not offer a discussion of Renaissance thought, and he rarely refers to authors from the Florentine Renaissance tradition. Pico della Mirandola only appears once in the *New Science* and that is a critique of his view of the universal flood (169). In the *Autobiography*, he does indeed praise the metaphysics of Pico della Mirandola and Marsilio Ficino and laments the fact that after the invasion of Cartesian thought these texts were "thought worthy of being shut up in the cloisters" (AU 132). He does not expand beyond that, however. Given this lack of text, what is it that convinces Berlin that the idea of microcosm is at the heart of Vico's thought?

Berlin's answer is curious. He argues that Vico does not have a theory of interpretation or communication. Because of this, he has to rely on a purely epistemological approach to history. Berlin makes the broad assertion, "Vico nowhere, so far as I know, fully or exactly explains the way in which men understand other men." He claims that there is no account of how to grasp "other ways of thinking" by "the language of empathy, or analogical reasoning, or intuition or participation in the unity of the World Spirit." Since Vico cannot explain how one can learn through interpretation, all knowledge must be grasped internally. So, in this view, individual humans must be microcosms. Berlin continues, "He rests his case on his conviction that what men have made, other men, because their minds are those of men, can always, in principle, 'enter into.' "[28] Berlin says this more succinctly when he writes that for Vico, "men can think of others only as being like themselves."[29] With this, Berlin reduces Vico's philosophy to one of sameness rather than difference. He praises Vico for recognizing that epistemological structures change radically over time, but he attributes this to the fact Vico posits a universal humanity that allows people of different eras to understand each other.

For my reading, Berlin has had to dismiss far too much of Vico's thought to arrive at this conclusion.[30] He passes over all Vico's efforts to develop accurate interpretations of pagan myths. Vico expresses his concern about the conceit of scholars and other sources of bias. He presents a way of using historical evidence to mitigate against the influence of contemporary ideas. Even if one dismisses or qualifies the results of his method, it is surprising Berlin would claim that Vico does not have a hermeneutic method.

For my study, the real problem with Berlin's reading is that it obscures Vico's entire discussion of class conflict. Berlin assumes that Vico's interpretation of pagan religion is that it is a unified cultural phenomenon. When one does this, one overlooks the point that the second comers to the asylums did not understand the rituals of poetic wisdom. As a result, one misses most of what Vico has to say about poetic wisdom as a method of communication. The rituals of the poetic characters were expressions of aristocratic self-discipline that communicated a poet's worthiness to remain in the upper class. By extension, the rituals express power and authority from the nobles to the plebeians. Because Vico emphasizes that imaginative universals were embodied concepts that had to be expressed physically, they were inherently communicative. Vico may not do the best job of reminding the reader of this point, but it is inherent to his account of poetic wisdom. In my study, I will try to think of poetic wisdom always as a form of thought that frames a world in such a way poetic thinkers must communicate their ideas through rituals.

Berlin's reading of Vico has been quite popular, and it is a good deal of fun. I do not want to stop anyone from drawing inspiration from it. To follow my study, however, it is important to let go of the temptation to think of mythical thought simply as a way to conceive the world. If one focuses too strongly on the theoretical problem of how to enter mythical thought, one can easily lose sight of the cultural and political context in which this form of thought occurs. Rather than worrying about how I can bracket my conceptual bias and think poetically, I will try to understand how poetic wisdom serves as both a conceptual and a political structure. This will help me read it as a critique of the oligarchy that dominated Naples.

Before I leave Berlin behind, I present a contrasting view. If anyone would have known that Vico was either kidding or a mystic, it would be Samuel Beckett. His only work of scholarship was entitled

"Dante... Bruno. Vico.. Joyce."[31] He describes Vico as a serious thinker and calls him "a practical roundheaded Neapolitan." This sets the tone for Beckett's anti-mystical reading of Vico. He dabbles with some of the same ideas that Berlin does. He connects Vico to the Renaissance thinker Giordano Bruno on the point of humanity as microcosm. He also discusses the way in which Vico combines action and thought. Yet, Beckett does not dismiss Vico's account of history.

Beckett acknowledges that Vico's originality was his interpretation of myth. From the outset, though, he points out that he sees myth as utilitarian. He writes that his account of myth is "as far removed from the mystical as it is possible to imagine."[32] He sees Vico's theory of myth as framed by the intellectual limitations of early humans. Beckett writes that for Vico, "The figurative character of the oldest poetry must be regarded, not as sophisticated confectionery, but as evidence of a poverty-stricken vocabulary and of a disability to achieve abstraction."[33] In the next chapter, I will make the poverty of language a central tenet of my reading of the poetic wisdom. Beckett then describes how the account of myth is integral to the evolution of both politics and language. While his essay is brief, he captures the depth of detail and consistency in Vico's account. At the end of Beckett's summary, he writes, "He may still appear as a mystic to some: if so, a mystic that rejects the transcendental in every shape and form as a factor in human development, and whose Providence is not divine enough to do without the cooperation of Humanity."[34] Beckett recognizes the central importance of human agency for Vico.

When Beckett connects Vico to Bruno's metaphysics, it is not to give an epistemological account, like Berlin, but to show how humans act in and on the universe. For Bruno, all extreme opposites—the maxima and minima—come together. As Beckett writes, "Maximal speed is a state of rest."[35] This signifies that both opposites and everything on the scale between them are identified with god and participate in him. For Vico, this signifies that all humans participate in the working of providence. History is not determined by divine control or the random acts of individuals. Human activity and providential control coincide. Beckett writes, "Individuality is the concretion of universality, and every individual action is at the same time superindividual." Hence human acts work as providence to produce religion, marriage, and burial and other universal human institutions. Beckett writes, "This is not Bossuet's Providence, transcendental and miraculous, but immanent and the stuff itself of human life, working by natural means. Humanity is its work in itself."[36] This supports the emphasis I placed on Vico's claim that divine providence can only work through free human choice.

When one takes Vico seriously, one can find a wealth of ideas in the *New Science*. Berlin's analysis goes into much more depth than I have related here. Nevertheless, he sacrifices a large amount of Vico's project to develop his reading. By taking Vico to be a serious philosopher and historian, Beckett gives a more comprehensive reading of the *New Science* in much less space. He goes on to connect the *New Science* to Joyce's major work. He does not expand on Vico's political philosophy or the problem of human sociability. This is where my project now turns.

The Giants and the State of Nature

There is a famous dispute in early modern thought that might connect Vico to his contemporaries. This is the debate about the state of nature. Early modern thinkers from Thomas Hobbes and John Locke to Samuel Pufendorf built their political theories around a contrast between humanity in the wilderness and humanity in civilization. Given that Vico describes civilization rising out of a time of giants, it seems that he is making a similar move. I will argue that there is a connection, but it is not the one that a contemporary reader might expect. The key difference is that on Vico's reading the time of the giants is actually not natural.

To begin, I want to frame Vico's account. The giants lived in the time between the fall of civilization and its rebirth. They were created during the barbarism of reflection, which becomes the barbarism of sense once the giants have fully adapted to life outside of civil institutions. He gives an intense description of the giants as physically large, solitary, and lacking any check on their passions (369). His fanciful passages about the giants inspire a good deal of speculation, and at the end of this study I will address the way Roberto Esposito thinks about it. To stick to the "getting things right" approach, I want to contextualize Vico's depiction by considering some of the sources from which he drew. Unlike most other early modern thinkers, he uses both literary and scientific evidence to build his view of humans living outside of civilization.[37] This is consistent with his commitment to drawing on as much evidence available to him as possible. His results are certainly problematic from a contemporary perspective, but they reveal Vico's position in this early modern debate.

His primary source is, of course, the Bible. He references Genesis 10, in which Noah's ark lands, and his sons—Ham, Japheth, and Shem—abandon him to found other nations (13). This means that the decedents of Noah who maintained the Judeo-Christian tradition never entered into the gigantic state. The others grew into solitary giants and forgot the institutions of the past (195). They needed to create pagan religion to reinvent civil institutions.

To expand his account, he draws on Greek and Roman mythology to explain what happened to the lost descendants of Noah. The stories describe a universe that was originally ruled by a race of titans or giants.[38] The gods, led by Jove, who was armed with lightning, overthrew them to establish their rule from Mount Olympus. Axiom XLII states, "Jove hurls his bolts and fells the giants, and every gentile nation had its Jove" (193). In his account, this mythic tale preserves an important aspect of the birth of civilization, since it is the invention of the imaginative universal Jove that stops the giants from their solitary wanderings. He then adds Homer's description of the cyclopes. He uses this image frequently to emphasize the solitary nature of the giants and the habit of the first theological poets to live independently (192, 296, 547). This tendency to live separately becomes important for Vico's argument about feudalism.

He then compliments this with scientific evidence. He refers to sightings of giant humans or bigfoot (*de los patacones*) in South America, and he references various discoveries of skeletal remains of large humans (170, 369). He refers to *De gigantibus eorumque reliquiis* by Jean Chassanion, published in 1580.[39] Vico rejects that specific account, preferring the evidence given by Caesar and Tacitus. This shows that he was thinking critically about the archeological evidence available.

More surprisingly to the contemporary reader, he uses science to support the idea that the descendants of Noah turned into giants when they stopped practicing good hygiene. He claims that when they lost the habit of washing and absorbed nitrous salts from the soil they grew large (369). Gustavo Costa demonstrates that this idea about nitrous salts was a widely held scientific view that was popular in Europe at the time.[40] Importantly, Vico takes this to a moral level. He argues that the solitary giants had to learn to live independently after they lost the infrastructure of civilization. Each learned a selfish morality based completely around individual survival. He calls this "bestial education" (195). This dimension of Vico's argument makes a certain amount of sense. Indeed, while contemporary post-apocalyptic science fiction novels do not usually depict a physical transformation into giants, they often emphasize the way that the requirements of survival without civil institutions would make humans more selfish, ruthless, and physically adept.

Vico holds consistently to the connection between civilization and cleanliness. A key reason why the Hebrew tradition did not fall into the state of giants, on his view, was precisely because of their strict rules concerning health. He writes, "The Hebrews, on account of their cleanly upbringing and their fear of God and of their fathers, continued to be of the proper stature in which God had created Adam and Noah had procreated his three sons; and it was perhaps in abomination of giantism that the Hebrews had so many ceremonial laws pertaining to bodily cleanliness" (371). This, of course, does not prove anything anthropologically about human beings before the dawn of civilization. They might be giants, and they might not be. When one ties these points together, an intriguing point becomes clear.

Vico never tells us where or how he thinks the ideal eternal history starts. When he describes it in the *New Science*, the time of the giants is placed in the context of a previously fallen civilization. After that apocalypse, humans learned how to become self-reliant while forgetting the importance of social bonds. As they grew more solitary, they bathed less and their bodies became disfigured. As conditions deteriorated, their passions grew even more fierce as experience taught them how to confront the dangers of the natural world. This learning did not occur in groups or even families, since mothers abandoned their children. The point I want to emphasize is that Vico presents this as a descent into an unnatural state. Humans have fierce passions that grow when unchecked, but this is not how they naturally exist. The time of giants represents a corruption of what humans actually are.

This makes Vico's view of the state of nature the opposite of the prevailing idea presented by early modern thinkers. Ordinarily, one might frame the state of nature as a time in which humans lived uncorrupted by civil institutions. One would then discuss how and why humans developed the ability to live in society. For Vico, the growth into the gigantic state was a corruption of human form, and giants had to learn how to live in a solitary manner. Of course, they then had to learn how to reconstruct human institutions and reenter civil life. In my reading, this is not because humans were leaving their natural state but because the physical corruption of their bodies and moral depravity of their passions was so destructive that it was difficult to restore humans to their rightful place.

When Vico discusses human nature, he does so in the context of civil life. In the first section of book 4 of the *New Science*, Vico describes "Three Kinds of Natures." He identifies a different human nature for each of the three ages of history. He does not include a nature for the deformed giants. During the age of gods, humanity had "a poetic or creative nature" ("*una natura poetica o sia creatrice*") (916). This allowed humans to create the pagan religion that tamed their desires.

He describes this as "a nature all fierce and cruel" ("*natura tutta fiera ed immane*") (916).[41] During the heroic age, the rulers "held themselves to be sons of Jove, as having been generated under his auspices" (917). This emphasized the distinction between the heroes and the plebeians. During the third age, Vico defines human nature as "intelligent and hence modest, benign, and reasonable, recognizing for laws conscience, reason, and duty" (918). By historicizing human nature, Vico solidifies the connection between it and the institutions of civilization. Human nature can adapt to changing civil institutions, but humans only manifest their nature when they are living in nations. When they are outside of civil life, they are living unnaturally.

When Vico uses the specific term *state of nature*, he often refers to the human nature that manifests itself in the age of gods. For example, axiom LXXVIII states, "The families cannot have owed that name, in keeping with their origin, to anything but these *famuli* of the fathers in the then state of nature" (257). His specific point here is that noble authority did not extend just to the offspring of a theological poet but to everyone in an asylum or fief. The point I want to make is that the "state of nature" is not the time outside of civilization but the divine age. He uses this term consistently. As another example, he describes people being found in Arabia and the West Indies in a state of nature. By this he means that they were found to be living in elementary fiefdoms (557). This is disorienting to the contemporary reader, since it was common practice among early modern thinkers to see the state of nature as a time before civilization or a time when there was no government. Vico is committed to the idea that human existence under a government is natural and so his idea of the natural state is one in which civil governments exist in some form.

He often emphasizes that feudal living was a prevailing natural state of humanity. He never leaves behind the idea that human nature changes with the evolution of civilization. In axiom LXXVIII above, he writes "*nello stato allor di natura*" with *allor* specifying that this state of nature occurs at this specific time. Nevertheless, this frequent connection underlines his point in axiom LXXX that "Men come naturally [*naturalmente*] to the feudal system" (260). He supports this point in axiom LXXXII when he says, "In all ancient nations we find everywhere clients and clienteles, which are best understood as vassals and fiefs" (263). One could make a case that the majority of human history has seen civilizations in feudal states. This case would depend on how broadly one is willing to define feudal institutions and feudal society. From Vico's perspective, ancient Western Rome was a feudal aristocracy much longer than an empire. This is based on his assertion that the Roman kingdom was an aristocracy rather than a monarchy. Further, after the Western empire fell, humanity existed in feudal institutions for another long era. Given how long humanity has spent under feudalism, it is surprising how reluctant contemporary philosophy has been to seriously consider it.

The civil nature of humans contributes to Caporali's idea that the barbarism of reflection is not something to be delayed at all costs as much as a safety net. Vico writes of it that "herein is providence above all to be admired, for it ordained that until such times as domestic education should supervene, the lost men should become giants in order that in their feral wanderings they might better endure with their robust constitutions the inclemency of the heavens and the seasons." The human ability to transform into giants in times of crisis means that they will always retain the possibility of domesticating themselves once again. Providence will always be there to guide human free will back to their civil state. He concludes this passage by writing, "providence ordained that, from the causes we are now setting forth, they [the giants] should shrink to the present proper stature of mankind" (524). This again emphasizes that human beings are not naturally giants but are suited to exist in civilization. This also suggests that philosophy should lead humanity forward at least into the third age rather than cautiously holding it back from the fall into barbarism. If a civilization does not choose to leave the heroic age, it will never escape feudalism. Given the help the giants in the forest will receive from providence, it is worth moving forward out of feudalism.

The civil nature of humans also contributes to the possibility that Vico has an intersubjective view of human beings.[42] One would not want to exaggerate this point to suggest he has a developed postmodern view of intertwined subjectivities. Nevertheless, if one understands *intersubjective* as meaning that politics cannot be separated from structures of thought, then Vico would have an intersubjective position. Axiom LXIX states, "Governments must conform to the nature of men governed" (246). This is not a piece of advice. Rather, it reflects Vico's idea that there is a basic connection between who people are and the government in which they live. One may not be understood without the other. Political change is, of course, possible, but it only happens slowly as human nature also evolves (249). This is an important idea from which to build a political reading of the *New Science*.

This point is alluded to in the frontispiece of the 1744 *New Science*. Originally, the volume included a title page with a small picture of winged metaphysic sitting on a globe and staring into a mirror. This is called *ignota latebat*.⁴³ Unfortunately, it is not included in the Bergin and Fisch translation. It presents the limited number of metaphysical ideas that are found through self-reflection. Upon seeing this, the reader is supposed to turn the page to see winged metaphysic now standing on a globe with a ray of light that comes from the sky and reflects off of her to illuminate the human world. Vico writes, "she contemplates in God the world of human minds, which is the metaphysical world, in order to show His providence in the world of human spirits, which is the civil world or world of nations" (2). Now that metaphysics examines humans in the civil world, it can reveal human nature as it exists in the wealth of institutions that are inherent to it. The only way to understand both human beings and their institutions is to look out into the civil world rather than simply inward.

Civil human nature also connects to the idea of free will and moral responsibility found in the *New Science*. It is impossible to think of humans as free creatures if they are removed from their civil state. Moral responsibility can only be seen in the context of civil life. This is reflected in his critique of the Stoics and Epicureans, whom he refers to as solitary philosophers. They both consider choice as an individual activity of decision-making without considering a social context. As a result, they understand human action as either random or causally determined. He writes, "For both deny providence, the former chaining themselves to fate, the latter abandoning themselves to chance" (130). Epicureans—he is thinking of Hobbes—deny the importance of an intelligent god and assume everything is material. As a result, they think the universe is all a matter of chance and that individual humans act randomly (1109). Stoics—he is thinking of Spinoza here—think everything is fully controlled by an intelligent God, leaving no room for free will. He writes, "Benedict Spinoza speaks of the commonwealth as if it were a society of hucksters [*mercadanti*]" (335). While "hucksters" is an appropriate translation, the key point is that it is a derogatory term for merchants and vendors. The idea is that all human activity, on this view, is controlled by forces of physics or even by market forces. For both, individual free choice cannot have a substantial effect. When one puts humans into a civil context, then one can see that human choice plays a role in the way civilization moves backward or forward on the path of the ideal eternal history.

Before moving from this topic, it will be helpful to bring Vico's view into focus by contrasting it with the familiar account of Jean-Jacques Rousseau about the evolution of human institutions. His account in the *Discourse on the Origin of Inequality* shares a number of vital insights with the *New Science*. It draws the opposite conclusion however, because it holds the more recognized idea that humanity naturally exists in the wilderness.

Like Vico, Rousseau uses anthropological evidence to support his view of humanity outside of civilization. Specifically, he uses Francisco Coreal's writings about Venezuela to support his position.[44] He also argues that humans without luxury would have been physically stronger. As in Vico's account, he argues that mothers in the wild would not have to raise their children. He writes, "Children [in the wilderness] enter the world with the excellent constitution of their parents and strengthen it with the same exercises that produced it, thus acquiring all the vigor that the human race is capable of having."[45] He describes how their strength and agility would allow them to withstand extreme weather, survive disease, fight some animals and flee others. These are not exactly Vico's giants, but it is a similar idea.[46] The two authors differ strongly on the way these creatures feel pity, as I will discuss in a moment. The key point the two authors share is that outside of civil society humans would have lived independently.

The remarkable similarity of the two views is epistemological. For both authors, because humans outside of society had no notion of luxury, they would not and could not imagine inventing it. Rousseau writes, "His [savage man's] desires do not go beyond his physical needs. The only goods he knows in the universe are nourishment, a woman, and rest; the only evils he fears are pain and hunger."[47] It would never occur to them to enter society to get the benefits of working together because they were surviving adequately without such support. Vico's axiom LXIV states, "The order of ideas must follow the order of institutions" (238). His giants would have to invent civilization before they could recognize what they had done. For both authors, explaining the origin of civilization becomes a major philosophical problem because neither can say that it was a product of a simple agreement.

This very important similarity masks an important difference in their approaches. For Rousseau, humanity lives naturally outside of civil institutions. The question for him is why humanity gave this up to enter into civil society. Why did they exchange their individual freedoms for the material benefits of living in society? This question becomes particularly difficult when one emphasizes that the lack of freedom in civilization entails relations of dependence and imprisonment in social classes. Vico comes at this from the opposite perspective. For him, humanity not only lives naturally in civil society, but there is also a substantial period in history in which the class divide is natural. He sees civil institutions and the class divide as a means of returning humans to their natural state. For him, the temporary sacrifice of freedom is worth it given the ultimate reward in the human age. This difference creates a fundamental disagreement in the way they describe the evolution of civil society.

Rousseau's answer to the problem of how humanity entered civil society seems straightforward to contemporary readers who are interested in the development of technology. Initially, small groups would occasionally form to hunt a particular animal, but they would have normally wandered apart afterward.[48] Only over an extended period of time would they have begun to work together on bigger projects and recognized the benefits of their associations. Eventually, some humans would happen to stop wandering long enough to feel the benefit of having a stable place to live.[49] These developments culminate, of course, in the invention of metallurgy and agriculture for which people lose their independence and become chained to society.[50] For Rousseau, the slow and accidental advancement of technology explains how humanity gradually left their natural state and entered civil living. It also explains how humans sacrificed their freedom. He even goes so far as to explain how this ultimately leads to the downfall of civilization, which he describes along the same lines as Vico.[51]

Vico's answer seems much less familiar because he is largely unconcerned with technological advancement. This will become a major theme in this study. There is a temptation to help Vico by reading technological development into his account of the evolution of civil institutions. I maintain that his refusal to emphasize technological development as Rousseau does is important for his philosophical argument. For Vico, the question of human development is always about how humans were able to tame their passions to return to their natural state. The purpose of poetic wisdom is to enable the nobles to begin that transformation through the imposition of self-discipline. Not only are technological developments accidental to this civilizing process, poetic wisdom itself is not particularly suited for technological advancement. As a result, Vico's account of early civilization is almost entirely about moral development while excluding technological concerns.

By framing Vico's position in this way, it is possible to see the conversation or debate that would transpire between these authors. On the surface, their dispute is about whether humans in the wilderness would be tranquil or violent. This is Rousseau's dispute with Hobbes. His debate with Vico is really about whether technological responses to practical concerns are enough to inspire the creation of civil society or whether a pagan religion is needed. There is a good deal at stake in this debate. If Rousseau is right, then the existence of technology is close to the heart of many social problems. Any sound political philosophy will need to figure out a way to justify human existence in civil society by eliminating the negative influence of technological thought. Of course Rousseau is concerned with the corruption of the upper class. As he describes in the first *Discourse*, their selfishness is greatly exacerbated by the presence of technology. If Vico is right, the problem with the upper class is not connected to technology. Instead, the problem is that their mentality is both inherently classist and also tenaciously resistant to any change. While these two positions stem from the same early modern culture and philosophical traditions, their diagnoses are quite different. Before thinking about how to resolve this dispute, I will give it even more historical context.

Passions and Interests

Our vision of early modern philosophy is shifting. In the past, there was much concern about how this tradition gave rise to the current idea of science and there was lively debate about what society had gained and lost with the rise of technology. Rousseau was a focal point of this discussion. The evolution of the scientific method is obviously still important. Now, however, much more interest is being taken in the rise of capitalism. Its ideological growth centered on the question of how civilization could effectively restrain human desire and instill morality without relying on religion. Capitalist ideology suggests not only that the free market can distribute goods effectively but that it can also stimulate civil behavior. Vico's *New Science* argues that capitalism is not strong enough to encourage morality. I do not see a reason to see him as an opponent of the free market in itself, and he never calls for an end to trade. His objection is that other institutions such as an effective judicial system are necessary to encourage civil behavior. Given the recent interest in the rise of capitalism out of the question of human sociability, I wonder if Vico's voice will take on more relevance in discussions of early modern thought.

In the early modern period, philosophers considered alternate institutions that could instill moral order to replace the church, which was losing credibility. The free market emerged as an obvious answer. Adam Smith did not recognize his argument about the invisible hand as relevant to the development of moral character.[52] He saw it more as an argument for allowing the free market to distribute goods without government intervention. Nevertheless, his position is often read with a moral presumption. It solves the problem of human socialization by suggesting that the free market will entice people to live in a civil fashion. On one level, self-interest will drive people to look for ways to survive, and the free market will channel that desire into the production of goods that people want and need. Given that commerce requires working together and building relationships of trust, people will also learn how to treat each other civilly. An important benefit of this system is that the free market can encourage moral behavior without the need for focused moral education. The free market seamlessly channels self-interest into civil behavior in a way that people do not resist, since they receive the immediate benefits from their labor.

To illustrate how deeply the connection between ethics and commerce exists in the United States, I turn to recent trends in university education. Universities profess to teach their students how to behave responsibly. At the same time, however, they are cutting requirements for humanities courses. This seems contradictory, but it is not as long as one intentionally or accidentally assumes that the market will channel self-interest into civil behavior. One can see this in the stereotypical career of college students in the United States. Many young students arrive at college to engage in binge drinking or other experimentally indulgent and destructive behaviors. Universities do not really believe that ethics courses will have an effect on this. Instead, they assume that students will wake up and realize that they will need to get a job to pay off their student loan debts. At that point, they will take their business and other pre-professional courses seriously. This will teach moderation in a way an ethics class on Aristotle never could. One could say that offices of career services rather than campus ministries become the center for teaching moral behavior. I am not sure how many people on campuses ever become aware of this mechanism for instilling civil virtue. The fact that this point goes unrecognized and unquestioned illustrates how deep this ideology is in Western society. One could add that as the price of tuition increases, more college students in the United States need to find jobs to supplement the loans they take out to finance their studies. I suspect politicians and administrators find this palatable because it cuts out the desire for dangerous indulgence. Fewer and fewer college students in the United States have the luxury of going to parties regularly. This helps instill in them the importance of civil behavior.

The connection between civil behavior and the free market seems so intuitive in the contemporary environment of neoliberalism that it can seem hard to formulate an alternative. In working on this study, I have thought about eighteenth-century authors who claimed they could not see an alternative to feudalism. They held that a civilization could not sustain itself if a class of aristocrats did not directly care for vassals.[53] When I consider how strange this looks now, I find hope that on the horizon there may be a stage after neoliberalism, or at least an improvement over the current system. Be that as it may, recent scholars have been returning to the early modern period to question whether the development of the market was inevitable.

In *The Origin of Capitalism: A Longer View*, Ellen Meiksins Wood discusses how early modern philosophers sought alternate solutions to the crisis of the seventeenth century that went beyond the market. She argues that capitalism's appearance of inevitability developed after the early modern period. Marxist theorists and free market advocates both argued, for very different reasons, that capitalism is a necessary stage in economic history. This view became so pervasive that contemporary thinkers have been discouraged from looking for alternate paths that Europe could have taken. Wood argues that early modern thinkers at the time did not assume that the development of capitalism was inevitable. They proposed many other directions for the development of European institutions.[54] European free market capitalism and democracy were not simply the result of organic evolution but resulted from key decisions and theoretical debates that could have gone differently. There was a lively discussion of this in the early modern period that scholars are now trying to uncover.

Albert O. Hirschman's *The Passions and the Interests* is one of the most important recent texts to rethink the theoretical origins of capitalism.[55] Hirschman reveals that it was not at all common sense to think that the market could instill moral behavior. He traces the history of the argument over whether commerce could be used to instill morality in the people.

He identifies authors in Northern Europe who argued that religious compulsion was necessary to instill morality in the people.[56] Nevertheless, advocates of commerce explicitly argued that the human passions for survival and luxury were so powerful that they would naturally evolve into enlightened self-interest as people came to recognize the benefits of civility or at least feigned civility. This position was strongly defended by Bernard Mandeville and then developed by d'Holbach and Hume.[57] As this theory gained traction, it expanded into other dimensions. For example, Montesquieu, Shaftesbury, and Hutcheson argued that commerce and moneymaking were ways not just to channel the desire to survive but also to generally soften the passions.[58] Hirschman's work, among other things, shows that the institutional connection between capitalism and moral order did not simply develop accidentally but resulted, at least in part, from the conscious application of these theoretical investigations.

Vico is one of the first authors that Hirschman identifies as interested in this discussion.[59] The *New Science* represents an early example of a philosopher identifying a mechanism by which selfish human passions could be turned in on themselves and transformed into moral order. He cites axiom VII as a key statement of how this mechanism operates in the course of human history. Vico writes, "Legislation considers man as he is in order to turn him to good uses in human society. Out of ferocity, avarice, and ambition, the three vices which run throughout the human race, it creates the military, merchant, and governing classes, and thus the strength, riches, and wisdom of commonwealths. Out of these three great vices, which could certainly destroy all mankind on the face of earth, it makes civil happiness" (132). Vico's point is that selfish humans unknowingly create the law that restrains the very vices that motivate them. Animalistic humans are unwittingly propelled to advance their selfish interests by developing the institutions that check their own passions. On this level, Vico is one of the authors who discuss the way society naturally directs humans to turn desire against itself in a way that people are unaware.

Hirschman does not recognize Vico's response. He asserts that Vico discovers this idea of transforming passions to interests, but then "there is no elaboration and we are left in the dark about the conditions under which that marvelous metamorphosis of destructive 'passions' into 'virtues' actually takes place."[60] Hirschman then drops Vico from the rest of the study. It is not surprising that Hirschman moves to safer territory. As with so many of Vico's ideas, his response to the problem is interwoven among many other issues. He does not simply dedicate a section to the answer, but expects the reader to piece it together. The basic point Hirschman missed, however, was the role of divine providence in Vico's account.

Vico's clearest statement about the problem of human sociability actually comes at the start of the section on "Method." In his view, the solitary giants in the wilderness were corrupted and so were concerned only with satisfying their immediate desires. He writes, "Seeking only what is useful for themselves and nothing for their companions, they cannot bring their passions under control to direct them toward justice" (341). Yet out of this self-love, they really do come to care about the safety of their families, cities, nations, and even the whole human race. This is because, in Vico's view, divine providence placed humans in a context by which they could choose to leave the wilderness. In this way, he writes, "That which regulates all human justice is therefore divine justice, which is administered by divine providence to preserve human society" (341). Vico does not think that it was simply self-interest that propelled humans to create the institutions that then checked their passions. It required an act of divine providence to put humans in a position where they could freely choose to take the path it offered. In this way, he preserves the roles of both free choice and divine truth in the mechanism by which humans rebuild civil institutions. This conforms with what I discussed earlier about the way that Vico incorporates both divine providence and human freedom into his science.

One can see this point in his discussion of the way the ignorant and passionate giants were able to reenter civilization. Inspired by a clash of thunder, the giants spontaneously invented a religion. He writes, "We must therefore proceed from a vulgar metaphysics, such as we will find the theology of the poets to have been, and seek by its aid that frightful thought of some divinity which imposed form and measure on bestial passions of these lost men and thus transformed them into human passion" (340). In other words, the first poets created an image so great and so terrifying that their fear stopped their selfish desires. This religion was created by free human agency. He writes, "The control over the motion of their bodies is certainly an effect of the freedom of human choice, and thus of free will, which is the home and seat of all the virtues, and among the others of justice" (340). The giants did not randomly create religion as the Epicureans would have it, and they were not compelled to invent it because of physical forces. It was a free act of will that occurred in the context offered by providence. Not every giant was able to invent the pagan religion. This implies that those who did had agency in its creation.

By introducing this notion of divine providence, Vico challenges the idea that the free market could instill civil behavior. Vico draws the conclusion that to further develop moral sensibility, it is not enough just to rely on the actions of the market. This will lead to his call to expand the resources of the judicial system to maintain order and provide equal justice for all. I will return to this argument much later. Now I discuss to the question of what would force humans to leave the wilderness.

Jove and the Problem of Human Sociability

The basic philosophical problem is how bestial humans who lack any inkling of the benefits of shared labor and communal living could choose to band together and create civil institutions. To understand the specifics of the challenge, it may be easier to first work through the problem through other early modern philosophers. I have already introduced Rousseau's notion from *Discourse on the Origin of Inequality* that small and incremental technological developments would draw humanity into civilization. Here I want to discuss the solution Bernard Mandeville offers in his "An Enquiry into the Origin of Moral Virtue," which he published as part of his well-known *Fable of the Bees*.[61] Hirschman talks extensively about Mandeville but does not focus on this particular essay. While Rousseau responds to Mandeville, I have not found evidence to suggest that Vico did or did not have access to it.[62] Nevertheless, it provides a helpful contrast.

Mandeville's *Fable of the Bees* is a dramatic argument to prove that the market rather than Christian virtue is best suited to promote civil behavior. It is an extended poetic allegory in which a beehive represents modern society. He argues that vices such as avarice drive the members of the hive to gather excessive wealth by manipulating the system. This greed-driven work ethic creates jobs and revenue for the hive, increasing overall wealth and prosperity.[63] When certain members of the hive start decrying vice and encourage the bees to be less greedy, the economy of the hive collapses, making things worse for everyone. The bees then regret having questioned the value of avarice.[64] Mandeville claims that the message of the fable is not that human selfishness resolves all social problems.[65] Nevertheless, the larger message of the fable does appear to be that greed unwittingly produces the enlightened sense of self-interest that produces social order and stability.

As part of his commentary on the fable, Mandeville wrote an essay entitled "An Enquiry into the Origin of Moral Virtue." There he directly confronts the problem of human sociability to identify the original motivation for civil behavior. He wonders what made people work together before there were institutions that channeled greed into productive behavior. He frames the problem by saying that those who had decided to first organize society had "to make the people they were to govern believe that it was more beneficial for everybody to conquer than indulge his appetites."[66] He claimed that what was stronger than holy reverence or even bestial greed was the human desire for flattery. As much as humans enjoy short-term pleasure, they enjoy even more the lasting joy they get from receiving praise, fame, and adulation. Fortunately for the first leaders, they could not only grant this attention but they could also manipulate it in such a way that people would do what the leaders desired. They created systems of honor and merit whereby people would be recognized for sacrificing immediate pleasures in favor of appropriate service to the community. This redirected the people's self-love toward social obedience and allowed the leaders to control their people.

Mandeville's account provides a helpful contrast to Vico because he makes use, albeit briefly, of ancient Greek, Roman, and Egyptian history. He explicitly denies the possibility that pagan religion itself could have instilled morality in people. He claims that the rituals of ancient religions were far too obscure and mysterious to be able restrain human passion. He writes, "It is visible, then, that it was not any heathen religion or other idolatrous superstition that first put man upon crossing his appetites and subduing his dearest inclinations, but the skillful management of wary politicians."[67] He supports his view by pointing to the lavish ceremonies the Romans used to celebrate virtuous service. He writes, "if we would know what made them [the Romans] excel in fortitude, courage and magnanimity, we must cast our eyes on the pomp of their triumphs, the magnificence of their monuments and arches."[68] It was the skillful flattery by Roman leaders that turned the human pride of the Roman people into a desire to serve the community.

Vico, of course, denies this view. As per axiom LXIV, the first leaders could not have foreseen what a community was or why they should organize it (238). The first leaders could not have seen the benefits of using flattery to instill order, so they would not have developed the scheme that Mandeville suggests. One can imagine that they would have developed this idea soon after a civilization was born, but it could not have founded a society as Mandeville suggests.

I present Mandeville's position as an example of how challenging the problem of human sociability was. Despite his understanding of it, he struggled to explain why humanity would ever begin to feel a sense of morality. I also present it to give another example of an early modern thinker who was trying to explain pagan religion. Many philosophers during this period wanted to incorporate pagan religion into their account of society. David Hume, for example, provides a long discussion of the development of it.[69] These parts of early modern philosophers often go overlooked. When one recognizes how prevalent they were during the period, Vico's turn to mythology becomes less strange.

Rousseau articulates much more clearly the problem of human sociability. As a result, he gives a solution that is much more developed and convincing. He takes issue with Mandeville on the moral value of pity. Rousseau famously claims that humans in the state of nature would not have been violent because their sense of pity would have restrained them from harming others. This argument is directed primarily against Hobbes, but it also challenges Mandeville. Both authors make the point that harsh and violent criminals are moved to pity when they witness some particularly tragic moment such as the murder of a baby. For Mandeville, this actually discounts the moral value of the passion. For him, it is nothing more than a universal programmed response that does not last past the initial impression. Any immediate response it inspires is not particularly moral, since it is just an instinct. Further, he is pessimistic about its ability to inspire long term moral behavior. This is part of the reason Mandeville attributes the birth of civilization to vanity instead.[70]

Rousseau, on the other hand, sees pity as the passion that checks selfish desire. It is the necessary feature that allows humans to begin working together. It is also needed to constantly restrain selfish desire to maintain and develop higher social orders. He writes that Mandeville "has not seen that from this quality alone [natural pity] flow all the social virtues that he wants to deny in men."[71] He specifically praises pity for its ability to turn the desire for immediate pleasure into the desire to work together to achieve a more stable existence. He writes, "pity is a natural sentiment, which, by moderating in each individual the activity of the love of oneself, contributes to the mutual preservation of the species."[72] In this view, pity was the emotion that allowed the evolution of human institutions to occur so that humans could recognize the benefits of social cooperation. Overall, Rousseau attributes the increase of human dependence on social institutions to the accidental discovery of labor-saving technologies, which inflame the desire for luxury. At the origin of human cooperation, however, is this sensation of pity.

As I alluded to earlier, Vico's main argument is that the bestial passion of the giants combined with their ignorance would be too strong for either pity or incremental technological advancements to civilize the first people. Vico holds that brutish mothers would abandon their children after weaning them. If mothers would not have pity for their own children, how could the giants be said to have pity at all? The giants would be too self-interested and emotional to show any possible interest in the suffering of others.

Vico often compares the giants to children, or at least he uses his experience of children to speculate about what the giants were like (186, 206, 211, 215, 231). The children he describes, however, do not resemble Rousseau's tranquil Emile, who pleasantly works in his garden unburdened by excessive human contact. They are children who impulsively do what they desire, occasionally fight on the playground, and rebel when ordered to behave. They act this way because their passions are strong. The passions of the giants were even more intense because of their bestial education, which taught them how to survive in the wilderness. In civil society, teachers and parents have ways of getting children to settle down long enough to learn the benefits of social behavior. In the wilderness, such education would not work. He writes that the giants "would be quite without that fear of gods, fathers, and teachers which chills and benumbs even the most exuberant in childhood" (369). If the passions of the giants were this strong, they would never notice the benefit of technological development or the rewards of flattery.

I would reinforce Vico's argument with the following analogy. A modern child would be considered out of control when she or he no longer has the fear of punishment or the desire for a reward. Generally speaking, an agitated child already tamed by civil institutions will eventually return to a tranquil state. The giant who has learned that survival depends on violent passions will not return to such a state. Being completely ignorant of civil institutions, she or he will never calm to a level of tranquility that would allow them to recognize the benefits of staying in one place. As a result, technology can never tame the giants. The civilizing force can only be provided by religion. This argument is foundational to the *New Science*.

From a postmodern perspective, there is no way to adjudicate this debate by arguing what humanity would have been like in a time outside of civilization. My goal has been to get to a point where one can understand the discovery of Jove and poetic wisdom. I now turn to this point. As strange as Vico's account of Jove may look, it makes sense when one thinks of it as a solution to a problem his contemporaries struggled to answer. Three criteria for an adequate account of the birth of civilization have come to light based on the problem of human sociability. The invention of Jove has to occur out of a state of complete ignorance. Further, the idea of Jove must be so powerful that it can tame the exceptionally powerful passions of the giants. Beyond that, Vico's account must also be entirely natural to adhere to the requirement that divine providence operates through ordinary physical causes. The last two criteria are fairly easy to meet. The first one is the problem.

Thunder is obviously a natural cause. Vico embellishes his use of thunder by connecting it to the biblical story. He fancifully claims that after the flood, it would have taken a long time for the air to fill up with enough water to create rain and lightning (192). This is part of what made the thunder so surprising to the giants. This aspect of his thought is not that critical other than to remind us that he is thinking his position through. The main point is he finds a natural event out of which a natural superstition may be invented. This is the natural context provided by divine providence from which the giants freely invented Jove.

Explosive thunder is legitimately terrifying. When a violent thunderstrike catches one unaware, it can make a person jump or duck as if being threatened. It can certainly make people stop what they are doing. This is what Jove's thunder does. Vico writes that this ability to stop human action is what creates "Jove's title of stayer or establisher" (504). It made the giants stop their aimless wandering. It also made them stop engaging in sexual intercourse out in the open. The thunder prevented the giants from satisfying their desires, "restraining their bestial lust from finding its satisfaction in the sight of heaven, of which they had a mortal terror" (504). The point is that the terror of Jove is far more intense than that which could be produced by other civilizing forces. Given how extreme the bestial passions were, the thunder needed to shake them physically and violently in order to instill such a sense of fright that they felt an overwhelming need to respond regardless of whatever desires they wanted to slake.

The giants would not have an instinctual response to the thunder. Vico writes that these giants "were frightened and astonished by the great effect whose cause they did not know, and raised their eyes and became aware of the sky" (377). When faced with natural threats, they would have either successfully responded in a bestial but automatic way or died. When the giants felt the fear of the thunder, there would have been no automatic response. Instead, they would have been terrified into generating a reaction that they had never had before. Since the thunder already made them halt, they would imagine that this is how they were commanded to respond. In this way, they connected their religion with moral obligation, although they did not recognize it as such. Indeed, their fear was so strong that it made them notice other unusual things that they also imagined to be commands of Jove. Hence Vergil's phrase, "All things are full of Jove" (379). The theological poets now found themselves surrounded by many auspices that commanded them to act in ways that crushed their bestial desires.

There is a temptation to ascribe to Jove's thunder a level of spiritual or metaphysical insight. One might want to relate it, for example, to Rudolf Otto's idea of the *mysterium tremendum*.[73] As I have discussed, however, Vico wants to avoid the conceit of scholars and so does not think of Jove as having metaphysical significance. He does, however, use the invention of Jove to connect morality to religion. He colorfully writes, "Just so the metaphysics of the poet giants, who had warred against heaven in their atheism, vanquished them with the terror of Jove, whom they feared as the wielder of the thunderbolt" (502). The basic claim is that religion was needed to instill morality in the godless giants. He continues, "From this nature of human institutions arose the eternal property that minds to make good use of the knowledge of God must humble themselves" (502). Because of the religious origin of morality, philosophy is then excluded from the task of moralizing people. He writes, "Religion alone has the power to make us practice virtue, as philosophy is fit rather for discussing it" (503). This does not mean that philosophy is irrelevant for the development of moral behavior in the human age. It just means that its task will be to understand justice and the workings of providence. Religion will still be necessary to instill civil behavior. By extension, material self-interest will also be unable to maintain civil order without the force provided by religious thought. Having explained why thunder is both natural and sufficient for taming the desires of the giants, I turn to the most difficult of the three criteria.

Given the ignorance of the giants, Vico presumes that the jump from the wilderness to civil society must entail the smallest cognitive leap possible that still entails the use of free will. To meet this criterion, he develops the idea of the imaginative universal, the big discovery he made between the 1725 and 1730 *New Science*.

At the core of Vico's entire epistemology of poetic wisdom is the assertion that the giants would have lost the capacity to reflect. It takes a great deal of mental effort and skill to be able to think theoretically. He describes the early humans as having "that infirmity of the human mind by which, immersed and buried in the body, it naturally inclines to take notice of bodily things, and finds the effort to attend to itself too laborious; just as the bodily eye sees all objects outside itself but needs a mirror to see itself" (331). This means that the giants could not have been self-aware, since they could not reflect on or recognize their own thoughts. They could not distinguish their ideas from the world.

Nevertheless, even if one cannot abstract, one could think by imagining. Ever since the *Study Methods*, Vico has maintained that children have powerful imaginations and later develop analytical capacities (SM 13). In the *New Science*, he carries this idea about modern children to the giants, whom he calls "the children, as it were, of the human race" (209). The first poets would have strong imaginations like the modern children. Axiom XXXVI states, "Imagination is more robust in proportion as reasoning power is weak" (185). The powerful imagination of the giants would be connected to the violent passions that poetic wisdom endeavored to restrain. The commentary to axiom LIII states, "The axiom is the principle of poetic sentences, which are formed by feelings of passion and emotion, whereas philosophic sentences are formed by reflection and reasoning" (219). By positing the first thought as a product of the imagination rather than abstraction, Vico can claim that the imaginative invention of Jove was the smallest cognitive leap that could be made out of sheer ignorance.

To be clear, it is important to combine the two points I have just made. The first poets thought through imaginative acts. These were not the ideas a modern thinker would ordinarily associate with the imagination. Any of us can decide to imagine a flying horse, and we can call a picture of Pegasus into our heads. We are aware that we have invented that image. The first theological poets could not reflect so they were not aware that they were creating a metaphor. They actively used their imaginations to see auspices in the world around them but they could not realize they were creating them. They created this world that commanded moral obedience without knowing they were doing it.

To build on this point, the first axiom of the *New Science* states that when people are ignorant, they use their own natures to explain the unknown (120). This is why philosophy has been held back by the conceits of nations and scholars. It also explains the content of the first human ideas. Axiom XXXII states, "When men are ignorant of the natural causes producing things, and cannot even explain them by analogy with similar things, they attribute their own nature to them. The vulgar, for example, say the magnet loves the iron" (180). At the very base of human thought is our imaginative tendency to anthropomorphize or, to put it more simply, to recognize one's own attributes in the world around them. Since the only thing the solitary giants could have had any awareness of is their own passions, they must have shaped their first images out of that awareness.

The first image in the mind of those giants was a metaphor in which the sky was a terrifying human who sent thunder and shouting as a form of punishment. As giants, they were "all robust bodily strength, who expressed their very violent passions by shouting and grumbling." In their minds, the sky became one of these violent giants. Those first poets, "pictured the sky to themselves as a great animated body, which in that aspect they called Jove, the first god of the so-called greater gentes, who meant to tell them something by the hiss of his bolts and the clap of his thunder" (377). The most elementary thought process, anthropomorphizing, enabled the first poets to create the image of Jove. This was a great leap, in one sense, because it enabled the return of humanity to their natural civil environment. It was, however, a small advancement in the sense that it was within the cognitive capacity of the rudimentary mentality of the giants.

One might think that the giants created an image of Jove as somehow a bearded toga-wearing man in the sky. One could also suspect that the giants, upon hearing the thunder, sat down to discuss what the cause was. To stay consistent with the requirements of the problem of human sociability, Vico assures us that this could not been the case. The first poets would only have been capable of spontaneous acts of ingenuity that would have lacked any sort of precision. To highlight this point, Vico emphasizes how strange and foreign this image of Jove would be to modern rationality. He writes, "it is naturally beyond our power to form the vast image of this mistress called 'Sympathetic Nature.'" Jove was not an invention akin to the writings of contemporary poets or cinematic computer graphic imaging. It was the product of a very basic imagination that was struggling to escape its own physicality. Vico writes, "It is equally beyond our power to enter into the vast imagination of those first men, whose minds were not in the least abstract, refined, or spiritualized, because they were entirely immersed in the senses, buffeted by the passions, buried in the body" (378). In my reading, Vico is emphasizing the foreign nature of this form of thought as a way to justify this as an account of the birth of thought from ignorance. It is a way of explaining the transition of the state of nature to civil society that does not have the problems of Mandeville's reliance of vanity or Rousseau's dependence on incremental technological development.

One of the ingenious aspects of Vico's account is that the poets themselves were able to create a superstitious religion without realizing it. This meant that they actually tricked themselves into believing and obeying a false god (236). He states, "the first theological poets created the first divine fable, the greatest they ever created: that of Jove . . . an image so popular, disturbing, and instructive that its creators themselves believed in it" (379). The power of the image combined with the fury of the thunder was strong enough for them to bow before a god that was not real. It is easy to speculate that pagan religion was created by a wise ancient leader to take command of an early nation. One might assume that all superstition was created by a charismatic person to trick people. This may have happened in history, but it cannot explain the origin of moral thought. Vico's account can because it relies not on a manipulative leader but on the crude but free imaginations of the first giants.

There are two ways, then, of talking about the truth of poetic wisdom. I think Vico struggles to express this point because the idea of an alternate epistemological structure was such a new and radical idea.

When one talks about the truth of poetic religion, one must realize that it depends on the perspective from which it is seen and lived. Because the first poets could not reflect, they could not recognize a difference between the real world and the imagined world. From their perspective, everything they thought had to be true. He says this in the commentary to axiom XLVII, which will become very important to my project. He writes, "These fables are ideal truths suited to the merit of those of whom the vulgar tell them; and such falseness to fact as they contain consists simply in failure to give their subjects their due" (205). Poetic wisdom creates a worldview that is so dominating in the minds of the first poets that they cannot step outside of it. Poetic wisdom is their reality, which they have created without realizing this.

From the perspective of the scientist, it is indeed possible to see that these pagan gods do not reflect actual reality.[74] He writes, "divine providence . . . permitted them [the first poets] to be deceived into fearing the false divinity of Jove because he could strike them with lightning" (385). The false religion of Jove was essential for reentry into civilization because the only thing that could tame the bestial passions of the giants was the belief in a divine threat. It is, nonetheless, still a false religion and a potential source of error in later human ages. He reinforces this point when he distinguishes between the first poetic language and divine knowledge. He writes, "that first language, spoken by the theological poets, was not a language in accord with the things it dealt with" (401). Because the first poetic language was based on anthropomorphizing natural objects, it was not actually suited to describing the world scientifically. Indeed, the language of the age of gods was based on the superstitious attempt to read natural signs sent from the gods. He contrasts this with the language of Adam, which was grounded in onomatopoeia and had God's authority. Whether Vico actually believes this last claim or whether the language of Adam is taking the place of his own metaphysics, the point remains that the language of Jove is not an accurate depiction of the natural or supernatural world. Jove and the mythology that follows is an invention. This view of ancient mythology puts Vico in line with Malebranche and other early modern thinkers who want to understand the sources of error and falsehood in the tradition.

Consistent with the emphasis Vico places on human agency, he explains how the first poets freely created Jove. He introduces the idea that the thunder inspired the awakening of conatus. In a manner that echoes Spinoza, Vico philosophically is not deeply interested in defending dualism, and he is much more concerned with depicting the mind and body as intertwined.[75] Nevertheless, he maintains enough of a separation for human agency. He writes that the creation of Jove produces "the conatus proper to the human will" (340). He uses the term *conatus* to signify immaterial self-determining causes. This is probably a reference back to Spinoza, but it also draws on an argument he made in the *Ancient Wisdom* (AW 77–79). In the *New Science*, he defends his view by cleverly critiquing the opposition with a conceit that amounts to a reduction to absurdity. He writes, "to impute conatus to bodies is as much to impute to them freedom to regulate their motions whereas all bodies are by nature necessary agents" (340). In other words, determinists attribute their own human nature to objects and fail to see the difference between the two. As a result, they assume that natural objects have conatus, which they clearly do not. The free incorporeal conatus of humans must be distinct from determined physical forces. This makes some sense as an attack on determinists and is consistent with Vico's idea that humans are inclined to use the known to understand the unknown. Nevertheless, it amounts to a circular argument because Vico assumes that conatus is free, which he is trying to prove. Vico may have better ammunition.

Vico makes another argument, which conforms to what was said about freedom and divine providence in the last chapter. It also clarifies his position in relation to Hirschman's concern about how Vico thinks divine providence works and his view on the invisible hand. Despite holding that human nature is inherently social, the barbarism shows that humans have the capacity to become corrupted by falling "under the tyranny of self-love." This corruption occurs when humans stop thinking socially and focus selfishly on the fulfillment of material needs. This is always a danger, given that "man desires principally his own utility" (341). To help humanity maintain its natural state, divine providence checks the ability of a human to satisfy material desires. He writes, "Unable to attain all the utilities he wishes, he is constrained by these institutions to seek those which are his due; and this is called just" (341). When humans discover they cannot get what they physically want, they are inspired to think freely. This breaks them out of the path driven by physical impulses and allows them to think about moral responsibility.

In this context, the Jove moment becomes an instant where divine providence offers human beings freedom by giving them the opportunity to consider something other than material needs. It is true that the thunder and the ensuing fear in the giants are physical phenomena, but the point is the giants cannot respond in an instinctual way. By checking their physical wanderings, the thunder invites the strongest of them to think of something other than physical impulses. This frees them from the material realm and allows them to invent a religion that is disconnected from physical desires. This makes civil society and moral behavior possible. On one level, this argument suggests that if Jove was not a free invention, then it would not represent the return to civil human nature. If Jove were an instinctual or determined response driven by selfish passion, humanity would not reenter civil society. On a grander level, it suggests that any mechanism such as the free market that tries to instill morality on the basis of material forces will not create a space for moral behavior. In this way, Vico's depiction of the invention of Jove is at the core of his rejection of the idea that the free market can directly transform selfishness into civil behavior.

Luigi Pareyson's reading of Vico helps explain how the creation of the imaginative universals could be free. When philosophers consider the possibility of free will, they generally think about whether it is possible to reflectively deliberate. They tend to overlook the fact that artists create spontaneously but also freely. Obviously, artists do deliberate when they work, but it seems that there are also moments of inspiration. One would not say that great works of art were simply determinate products of natural stimulation. In a similar way, one should not say that Jove was an automatic response. Instead, it was a rudimentary work of art that came from human agency. Pareyson reads the *New Science* as a defense of the value of the faculty of *ingegno* as producing free and creative acts. He asserts that even though Jove is simply an act of imitation in which the sky is thought to imitate the bodies of the giants, this is still an act of creativity. For Pareyson, because civilization was born and then develops by means of these ingenious acts, Vico shows the importance of studying the faculty of *ingegno*.[76] I maintain that by putting human agency at the start of civilization, it demonstrates the importance of human responsibility throughout Vico's work.

To end this discussion of Jove, I must return to the point I made in response to Berlin. Poetic wisdom is inherently communicative. It is important to explain how the first imaginative universal functions as a means of sharing meaning.

The invention of Jove was an act of imaginative imitation. It had to be in order to be the smallest leap from pure instinct to thought. As axiom XII says, "Children excel in imitation; we observe that they generally amuse themselves by imitating whatever they are able to apprehend" (215). The issue this raises is that Vico thinks of poetic imitation in two different ways. When he discusses children and the embodied thought of the first poets, he emphasizes the way they thought by physically performing their ideas. In this sense, imitation means literally recreating a past idea or experience. When he discusses pagan superstition, he emphasizes the way the poets assumed the sky imitated their own passions. He says directly, "They believed that Jove commanded by signs, that such signs were real words, and that nature was the language of Jove" (379). The poets imagined the sky to be a being that was in some way an imitation of themselves. The ability of this being to create fear, however, gave it the authority to demand obedience from the poets. Poetic wisdom is connected to imitation in the sense of mimetic performance and in the sense of anthropomorphizing the natural world.

When commentators have explored poetic wisdom, they have tended to emphasize one of these two aspects of imitation. Gianfranco Cantelli tends to portray the poetic characters as speaking through nature. Donald Phillip Verene, on the other hand, stresses the importance of mimetic activity for remembering the poetic characters.[77] I read Vico as holding these two dimensions together.

He writes, "by that trait of the human mind noticed by Tacitus whatever these men saw, imagined, or even made or did themselves they believed to be Jove" (379). The mental trait he refers to is found in axiom XXXIV. Tacitus claims that once human beings start to rely on superstition, they see superstitious forces everywhere (183). This makes a certain amount of sense. When one succumbs to superstition, one stops using objective data to verify or discredit the causal relationships one imagines. At that point, there is nothing to prevent a person from finding superstitious forces everywhere. Vico pushes this notion to its extreme limit. If the poets are going to see the superstitious commands of Jove everywhere, then they will also see Jove in their own behavior. This means both that the poets are commanded by Jove when they see the natural forces in the world, and that they transmit the commands of Jove when they imitate him.

In this way, the poetic character Jove communicates in two ways. The poets unwittingly imagine the commands of Jove coming from a wide range of natural phenomena. They struggle to obey these commands for fear of some sort of punishment. The earliest poets do not have the capacity to reflect or deliberate, so they should not be thought of as carefully interpreting these signs. Rather, their lives are a series of spontaneous but freely creative responses to the passions evoked by divine signs. From their perspective, life would be constant obedience to divine commands. Of course, the scientist can recognize that both the commands and the responses are imagined in the mind in the poet. In this sense, the invention of Jove is an act of self-discipline. The poets imagine that Jove communicates, but in reality they are controlled by their own spontaneous desire to control their passions. In this sense, they think Jove is communicating when really it is their own imaginations that drive them to check their passions.

In another sense, however, communication is happening even if the poets do not realize it. Because the poets think of their own behavior as the activity of Jove, they communicate Jove's commands to others. They do not recognize their own agency in this because they superstitiously attribute everything, even their own behavior, to Jove. Nevertheless, their mimetic performance of Jove signals to the other poets that divine commands need to be obeyed. This turns the individual self-discipline of the poet into a network of social pressure to listen to the superstitious commands of Jove as they are communicated by the other poets. In the first asylums, the theological places felt the divine commands transmitted by natural forces and each other and responded by checking their material desires. In those asylums, poets would learn to watch each other carefully to see if commands were disobeyed. This pressure compelled the poets to restrain their passion and reenter civil society. It also forged a powerful sense of social identity based entirely on showing obedience to traditional rituals in order to maintain a position in the community.

It is hard to imagine anthropologically that humanity began this way. Vico's account is compelling because it lays the groundwork for an explanation of why the aristocracy behaves the way it does. Vico's view of the birth of civilization is not one in which early humans feel a spiritual connection to the earth unburdened by the demands of technology. Rather, the world of the poets is a desperate one in which they feel constant pressure from nature and from each other to demonstrate proper self-discipline. This matches a popular vision of aristocratic behavior. Nobles feel a profound sense of tradition. It inspires in them a strong sense of self-discipline that justifies to themselves the authority they wield over the lower classes. This self-control is motivated by intense social pressure exerted by other members of the aristocracy. Hence, the aristocratic life is dominated by constant worry about behaving inappropriately. If Vico's account is superior to Mandeville's or Rousseau's, it will not be because he accurately explained the origin of humanity. It will be because he diagnosed better the forces that cause the aristocracy to prevent progress.

In this chapter, I have tried to go from what is familiar and work toward what is unusual. Contemporary readers are accustomed to thinking about pagan religion in terms of a magical connection to the natural world. This is what Berlin found in the *New Science*. Contemporary readers are also used to thinking about the state of nature as a place where humanity demonstrates their fundamental characteristics outside the control of a central government. The *New Science* does not conform to either view. Once those ideas are cleared away, it becomes much easier to see how Vico builds a theory of myth to explain class domination. The invention of Jove is a free and spontaneous act of great ingenuity. At its core, however, is the imposition of discipline not just on oneself but on all others. The invention of Jove represents the birth of noble authority as an expression of obedience to tradition. This defines the aristocratic world view. Before showing how this applies to Vico's historical context, I want to use this discussion of Jove to build a focused account of poetic wisdom as an epistemological structure.

3

Imaginative Universals

Vico's Discovery

Poetic wisdom is an alternate epistemology because it organizes perception by using a unique type of concept. Vico called these *imaginative universals*, or *universali fantastici*. Each one is a paradigm that identifies a group of objects, actions, or people without abstracting particular qualities from them. Because poetic wisdom does not think reflectively, it does not separate essence from attribute or the essential from the accidental. For a particular entity to be included in an imaginative paradigm, it must reproduce all elements of that paradigm. Otherwise, it is not recognized as a manifestation of the imaginative universal. Each pagan god is an imaginative universal. To witness or become a manifestation of the god, one must reproduce that god exactly. This chapter will try to make sense of what this could mean. This is a challenging idea, but that is to be expected. If poetic wisdom is an alternate form of thought, then it must require reformulating basic structures of knowing.

Vico alerts us to both the difficulty and the importance of the imaginative universals. He writes, "This discovery, which is the master key of this Science, has cost us the persistent research of all our literary life, because with our civilized natures we [moderns] cannot at all imagine and can understand only by great toil the poetic nature of these first men" (34). In *Vico's Science of the Imagination*, Donald Phillip Verene comments, "It is rare that an author gives such a direct statement of the central premise of his thought, and surprising that he provides such clear guidance for its interpretation."[1] Nonetheless, his account is still difficult to grasp.

Beyond the inherent difficulties involved in engaging an alternate rationality, Vico's style of presentation adds two further obstacles. First, while one can see that Jove presents a solution to the problem of human sociability, it is unclear beyond that why the poetic wisdom is so significant to the *New Science*. There is no clear statement as to what the scientist is supposed to learn from the discovery. If Vico had indicated that more directly, it might be easier to understand what they are. Second, as Verene discusses, Vico does not dedicate a section of the *New Science* to the epistemology of the imaginative universals.[2] Book 2 combines his account of the poetic wisdom directly with his history of the civil institutions of the first two ages. It does not include a passage that simply defines poetic wisdom as a structure of rationality. This textual structure conforms perfectly to his method. To show that his interpretation seamlessly collects all the available evidence into one narrative, he intertwines his description of pagan religion, civil history, and epistemology. The closer he can embed these three elements together, the more accurate his science would be. This is a commendable objective, but it does not help the contemporary reader approach the epistemological structure of poetic wisdom.

Over the last fifty years, research on the imaginative universal has tried to make sense of it by orienting its discovery toward a philosophical purpose. Authors have explained why knowing pagan religion is philosophically important and used that to shape their interpretations. They have all been vital for me in developing my own approach to poetic wisdom. At the same time, I think the significance of my approach will be helped by contrasting it with these other ways. The fundamental difference between our approaches is that the others try to find a positive use for comprehending and even using poetic wisdom. I see poetic wisdom as a problematic form of thought that is a danger for just rule in the human age. I propose that poetic wisdom must be understood in order to reform it.

Before exploring my critical approach, I will present some of these other approaches. Many have seen the discovery as part of Vico's defense of the philosophical value of the imagination. Vico claims that in searching for the imaginative universals, "we encountered exasperating difficulties which have cost us the research of a good twenty years" (338). This places the start of his journey around the time when he was writing the *Study Methods*, his most determined call to balance the ancient study of rhetoric with the modern critical method. Verene observes, "The force of Vico's remarks is that he intends us to regard all his thought as pointing not only to a conception of a new science but specifically to the conception of the imaginative universal that makes it possible."[3] Verene's position is that Vico's most significant project was the defense of rhetoric and the imagination. The discovery of the imaginative universals completes it.

As discussed in the last chapter, the *Study Methods* defends the use of both ancient and modern study methods. It does not present the critical method as inherently inferior, but it does argue that the ancient imaginative approach can do certain things better. The imagination's strength is making connections between disparate topics. If one can train the imagination, one can uncover practical solutions to difficult problems and establish a common ground with the audience. The *Study Methods* makes these points practically. Unfortunately, it cannot really explain why the modern critical method could not eventually make the imagination obsolete. In other words, his argument does not eliminate the possibility that the theoretical method could develop its own problem-solving and communication strategies. With the discovery of the poetic wisdom, this is now explained. If these two forms of thought are epistemologically distinct, then critical or technological thought could never grasp the world the way poetic wisdom does. Given that the poetic wisdom existed at the dawn of civilization, it would be necessary to study it to understand human culture and then use it to develop political prudence. This makes it imperative that philosophers study rhetoric and develop their imaginations alongside other modern approaches. One needs to know the mythic tradition underlying culture to communicate with people in it.

This path opens a variety of possibilities for finding value in studying pagan thought. Some argue that it is important for understanding modern civilization. Gianfranco Cantelli, after having given an extensive account of the poetic characters, claims that the vulgar language of the third age of humans comes out of divine and heroic language.[4] The imaginative universals and the intelligible universals limit what human beings can know and the nature of their institutions. Humanity thus needs to respect the imaginative universals that make up half of human creation.[5] Jacques Chabot contrasts Vico's view of imaginative making with Hegel's view of reason as an external structure that directs humanity. By acknowledging that humans actually make the social world rather than following the path of reason alone, we can recognize the value of imaginative activity.[6] Hence, humanity should learn to value and respect the imaginative cultural products of myth in addition to more rational institutions.[7]

Other authors connect Vico's defense of the imagination to epistemology and art. As discussed in the last chapter, Pareyson uses the creation of Jove through an act of *ingegno* to build a case that the *New Science* as a whole defends the importance of spontaneous creativity. Marcel Danesi argues that since the birth of human reason is imaginative rather than logically systematic, scientists ought to consider its role in human psychology.[8] In her work on the reception of Vico in Italy in the nineteenth century, Martina Piperno identifies the way the discovery of poetic wisdom provided authors a way of articulating the natural forces that influenced the lives of ancient thinkers.[9] She further argues that Vico's identification of poetic wisdom as a separate mode of thought had a substantial influence on later Italian attempts to interpret and use ancient images and myths.[10]

Other authors look for a more moral or political significance to the discovery of the imaginative universals. Verene suggests that philosophers must understand the imaginative universals in order to recognize their contemporary philosophical equivalents, which he identifies as recollective universals. These universals, which Verene connects to Vico's new art of criticism, present a way for philosophy to deploy *fantasia* to remember the past, understand the workings of the mind, and grasp the course of history. They help reveal the metaphysical truth in the rise and fall of civilizations. This gives solace for—but not an antidote to—the oncoming barbarism of reflection. He writes, "This praxis [of thinking with recollective universals] can refresh mind in the last days of rust and misbegotten wit, but it does not thereby convert a negative into a positive."[11] By studying the powerful imagination of the first people, contemporary philosophers can use their imaginations to recognize the decay of humanity and mitigate against the stresses it causes even if it cannot be prevented.

Other authors have suggested that poetic wisdom must be accounted for when one considers how to maintain and improve modern society. For example, Battistini carefully examines Vico's use of Vergil and concludes that the *Aeneid* could be understood as a Homeric epic for the human age. Vergil presented virtue poetically in a way that tapped into the power of pagan religion without regressing into superstition. Thus, he presents a model for using the structures of poetic wisdom in a modern way to inspire civic duty and to forestall the barbarism of reflection.[12] Paolo Cristofolini calls this use of poetic wisdom a *rimbarbarimento*. This is not a return to barbarism but reflects the Roman ability to recapture pagan wisdom without losing their modern rationality. He emphasizes that, for Vico, Naples has yet to reach the heights of Cicero and Augustus and that his discussion of poetic wisdom is meant to help moderns develop their *fantasia* to reach the heights of the past.[13] These authors do not see Vico as simply defending tradition and community. They present him as unveiling past forms of knowledge that could be redeployed in ingenious ways that do not undercut contemporary rationality.

One of the most thorough uses of this approach is David L. Marshall's *Vico and the Transformation of Rhetoric in Early Modern Europe*. He draws on all of Vico's works to show how they defend a new and modern idea of rhetoric. For him, Vico's early texts expand what counts as worthy of interpretation.[14] This transforms the study of rhetoric from a simple discussion of persuasion to higher epistemological and sociological investigations. This is the road Marshall takes to finding an intersubjective view of humanity in Vico's earlier writings. Politically, this position propels Vico to argue that modern governments need to communicate with people by recognizing the *co-presence* of individuals who exist in multiple relationships with others.[15] He writes, "This is the core of Vico's sublimation of rhetoric. The epicenter is located at the intersection of *institution* in its spatial and temporal senses. Vico insists that the senate be *presente al popolo*."[16] Marshall clarifies that *presente* here means that "the patricians and the plebeians witness each other reciprocally." It also means that the plebeians have rights to information and actions by which they can express themselves and evoke change.[17] This is a modern view of rhetoric and politics because it is a profound expression of what would be really necessary to have a society in which there was true participation.

The poetic wisdom plays an important role in this deep idea of *presente*. Marshall sees the *New Science*'s division of humanity into three ages as describing a primary barrier to communication and political discussion. Marshall calls this "desynchronization." The study of the imaginative universal and poetic wisdom allows a society to understand and maintain institutions of the past so that it is possible to comprehend historically distant cultures. This creates the possibility for, as he writes, "A society that possesses institutions where citizens gather, debate, decide, and act in a society that synchronizes its members, so that they all share basic points of reference in past, present and future."[18] Roberto Esposito emphasizes the way Vico does not draw strong borders between the ages but shows them as overlapping and intertwining.[19] Marshall builds on this point to show how rhetorical knowledge of the interconnection of the three ages allows for the creation of a just society. Further, I think Marshall is correct to suggest that Vico has a complex view of what participatory government might look like. Unlike other early modern thinkers, he recognized the vast differences that exist between ways of thinking and communicating. If these epistemological distinctions exist, then, for example, Rousseau's idea of a general will rising effortlessly out of political discussion becomes less believable. Marshall lays out a path for grasping this complex idea of political community in Vico.

These authors provide valuable insights that have helped me build my reading of poetic wisdom as an epistemological structure.[20] What I find lacking in these accounts, though, is a focused investigation into what Vico says the Roman myths actually mean. They do not ignore his interpretations entirely, but their focus is more on understanding poetic wisdom as a structure of thought rather than as an element of Vico's account of the history of civil institutions. As a result, they do not consider the way poetic wisdom directs the action of the theological poets and the heroes. Further, they do not connect the operation of poetic thought to the cruel behavior of the nobility and their oppression of the lower classes. I propose that Vico saw this connection. He does not write a strong manifesto calling for the removal of the civil institutions of poetic wisdom. Even in the human age it is important to restrain human self-interest, and those institutions could be helpful in that. Nevertheless, he does discuss the way that poetic wisdom needs to be resisted and contained in the human age.

As discussed in the first chapter, Bobbio rightly points out that Vico does not describe corrupt forms of government. Rather, he shows how forms of government are appropriate for each age and how the class struggle provides the mechanism for political evolution. Nonetheless, the borders between historical eras are not clearly defined. In the transition from the second to the third age, a heroic government and a popular government could coexist and, indeed, compete with each other. The poetic wisdom of the heroic age would compel the nobles to protect the institutions of authority. The people and the monarch would fight against that in order to impose a government that would be suited to the mentality of the human age. The philosopher would use human reason to promote the cause of justice and fight against the traditional aristocratic government. This would entail engaging the political fight for democracy and monarchy against aristocratic feudalism.

Vico address this point specifically at the end of book 4, where he explains how a government of a new era can be impeded by the institutions of the old. Vico asserts that new governments must retain old institutions over the course of the transition (1004).[21] This derives from axiom LXXI, which states, "Native customs, and above all that of natural liberty, do not change all at once but by degrees and over a long period of time" (249). The specific example he gives involves the dictator Quintus Publilius Philo and the Publilian Law. In response to a major uprising in 339 BC, this law dictated that the nobles could not overturn a plebeian plebiscite (112). This change, however, did not clarify how the plebeians would administer the government. Authority naturally drifted back into a type of aristocracy in which the plebeians became wards of nobles. He describes this state of coexisting governments by writing, "they were by nature free commonwealths, administered aristocratically" (1006). This suggests that the society had temporarily overthrown feudal structures but then regressed back into them despite the granting of superficial freedoms.

Vico's discussion represents a moment when he sees older and newer forms of political authority competing. The result of this particular encounter was that the plebeians gained some freedoms but failed to get substantial control of the government. Individual plebeians were unable to restrain their self-interest and slid back into the stability of feudalism rather than contribute to a new government. This did not stop the development of Rome, but it steered it toward the creation of a monarchical empire under the Caesars rather than a popular democracy. The efforts of the plebeians were positive but not as effective as they could have been. Had the plebeians better understood poetic wisdom, they would have better known how to reform it and avoid falling back into aristocratic rule. The lesson I draw from this is that Vico supported the idea that the political institutions of poetic wisdom needed to be reformed to enter into the human age. Moreover, it is important that such political evolution be executed carefully to avoid possible missteps. This passage is buried at the end of book 4, but it is a call to use human freedom to supersede the aristocratic authority of poetic wisdom.

These overlapping governments did not merely intensify conflicts between the rich and poor. They were the product of a clash between different epistemological systems. I suspect that Vico looked at the feudal institutions dominating Naples and wondered why reform had not been possible. He realized that the only answer to this question is that the feudal aristocrats framed the world differently that the monarch or the people. They blocked substantial reform because their mentality was oriented toward something other than the sort of social and economic progress that everyone else desired. This contributed to his discovery of poetic wisdom as an epistemological structure. Vico's discovery was that inefficient but tenacious feudal rule was not just the result of ordinary superstition. The noble resistance to any sort of philosophical discussion or compromise existed because the aristocracy had an entirely different way of conceptually framing their world.

The discovery of Jove revealed that the primary function of poetic wisdom was not to care for practical needs but moral needs. The imaginative universals were unwittingly invented by the first theological poets to provide the ritualistic self-discipline necessary to return the giants to their social human state. I will show that all the gods of the greater gentes function in this way. The imaginative universals instill familial control over fiefdoms (Juno), demonstrate noble breeding (Venus, Apollo), protection of the pagan religion (Diana, Vulcan, Saturn, Vesta, Mercury) and a willingness to fight against rebellion (Mars, Minerva, Neptune). These rituals of self-discipline spring from a mentality oriented to maintaining a separation between nobility and the animalistic lower classes. This means that poetic wisdom, at its core, was invented to frame the world in a way that resists the possibility of change. While this had value in the first ages of humanity, once the third age arrives it blocks positive development. From this perspective, poetic wisdom needs to be understood in order to find a path to reform.

As I discuss the imaginative universals in this chapter, my focus will not be on the power of the imagination or the importance of religious tradition. It will be to understand how restrictive poetic wisdom is. While the gods are created by fantastic leaps of imagination, their lasting effect is their ability to restrict the passions and actions of the nobility to return them to civil life. In later chapters, I will show this in Vico's specific portrayals of the imaginative universals. Here, I will focus on how poetic wisdom exists as an epistemological system.

The Origin of Poetic Wisdom

Vico makes his momentous discovery between the publication of the 1725 and the 1730 edition of the *New Science*. As mentioned above, he is fully aware of its importance. He disavows the first edition, and he claims that only three ideas carry over from it: the science of blazonry, the discussion of the origin of letters, and the idea of a universal mental dictionary (28, 33, 35). Despite this, when one reads the first edition, one sees many ideas about mythology that carry over. The texts of the two editions are so different that they could be considered completely different works rather than different editions of the same work. Nevertheless, the 1725 edition has many of the key elements of the Jove story that appear in the later work. It maintains that the thundering sky was the first thing people noticed, and they gave it the name *Ious* through onomatopoeia (NS25 369). They believed the sky to be a powerful deity that gave them commands. He identifies poetic characters as the basic ideas of poetic reason (NS25 261). He even argues that the function of pagan religion was to civilize the early humans by stopping their wanderings. He writes of the earliest society that, "This is the time in which the great principle of the division of the fields begins through worship of the thunder that drove the impious, vagabond giants underground, i.e., held them fast on certain lands" (NS25 413).[22] Given that Vico recognized the significance of his discovery, it is remarkable how difficult it is to pinpoint what changed about his view of poetic characters.

By isolating the differences between the two works on mythology, it will be possible to bring into focus the epistemological account of myth presented in the later edition. Further, it will reveal how Vico's view of ancient myths transforms from moral admiration to moral condemnation. I will find these differences through a discussion of two of Vico's sources that were highly influential in the 1725 edition but are then rejected in the later work. These sources are Gianvincenzo Gravina and Dutch classicist Gerhard Johann Voss, also known as Vossius (1577–1649). These two thinkers present ideas about mythology that one might expect from an early modern theorist of myth. As Vico parts from them, his radical and critical view of myth emerges.

In the 1725 edition, he uses the term *ragione poetica* or *poetic reason* (NS25 313, 315, 328). This changes to *sapienza poetica* or *poetic wisdom* in the later work. This does not seem like a dramatic change until one realizes that his friend Gianvincenzo Gravina had previously used the term *ragione poetica* in *Delle antiche favole* and *Della ragion poetica*.[23] He passed away in 1718 before Vico had completed the *Universal Law*. Nevertheless, he was a significant thinker in Italy who was a professor at La Sapienza university in Rome and was one of the co-founders of the Accademia dell'Arcadia. He published prolifically on natural law and poetry.[24] When Vico used the term *ragione poetica*, readers would have recognized it as a reference to Gravina's work. It would make sense to read the change of terms as a rejection of part of Gravina's view. What changed?

Gravina and Vico share the basic idea that the first poets thought in an embodied manner and were incapable of abstract thought. Gravina portrays this as an important advantage for the poets. He holds that abstract thought can corrupt the idea of natural objects and civil customs in a thinker's mind. Whenever one conceptualizes an image, there is a danger that a thinker will add or subtract attributes from the totality of the idea. Since the ancient poets did not have this temptation, they saw directly into the reality of things. This meant there was great wisdom in ancient writings. Any modern author who can read ancient poems properly can gain metaphysical insight. Gravina contends quite strongly that "[Homer], who under the direction of these principles fixed his gaze in the *Iliad*, caught sight of all the customs of men, all the laws of nature, all the orders of civil government and, universally, the entirety of the being of things, presenting in disguise under the representation of the Trojan War which was the canvas on which he wanted to draw his marvelous embroidery."[25] In saying this, Gravina is attributing not just political but also true scientific and political wisdom to the ancient poets.

The two authors also share the idea that the embodied poetry of the ancient poets like Homer gave them a way to speak directly to the people. Whereas a modern reader might find Homer's works to be fantastic and exaggerated, Gravina holds that they were adapted to teach morality to the early nations. Because ancient people had powerful imaginations but thought in a crude manner, Homer needed reach them through fantastic and passionate metaphors that communicated sublime ideas in sensual images.[26] His epic poems taught both moral lessons and scientific principles to his audience by deploying poetic reason in a way that his audience could grasp. A large section of *Della ragion poetica* explains how specific stories in the poems contain moral messages that would inspire Homer's crude audiences.[27] In this way, Homer's poetry was instrumental in taming the passions of the Greeks.

In the 1725 *New Science*, Vico was unwilling to claim that the ancients had knowledge of natural science. In moral philosophy, however, Vico's position was quite close to Gravina's. The first edition divides the history of poetry into three ages. The first poets who founded the nations were "severe" (NS25 288). This strict discipline was necessary for the establishment of the first communities, and their myths were appropriate for this. These poets had the moral discipline necessary to tame the passions. This dedication was corrupted by the poets of the second age, who exaggerated them and filled them with tales of licentiousness (NS25 292). Their textual distortions explain why modern interpreters must work so diligently to reveal the original meanings of the myths. Vico places Homer in the third age of poetry, "in which individual poets collected the fables of these nations i.e., their corrupt histories, from which they composed their poems" (NS25 288). Because Homer was given bad information, he sometimes misrepresents Greek history (NS25 457). This should not obscure the powerful role that Homer had. He was able to reformulate the stories in a way that helped Greek civilization advance. This is more subtle and historically contextualized than Gravina's account. Nevertheless, it concludes with Homer imparting a positive morality that is worthy of philosophical study.

The 1725 *New Science* makes a claim about heroism that I do not think appears in the later edition. Vico writes, "This heroic nature, which lies halfway between the divine and human institutions of the nations, has hitherto lain unknown, because we have either relied solely on our memory of it or imagined it other than it was" (NS25 89). This is an early formulation of the conceit of scholars. What is peculiar is Vico's claim that the heroic age served as a middle ground. This allows him to make two claims about Homer. On the one hand, he describes him as "the first certain Greek author and the first certain father of the whole of Greek erudition" (NS25 34). On the other hand, he writes, "to Homer himself we attribute no wisdom other than the civil wisdom that was proper to the sect of heroic times" (NS25 296). Because the heroic age serves as a border between the other two ages, Homer can be in the heroic age and yet convey ideas from the divine era into the human era. This echoes Gravina's conception. Homer's natural sensibilities were unencumbered by abstract thought and allowed him to help humanity move forward by transmitting a moral sensibility that has eternal relevance.

In chapter 20 of the 1725 *New Science*, Vico clarifies his position. He writes that after many years, "the Greek religions were defiled," but then Homer arrived to correct this and restore the ancient wisdom to that of the first age of poetry. Vico writes, "Reflecting upon the corruption of his times, he organized the whole system of the *Iliad* on the basis of Providence, which we established as the first principle of the nations, and on the religion of the oath." Homer understood the importance of the restraint of passion, but he lacked philosophical awareness to argue for it. So, he included in the *Iliad* a metaphor to describe the importance of fealty and devotion. This metaphor was, in his words, "the oath which Jove took when he solemnly swore to Thetis that he would restore the honour of Achilles, which had been abused when Agamemnon took Chryseis by force" (NS25 295). In this way, as Gravina also describes, Homer used physical images to illustrate the importance of moral behavior to the Greek people.

Vico gives other examples of Homer's morality. Since the Trojan war was caused by Paris's incontinence, the fact that Troy loses teaches the importance of loyalty in marriage. Achilles is praised for refusing a foreign queen and marries a woman from his own nation with whom he shares the auspices. When Ulysses kills the suitors of Penelope, it teaches the evils of gluttony and laziness (NS25 295). Homer did not reason through these moral points by abstract conceptualization. He uses his natural understanding of goodness to communicate to his fellow heroes the importance of moral discipline. In this way, the paragon of the heroic age was able to bring the Greeks out of their corruption and steer them in the direction of philosophical thought. In the 1725 *New Science*, Homer is a source of moral insight that still has value in the modern age. Even if he lacked philosophical erudition, he understood the values of fealty, loyalty, and devotion. One could still read the epic poems today and learn about morality.

In the 1744 *New Science*, this position radically changes. There is still this basic idea that poetic thought is embodied in a way that allows for people in early civilizations to communicate. He pushes that idea to the point of saying that Homer was not an individual thinker but the oral tradition itself. This means that the poems could not have directed the Greeks toward morality but instead were expressions of their moral world view. When read honestly, the poems reflect a brutal culture that celebrates rather than condemns the excessive passions of the gods and heroes. The works encourage passionate behavior that would be criticized by anyone who considers morality from a philosophical perspective. He directly contradicts his earlier view: "if the purpose of poetry is to tame the ferocity of the vulgar whose teachers the poets are, it was not the part of a wise man, versed in such feelings and customs, to arouse admiration of them in the vulgar in order that they should take pleasure in them and be confirmed in them by that pleasure" (782). Now, instead of praising Achilles, he condemns him for risking the Greek army because of his love for Briseis (783). He refuses to admit that the depiction of brutal violence in the epic poems was simply necessary to communicate to the audience. He sees the epics as evidence that heroic civilization could not have been "touched and humanized by any philosophy" (785). He further claims that a key aspect of philosophical morality is acting in a consistent manner, but the characters in the epic poems do not do this in any way (786). He even criticizes the Homeric tradition for celebrating drunkenness (784). In the 1744 *New Science*, the epic poems reveal a culture deeply entrenched in a brutal morality that may have restrained and channeled heroic passions but not in a way that has any connection to a philosophical sense of morality.

At a key moment, Vico makes clear that the epic poems had moral value in the heroic age but no longer do so. After describing the way in which Achilles is so childish and easily offended, he writes, "Here is the Homer unrivaled in creating poetic characters, the greatest of which are so discordant with this civil human nature of ours, yet perfectly decorous in relation to the punctilious heroic nature" (783). If one is going to take seriously the idea that the Homeric poems were a product of their cultures, then one must admit that those cultures had a radically different morality than the one that modern philosophers describe. Their harsh cruelty would have no place in a society driven by human reason.

Book 4 of the *New Science* gives another example of this criticism. He claims that people in the heroic age can "apprehend human customs only in terms of characters made famous by luminous examples" (809). He then gives examples of the exceptionally harsh portrayals of the Homeric heroes. Achilles contains all the properties of "heroic valor." It includes feelings such as "quick temper, punctiliousness, wrathfulness, implacability, violence, the arrogation of all right to might." Ulysses contains "all the feelings and customs of heroic wisdom," including "wariness, patience, dissimulation, duplicity, deceit, always preserving propriety of speech and indifference of action, so others may of themselves fall into error and may be the causes of their own deception" (809). These are not virtues that would have any place in a just system of government.[28]

With the rejection Gravina's view, Vico's political philosophy comes into focus. Gravina himself was no particular fan of the aristocracy.[29] If anything, I think he hoped that the nobles would look at Homer in a new light and rule in a more progressive manner. Regardless, anyone who claims that ancient morality represented "the innocence of the golden age" makes a political claim that society ought to return to the political structures and morals of that previous era (518). This is because the ancients had a moral wisdom that has been lost. When Vico rejects this idea, he recognizes that ancient systems of thought were an obstacle for progressive change.

In a key passage, Vico appears to connect the Homeric portrayal of Achilles to knights of the middle ages while placing heroic virtues in opposition to philosophical virtues. In the human age, philosophers value justice, glory, and the immortality of the soul as per the three principles of his science. Achilles rejects them. Rather than recognizing Hector as an equal, he treats him unjustly by dragging his body around the walls of Troy. Rather than valuing glory, he sacrifices it when he withdraws his forces to spite Agamemnon. Rather than valuing the immortality of the soul, he scorns it when he tells Ulysses in the underworld that he would rather "be the meanest slave in the land of the living." The Homeric tradition praises Achilles's virtue from a heroic perspective. From a philosophical perspective, it is nothing but arrogant and spiteful. Vico ends his analysis by connecting Achilles's behavior to the mentality of the knights after the fall of Rome. He writes, "What he preaches is thus the virtue of punctiliousness, on which the duelists of the returned barbarian times based their entire morality, and which gave rise to the proud laws, the lofty duties, and the vindictive satisfactions of the knights-errant of whom the romancers sing" (667). Obviously, he is referring to the heroes of the epics written during the Renaissance. Nonetheless, it would not have been lost on his readers that the practice of dueling was still prevalent in Vico's Naples.[30] This would make a connection between the mentality of Achilles and the mentality of the Neapolitan barons. This represents not only the full rejection of Gravina's depiction of poetic reason but also invites the reader to think about the imaginative universals as being the driving force behind aristocratic thought.

This provides evidence to justify my interpretation of poetic wisdom as a civilizing force in the first two ages but a regressive barrier in the human age. This gives a context for exploring poetic wisdom as an epistemological structure. His primary tool for understanding ancient myth was literary tropes. These provide approaches for considering different ways names and words may be connected with people and objects. Contemporary readers might consider literary tropes to be sophisticated and technical mechanisms for interpreting the construction of images in great literature. One may consider metaphor, synecdoche, metonymy, and irony to be profound ways of evoking emotion through vivid descriptions. I do not think this is helpful when considering tropes in relation to mythical thought. It is more helpful to consider tropes as ways of creating vulgar nicknames. One could think of the "Arthur 'Two Sheds' Jackson" sketch from Monty Python. In the sketch, an interview with a composer is sidetracked by a discussion about the composer's supposed desire to buy a second shed. The nickname is a sort of metonymy in which the composer's association with two sheds comes to represent the man. I think this is the level at which Vico is thinking to understand how ancient religion conceived of the pagan gods.

Andrea Battistini has identified a key shift in Vico's thought by looking at the influence Vossius had on the 1725 *New Science*.[31] He had explored the relationship between tropes and ancient poetry and realized that connections between the names of people and their characteristics were far more fluid than they are now. He developed the important idea that proper names did not simply identify individuals but could be used to name everyone with a certain characteristic. Hence, "Hercules" did not just identify a man named Hercules as one particular hero; it identified anyone with great strength. This could explain how myths might attribute a wide variety of deeds to the same hero. It could also explain the reason why metamorphosis happens so often in myth. When a mythic figure changes a characteristic, their identity also changes.

Voss explored the possibility that the first poets used antonomasia as a fundamental structure of early language. Antonomasia uses a particular characteristic of a person to identify that person. In a way, it is a nickname derived from an attribute or activity associated with someone. Clear examples of this are Shakespeare being called "the bard" and Aristotle being called "the philosopher." It can have more general uses, though. One could call anyone who is good at crafting objects "MacGyver" or one could use a person's university, such as "Yale," to refer to a person.

Battistini breaks down the way that Voss related antonomasia to metonymy and synecdoche. All three are ways that a particular thing may identify an entire object. Metonymy, the broadest category, uses the name of something identified with an object to identify the object itself. Two common examples would include using *brass* to refer to high-ranking military officers or corporate managers or using *Wall Street* to refer to the economic world. Synecdoche refers specifically to using the name of a part of an object to refer to the whole object. For example, *wheels* can refer to a car or any vehicle. In the expression "there are many mouths to feed" the word *mouths* signifies whole human beings. Synecdoche can also go the other way when one uses a general word such as *police* to indicate just a part of the whole such as one or two officers. The distinctions and connections between the two tropes can be blurry. The question here is how ancient poets would have thought about antonomasia in relation to the other two tropes.

I characterize the distinction between the two tropes in this way. In metonymy, the connection between the associated object and the object itself can be quite distant. When one uses the expression *top brass* to mean corporate executives, it is entirely likely that those executives have never actually worn anything brass. On the other hand, if a vehicle did not have wheels or, much more disturbingly, if a person did not have a mouth, there would be a question as to whether it was still a vehicle or a person. So synecdoche relies on an object with a much tighter connection than metonymy. Ordinarily, antonomasia would be thought of as a subset of metonymy. This is because a modern thinker ordinarily thinks of a characteristic as something associated with a person rather than as an actual part of a person. One could imagine Shakespeare in retirement and still being called the bard even if he did not engage in playwriting anymore. Nevertheless, if one were to think of characteristics as a part of someone, then it would be more like a synecdoche. It is often said in the United States that where one goes to university shapes who they are and becomes a part of them. In this case, calling someone "Yale" would be more like a synecdoche. Indeed, one could use the term "the bard" to refer just to the time in the past when Shakespeare was composing and, once he stopped performing the action, one would not call him "the bard" anymore.

Battistini's point is that Voss recognized that the early poets would have used antonomasia much more like synecdoche.[32] Their rudimentary minds would not have had the reflective ability to separate attributes from objects. Any characteristic of a person would be a literal part of that person. So if Shakespeare stopped writing or MacGyver could no longer craft remarkable tools, then they would no longer be Shakespeare or MacGyver. This is similar to the way that a car without wheels would be a large piece of metal and plastic rather than a vehicle. For the poets, names were much more characteristics than means of identification for specific objects. When one lost the characteristic, one would no longer get to use the name.

Voss's analysis leads to the idea that the word *Hercules* was not originally understood as a name for an individual person. It was the name of any person who displayed strength or power. One could say that the early poets did not clearly distinguish proper names from adjectives and, indeed, names actually functioned more like adjectives. Over time, people forgot this point and thought that one individual Hercules did a wide range of deeds. Originally, however, there was one strong man who was Hercules who was followed by a number of other Herculeses. So all of these deeds were performed by different men who had the same name because they shared the same characteristic.

Up to this point, Voss's view is close to Vico's. Nevertheless, from his perspective, Voss makes a key mistake by falling prey to the conceit of scholars. He holds, as Gravina did, that the early poets combined their inability to abstract with heightened physical perception to have a special insight into the world and an ingenious clarity of expression. They used antonomasia so well that they spoke with a profound eloquence and remarkable philosophical depth. This meant that Voss saw the twelve labors of Hercules as revealing metaphysical insights into the zodiac. Vico rejects this and interprets the labors of Hercules as documenting civil institutions of ancient civilizations (NS25 460–470).[33] He does line up the labors with ages of different gods, but he sees them as representing expressions of noble ownership and the repression of plebeian rebellions, among other things. In the 1725 *New Science*, Vico agrees with Voss's basic idea that the name *Hercules* represented a group of people with a shared characteristic but disagreed with the way he interpreted the myths themselves.

Voss makes a graver error, however, but Vico does not recognize this in the 1725 *New Science*. Voss's analysis of antonomasia leads him to a basically euhemerist view of ancient myths.[34] This position, as many are aware, is the view that ancient myths were actually distorted histories of the past. In Voss's view, there must have been an initial Hercules who was the original strong man. This established the word "Hercules" that then represented characters in all the subsequent stories. The point is that one could then, at least in theory, figure out the actual events. This assumes that the poets recorded the myths to preserve their historical value as modern historians would today. Vico does not recognize this error in the 1725 *New Science*.

Vico's euhemerism in the earlier edition is subtle in that he does not say directly that ancient fables are distorted histories. His focus is more on careful interpretation and showing similarities in fables across cultures. It is not hard, however, to find him assuming that meanings of words came from original descriptions of things or people. One can see this most immediately where he writes directly about antonomasia. He claims that the first poets used it because they had limited vocabularies and difficulty conceiving characteristics abstracted from particular examples of objects (NS25 384). When they met a person from a particular region with a new characteristic, they used the name of the region to signify the characteristic. He writes, "Thus when the Romans were ignorant of refined customs and first observed them among the Tarantines, they used the word 'Tarantine' for refined" (NS25 384 also 263). In a similar way, "Capuan" signified proud. So, "Tarantine" and "Capuan" did not signify the places or the tribes as much as the associated characteristic. One can see such uses of geographic names in contemporary society. Vico presents this etymology as historical. He specifies that the Romans met these tribes from particular regions and learned of these characteristics. The words *Tarantine* and *Capuan* become names that simply blend different meanings together. These words are used in a peculiar but not mysterious or challenging way.

One can see further examples of euhemerism in the interpretations of myths presented by the 1725 *New Science*. As just one example, Vico has a very peculiar interpretation of the fable of the apple of discord, otherwise known as the judgment of Paris. He calls this a "native history" or "istorie natie" (NS25 454). This is the noted tale that recounts Eris, the goddess of discord, throwing a golden apple as a prize in a contest between Venus, Pallas, and Juno. Vico reads this as a fanciful but historical document of a class uprising. Juno represented marriage and Pallas represented the noble ownership of the fields. The plebeian Venus represented an incident where the lower class fought for the rights guaranteed for the upper class by the other gods. In similar future situations, the names of the goddesses would be applied to the people taking those roles in those situations. He actually cites Plutarch's claim that the idea of this being a beauty contest was a later addition to Homer's epic. This helps Vico maintain that the ancient poets would have been too unrefined to have a sense of beauty (NS25 454). The point is that his interpretation is euhemerist in that the idea of the apple and the contest are a rendition of an important event in the past.

This approach to ancient myths is appealing because it is so straightforward. Nevertheless, it is highly problematic. Besides risking the conceit of scholars, it is simply difficult to believe, given how odd the stories are. No matter how much one might want to say that the ancient poets exaggerated their histories or that they were embellished over time, it is hard to read the fables honestly, as Vico at least tried to do, and then think that this was an attempt at history. Vico thus abandons Voss's approach. Voss only appears in three passages in the 1744 *New Science* and two of them are critical (428, 641, and 858).[35] More importantly, he stops referring to his interpretations of myths as histories. At times, the substance of his interpretation actually stays the same, but he no longer suggests that the myths sprung from a description of an original event. This is true of his interpretation of the judgment of Paris. He more or less maintains the institutions the three goddesses represent, including the fact that it was the plebeian Venus rather than the noble Venus involved. He even includes Petrarch's caveat (652). The key difference is that Vico does not hint at the fact that this represents a particular historical event. Instead, he keeps his description general. He writes that "the first discord arose over the fields which the plebeians wanted to cultivate for themselves" (652). The myth now represents a general trend in the development of civilization. Whether or not there was a first event, the story has significance because the oral tradition preserved it as a representation of the evolution of political institutions. Vico moves away from euhemerism completely.

There is a much more important difference, though. In the conception of Voss and the 1725 *New Science*, the focus was on the way words name people. Through antonomasia, one word or name, like "Hercules," could become a nickname for an entire set of individuals with the same characteristic. In the 1744 *New Science*, the concern is with the way the use of names by poetic thinkers shapes the way they recognize people. Imaginative universals become concrete concepts or images by which poetic thinkers recognize concrete manifestations of a person in a category. Imaginative universals are no longer just shared names for people who share a characteristic. They are the images poetic thinkers use to identify a person with a concept. Imaginative universals are metaphors in the sense that they find identities between mental images and particular instantiations of them in the world. The basic point is that now poetic wisdom is primarily a way of thinking and knowing rather than a way of identifying.

Vico's clearest description of the imaginative universals may be axiom XLIX. He writes, "the first men, the children, as it were, of the human race, not being able to form intelligible class concepts of things [*generi intelligibili delle cose*], had a natural need to create poetic characters; that is, imaginative class concepts or universals [*generi o universali fantastici*]" (209). By "intelligible class concept," he is referring to the now ordinary process of looking at a group of different objects and finding a characteristic they all share. This process would require the ability to abstract—which, presumably, the first poets could not do. So, the question becomes "How could someone who lacked the ability to separate mentally universal characteristics from particulars make any sort of concept?" That is the question the imaginative universals answer.

When I am asked to explain Vico's theory of poetic wisdom, I have found that a major obstacle is helping readers recognize a basic point about contemporary reflective thought. Thinkers of the third age can deduce a universal concept from a variety of individual objects that share a characteristic. For example, one can understand the general concept "apple." One can also recognize that particular objects such as red, green, and yellow apples can all fit under that general term even if they have different colors. It is not difficult to see that these objects can have a range of colors and still fit into the category. This conceptual mechanism is so fundamental and obvious to abstract thought that one might not notice it. It does not seem like a noteworthy mental capacity and so it is easy to overlook. When I try to highlight it, others think there must be more to it, since this idea seems so fundamentally obvious. One has to recognize this function of the reflective mind in order to make an important distinction between reflection and memory.

When one remembers an object, one calls an image of the entire object to back to the mind. Memory does not have the same critical engagement that reflection does. Rather than isolating particular characteristics, memory recreates entire past experiences. Memory is a function of the imagination rather than abstraction. This means that it comes more easily to the human mind than reflection does. This is what gives memory such a vital role in poetic wisdom.

Even if the human mind comes to use memory more rapidly, there is no reason to think that it is simply passive. It is an active mental faculty by which the imagination pieces together past sensations to form a new image that resembles a past experience. This new image does not reproduce a photo of the previous experience but builds on the past. Vico was insistent on the fact that the faculty of memory was a creative aspect of the imagination (699).[36] This idea is not that far away from Descartes's point in the *Meditations* that sensation is a faculty of judgment. He famously uses the example of someone seeing three men when in reality they were three automata. The viewer judges in the very act of sensation that the robots are human when they are not. This shows how sensation and imagination are active in the creation of images.[37] The point is that an act of memory creates images from the past by including and excluding certain details.

What would happen if someone had the ability to remember but not reflect? Could that person still use a type of concept? Without reflection, one could not recognize that a particular object had characteristics that were separate from the general category. Despite that, one could use memory to recall that a new experience was the same as a previous experience. One would recognize a category, but every object in the category would be identical. Any differences between particular objects in the category would be overlooked. One could have the category "apple," but every individual apple would appear exactly as the rest. This seems outlandish from the perspective of reflective thought. It is helpful to remember, however, what Descartes said about the automata. Sensation judges the automata are humans without careful analysis. In a similar way, each apple would be imagined as identical to the previous one. With each experience, the imagination would modify and develop the idea of what the category "apple" meant. Yet, they would all appear the same.

This example of the apple gives a sense of what Vico is describing. Imaginative universals are a little different, however. They generally come from the imaginative identification of a human attribute with a sensation or an activity. Jove is the identification of an angry person with thunder. This explains the origin of superstition. Vico emphasizes that poetic thinkers metaphorically attributed their own passions to natural features. More commonly, however, he connects imaginative universals to human attributes. So whenever someone demonstrates "an idea of valor common to all strong men," that person is imagined to be Achilles.

Every time someone shows "an idea of prudence common to all wise men," that person is identified as Ulysses (403). In these cases, it is easier to see how each new instance could be imaginatively identified with the last. With every new prudent or valorous act, Ulysses or Achilles reappears, identical to the previous instance in the mind of the poetic thinker. I will return to this passage in a moment.

From both directions, the effect of the imaginative universals is to restrain human passions. Superstition controls them externally by convincing people to obey signs that are seen in nature. The first people obey the commands of the thunder god Jove and build altars. When figures such as Ulysses or Achilles reappear, the people will follow their commands as they did in the past. More importantly, those who want to rule will have to control themselves to imitate the paradigms as closely as possible. There is a creative dimension to the poetic characters because it takes powerful acts of imagination to invent them. From there, however, the mimetic nature of them requires an exact imitation of the past.

Vico defines imaginative universals as "certain models or ideal portraits, to reduce all the particular species which resembled them" (209). The poetic wisdom obscures particular characteristics in order to identify new experiences with past paradigms. In other words, the only way a poetic thinker can apply an imaginative universal to an object is to see that the present manifestation is an exact replica of the image of the past. The poet can only do this by ignoring particular differences or creatively incorporating new characteristics into the image. Either way, the end result is that the new manifestation is identified with the past no matter how different the past and present object might be.

Axiom XLIX gives a remarkable example of this. He writes, "the Egyptians reduced to the genus 'civil sage' all their inventions useful or necessary to the human race which are particular effects of civil wisdom." This shows the imaginative tendency to see the same particulars over and over again and identify them with each other. Instead of trying to create new categories, the poetic mind will try to reduce many different objects into the same image. Going further, because the imaginative universals are usually tied to human activity, all of the actions within the genus are often reduced to one person. He continues, "because they could not abstract the intelligible genus 'civil sage,' much less the form of the civil wisdom in which these Egyptians were sages, they imaged it forth as Thrice-great Hermes" (209). In the poetic mind, every act of civil wisdom was identified with Thrice-great Hermes or Hermes Trismegistus. Further, every person who did an act of civil wisdom was identified with the imaginative universal Thrice-great Hermes. It was not that "Thrice-great Hermes" was a category name that was separate from particular instances like an intelligible universal. The poetic mind immediately identified all civil sages and acts of civil wisdom with Thrice-great Hermes.

At the end of the first section of the "Poetic Logic," Vico gives a helpful discussion about allegories in relation to imaginative class concepts (403). I already drew from this section when I used the examples of Achilles and Ulysses. I want to discuss it further because he makes a helpful distinction, but it requires some context. The purpose of this passage is to make a point about the value of etymology in relation to ancient mythologies. He clarifies that imaginative universals can be called fables and that mythologies are longer allegories that derive from them. These poetic allegories are thus grounded in the same immediate connections between physical characteristics and members of a set. They have a "univocal signification." This connection is not as immediate in contemporary allegories, which are based on "analogical" relationships. This means that ancient allegories with their immediate basis in characteristics that connote "a quality common to all their species and individuals" are going to have etymologies that have a basis that is shared among different civilizations, while contemporary allegories will not. This is important for that part of Vico's science that is proving the universality of the ideal eternal history.

While I am not interested here in that argument, I am interested in his specific claim that "Allegory is defined as *diversiloquium* insofar as by identity not of proportion but (to speak scholastically) of predicability, allegories signify the diverse species or the diverse individuals comprised under these genera" (403). In ancient poetic allegory, which I take to rise from fables, the characteristic is a predicate of the subject and identified with it. In contemporary thought, allegory is a proportional relationship. I imagine it this way. One could make the following metaphor: "That person is an ox." For the contemporary mind, this would mean that the person's strength is proportionally larger than other people's just as oxen are stronger than other animals. The poetic mind does not work this way. For them, the person would have the predicate of "ox" and be identified as such. The ancient poet would see the person as an ox. I would speculate that this might explain why animals appear intelligent in many mythologies. Vico, however, does not talk about this, and he uses the examples of Achilles and Ulysses in this passage as he had used Thrice-great Hermes elsewhere. What I take to be important here is Vico's emphasis on predication and identity. I take this to mean that in the minds of ancient poets, the concepts they used to identify individuals were seen as identical to the individuals in the category.

This idea can be challenging to grasp because the modern mind has become habituated to fitting individual objects into general paradigms without sacrificing the individuality of a particular object. We moderns can look at a set of objects, such as bowl of fruit, and recognize the different apples in it. Despite the obvious differences between the apples, the modern mind is accustomed to identifying common characteristics and using them to create groups of individual objects and separating them from the group. When one recognizes that this trait is not obvious but, instead, is a product of a mental faculty, one can see that the mind could actually take an easier path. If the mind concentrated solely on similarities and did not think at all about differences, it could recognize objects in the set without mentally registering how the objects are different. It is helpful to compare this to our experiences with unfamiliar sets of objects. Most of us do not know differences in species of bees. When we see a bee, we recognize it as such and act accordingly. An expert would immediately recognize subtle but distinct characteristics that most of us would not bother to identify. For most of us, all bees are identical, practically speaking. In this way, we make a mental move similar to the imaginative conceptualizations performed by the first poets. They lacked any sort of detailed knowledge. So their way of thinking was based entirely on acts of identification that obscured all difference. In this way, the poets used categories, but everything in the category was the same.

So far, I have just tried to give a picture of the imaginative universals by contrasting them with intelligible universals. I have not tried to outline the characteristics of poetic wisdom. I am nowhere near broaching the question of whether any of Vico's account might in some way be true. I will broach that topic near the end of this chapter. What I think will be most helpful next is to draw two images of imaginative universals from popular culture.

Godfrey and Darmok

Torquato Tasso's epic poem *Jerusalem Delivered* was published in 1581. It had a lasting impact on Italian culture. The poem was often read, memorized, and recited publicly.[38] Many Italians had a deep personal connection to its characters. Between the 1730 and 1744 editions of the *New Science*, Vico added an example from it to the end of the commentary on axiom XLVII. I cited this commentary earlier, since it expresses well the way in which the myths were true for the ancients but do not reflect reality. In the later edition, he adds the example of Godfrey the war chief (*capitano di guerra*).[39] It is very unusual for Vico to draw on what could be considered a relatively contemporary popular image. When Vico refers to poetry, it is usually to ancient sources or Dante. This appears to be a unique moment when Vico turned to popular culture to explain his position.

Axiom XLVII opens with the statement, "The human mind is naturally impelled to take delight in uniformity" (204). It concludes with this description of Godfrey, the leader who captured Jerusalem in the First Crusade: "Thence springs this important consideration in poetic theory: the true war chief, for example, is the Godfrey that Torquato Tasso imagines; and all the chiefs who do not conform throughout to Godfrey are not true chiefs of war" (205). In poetic thought, all war chiefs are identified as Godfrey. Whenever one properly performs the activities of a war chief, people will see another Godfrey. This conforms with the above discussion of the imaginative universal.

This example becomes more instructive when it is found in popular culture. People do not ordinarily define the characteristics of celebrities and public personalities. It takes reflective effort to define the distinctive features that make a person great. Instead, people tend to identify new great people with figures from the past. One sees this often in sports. Fans are quick to identify talented new players as the next Michael Jordan or Lionel Messi. Experts may break down specific talents and qualities, but fans want to see the new player as conforming to the greatness they have already witnessed. This can be seen as well in art, politics or, presumably, war. The people are fond of Godfrey for his heroic deeds. They want another one to come along and repeat those feats of the past. When such a leader comes, they will use their imaginations to see another Godfrey. This is the contemporary tendency to which I think Vico directs our attention.

For the first poets, this act of identification was much more necessary and totalizing. Because they could not engage in abstraction, their prime way of understanding activities was by using their imaginations to have past figures reappear in present manifestations. To use images from the past, they had to project them into the future and identify them with new experiences. This act of identification obscured the differences in the past and future events, but allowed the poets think about what they were seeing.

In the modern age, we certainly have the choice to identify two distinct figures. We can certainly compare attributes of two people rather than identifying their images. When we reflect epistemologically on our capacity to recognize objects, our ability to isolate distinct qualities takes center stage. Vico asks us to notice, I think, that in the ordinary course of life, we much more regularly identify unfamiliar objects with each other without looking carefully. It simply requires less effort. Poetic wisdom is an entire mode of thought that operates by relying entirely on these acts of identification.

Vico added another passage to this group of axioms between the two later editions. Axiom LII, which does not appear in the 1730 edition, states, "Children excel in imitation; we observe that they generally amuse themselves by imitating whatever they are able to apprehend" (215). He then claims that this tendency also appears in the poetic nations, since "poetry is nothing but imitation" (216).[40] I take this to signify that as his idea of poetic wisdom developed, he thought more about the importance of imitation as integral to poetic wisdom as a form of thought. It also signifies that he was considering the way that poetic wisdom leads to performative conformity.

I suggest it is helpful to think of Godfrey not just from the perspective of a known object but also as someone who wants to be known. Any war chief would have felt pressure to conform to the paradigm Godfrey provided. Given that poetic thinkers could not easily separate the accidental from the essential, war chiefs would have had to struggle to conform exactly. When I think of this aspect of the imaginative universals, I consider how ancient religious rituals would have to be repeated in their entirety if any mistakes were made. In ancient Roman religion, this was called an *instauration*. Priests would have to make absolutely certain that every word in a ritual was said perfectly or the ceremony would be considered invalid. This must have put tremendous pressure on them to speak in a manner that absolutely conformed to the tradition.

As I build my account of the poetic wisdom, I will emphasize how the limits of its epistemological structure served to restrain bestial passion. Vico discovered that the images of gods and heroes do not simply persuade people to obey. My contention is that the entire form of thinking restricted their ideas and their actions. The connection between idea and imitation compelled them to act certain ways in order to think. I will develop this in chapter 5. Here, however, I turn to another depiction of poetic wisdom in popular culture. This one is much more contemporary.

Vico's notion of poetic characters made a remarkable appearance in 1991 in an episode of *Star Trek: The Next Generation* entitled "Darmok." The teleplay was written by Joe Menosky. He also wrote the teleplay for "Hero Worship," which aired in 1992 and features the SS Vico, so there is evidence he was thinking about Vico as he developed this script.[41] He downplays the political dimension of the poetic wisdom. Nevertheless, his account is interesting because it highlights the gap between imaginative and intelligible universals. The frustration the Federation officers show with themselves and their translating computers highlights how hard it is to make the leap from one form of thought to the other

The episode also gives a remarkable picture of how a society might operate using just poetic wisdom. It seems unlikely that a civilization could ever make such technological advancements while relying on poetic characters as the primary mode of communication. Poetic wisdom would not appear to allow for the richness of conceptual ideas that would be necessary to develop such machinery. Nevertheless, science fiction is particularly suited for this type of speculation and may serve as a further illustration of the philosophical point. In the episode, the Enterprise and its Captain Jean-Luc Picard encounter an alien race, the Tamarians. The universal translator allows the two cultures to recognize the words each other uses but not their meaning. The Federation cannot understand the metaphorical language of the Tamarians, who cannot grasp the conceptual language of the Federation. The Tamarian Captain, Dathon, teleports himself and Picard to the planet El-Adrel to try to bridge the gap. Dathon says such expressions to Picard as "Darmok and Jalad at Tanagra," "Mirab, his sails unfurled," and "Shaka, when the walls fell." The Federation officers cannot see why Dathon keeps citing random mythical stories. Dathon uses these images in the hope that Picard will imitate these characters, but Picard doesn't understand. Picard slowly realizes that "Darmok and Jalad at Tanagra" represents a specific battle tactic, "Mirab, his sails unfurled" means running away, and "Shaka, when the walls fell" represents failure. Dathon's language and understanding of the world is based not on concepts but on metaphorical images that use the past to plan courses of action for the future. This language does not create new words but uses historical paradigms to prescribe future action. This episode gives remarkable insight into how poetic wisdom functioned.

Star Trek emphasizes the communication barrier between poetic wisdom and reflective conceptual thought. From the perspective of a thinker of the third age, the easiest way to present an idea is by using clearly defined concepts. If one uses a proper name that clearly identifies just one object, this is not necessary. Otherwise, a speaker can express one or more concepts until it becomes clear which particular is being described. The contemporary assumption is that images and metaphors can add color and depth to an account, but they are not necessary to communicate about a particular object or express a specific command. In fact, it is thought that distinct categories are the best way to specify an object in a detailed manner. When the Tamarians speak, the Federation officers cannot understand why they do not just tell them their thoughts in a clear and direct manner.

If we were to consider this from the Tamarian perspective, we would have to imagine how metaphors could be the most explicit way of communicating. For them, the separation between universal and particular would actually open up the possibility of ambiguity. A metaphorical image or poetic character contains all the relevant details immediately within it. One can use the image to identify precisely what is being referenced. If the present manifestation does not display all the details, then it does not fit into the imaginative universal. In that case, the leader would fail to be the war chief Godfrey, or Picard would fail to be Mirab. When the manifestation does perfectly match the past image, then the imaginative universal quickly and concisely represents it in every relevant way. For the Tamarians, this is what it means to communicate clearly. One could say that in poetic wisdom, one gets the certainty of using proper names with the added bonus of incorporating many characteristics into those names. From the Tamarian perspective, this would be a huge advantage.

Of course, in the act of identifying the poetic character with a present manifestation, the poetic thinker obscures many accidental attributes. To be fair, however, modern conceptual thought also does this. It would be impossible to use discursive concepts to describe every attribute of an object at an atomic level. The fact that poetic thought obscures details is not, in itself, a disadvantage.

Nevertheless, poetic wisdom encounters the same disadvantage as discussed above with Godfrey. A discursive thinker could easily distinguish important attributes from unimportant ones. For example, one could ask for an apple and say that its variety does not matter. A poetic thinker could not do that. All the attributes identified within a poetic character are essential. Following Vico, when Dathon issues the command "Mirab, his sails unfurled," he is not just telling Picard to retreat but to retreat in a particular way to match the image. One wonders if there are other images of Mirab that Dathon could use to tell Picard to flee in a different way. In Vico's account, it seems like there would have to be. Since each image is a self-contained whole, one would need a new image to communicate each specific course of action. Perhaps one could draw an image from the same narrative or from the tales of the same character. A poetic thinker could not, however, articulate that one should run away like Mirab in one regard but not in another. This would require an analogical metaphor which poetic wisdom does not use. Because poetic wisdom depends on allegorical metaphors and identity, it has to present exact images and calls for exact imitation. This is a key limitation of poetic thought.

The episode ends with Picard committing to rereading Homer to deepen his understanding of poetic thought. He has now recognized the enduring value of the imagination as a way to experience the world and communicate ideas about it. I find it worthwhile to imagine Godfrey and Darmok as a way to enter into poetic thought and envision how poetic characters could be used as commands in a poetic society. This imaginative exercise helps to check one's philosophical tendency for critical analysis. Poetic wisdom is a way of thinking that is inherently unreflective, so conceptual arguments for it will not work. Therefore, using images to envision how it functions is invaluable. This may also start one on a road to use Vico's account of poetry to develop ideas of aesthetics.

At the same time, however, both Godfrey and Darmok show how limiting and restrictive poetic wisdom can be. Because this form of thought depends on allegorical metaphors and identity, it demands a certain exactness of expression. Because it cannot separate universals from particulars, it lacks flexibility of expression. While the Star Trek episode romanticizes this form of thinking, it forces one to acknowledge that the civilization it is depicting is impossible, at least from the way Vico is portraying poetic wisdom. This is not meant as a criticism of the episode, which is a remarkable use of speculative science fiction to explore a philosophical idea. Nevertheless, while I do not want to deny the ingenuity and force of poetic wisdom, I want to build a case that as it enters the third age of humanity, it becomes an impediment for the development of justice. While it serves an essential role in restraining bestial passion to maintain society, it also impedes developments that could help civilization thrive. While I encourage the reader to use Godfrey and Darmok to imagine the genius of poetic wisdom, I also suggest that reader should also use them to consider the limits of this way of thinking.

Nobility and Fandom

When I first started studying Vico, I used to explain poetic wisdom by describing how kids on the playground would imitate popular sports personalities. They would use their powerful imaginations to reproduce physically their idols. I used to think of this primarily epistemologically as a way for children to know what an excellent athlete is. As my thinking about this grew, I began to consider it more as an exercise in self-discipline. Children could use the image of the athlete to motivate themselves to learn the practice of training to get better. While many talk about such inspiration, I am not certain how often this actually happens. Instead of pursuing this path, I want to discuss another way in which conformity to ritual inspires self-discipline in the contemporary world.

In her recent work, *The I in Team: Sports Fandom and the Reproduction of Identity*, Erin C. Tarver turns attention away from the exhibition on the athletic field and toward the spectators.[42] Her contention is that contemporary fandom is a means of producing identity through self-cultivation. For many, of course, sports are just a means of light entertainment. Those who consider themselves to be truly dedicated fans, however, feel compelled to demonstrate their devotion to the team and the other fans by participating in rituals that require self-control. I want to discuss this phenomenon as an analogy for the functioning of poetic wisdom. This is limited because contemporary sports fandom is not a complete epistemological structure. In modern society, people have the ability to reflect. While the fans' rituals contribute to the lifeworlds with which they frame their surroundings, they are not totally immersed in them. Nevertheless, my reading of poetic wisdom centers on the way the myths functioned to civilize passions through the imposition of discipline. I present this idea of sports fandom to consider how imaginative universals worked to civilize the earliest giants.

Tarver's analysis reveals three levels at which the rituals of fandom encourage self-discipline. On the first level, the performance of ritual enables the fan to build a sense of identity through personal rituals of self-control. Tarver's analysis explores how the personal rituals of the self-discipline of fandom can permeate the life of a fan. Loyal supporters do not just perform rituals at games but demonstrate their devotion through clothing, home decorations, body tattoos, and special devotions at weddings and other public gatherings.[43] Tarver maintains that sports pageantry is not mere entertainment or marketing. Rather, loyal fans incorporate these activities throughout all aspects of their lives so that they constantly control and direct their desires to reinforce continually their identity as fans. She writes, "The performance elements of sports fandom are able to function in this way because they offer an immediately tangible means to cultivate one's sense of self and place in the larger social order, by incorporating reiterations of that identity in virtually any feature of everyday life."[44] On the reverse side of this, these fans can feel shame when they fail to perform a ritual or inadvertently perform an action that supports an opposing team. This fear reinforces the pressure they put on themselves to control their desires in conformity with their self-understanding.

On the second level, the personal need for self-discipline is connected to the larger community of fans. Tarver's account of fandom follows Michel Foucault's emphasis on the connection of self-knowledge to discipline and social behavior. As she explains, Foucault shows that while the object of self-knowledge is the self, the associated performative activities always occur within social relations.[45] They work through the reinforcement that comes from communal activity and social acceptance. Tarver writes, "the performances of sports fandom are practices of self-cultivation—specifically, they enable fans to cultivate a robust sense of themselves as individuals belonging to a particular community."[46] It is the shared sense of discipline that happens in a social context and is communicated among group members that strengthens the production of self-knowledge. In the mind of the fans, while particular rituals may be practiced in individual contexts, they are always understood in connection to a larger group to which they want to stay attached.

On the third level, Tarver discusses the way in which these rituals cultivate a distinction between the fan group and the other. This happens most obviously when the supporters of one team distinguish themselves from those of another squad. She pushes this further as she identifies ways in which the communal self-discipline of fan groups reinforce ideas of class, gender, and racial superiority. As an example, she examines specific rituals and traditions associated with the University of Mississippi that celebrate racial supremacy.[47] She describes the role that the practice of naming teams after marginalized groups plays in fan behavior.[48] She examines how the language in which fans describe athletes codes positive and pejorative attitudes toward them depending on their perceived connection to the superior group.[49] Specifically, when star athletes are white and come from a socially acceptable class, they are celebrated as heroes because they embody the values of the community.[50] When athletes come from lower-class backgrounds outside the elite fan base, they are treated as mascots. The fans delight in taking a patronizing attitude toward those athletes in a way that allows them to celebrate ritualistically their own superiority.[51] The interesting point for this study is how the rituals that encourage self-discipline lead organically to the celebration of that discipline in contrast to groups that are seen as inferior.

As one imagines how the poetic characters functioned in the *New Science*, it is important to think about these three characteristics of self-discipline, social pressure, and class distinction. For a theological poet, thinking an imaginative universal required either seeing it physically represented or actually performing it. The proper performance of the ritual demanded that a poet recreate the paradigm as exactly as possible. This could only be done if the poet restrained any bestial desire. The rigidity of poetic wisdom required that the poet engage in self-discipline to think and communicate an image. This is the inherent connection between poetic wisdom and the civilizing of humanity in the first two ages.

This always happened, however, in a social context. The poets constantly watched each other to see whether they could perform the rituals of the pagan gods. If poets could not restrain their desires and fulfill their religious obligations, they risked being shunned by the community beyond the intense internal shame they felt. When the other poets could not recognize one as performing an imaginative universal properly, they would stop acknowledging that poet as a member of the aristocracy. In this way, the rigidity of poetic wisdom instilled an inherent dimension of social pressure into the first asylums.

In order to make this pressure tangible, the aristocrats understood themselves as separated from the animals. These creatures included the *famuli* who had not heard the original thunder but wandered later into the asylums seeking protection. Inherent to poetic wisdom is the idea that those who can perform the rituals are human and those who cannot are animals. This means that the imaginative universals often contain demonstrations of superiority by the nobility to assert their authority. The rituals call on the nobles to oppress the plebeians as a way of demonstrating their dominance to the other nobles as much as the lower class. Hence, this class separation is also inherent to poetic wisdom.

I will discuss this in detail after I say more about the Neapolitan feudal aristocracy that I think is inspiring Vico's account. Here, however, I offer the example of Vico's depiction of the imaginative universal Venus. When Vico described the judgment of Paris, he referred to the plebeian Venus. Here, I refer to the Venus of the greater gentes. Vico specifies that this Venus represents civil beauty rather than natural beauty or the beauty of virtue, since those ideas of beauty could only develop later (565). Civil beauty is specifically the recognition of the superiority of the nobility to the plebs. Vico writes, "The idea of civil beauty must have been engendered in the minds of the theological poets when they saw that the impious creatures who had taken refuge on their lands were men in aspect but brute beasts in their habits" (566). This recognition entered into the core of the poetic world view. It oriented the poetic mentality toward defending the institutions of the nobility against the plebeians. The poets were not consciously aware of this, since they could not critique their own worldview. Nevertheless, they maintained their self-control through the imitation of the imaginative universals, which entailed protecting the rituals from the plebeians. The poetic mentality did not include the plebeians in their idea of humans. This is tied to the self-discipline inspired by Juno. The nobles had to restrict their desire to copulate. If they did produce a child with a plebeian, the child was considered a monster (567). This classicism is ingrained in the poetic wisdom.

The Poverty of Poetic Speech

There is one other characteristic of poetic wisdom I want to introduce before moving forward. Vico writes, "Now the sources of all poetic locution are two: poverty of language and need to explain and be understood" (34).[52] Contra Berlin's characterization, Vico emphasizes that communication, expression, and interpretation are essential elements of all poetry. He also emphasizes that poetic wisdom forms out of a linguistic limitation. This characteristic has also been undervalued by scholars who have emphasized the philosophical importance of the imagination in Vico's thought. This characteristic is important for understanding how he depicts the evolution of poetic wisdom. I will argue later that it is also important for understanding how intelligible universals come to displace imaginative universals in civilization. Here, I want to focus on the point that the poverty of language directs poetic thinkers to expand existing images rather than invent new words.

When early modern philosophers discussed the origin of language, they often considered how the physical limitations of early humans would have restricted their ability to speak and how this shaped their course of development.[53] Vico takes a similar approach to emphasize that it would not have been easy for the first poets to invent new words. Mentally, their inability to abstract meant that they would have struggled to identify the unique characteristics of objects so they would overlook new things to name. Physically, they would not have had the muscular skills needed to make precise articulate sounds. As a result, poetic language had a small vocabulary (NS25 97, 308; NS44 581). In the 1744 *New Science*, he calls this the "poverty of speech" ("povertà di parlari").

It is important to note that this phrase does not simply imply that these vocabularies were small because many words had yet to be invented. Vico's language reveals that the *povertà di parlari* is more of a limitation on poetic thought than the literal shortage of words. *Parlari* is translated as "words" or "languages."[54] Yet he often uses *voci* to speak about actual words (e.g., NS25 277). He also generally uses *lingue* for languages, especially when he is referring to lexicons and the evolution of languages (e.g., 35, 928). *Parlari* is the noun form of the verb *parlare*, which means "to speak" or "to talk." His use of that term seems to refer to the manner in which poets spoke and expressed themselves. The poverty is not the number of words or languages but of their capacity to speak. Vico, at times, does use *povertà di lingua*, particularly when he is actually discussing the small vocabularies of the first people (NS25 284, NS44 456). Nevertheless, he uses *parlari* more frequently than *lingua*, and I think this shows his general interest in how poets work to express themselves using fewer words (e.g., NS25 98, 308, 326, NS44 34).

Vico maintained this idea of the poverty of speech from the *Universal Law* to the *New Science*. He revised it as his thought developed, but he discussed it throughout. This concept helps him make a case for a fundamental principle of his system. It is an important piece of evidence for his claim that poetry developed before prose (472). The words of the first languages would have had one syllable and been based on onomatopoeia (447–448). Since the first poets would not have the physical dexterity to make many sounds, they would intonate the sounds they did make to have a wider range of expression. This would help them learn poetic rhythm. Part of his evidence for this is that "stammerers by singing teach their tongues to pronounce" and that "men vent great passions by breaking into song" (228–229). Here, the poverty of speech is this inability to speak using a complex range of sounds. It drove the first poets to make complex songs out of their few words rather than invent new ones. Since all people would have had difficulty speaking, this also leads to his claim that poetry was not created just for special ceremonies but that it was widespread among the people.

Further, the poverty of speech lends support to the idea that the history of poetry, religion, and law accurately portrays the history of civilization. Because the poets had a limited ability to communicate, they would also have found it difficult to distort intentionally the nature of human institutions. Despite the fact that the myths are hard to interpret, one could have relative confidence that they accurately represented past cultures if they could be interpreted properly. In the 1725 *New Science*, he writes that "we find that these characters were histories of the oldest superstitious customs of the peoples of Greece, described in a natural theogony which unfolds the mode of their generations" (NS25 267). Hence, there is a real connection between the poems and the institutions that produced them.

While these points are important, I am more interested in his claim about the way poetic wisdom develops. The poverty of speech has a limiting effect on the development of language that becomes a positive impulse. When confronted with a new experience, poetic thinkers will be inclined to stretch an existing poetic character rather than invent a new one. An extreme passion can inspire poets to invent new gods. Usually, however, these passions will be channeled into existing imaginative universals such that the symbolism associated with the god enters more territory. I would imagine that this would be restrictive because the limited number of gods would often encourage the poets to ignore stimuli without considering them at all.

On the positive side, however, this limitation would be the source of great creativity. Artists will often place restrictions on themselves to force them to explore new pathways to inventive inspiration. The poetic thinkers develop a variety of linguistic tools to stretch existing metaphors to cover a wider range of experiences. He calls these the "first lights of poetic style," that are "vivid representations, images, similes, comparisons, metaphors, circumlocutions, phrases explaining things by their natural properties, descriptions gathered from their minuter or their more sensible effects, and, finally emphatic and even superfluous adjuncts" (456). He offers, as an example, "the blood boils in the heart" as a poetic description of hatred (460). This is an example of the way poets can use comparisons between objects to vividly express an intense passion. The point I want to emphasize, however, is all of these tools work to expand the range of the poetic characters. These imaginative tools enhance the organic complexity of mythic images, which then get preserved as a seemingly discordant group of stories and symbols.

This position explains why the interpretations of myths in the *New Science* are so complex. While the imaginative universals may have been invented as clearly defined ritualistic actions, over time they evolved. Because of the poverty of language, the poets often attached new associations to the old rituals rather than inventing new paradigms. While these additions may have seemed natural when they were first imagined, the original connections are often lost over time. As the images of the gods were preserved, they rarely had clearly defined categorial meanings. Instead, each god has a network of associations that may be disconnected or even contrary. When one looks at the sphere of influence of each Roman god as we now understand it, one sees how confused and jumbled the images are. This is because of the poverty of poetic speech. Since Vico is trying to understand the history of civil institutions, he does not simply drill down to the original invention of the imaginative universal. Instead, consistent with his method, he wants to trace the curious ways in which the rituals expanded. As I present my interpretation of the gods, I will try to keep this in mind. Further, I will discuss how this tendency to expand the pagan gods may lead to the disruption of poetic thought when I introduce the idea of overinclusion.

Vico's account of the poverty of poetic speech reveals another way in which his mistrust of the nobles grew. In *On the Constancy of the Jurisprudent*, his discussion is most straightforward. He already had an idea of poetic characters, although it was far from his final account. Here, the first poets simply notice what is most striking in objects and arrange those features in suitable ways that add emotional energy to them. This produces "sublime poetic characters" (CJ 79).[55] This was a tremendous power of the early poets that contemporary thinkers struggle to recapture. He writes, "If someone should wish to excel in poetry, he must first completely unlearn what people call proper language and limit himself to the impoverished vocabulary of the most ancient times" (CJ 83). This is similar to what Gravina had asserted.

He draws on contemporary evidence to support his view. He writes, "we have observed that children and peasants and all people with limited vocabulary speak very little because they have insufficient language" (CJ 81). This limitation, however, leads them to make very profound statements based on emotionally charged images. Vico writes, "If to this lack of words one adds a good judgment, their words will be adequate to things; if they have a lofty soul, they will speak of the sublime; if they have imagination, they will speak pointedly of many things" (CJ 81). This allows their words to be persuasive to an unsophisticated audience. He writes, "Thus filled to the brim with images, everything he [the poet] sings will be elevated, and at the same time accommodated to the sense of the common people" (CJ 84). In this text, this is how poetic language established the first religion and the first law (CJ 90).

Vico emphasizes, however, that this poetic form of communication is not true in a philosophical sense. Given that the audiences of the poets would have been crude, the poet's images would have to be extremely passionate but unrefined. Drawing on Horace, he identifies that the two "most profound precepts" of poetry are to moderate the common beliefs of people and to "choose as the most suitable material a credible impossibility" in order to communicate effectively. This shows that poetic thought is effective but based on false ideas. He writes, "These two precepts, I say, show the poetic faculty thrives on errors and opinions, and disappears with philosophy and truth" (CJ 81–82). This is a clear expression of his political position that philosophical reflection is necessary to develop a just society. In this work, the poverty of speech inspired the poets to create remarkable images out of a small vocabulary that would connect to the minds of the people even if the ideas were flawed.

The 1725 *New Science*, Vico expands this account to explain how the poverty of poetic speech influences the development of human thought. He writes, "For a poverty of words naturally makes men sublime in expression, weighty in conception and acute in understanding much in brief expression, which are the three most beautiful virtues of languages" (NS25 250). He now seems to be referring more generally to the way the poverty of poetic speech helps to expand the imagination of the first poets. Because poetic thinkers cannot think abstractly, they must communicate using images closely tied to their objects. He writes, "they express themselves by means of things and actions that have natural relations with the ideas they want to signify" (NS25 251; see also NS25 306). The poverty of poetic speech now combines with the incapacity for abstraction to create a language that immediately symbolizes human institutions. In this edition of the *New Science*, Vico already sees how the poverty of language would have caused the first poets to use the same name to describe all things that share an attribute (NS25 262). He even sees that the first poets used allegorical metaphors rather than analogical (NS25 265). Again, this is close to Gravina's view.

This emphasis on the authentic connection of poetic speech to institutions is what leads Vico to be very concerned about how the myths became corrupted. The ancient poems as they are handed down range from being too sophisticated to be products of the poets to being so violent that they could not stabilize a civilization. Vico proposes hermeneutic strategies that I have already discussed. He presents a series of principles concerning the corruption of the original stories. This does include the general deterioration of morality. He claims that customs "tend naturally to change for the worse and toward their corruption in all states" and that this "drove the fables toward highly corrupt meanings that were completely contrary to the religions, good laws and customs [that they formally signified]" (NS25 286). As the hold of poetic morality and law weakened, human licentiousness inverted the original stories. For example, he assures us that the early pagan religions would have been so powerful that adultery was impossible. So, the earliest images of

Jove actually presented him as completely loyal to Juno. As this religion lost its grip on the heroes, storytellers began to portray Jove's children as being born to other mothers (NS25 287).

He also presents the history of poetry discussed earlier in this chapter that claims the heroic poets corrupted myths but that they were salvaged by Homer and other poets. The poets of the first age represented the customs that founded the nations. During this age, the poverty of poetic speech connected mythic images directly to history. The second age of poets, however, "was an age of wholly corrupt poets" (NS25 288). These poets inverted the morality of the fables and incorporated stories of shameless and licentious gods (NS25 292). It was late in the evolution of poetic thought that the hold of pagan religion weakened. The third age of poets, including Homer, were then the ones that preserved the myths, but only after they had been corrupted.

I have already discussed how his view of Homer changes radically in the 1744 *New Science* in terms of both the message of the poems and the source as an oral tradition. I want to emphasize that he stops discussing the idea that a third type of poet contributed positively to the morality of civilization. He does not exclude the possibility that contemporary poetry has value and, being a poet himself, I have no reason to think of him as opposed to it. Nevertheless, he stops looking for a positive use in the human age for the poetry that was produced by poetic wisdom in the first two ages. This is because he now talks about the way in which the poetry of the heroes collapses and falls into conflict with human reason. This happens because of the poverty of speech.

When poetic speech was first invented, it relied on natural comparisons to present objects (456). As civilization develops, the poets will invent new characters and expand existing ones. Eventually, the heroes reach a point where they fight against this limitation. They develop a desire to express more ideas but lack the ability to invent new words. Instead of turning to human reason, they expand poetry beyond its boundaries. Vico writes, "Digressions were born of the grossness of the heroic minds, unable to confine themselves to those essential features of things that were to the purpose in hand" (457).[56] He describes the way the heroes would use inversions to expand what they could express. This is the practice of reversing word order to expand the way they express themselves within the poverty of linguistic resources (458). In this way, the poetry of the heroes loses its connection to objects and institutions because their poetic resources are not adequate to the task.

At the same time, the people find a way to promote the use of intelligible universals to express what the heroes cannot. They realize that complex images can be reduced to simple words. "The blood boils in my heart" becomes a single word such as "hate." Vico describes the transformation by writing, "For after the poets had formed poetic speech by associating particular ideas . . . the peoples went on to form prose speech by contracting into a single word, as into a genus, the parts which poetic speech had associated" (460). He asserts fairly clearly that the contraction of the images is a positive development. He writes, "By means of these vulgar genera, both of words and letters, the minds of the peoples grew quicker and developed powers of abstraction, and the way was thus prepared for the coming of the philosophers, who formed intelligible genera" (460). As reflective thought enters the stage, certain humans learn to think more keenly. Lawyers develop the ability to think rationally about what justice means. Philosophers develop the ability to direct humanity toward a better republic.

In each of these three works, Vico praises the way poetry confronts the restrictions that arise from the poverty of speech. He also sees its limitations. More importantly, he always presents philosophy as a way to overcome the confusion of poetic wisdom. Over the course of the three works, the stakes become higher as he becomes less confident that poetic wisdom ever had a connection to true morality. As he describes the brutality of the heroes in the 1744 edition, one feels a more serious call to find a way to check the injustice of the nobility. This makes the *New Science* an anti-baronial work. To connect his account of poetic wisdom to the feudal aristocracy that dominated his nation, it is necessary to look directly at the political situation in Naples.

4

Feudalism

Merging Traditions

Vico claims that after the flood the Hebrew and gentile traditions separated. The Hebrews retained their knowledge of civilization and prohibited the use of divination, while the gentiles fell back into superstition (167). This has always been regarded as a curious point. Vico may have included it to avoid the inquisition. It may also have been a legitimate attempt to make the evidence of the Bible square with the history of Roman law. Either way, it is important to recognize that he was not alone in making such a separation. In the fifth *Discourse on Method*, René Descartes himself claims he will not apply his geometric method to this world that God created but to a theoretical world. He claims this will make the topic easier to discuss.[1] In *La vita civile*, Vico's friend Paolo Mattia Doria splits the gentile and Hebrew traditions. He claims that the story of Cain and Abel truly reports the early cause of political turmoil, but the gentile tradition lost sight of it and developed accounts of history that were based on natural causes.[2] Further, Doria claims that there was a period in ancient Egypt where overpopulation led to great instability. The Hebrews did not have to endure this stage because they had the wisdom of God's teaching.[3] By putting Vico's claim in context, one realizes that it is not simply an eccentricity but part of a widely used rhetorical strategy and topic of study.

Vico's variation of the split does not successfully hold to the Christian tradition. In 1769, G. F. Finetti published a work accusing Vico of contradicting the Roman Catholic faith. His key argument focuses on the tower of Babel. In Vico's account, the descendants of Noah lost their shared language as they transformed into giants. Finetti points out that in the Bible separate languages were created when the tower was destroyed.[4] These accounts are chronologically incompatible. He then makes many other arguments against the *New Science*, including referring to anthropological evidence of early races of pygmies that would have been the opposite of giants.[5] Evidently, he wanted to go further, as Croce reports that he planned to publish two more volumes but never did.[6] Finetti's ire is indicative of the lasting impact Vico had on the Neapolitan intellectual community.

Vico's claim about the division of nations inspires both curiosity and frustration in contemporary readers. I suggest that it raises an intriguing question. If one provisionally accepts the idea that there was such a division, what does Vico think happened to it? If the fall of the Western Roman Empire was a return to barbarism like the flood, what happened to the divide between the gentile and Hebrew traditions? Vico did not highlight his answer to this question. Nevertheless, he does claim that the two traditions merged.

At the end of book 4, he includes a chapter about the "Guarding of the Laws." This is a summary of the history of Roman law from the Twelve Tables to its culmination in the reign of Constantine. This was the ultimate stage in which Rome achieved a government in which people were justly rewarded for their hard work (1001). It would not be lost on his readership that Constantine converted the Empire to Christianity. While Constantine really did implement judicial reforms, I interpret this as saying that his reign finally brought the pagan tradition back to the level of development that the Hebrews had never forgotten. At that point, the traditions merged. These Christian and pagan traditions came together to live at the summit of the human age for two centuries. When Rome fell, nearly everyone forgot Rome's civil institutions. No group or nation in Western Europe escaped this collapse as the Hebrews had escaped the flood.

This point is reinforced by Vico's assertion that after the fall, Roman law fell out of use by everyone in Europe. He writes, "in the rude days of the recourse of barbarism the nations forgot the Roman laws, so much so that whoever invoked one on his behalf was severely punished in France, and in Spain even suffered death" (1002). While Vico does not make this point directly, this passage strongly implies that even the Vatican had lost the legal traditions of the Roman Empire. He qualifies his claim because he has to acknowledge that some of the legal documents were preserved. He writes, "Among all the aforesaid nations we find documents only in barbarous Latin, understood only by a very few nobles, who were also ecclesiastics" (1051). This implies that there were a few scattered scholars who managed to keep some of the documents alive. It does not suggest that there was a nation who kept alive Roman traditions as the Hebrews had done. In the returned barbarism, there was now only one tradition in Western Europe and that was dominated by poetic wisdom.

Moreover, despite his reluctance to assert that the Catholic church had fallen into paganism, he actually justifies why divine providence allowed this to happen. He writes, "he [God] permitted a new order of humanity to be born among the nations in order that [the true religion] might be firmly established according to the natural course of human institutions themselves" (1047). I interpret Vico in this way: the Hebrews remembered the institutions of the human age but had no memory of pre-diluvian history. The gentiles passed through the three ages but separately from the Hebrews. When these two traditions came together, they produced a government worthy of the human age, but because of its historical division it was not as stable as it could have been. With the returned barbarism, divine providence now offers an opportunity for one tradition to establish a human civilization that authentically traces the ideal eternal history in conjunction with the Christian faith. If Europe follows the guidance of providence, it could now produce a government even greater than Constantine's. This reading of the fall of Rome is consistent with the idea that the barbarism is not a punishment to be feared but a positive mechanism by which civilization can protect and develop itself. More importantly, it underlines the point that after the fall there was one tradition in Europe that was based on poetic wisdom.

Whether or not Vico's account—and my interpretation of it—is historically accurate, it invites the reader to consider Western Europe after AD 500 or 600 to be dominated by poetic wisdom. Vico dedicates book 5 of the *New Science* to this point. He omits any involved discussion that would relate the cult of the saints to the imaginative universals. If he had done so, the book would be much clearer, but I assume this would have been problematic for the censors. Regardless of his motive, he does show how many other specific features of poetic wisdom manifested themselves during this time. Despite the fact that there were isolated pockets of aristocrats who preserved Latin, there was a return to reliance on mute gestures and hieroglyphs (1051). The reliance on auspices also returned. He shows this through a discussion of medieval warfare. I will discuss later that when the first fiefdoms did go to war, it was always war over their gods. This aspect reappears in medieval warfare, since wars were once again fought to preserve or destroy the gods of other nobles. Vico presents as evidence the fact that saints' relics were revered at this time. Since the goal of these wars was to steal the auspices of the enemy, medieval nations would work protect their relics.

He writes, "the peoples of those times were very careful to bury or hide them, and such repositories are everywhere found in the innermost and deepest part of churches" (1050). This invites the reader to think about saints as imaginative universals without emphasizing it.

Book 5 also presents many examples of ancient Roman law reappearing in feudal law. This was not because the law had been preserved but because it had been reconstructed over the course of the ideal eternal history. The original fiefs of ancient Rome returned because feudalism once again became the most useful way for distributing goods (1063). He then traces the same evolution of property and ownership (1065–1066, 1073). He was even willing to say that bishops and abbots were the leaders of early fiefs (1056). The ancient Roman laws of the census return (1069, 1078). He even addresses specific Neapolitan institutions. Notably, he describes the returned heroic assemblies. In ancient Rome, one could not appeal a decision by a noble assembly in any way other than appealing to the assembly itself. This shows that the these governments were oligarchies, since the monarch did not have the power to overturn the aristocracy. In the returned times, the nobles could only to appeal to the king when he was part of the assembly (1081). So, again, the king does not have the power to veto the aristocracy. His main example is France, but he says this is also true of the "Sacred Council of Naples" (1082). This demonstrates that both ancient Rome and Naples were driven by aristocratic rule.

While book 5 is brief relative to the others, Vico reveals many connections between his depiction of ancient Rome and medieval Europe. The thoroughness of his account conforms to his assertion that he studies ancient Rome as a way to understand modern Europe (1047). It also supports Giarrizzo's idea that the *New Science* is more about modern Naples than ancient Rome. I see this as an invitation to think about poetic wisdom as a description of the mentality that dominated Neapolitan aristocrats in Vico's day. I will not try to line up the Roman gods with specific prominent saints during this period. Instead, I will explore the way his interpretations contain elements of feudal institutions and build to an overall description of the way feudalism is driven by an epistemology that is separate from the people. To build this interpretation, it will be necessary to look at the feudal institutions that dominated Vico's Naples. This chapter is dedicated to this topic.

Research into the feudal structure of Naples from the fifteenth century to the rule of King Charles of Bourbon has grown substantially since the 1960s. As Jennifer D. Sewlyn comments, studies of this period had been dominated by Antonio Gramsci, who had an idyllic view of the peasants, and Benedetto Croce, who portrayed the masses as holding back an intellectual elite.[7] Since then, researchers have revealed the complexity of the systems of power circulating in the province, particularly during the rule of the Spanish viceroys from 1504 to 1714.[8] Much of this research has been focused on why, after a period of relative growth in the fifteenth century, Naples failed to capitalize on it and then struggled to recover from the political and economic crisis of the seventeenth century.[9] There has also been a growing number of cultural analyses of life in Naples during this period.[10] In the first section of this chapter, I will draw on this research to sketch a picture of the evolution of feudal politics in Naples.

I will begin with a discussion of the Spanish administration of Naples to explain why the nobility was able to entrench its power while it faded in other parts of Europe. This is useful for understanding why Vico and his compatriots had a unique political outlook. Then I will discuss the most important point I want to make about Neapolitan feudalism. The authority of the barons was based on the judicial privileges they held in their fiefs. Each baron was given the responsibility to run the police, courts, and prisons in his or her fiefs. While they certainly profited from the labor of the vassals on the farms, they also benefited monetarily from fines and fees associated with their control of the courts. They also used this power to preserve their authority. This blocked not only the development of commerce but also fair and equal law enforcement. This represented a major obstacle for the reform for which Vico hoped. In the final section, I will discuss the growing middle class of lawyers in Naples who were in tension with the nobility. I will look specifically at the arguments of Francesco D'Andrea and Paolo Mattia Doria, both because they give more context for the *New Science* and because they flesh out the picture of life in Naples under Spanish rule. I end with a discussion of some of Vico's direct remarks about feudalism in this context.

It is important to remember that John Locke, author of the prevailing political model to come out of early modern thought, was allied with the aristocracy. At least tangentially, he participated in Lord Shaftesbury's attempt to overthrow King Charles II. While he frames his social contract theory in terms of a check on the power of a monarch, he does so from within aristocratic assumptions about who will participate in political discourse. Indeed, one could argue that his defense of private property actually justifies keeping wealth in the hands of the upper class.[11] Further, as many are aware, when Locke's system was implemented for the US Constitution, it produced an aristocratic document that not only allowed slavery but also denied the right to vote to women and to men who did not own land. Vico was not an aristocrat, and so he was in a position to problematize the power of oligarchy. The better one can understand Vico's context in the Neapolitan feudal system, the easier it will be to see how his philosophy may provide an alternative to the aristocratic one offered by Locke.

Neapolitan Feudalism and Spanish Colonial Rule

Axioms LXX to LXXXII defend the claim that aristocracy, rather than monarchy, was the first form of government. This position was so important to Vico that he drops his rule against referring to other authors and dedicates an entire subsection of his science to challenging Jean Bodin's argument for the primacy of monarchy (1009–1019). In these axioms, one can see the connection between feudal rule and poetic wisdom (254). The first priests used a pagan religion to rule over their families in separate clearings (250). Each theological poet extended his (or possibly her) authority over the giants who wandered into their asylums. These giants became the *famuli* (256). Axiom LXXXI asserts, "it is a mark of the strong not to lose by sloth what they have gained by valor" (261). Because of this, the leaders of the families defended their institutions from the latecomers while exploiting them. This principle is one of the "perennial sources of fiefs" (262) and it implies that all early nations will originate in a system of vassals and fiefs (263). Other early modern thinkers tend to frame the question of government as a debate about rule by all versus rule by one. Vico maintains that aristocracy is the primary form of government, that it is the primary obstacle to reform and that it is driven by poetic wisdom.

For the Neapolitan intellectual community, feudalism was not a relic of a distant past. The hills and mountains of Naples and Sicily had many castles that oversaw fiefs. They contained farms that were worked by peasant sharecroppers as well as small villages called *università*. Historically and practically, the authority of the barons stemmed from their management of the judicial system in their territories. The lawyers in Naples would be quite familiar with the system in the countryside. Many would have either moved to the city or their parents would have. Vico's grandfather was probably a *contadino* around the town of Maddaloni, about twenty-five kilometers north of Naples. His father came to the city in the 1650s to establish his bookshop.[12] Further, there was a growing desire among noble families to have palaces in Naples to arrange marriages and make deals. The legal class in the city would have known or worked for these barons.

Twenty years before Vico's birth, the Masaniello peasant revolt threatened Spanish and baronial control of the province. It was the largest peasant rebellion in Italy, but it was successfully suppressed. It was only on August 2, 1806, that an occupying French government was able to revoke the judicial privileges that the barons had over their fiefs. During Vico's lifetime, Neapolitan law students interested in political reform would have had to consider it as a significant obstacle.[13]

For nine years, Vico himself worked in the feudal castle of Dom Domenico Rocca, now the Castello de Vargas Machuca di Vatolla.[14] At a chance meeting in a bookstore, he made a contact with the Marquis's brother, who recommended him for a job as a tutor for the noble's children. Vico writes, "He was assured that he would be treated in every way as a son of the family, and so it proved to be the fact" (AU 119). Vico became immersed in the cultural life of a rural fiefdom. He would have also seen how Don Domenico would have used his authority over his vassals. He was such a good administrator that he was able to double the size of his holdings before his death in 1699. As I will discuss, it was typical for successful nobles to reinvest excess funds into purchasing more land.[15] Nicolini tells us that Vico remained friends with the family and sent a copy of the first *New Science* to the Marquis Francesco Rocca, Don Domenico's successor.[16] While Vico spent most of his life in the city, he had direct experience of life on a fief.

When Vico was born in 1668, Naples had been a colony in the Spanish Empire for approximately 164 years. Naples had been one of the five main city-states in Italy. The death of King Ferrante in 1494 gave a pretext for King Charles VIII of France to invade and take the throne. This started the series of wars that would destroy the power of the Italian city-states and eliminate the immediate hope of Italian unification. France briefly took control of Naples, but they were defeated by Spain at the battle of Cerignola, which led to Spanish control of the province in 1504.

From the rule of King Alphonsus the Magnanimous in 1442 to the early years of Spanish Habsburg rule, the economy of Naples thrived. As the sixteenth century wore on, however, the situation worsened. Spain came to rely on Naples as a vital source of money and troops to maintain its war efforts in Northern Europe. As Antonio Calabria argues, because Naples was distant from the fighting, it became a safe place from which Spain could draw resources.[17] By the end of the sixteenth century, the burdens that Spain placed on Naples started undoing its earlier economic progress. When Spain decided to commit fully to maintain its influence in central Europe by entering the Thirty Years War, it made even stronger demands on the resources of Naples. This sent its economy into a severe and lasting crisis that would lead to Masaniello's peasant revolt in 1647.[18]

After the war, Spain had lost its influence in Europe, which eased the burden it had imposed on Naples. Nevertheless, it also lacked the resources to rebuild its infrastructure. Further, a devastating plague hit Naples in 1656, which killed hundreds of thousands and impeded any economic recovery.[19] When the War of Spanish Succession broke out in 1701, Spain had lost so much influence and economic strength that it was other important powers of Europe—France, Austria, and England—that fought for control of the Spanish throne. At the war's end in 1714, the Bourbon king with French support was able to retain the throne, but Austria won a great deal of territory, including Naples. They would only hold onto the territory for a couple of decades. Spain was able to regain influence over the province when King Charles of Bourbon took the throne of Naples in 1734. He ruled it as an independent nation although clearly in the sphere of Spanish influence. He ruled until 1759, when he abdicated the throne of Naples to become King Charles III of Spain.

The crisis of the seventeenth century had a lasting effect on the economic development of southern Italy. Calabria's study shows in great economic detail how the burden Spain placed on Naples devastated its development. My interest lies more in the political dimension of this crisis. The period of Spanish occupation saw a complex relationship between the Spanish viceroys and the local barons shape a distinct brand of feudal rule. Since Spain could not help Naples recover, it decided to maintain stability by leaving much of the authority in the hands of the aristocracy rather than trying to centralize power. While noble privileges were being revoked in areas like Piedmont, they were still firmly in place in Naples.[20] To maintain this authority, the barons adopted an exceptionally conservative view of politics that emphasized the importance of their control.

There is much debate about how the rule of the Spanish viceroys allowed the nobility to entrench themselves. In his work on the revolt of Masaniello, Rosario Villari paints a bleak picture of Spanish taxation and neglect that eliminated any possibility of anti-baronial opposition. He writes, "In southern Italy, however, it [the economic crisis of the seventeenth century] brought about the absolute decline and elimination of progressive development. The social structure was simplified: aristocratic domination was consolidated and extended, and those of the new groups that resisted subjection to feudal authority were marginalized and crushed."[21] Since then, many authors have argued that Villari exaggerates the point. In a polemical review of the literature, Eric Cochrane wonders how the Academies and Universities in the province could have developed and questioned feudal authority if the nobility had the authority that Villari described. He further suggests that the increase in sales of fiefs during this period could have actually increased social mobility rather than restricting it.[22] John Marino questions whether the Spanish administration was uninterested in bringing their authority to the countryside. He analyzes advice given by the outgoing Spanish viceroy Zuñiga for supplying the population, collecting taxes, and defending the territory to show the strategies the viceroys used to expand their power in the countryside at the expense of the barons.[23] Much research is still to be done to understand the extent to which feudalism did or did not evolve during this period. It is clear that the aristocracy fought to maintain their authority and to protect the political traditions that supported it. They adamantly resisted any substantial political or economic reform.

The Spanish government made two major decisions that help explain and illuminate the authority of the barons during the modern period.[24] First, especially during the Thirty Years' War, the Spanish demand for resources outpaced the ability of Naples to pay. Not only had levels of taxation been pushed to the limit but also demand for Neapolitan goods had dried up. Revenue could not be raised by tariffs or other mechanisms. So, Spain decided to sell its possessions in the province of Naples to raise needed funds. Rosario Villari quotes this order from King Phillip IV from 1637: "His Majesty commands that provision be made for the sale or mortgage of everything he still has in his kingdom."[25] As a result, as Anna Maria Rao reports, "At the beginning of the eighteenth century, only about 100 of the approximately 2,000 communities were directly under royal jurisdiction; all the others were subject to feudal jurisdiction."[26] Before the sale, many towns were under the direct control of the state. The police, courts, and prisons were run by representatives of the viceroy in the capital. The sale allowed existing barons or new barons to purchase these communities and incorporate them into their fiefs. In these towns, the judicial systems went from being state run to being run by individual barons. This would not apply to larger towns and cities, which were always under the authority of the state. Nevertheless, the sale put many citizens under the direct authority of the nobility rather than the viceroy.

As I have researched this project, I have had a hard time conceiving the infrastructure of the province of Naples. I am used to think about territories having central governments that administer the law throughout the land. In this province, the central government actually had very little direct authority over most villages. Outside of the cities, most people were concerned not about the viceroy's law but about the judicial authority of the barons. As this picture comes into focus, it becomes much easier to understand why Vico was concerned about an oligarchy rather than a monarchy. Further, one can see why Vico's description of the evolution of civil institutions emphasized the growth of the judicial system rather than technological development.

Returning to the Spanish sale of fiefs, Cochrane suggests this may have allowed for more class mobility. It also created tension within the aristocracy. The new barons were indebted to the viceroy and were in conflict with the old barons, who fought to maintain their independent authority.[27] Overall, it greatly weakened the infrastructure of the Spanish government. The expanded number of fiefs made it harder for the central government to supervise the authority that the nobles wielded over their vassals.

Villari describes a number of ways in which the Spanish sell-off impeded the ability of the viceroy to govern. The sale of defensive works, for example, put the province at risk of both piracy and French invasion.[28] More importantly, the viceroy came to rely more heavily on the barons to collect taxes.[29] Typically, the Spanish government would allow third parties to collect tax revenues for a fee. As the pressure for revenue grew and Spanish territory was sold off, the Spanish turned directly to the nobles to collect revenue. This meant that the viceroy had to give the nobles more power over their fiefs to protect the revenue stream. Villari writes, "the expansion and consolidation of feudal ownership . . . was itself realized through the ever-widening domination of the political and administrative apparatus which the aristocracy managed to secure during a period of weakened state power."[30] This impeded the ability of the Spanish government to protect the rights of the vassals in noble estates.[31] One could question whether Villari's account underestimates the extent to which the Viceroy still managed to exclude the nobility from government decision-making.[32] Nevertheless, it is not disputed that the nobility was able to consolidate its power over its vassals in this period.

The other decision of the Spanish government was to maintain and support traditional structures of local authority rather than commit to a strong colonial rule with a powerful central administration. The Spanish never emphasized making the Neapolitan culture more Spanish or making the political institutions of Naples conform to a Spanish model.

Moreover, the government in Madrid was so committed to maintaining stability in Naples that it actually supported the nobles against the viceroy. A key element of this support was a decree, made in 1540, that all taxes in Naples would have to go through the noble parliament. This meant that the aristocratic class rather than the viceroy had the power to level taxes. The Spanish monarch also voided taxes imposed by the viceroy when the Neapolitan barons did not support it.[33] Madrid also gave the barons the right to privately send delegates to the monarch to complain without the approval of the viceroy. This, at times, could cause the viceroy to be replaced.[34] This sharply cut into the viceroy's capability to centralize his authority. I do not want to overstate this point because recent research suggests the viceroys did still wield a good deal of power, especially in making decisions for the province as a whole. Nevertheless, particularly within their own fiefdoms, the authority of the nobles was largely unimpeded by the Spanish administration.

By looking at the relationship between Spain and its colony, one can see how the oligarchical power of the aristocracy in Naples was growing while power was being centralized in other parts of Europe. While there was a large movement of population into the cities, more citizens in the countryside came under feudal authority. This context helps one understand why the *New Science* would be dedicated to a discussion of the power of oligarchy. To further dig into Vico's project, it is necessary to look specifically at how barons wielded their authority over their fiefs.

Feudal Judicial Authority in Naples

The historiography of the term *feudalism* reveals how difficult it is to develop a universal definition of it.[35] My interest here is limited to feudalism in the province of Naples as it continued into the seventeenth and eighteenth centuries. The point I want to emphasize is that it was a system in which feudal lords were given judicial privileges and responsibilities to maintain law and order in their individual fiefs.

From a contemporary perspective, one might be tempted to think of a baron managing a fief like the owner of a company. The vassals would function as if they were employees and the baron would try to profit as much from their labor as possible. Sharecropping was an essential dimension of baronial rule, and it was important for the survival of the fief. It was not, however, the main instrument of noble authority. A better contemporary analogy would be that the baron was a private individual who was subcontracted by the central government to manage the police, courts, and prisons in the baron's territory. Each baron had the responsibility to make sure that the laws of the province were enforced by the private police service and law courts. In exchange, the baron could profit from charging fees, setting tariffs, and collecting fines. They could also administer the law to protect their ownership of the territory. In some ways, a Neapolitan fief is analogous to a contemporary gated community with its own private police force. The difference is that the residents of the gated community share the cost and responsibility to administer the police, while the baron had the title for the land and almost complete authority.

Villari's description of Naples before the 1647 revolt focuses on two points: "firstly, in the social disintegration and sharp class polarization distinctive of the modern South; secondly, in the permanence of important extra-economic factors in the exclusive rule of the nobility, such as propensity to anarchy and the revival and reinforcement of aristocratic rights and privileges."[36] His second point emphasizes "extra-economic factors," which included the judicial rights of the nobles to enforce the law. He emphasizes that the aristocracy fought to defend and expand their judicial privileges on their fiefs. He calls this anarchy because the efforts of the nobility reduced the power of the central government. As the noble authority grew, they got more freedom to rule their fiefs as they desired. Over time, Naples functioned less like an organized nation and more like a network of independent municipalities that were administered by a class of oligarchs rather than a central administration. This contributed to Villari's first point: that the increasing power of the nobles promoted a strict class division. While wealth was a part of this, it was the judicial privileges of the aristocracy that fed their superiority and political control.

In *Fiefs and Vassals: The Medieval Evidence Reinterpreted*, Susan Reynolds looks at the early history of feudalism in southern Italy and supports the idea that it was originally a judicial system. The evidence from the eleventh and twelfth centuries is often unclear and her work is, admittedly, somewhat speculative. Nevertheless, she has significant evidence. The Normans brought the feudal system to Sicily with their invasion in 1061 and then took it to the mainland in the early twelfth century. She emphasizes that when the Normans came, they did not have a fully developed idea of feudalism as a system. As it was implemented, it incorporated elements of the existing Lombard system of ownership and developed its own traditions over time.

She makes two key claims. On the one hand, she cannot find evidence that distribution and ownership of property was based on a special feudal relationship with the king. She asserts, "At all events there seems to be no evidence of any myth that derived rights of property from grants of land by the first Norman conquerors."[37] It is possible that ownership was still based on Lombard traditions or that the king actually thought that all the land was his. The idea that the king gave the nobles land to work does not hold in this case. Conversely, there is evidence to suggest that the soldiers were tasked with protecting territory. Reynolds writes, "When Norman soldiers were first given fortresses or lesser properties they were presumably expected to help defend them and extend their lords' conquests."[38] This would have solidified into traditions over time. Out of this developed the idea that the new barons would be obligated to supply soldiers to the king when so called.[39] Connected to this military idea of protection from invaders was the judicial idea of enforcing the law to protect the territory from criminals. Reynolds claims that feudalism developed on the model of a "hierarchy of jurisdiction" as was found in France.[40] She describes the French model in this way: "property rights were not in reality very significantly distributed through the hierarchy: what lords at its intermediate levels enjoyed were much more like governmental rights."[41] The land was actually owned at the level below the baron by the person who oversaw the vassals working the land. The baron profited from using governmental privileges to assess fees that were imposed onto the landowners.

Tommaso Astarita emphasizes that the geography of the southern Italian region made the physical layout of Neapolitan feudalism distinct. In northern Italy, farmhouses were dispersed across the countryside. He writes, "In the South, on the other hand, villages developed on hilltops or mountains, where they were better protected from attackers (pirates or soldiers) and the malaria that lurked on the plains."[42] Feudal lords would live in a castle in the center of town, while the peasants would walk great distances to work the fields. This village structure made it easier for the nobles to administer the fiefs and monitor their vassals. Over the ensuing centuries, the class divide became more rigid as the nobles stabilized their authority.

Frederick II of the house of Hohenstaufen ruled, more or less, from 1198, at the age of four, until 1250. He greatly increased the economic and cultural influence of Naples in Europe as well as founding its university in 1224. Some of his decisions, however, damaged the long-term economic development of the province. On some goods, he maintained a royal monopoly that weakened the growth of commerce and manufacturing. Beyond that, Astarita writes, "The spread of the feudal system in the countryside increased peasant subjection and dependence and reduced the chances for more innovative agriculture."[43] During this period, the majority of people in southern Italy became harshly exploited.[44] The economic dimension of feudalism grew during this time. The more important transformation, however, was from feudalism as a military institution to a judicial one.

Feudal authority grew dramatically during a period of profound uncertainty between 1343 and 1435. While the black plague contributed to this crisis, especially from 1347 to 1350, the primary cause was the instability of the monarchy. Two queens, Joanna I (1343–1381) and Joanna II (1414–1435), struggled to assert their authority during this period. Since the monarch's role was understood to be primarily military, feudal lords did not respect the power of female rulers. There were no firmly established traditions or institutions to explain how a queen could rule or what the role of her consort should be, so the various husbands of the queens struggled to aid the monarch.[45] The barons used this ambiguity and instability to assert their judicial control over their fiefs. They did this primarily by exchanging their support to the monarch for special judicial privileges. Astarita writes, "More and more feudal barons won the right to exercise criminal jurisdiction over their vassals, even in capital cases."[46] The local authority of the nobles was eclipsing the central authority of the province.

Astarita makes the important claim that monarchies were generally quite unstable during this time. He writes, "Neither the conception of monarchy nor its institutions were strong enough to withstand the problems caused by a weak sovereign or a dubious claim to succession."[47] One might have an image of this period as one where strong monarchs were the clear center of power over a territory, but this is problematic. The lack of clarity about rules of succession indicates how tenuous the authority of monarchs was. More importantly, there was not a clear understanding of what a monarchial administration should look like and how it should govern a territory. This lack of a clear definition of monarchical authority was compounded by limitations of technology that made it hard for individual monarchs to communicate across large territories. The class of feudal lords, on the other hand, could use their immediate connection to the people to provide stability. While individual nobles sometimes ran into difficulty maintaining their estates, the class of nobles as a whole was quite strong and cohesive. This is important to remember as one considers the order of governments in Vico's ideal eternal history. For him, the first two ages were characterized by theocratic and then aristocratic rule. Stable monarchy was only a product of the third age (925–927). This reflects the traditional stability of the nobles that outlasted the ability of individual families to maintain monarchical authority. While histories and romances often highlight the power of the monarch, it was the nobility who controlled the real institutions of authority.

The period of instability in Naples ended after a seven-year civil war and King Alfonsus the Magnanimous came to power. In order to stabilize his control, he had to appease the barons. He gave them the hereditary right to full control over the law in their fiefdoms. Astarita writes, "In 1443 the king granted all Neapolitan barons the *merum et mixtum imperium*, or full civil and criminal jurisdiction over their vassals, including most capital cases."[48] With this, he claims, the feudal lords had been fully transformed from soldiers to judicial authorities. The people living in the fiefdoms were no longer serfs without rights, but they were firmly under the legal and economic authority of the lord. Astarita writes, "Villagers owed dues to their lords and were subject to the latter's growing jurisdictional authority, but they rarely owed labor services, they could sell their own land, and they could leave the village."[49] Vassals were not slaves who could be bought and sold. They were free to find better living conditions and shift from fief to fief as they wanted and were able. They were subject to the law of nobles however. In connection to this point, Vico insists that the vassals were not slaves and that the only slaves during the heroic age were captured in war (608, 443).

As a result of this evolution, the term *feudo* in Naples takes on special meanings. Astarita explains that it refers to land that has "special legal characteristics" that are different from "allodial land." "Allodial land" (also spelled "alodial") is land that is fully owned by a private individual to the extent that it has absolutely no connection or obligation to the government. This sort of ownership is rare today. In the United States, for example, the federal government retains the right to buy back any private property. This means that the ownership is not allodial. In feudalism, granting allodial ownership was more common than now. Nevertheless, ownership of a *feudo* was still the most common. Astarita writes, "the transmission and acquisition of a *feudo* took place according to old feudal traditions and usages, complemented by royal laws."[50] Ordinarily, this would mean that there was an agreement between the baron and the central government about rights and responsibilities. The terrain in Naples, however, made those rights distinctive. Because the mountainous territory made travel so difficult, ownership of a *feudo* gave barons judicial authority over entire towns. The term, he writes, "was also used to describe any village or town in the kingdom, constituted as a community, over which civil and criminal jurisdiction, at least in the first degree, was wielded not by the royal government, but by a private individual recipient of a royal investiture of that purpose."[51] This meant that the pervading idea of a fief or *feudo* in Naples was that a baron was a private authority contracted to maintain order over entire towns. The larger towns and cities would still be in the hands of the central government, but many villages would be under the direct judicial authority of a baron.

Vico also refers to the distinction between allodial ownership and ownership of a *feudo*. He claims that in the returned barbarism, allodial ownership returned as strong heroes took control of territories. Over time, however, they had to cede some control of them as the heroes banded together to face the plebeians who grew in power. As a result, allodial ownership disappeared. Through a fanciful etymology, he claims that allodial ownership came to be known as "goods of the distaff" or of the spinning wheel because it collapsed as the heroes became weaker (657, 1076). Throughout book 5, he makes reference to the idea that the vassals had freedoms but had to swear loyalty to the barons (1057). He also emphasizes that in the heroic age, ownership was controlled through the aristocracy and not a central government (1072, 1074, 1080). I read this as all centered around an understanding of fiefs as involving judicial authority rather than just material ownership.

The rights that feudal lords had in Naples were quite diversified. They offered many opportunities for generating revenue while, at the same time, being quite invasive in the lives of the vassals. Astarita categorizes the four categories of rights.[52] First, the nobles could exercise a series of royal powers. This included, for example, imposing fees on goods and people passing through the fiefdom, fining people who transgressed the law, charging fees for using the civil courts, and collecting fines for people who violated local standards of weights and measures in trade.[53] Second, the nobles could maintain certain monopolies on things such as "mills, ovens, and inns of their fiefs."[54] Third, the nobles could charge a fee on the use of farmland and grazing land. Fourth, the lord could demand certain types of work for the maintenance of the fief or a fee in lieu of doing this work. For example, vassals could pay a fee instead of standing on defense of the castle.[55] This made the fiefs a remarkable investment, which is why the Spanish had no trouble selling them to raise money for the war effort.[56] It also could allow for oppressive control of the vassals for barons who decided to rule with cruelty.

As profitable as the fiefs were, however, it was still extremely challenging for an individual family to maintain control of its noble privileges. If a family went into too much debt, it could be forced to sell its fiefs and, in extreme circumstances, it could have to liquidate altogether, perhaps permanently ending its place among the nobility. Particularly during times of crisis, this was a very real and present threat. To maintain their feudal privileges, families had to maintain strict control over their territories, their spending, their moral conduct, and even their reproductive practices. These restrictions promoted an exceptionally conservative mindset that was resistant to any sort of change. While this system maintained stability and had some advantages, it blocked the development of commerce and the expansion of legal rights to the vassals in order to retain judicial privileges that were the family's source of authority and revenue.

Astarita's study of the Caracciolo di Brienza focuses on the way in which this ancient family used feudal institutions to maintain its power through the centuries; this is the "continuity" to which the title of his study refers.[57] He illustrates how the family rigorously adhered to the customs and institutions of feudalism to avoid calamity. From his archival research that documents the family's economic resources, he paints a profound picture of the conservative mentality that drove noble families. While feudal institutions did evolve and adapt somewhat to changing conditions, they produced a mentality that tenaciously held onto traditions of authority while resisting innovation.[58]

It is important to realize that the barons did not have much other than tradition to maintain their control. Because their judicial privileges stemmed from a weak central government, they could not rely on a Spanish viceroy to support them. Economically, the nobles were certainly much richer than the vassals. Nevertheless, because their fiefs contained small-scale agriculture production without much industry or trade, they did not have much wealth to draw on in times of crisis. Socially, because rural nobles usually operated in separate castles in distant towns, the fiefs were managed independently and they could not easily call on others for help.[59] When the nobles were tested by Masaniello's revolt, they managed to band together and get military support from the Spanish. It was not easy, however, and it took a year to restore order. The overall point is that the lack of noble infrastructure and resources meant they had a strong motive to maintain the traditions of authority as much as possible, since that was the primary source of their authority and stability.

This meant that the nobles were reluctant to allow any sort of change. Since any alteration might lead to a larger questioning or erosion of noble privilege, the nobles dug in against reform. In the noble worldview, survival and tradition were closely connected. Whether they were self-aware of this association or not, their decision-making was always directed toward stability rather than innovation. They then impressed upon the vassals the idea that tradition needs to be maintained to ensure their survival as well. Astarita writes, "Presumably the aristocracy shared the belief, expressed by many jurists in Spanish Naples, that the rural community—vassals and lord—was tied by mutual obligations to ensure the maintenance of all its members, what Aurelio Lepre has called the 'ethics of survival.' "[60] The idea that the feudal institutions needed to be protected thus permeated to both the vassals and the intellectual elites.

Astarita's analysis shows how this conservative worldview went far beyond a straightforward political stance. The desire for stability permeated all aspects of the noble lifestyle. They had to maintain rigorous self-discipline in their economic activities and even their personal behavior. Their actions stemmed from a worldview that demanded self-control not just to use resources effectively but also to make sure that all traditions were strictly followed. Obviously, some nobles lacked self-discipline, and many of them paid dearly. Nevertheless, Astarita shows how the desire for continuity was a pervasive part of the feudal worldview.

Tradition and practical concerns dictated that the nobles had to spend conspicuously in order to maintain their class status. They had to show their wealth to the other nobles to maintain their position in the aristocracy. They had to display it also to their vassals as a sign of their authority. This conspicuous consumption put a constant drain on their resources. Indeed, most additional revenues, which normally were not that large, went to some form of demonstration of class status or the purchase of more land for the expansion of fiefs. This meant that the Neapolitan nobility did not develop habits of saving or investing money.[61] They maintained traditionally stable sources of revenue and then focused on limiting their spending to sustain their fiefs and their position in the aristocracy. Often the small profit margins on fiefs would drive families into deficit spending, which put more pressure on them to economize. Social and economic pressure on the noble families largely prevented them from seriously considering long-term investment as a means toward long-term stability.

An interesting dimension of Astarita's analysis is his discussion of the relation of rural nobility to the city of Naples. Over the centuries, pressure grew on the nobles to spend more time in the city. Nevertheless, Astarita shows that many noble families limited their time there, going primarily for making deals or negotiating marriages.[62] Their desire to display their affluence did not lead them to building major palaces or contributing to great building projects as they did in Florence.[63] Just as they were not looking to open larger revenue streams, they also did not desire to make grand statements in the architecture of the city. This appears to be a major indication of the conservative orientation of the nobility.

Astarita's research reveals how averse the barons were to financial investment, speculation, and risk. He writes, "The analysis of baronial revenues shows that the Caracciolo di Brienza, similarly to many another aristocratic family in the kingdom, did not as a rule try to innovate in the way in which any of the revenues of their fiefs were administered. With a few short-lived exceptions, over two centuries renting out feudal and monopoly rights and feudal and allodial lands was the common practice."[64] In the case of agriculture, the family limited themselves to renting out small plots of land to the vassals for farming or grazing.[65] They could have tried to implement more modern managerial styles that would have consolidated land together to farm them on a larger and more efficient scale. Astarita can find just one instance where the Caracciolo di Brienza experimented with such a method. In 1611, they purchased five larger estates, which the marquis would directly manage and fund. The experiment was soon scrapped and not repeated, indicating a lack of commitment to the project.[66] Neapolitan nobles also did not engage in much trade. Especially in the seventeenth and eighteenth centuries, the grain that was produced was sold in the local villages. On occasion, the barons would facilitate the development of trade to more distant lands, but generally the produce from the fields remained in the region.[67] When the family had surplus money, it invested it back into more fiefs, who would produce goods in the same traditional way. Astarita summarizes by saying, "Though his patrimony had more solid bases, in most respects the marquis of Brienza in the 1780s was still making his money in the way his ancestors had two centuries before."[68] Given the technological developments that were occurring in Europe during this time, it is remarkable how unchanged the economic system of southern Italy remained.

It is true that the geography of the province was a disincentive to innovations in trade or large-scale farming. The mountainous territory did not lend itself to obvious ways to develop either one.[69] Nevertheless, the traditional conception of the nobility was probably the greater disincentive. There was a long-standing cultural belief that nobles should not engage in trade. There was even a belief that families who engaged in trade should lose their noble status. It was not until the 1680s that the Spanish government made clear that the nobility could engage in such practices without fear of losing their noble privileges.[70] This announcement did not really have an influence on how the nobles approached generating revenue. As a class, they resisted changing the economic structure of Naples.

One of the most significant and personal ways in which a noble family had to control itself was in the area of reproduction. Before 1550, families had many incentives to have children. They could get more representation in the noble parliament as well as open more roads to survival during periods of instability. By fragmenting the family fiefdoms, there was great hope for retaining control of the entire territory. Once Spain solidified its control in 1550, these incentives diminished. Noble families turned their attention to keeping fiefs consolidated together to maintain revenue. They also petitioned the government for entails, which would guarantee that a family could perpetually retain property rights for a territory.[71] Fundamentally, noble families tried to control reproduction so competing sons would not split the feudal estates. Theoretically, it would be ideal for a family to have just one son, who would keep all the lands together. This, however, would be a risk since the death of that son could end the line. Additional sons, called cadet sons, were often prohibited from marrying and were blocked from receiving inherences. Families would place them in the military or other professions, and then they would just retire on the family wealth.[72] Because of the need to pay dowries, an excess of daughters could be a tremendous economic burden. Not only would families set up special funds for marriages, but also groups of nobles would invest in shared accounts that they could draw on as dowries needed to be paid.[73] Astarita goes into much more detail about how the control of reproduction was seen as vital to the survival of the noble family. I raise this aspect to underline how pervasive the pressure was on the lives of the nobles to control their actions to maintain their status.

Vassals and Fiefs

The Neapolitan nobility's focus on stability and self-control depended on a strict separation of classes. The nobility were motivated to use their judicial privileges to generate revenue. This meant that the life of a vassal required careful navigation of a variety of fees and policies designed to exploit many aspects of daily life on a fief. More importantly, the barons needed to reinforce constantly the point that they had judicial privileges and the vassals were not in a position to question them. This meant that both the courts and the daily rituals of the barons were displays to remind the vassals of the separation of the groups. Neapolitan vassals were not slaves, but they had little practical opportunity to appeal to the central government for help and lacked substantial opportunities for class advancement. During the eighteenth century, some vassals were able to move closer to middle class status, usually by entering the growing legal profession. Some vassals, whom Astarita refers to as notables, became leaders in the vassal communities. This did not really translate into real political power, however, and they had little influence on the way the barons ruled the fiefdom.[74]

This system of oppression created constant tension between vassals and barons. This erupted into two major rebellions during the Spanish rule. The first, in 1585, was the result of a price increase on grain that coincided with a stagnant economy. Merchants and craftspeople joined the peasants in a mass uprising in the city of Naples that threatened the city administration. The legendary Masaniello revolt of 1647–48 was a major peasant uprising that threatened nobles throughout the province. The people were able to organize, take control of territory, and declare an independent republic, which received some French military support. The movement ran out of steam in April of 1648. The Spanish government and the nobility were able to work together to use the military force to put down the rebellion. Masaniello, a fisherman who became prominent at the beginning of the revolt, was assassinated in the first days of the uprising. Nevertheless, he and the rebellion became symbols of the possibility of popular movements. The rebellion was well known throughout Europe.[75]

When the rebellion was put down, the instigators were treated harshly. Astarita suggests, however, that many of the nobles had learned their lesson. They tried to build more positive relations with their vassals. They tried to present themselves as more benevolent and to emphasize their commitment to protect the vassals' interests. Perhaps more significantly, the nobles compromised more often with the vassals rather than using force or going to the central government.[76] This, however, should not overshadow the fact that the government always sided with the nobility in legal conflicts. The last Spanish viceroys and then the Austrians did nothing to challenge the judicial authority the barons had over their vassals. Even after Naples became an independent republic with its own king, public sentiment to change the system did not really gain popular support until the end of the eighteenth century.[77]

Villari discusses at length the abuses of the nobility leading up to the 1647 rebellion. I will discuss one example. Villari sees the situation in Naples as much more grave than other scholars, and it is hard to get a sense of how cruel or kind the typical Neapolitan baron was. Nonetheless, the story shows how the barons protected themselves as a class. A report in 1643 argued that Gian Girolamo Acquaviva, Count of Conversano, had murdered eight people, although many thought the number was quite higher. This only scratched the surface, however, of the injustices he committed against his vassals. The report listed a total of fifty-six charges against the count. Among his victims were both his own mayor of the commune of Nardò and, in order to cover that up, the mayor's assassin. Part of the reason for the assassination of the mayor, Villari writes, "was the latter's campaign to ensure that the election of administrators of the commune took place under the supervision of the royal governor rather than a feudal minister."[78] The mayor was working to free the people from the massive tax burden imposed by Conversano. Villari argues that Conversano's actions were especially harsh, but that they were representative of the actions of the nobility given that the viceroy did not intervene.[79]

What is remarkable about Conversano's story, however, was how the network of barons and the viceroy worked to protect him. Villari reports that he had been pardoned in 1631, 1635, and 1638. It was only after the mayor of Nardò was assassinated that a special commission was called to investigate him. As that tribunal was going on, two events occurred. In 1640, Conversano organized a protest against Bartolomeo d'Aquino, a man who had risen from outside the nobility to acquire enormous wealth by controlling the market for the rights to collect taxes for the Spanish government. When the viceroy moved against Conversano rather than d'Aquino, the nobility closed ranks to protect the traditional feudal lord regardless of how harsh he might have been. The viceroy, realizing that he would have to fight the entire class of nobles to prosecute him, did not punish him for his actions.[80] Moreover, in 1643, while the investigation was still ongoing, it was discovered that Conversano was contacting the French about the possibility of an anti-Spanish rebellion. Again, the viceroy, maintaining the policy of non-intervention against the nobility, simply made him agree to stop contacting French agents. He then trusted him enough that he charged him with raising 1,000 cavalrymen for Spain.[81] It came out, however, that Conversano had no intention of ending contact with France, and he was going to use the troops for his own purposes. At that point, he was arrested. The nobles responded by cutting off loans to Spain in support of Conversano. He was then called to Madrid by the King of Spain. Philip IV got him to agree to stop his acts of sedition, but in exchange he granted him more feudal privileges, which gave him complete jurisdiction over his fiefs. While the government in Naples was eventually able to roll that back, it shows how effectively nobles could work the system.[82] Feudal traditions had created a strong network among the nobility that helped them maintain their authority at the expense of Spanish rule and, more importantly, at the cost of any sort of justice for the vassals.

Villari points out that an important way the barons abused their power was through banditry. This had been a difficult and complex problem in Naples for quite some time. Bandits were pervasive throughout the province and could make travel and trade challenging. In 1585, Marco Sciarra organized a bandit army of about 1,000 soldiers who would regularly attack towns for seven years.[83] In general, bandits would be willing to work for nobles or other authorities. By the seventeenth century, the nobles were able to employ the services of bandits to make sure that tolls and fees were paid and also to impede the Spanish administrators. The bandits could work knowing that the noble—their employer—had control of the police and court system and would not prosecute them. Especially before the Masaniello revolt, barons regularly employed bandits to tighten their control and protect their sources of revenue.[84] By the end of the seventeenth century, the viceroy had made inroads toward stopping banditry, but there was still the threat of violence even as the barons turned to more legal means of maintaining control.[85]

Astarita's research supports Villari's claims that before 1647, the barons worked to expand their feudal judicial power. He examines a report by Giovanni Maria Novario produced in 1634 about the types of grievances vassals were bringing against their lords to Spanish courts. The majority of the complaints were against the way the barons applied their judicial authority, while very few had to do with economic interests.[86] After the rebellion, grievances in the Caracciolo di Brienza fiefs were more often tied to specific issues dealing with use of land than to juridical authority. This is the basis for Astarita's claim that after the rebellion the barons were more inclined to negotiate and compromise with their vassals. Nevertheless, as mentioned above, the central government still supported existing feudal juridical privileges rather than making a concerted effort to centralize power.[87]

Neapolitan feudalism was a decentralized legal system in which distinct estates were policed by private landowners who could work together as a coordinated aristocratic class. The nobles directed their efforts toward maintaining those traditions that safeguarded their privileges in order to protect their survival. Their hold was so strong that the political institutions in Naples did not substantially evolve for hundreds of years. While they could adapt somewhat to changing conditions and even thought philosophically about justifications for their authority, as a class they did not seriously entertain the possibility for substantial change in their political rule. Their conservative mentality prevented them from seeing social and economic changes that could be quite beneficial for themselves and everyone in the province. My interpretation of the *New Science* will read it as an attempt to explain this mentality as a way to see how to change it. At the core of poetic wisdom is the idea that powerful imaginative concepts were necessary to impose self-discipline on the giants. This is the origin of the noble mentality that centers its worldview around the need to protect their political institutions. In other words, the *New Science* proposes poetic wisdom to explain why the nobility cannot recognize obvious ways in which a more just government could improve the situation in Naples. When one goes into Vico's account of the imaginative universals, one can recognize this noble mentality.

Vico and *i Togati*

In the midst of this powerful oligarchy, Vico took the only real path available to the middle class, which was the study of jurisprudence. Anna Maria Rao describes how popular and how pervasive this option was. Qualitatively, many visitors to Naples in the eighteenth century were astonished by how many lawyers there were. Quantitatively, while the numbers are difficult to pin down, it appears that by the end of the century there were between 20,000 and 30,000 lawyers who were serving around five million inhabitants. This meant that there was a ratio of one lawyer for every 200 citizens, which was substantially higher than in England.[88] Since other typical paths to wealth and the middle class such as commerce had been stifled, this was the professional path that remained. The popularity of law was also the result of the structure of the central government under the viceroys.

When the Spanish established their government in Naples, the Consiglio Collaterale was the viceroy's main advisory body. As the Spanish consolidated their control, its influence eclipsed that of the parliament, which was the highest administrative body of the nobles.[89] By 1542, the important viceroy Pedro Álvarez de Toledo ruled that the Consiglio Collaterale would consist only of people who had a legal training. It was no longer enough just to be just a hereditary noble to serve on it.[90] This created a class called *i togati*, or "the robed," who managed the administration of the government. While the hereditary nobles still had important positions of power, including the *seggi* and the *giunta degli eletti*, *i togati* managed the main functions of the administration.[91] Hence there was an enormous demand for trained lawyers. This is why the seat of the professor of jurisprudence at the University of Naples was so coveted by Vico and his rivals. Law degrees were desired both by ambitious members of the middle class and by some hereditary nobles who wanted to expand their power.

While the Spanish government used lawyers to expand the power of government, the nobility also used them for protection. Indeed, a powerful bond grew between lawyers and nobles. It was prestigious for a baron to wield a legal team. Many lawyers wanted to serve the nobility, since that could open a path to buying a fiefdom. When the Austrians took control, they considered taking away the judicial rights from the barons, but the Consiglio Collaterale opposed it. Rao claims, "Feudalism and the judicial apparatus, in reality, supported each other."[92] This alliance was maintained into the rule of Charles of Bourbon, since his attention was focused on other needs of the new republic, including the military. It was only in the 1760s that popular opinion started to turn against the barons.[93] So the alliance between lawyers and the nobility was dominant in the political culture throughout the early eighteenth century.

This alliance may explain why Neapolitan intellectuals directed their criticisms toward the church rather than the nobility. Part of this was anger about censorship. In 1688 there was the noted trial of the atheists, in which the inquisition investigated four young lawyers for their atomistic views. This evolved into a dispute between the city, the church, and Spain. While this was one of the last major fights between Naples and the inquisition over jurisdiction, an atmosphere lingered where scholars were afraid of censorship.[94] There were issues that went well beyond intellectual freedom, however. There was concern that the church had been able to exert undue influence on the workings of the government. Many intellectuals, including Pietro Giannone, were concerned that Rome had the right to invest priests in the city and province, a right it did not have elsewhere. This meant that Rome had special influence over the direction of Neapolitan politics. Giannone and other intellectuals were concerned that while they had connections with both the viceroy and the baronial class, they were excluded from the real source of political and economic power, which was the Vatican.[95]

In the early eighteenth century, many Neapolitan intellectuals were also concerned that the church had too much power because it controlled too much land. Throughout the period of the Spanish viceroys, a variety of Catholic orders were able to expand their holdings in the province and acquire economic control over various industries.[96] It turns out, however, that they overestimated the amount of territory the church owned. In his extensive account of the debate over feudal authority after Vico, Pasquale Villani charts a slow shift in intellectual criticism from the church to the nobility. Antonio Genovesi (1713–1769), who would earn fame as the first professor of political economics, focused his attention on the power of the church. He thought that the church owned approximately two thirds of the property in the kingdom, while the nobles only owned a fifth. His idea of what the church owned was highly inflated, and the nobles actually controlled much more territory than Genovesi realized.[97] It was not really until the second half of the eighteenth century that authors understood how much territory was in the hands of noble judicial systems. This turned their criticism toward the upper class. In his *Scienza della legislazione*, which started to appear in 1780, Gaetano Filangieri addressed directly the problem of too much property being under noble judicial authority. Giuseppe Maria Galanti did a sociological and economic survey of the whole province, which showed how unsustainable life in the provinces under the nobility was becoming and clarified how much territory was owned by the church.[98] These arguments would develop well after Vico, however. During his time, the intellectual focus was on the church.

Despite the fact that Vico's collegaues like Giannone in the early eighteenth century were focused on the church, some did argue against the power of the nobility. Vico's friend Paolo Mattia Doria was a lesser noble from the famous family that ruled Genoa. He moved to Naples and wrote extensively on both mathematics and political philosophy, including his major work, *La vita civile*, which was first published in 1709. As the War of Spanish Succession was ending and it was becoming clearer that Austria would take control, Doria wrote a description of the city and province of Naples.[99] He discusses both class differences in the city of Naples and the characteristics of different regions in the province. The work includes an extended critique of the way Spanish mismanagement allowed the barons to impede the growth of the province. His argument includes the way that the church was also able to grow economically and politically during this period, but I am focusing on his early critique of the nobility.[100]

He affirms that the Spanish objective was to maintain their authority in an easy but enduring manner.[101] He argues that their main strategy was to divide and conquer. He identifies five ways the Spanish accomplished this during the reign of King Phillip II (1556–1598). They permitted the church to increase its influence, thereby creating conflict with the barons. They prevented commerce and did not allow the vassals to engage in business, while at the same time "removing all obstacles from the vain ambitions of the barons." They also stirred discord between the higher and lower barons. In order to impede the development of moral character among the nobles, the Spanish prevented them from getting access to education while encouraging their pride so they would believe themselves superior to northern aristocrats. Finally, the Spanish encouraged barons from other city-states to come to Naples to threaten the power of the local barons.[102] This situation improved after 1647, particularly during the rule of the viceroy the Marquis del Carpio (1683–1687). He was able to limit some of the judicial rights of the barons and their use of banditry while at the same time bringing a sense of civility. Despite this, the damage to the baronial class had been done. Doria describes a nobility that had fallen into decadence. It is worth looking more closely at his argument.

Doria asserts that the barons were vain and so desired to look important rather than develop a real sense of virtue. This is not an uncommon claim to make about nobility. What is intriguing is that Doria makes a distinction between traditions or customs (*costumi*) and rules or maxims (*massime*). On the one hand, he claims that the customs that would help the nobility develop character are fading or are being replaced. On the other hand, however, the maxims dictating how one should be a noble are not. He argues that the nobles were paying strict attention to following rules of behavior centered around manners and dress, but they have lost the context of these rules, which were originally meant to help one live well. Doria argues new maxims must be imposed to provide a foundation for virtuous behavior. He blames other nations for failing to do this. He writes, "New nations [France and Austria], coming to occupy the kingdom, spread around examples of their traditions yet without creating new corresponding maxims. The kingdom is becoming a chaos of feelings and measures to fight it but they do not entirely satisfy the need for virtue."[103] The problem is that a gap has opened between the traditions the nobles follow and substantial encouragement for virtuous living in a modern context.

Doria gives a number of examples of this. The barons study the rules of language and courtesy, but they do so primarily so that they can show themselves to be superior to the others. The higher nobles study the language so they can talk down to others while the lesser nobles hope to take advantage of mistakes. These rules of speech, however, have lost their connection to virtuous behavior.[104] Because the nobles lack character, they often fight duels. Rather than thinking about a duel's inherent danger, they carefully study the rules for dueling so they can follow them properly.[105] Doria also argues that changing customs are giving women more liberty, but the rules as to how they should be treated are not changing. The nobility still treats them as servants and severely criticizes them, as was dictated by the old maxims. As a result, the women have more freedom to speak but they have little to say because their energy has been drained by the nobles, who still impose old rules of behavior on them.[106] In all three cases, in the absence of old or new traditions, the nobility have figured out ways to use the old maxims of etiquette to their own personal advantage. They study the rules of behavior not to live well but to dominate others.

Once again, Doria blames the Spanish for promoting this behavior by keeping the barons ignorant, particularly of world affairs. If the barons had paid more attention to the broader political situation in Europe, they could have developed an *amor di patria*, or a love of the nation, which could have created new customs and maxims directed toward virtue. Instead, the barons had a limited sense of *amor proprio*, which, for Doria, signified just a sense of self-interest and self-preservation. Hence the nobles looked to increase their own vain interests locally without seeing the greater needs of the kingdom.[107] He maintains that the conspiracy of the Macchia to rise up for Austria was a disaster precisely because their lack of understanding of European affairs kept them from recognizing how difficult such a rebellion could be.[108] Doria suggests that the people of Naples had the numbers to rise up against the nobles or the Spanish, but they had been trained to follow the model of the barons so they also learned to act solely out of vanity and immediate self-interest.[109]

Doria's argument alludes to the problem with baronial judicial privilege. Originally, the nobles were granted these privileges on the basis of a real manifestation of virtue. Now they use their judicial privileges to defend their authority, but this no longer has anything to do with virtue. As the barons engaged in more duels, banditry, and violence against the vassals, they used their judicial rights to defend that behavior. Doria's account suggests that as the character of the barons eroded they lost the capacity to enforce laws justly. By tenaciously holding to the language of tradition but not its deeper content, they held their authority but lost their virtue. I will argue that this argument echoes Vico's larger claims about the decay of poetic wisdom.

Vico's famous law professor, Francesco D'Andrea, also argued against the power of the nobility. He was a member of the Academy of the Investigators, who defended the new Cartesian method against Aristotle, so he was probably one of the thinkers Vico was describing when he discussed the way Naples had been overrun by Cartesians.[110] Nevertheless, D'Andrea's ideas about law were probably a major influence. In 1696, he published his major work, *Avvertimenti ai nipoti* or *Caution to My Nephews*.[111] On one level, he recommends that people take up the legal profession because it is the best way to improve one's class status. More broadly, it is an argument about the importance of the class of lawyers for effective government. This may seem an unusual topic for an argument about political philosophy. Particularly in our society, we may assume that lawyers are necessary but costly bureaucrats or, more pejoratively, impediments to the smooth running of business or government. Naples is interesting, however, because it so stifled the development of both commerce that intellectuals who wanted to defend the growth of the middle class had to defend lawyers. While the legal profession had grown organically under the viceroys, thinkers like D'Andrea had to advocate for it in order to grow its influence. This causes him to develop an argument that Vico would later defend.

His argument against the nobility can be found in the brief document *Discorso politico intorno alla futura successione della monarchia di Spagna*. This was written before the death of the Spanish King Charles II while France was putting pressure on the nobility to rebel. D'Andrea had won favor with the Spanish by arguing that it would be better for Naples to remain with Spain than be subject to French tyranny.[112] Despite the temptation of a new French government, D'Andrea remained on the side of the Spanish and held that it would be easier to reform their rule than try to win a better deal with the French. In this text, he outlines the problems with the Spanish administration and the nobility.

He argues that King Charles I, who became the Holy Roman Emperor Charles V in 1519, ruled effectively because he understood Spain in the context of larger European interests. When Spain was divided from the rest of the empire, it turned inward. King Phillip II and later kings lost their ambition for empire and global influence, and they concentrated primarily on preserving what they had. As a result, they acquiesced to the demands of the nobility out of convenience. D'Andrea argues that the king gave up so much power that the barons essentially took control. He goes so far as to say it was a monarchy in name only. It was actually an aristocracy because the king followed the wishes of the barons rather than the other way around.[113] While this has created problems, D'Andrea suggests that lawyers can help ameliorate the situation.

The monarch needs to be strengthened so that he can serve the interests of the people instead of simply obeying the barons. Lawyers are in a special position to help with this. On one hand, they can help mediate between the king and the people so that the king can serve their actual interests and not simply respond to popular opinion which may be easily misguided. At the same time, the lawyers could make sure that the traditional authority of the nobles was not so rapidly overturned that it would cause too much instability.[114] Salvo Mastellone argues that this makes D'Andrea much more a precursor to Vico than to Giannone. In the next chapter, I will highlight this argument when Vico makes it in the *Study Methods*.[115]

So there were arguments being made against baronial power. Nevertheless, there is an important point to be made here. None of these thinkers call for the elimination of the nobility or the complete elimination of their privilege. In 1783, Filangieri published his third volume of the *Science of Legislation*. There he argues straightforwardly that feudal jurisdiction divides the province and creates a network of small tyrants who are in a position to corrupt the courts. He is unconcerned with the possibility that removing this noble privilege will cause too much anarchy.[116] This was a position that had to evolve. From the generation of D'Andrea to Giannone to Genovesi, authors could not conceive of a world without baronial control of the judicial system. Just as intellectuals today struggle with envisioning a world without stock markets and boards of directors controlling the distribution of food and other necessities of life, thinkers of that time could not see clearly how the masses could be controlled without the immediate jurisdiction of the barons. So, they argued for ways to moderate baronial authority by increasing the power of the monarchy but not to eliminate it. Villani traces in the development of the writings of Genovesi a shift from using models of just and paternal nobles to a discussion of the need to redistribute the wealth. Yet he still does not attack the nobles directly.[117] They could, however, see quite clearly what life would be like without the influence of Rome and if the government took land from religious orders. So, the earlier generations of thinkers focused on arguing against the clergy instead of the barons.

In his work on Giannone, Lino Marini makes an important observation. Another important reason why the intellectuals were not working against the nobility was that the nobility were among them. As much as anyone else, the nobility did not want to return to the chaos at the end of the fifteenth century. Some saw that there was need for reform and strongly advocated for it. Beyond Doria, the Duke of Torre Orsaia and Marzio Carafa Duke of Maddaloni were highly active among the Neapolitan intellectuals in talking about ways of reforming the feudal system. Beyond their theoretical contributions, they also embodied the potential of the barons to serve as allies in the cause of justice. Their active engagement in the discussion encouraged others to think more about reform than eliminating baronial privileges.[118] As the eighteenth century moved forward and it became less likely that aristocratic reform would happen, the critiques became stronger. As Vico was writing, however, there was still the possibility that the nobility would work with *i togati* toward finding new ways of promoting justice in the province.

In this context, I think we are in a better position to evaluate the *New Science* as a work of political philosophy and as anti-baronial. From a contemporary perspective, the fact that Vico defends monarchy seems peculiar. As one understands better the political situation in Naples, one can see how it was a call for reform against the conservative mentality of the nobility. The *New Science* does not call for profound changes to the feudal structure of Naples. Others in Vico's circle, however, also were not calling for radical changes. The more radical thinkers spoke out primarily against the church instead of the barons. Some of those who were speaking out against the barons called for lawyers to help guide the monarchy and for people to recognize that the rules of noble authority were no longer connected to real virtue. Vico repeats these arguments, I will suggest, in the *New Science*. From this perspective, the *New Science* is anti-baronial. I should mention that during Vico's lifetime, Naples was a rich intellectual community and there were many other voices. From at least this limited context, one can see the political dimensions of the work.

Outside of his philosophical writings, is there reason to think Vico thought there needed to be reform of the barons? There is no dramatic document where he launches a major invective against the baronial class. In his *Autobiography*, as he gets to the publication of the *New Science*, he focuses on his quest for attention and his attempts to respond to his detractors. While he was frustrated with how his career went, he does not blame the nobility, perhaps in part because there were nobles helping him. There are passages elsewhere, however, where he suggests that he had problems with the nobility.

In his early *Conspiracy of the Prince of Macchia*, he makes an interesting reference to Masaniello's rebellion. In 1701, a group of nobles tried to take advantage of the death of the Spanish king to overthrow the Spanish viceroy in favor of Austria. In Vico's account, the prince wanted to get the plebeians on his side and went to talk to their leaders. A plebeian leader responds that the nobles did not help the plebeians in 1647 so the plebeians now have no incentive to help the nobles. Vico has the plebeian argue, "With Masaniello as our leader we tried to alleviate the city from the weightiest taxes and reclaimed the rights obtained from Charles V. It was equitable for the patricians to support the wishes of the weaker order, but you, O Nobles, instead opposed us!"[119] This implies that Masaniello was engaged in a just rebellion against the unfair oppression of the Spanish as popular opinion held. Vico then makes clear that the plebeians who did join the prince's rebellion were the worst among them.[120] This leads one to believe that the plebeians who saw the significance of Masaniello's rebellion and rejected the prince were reasonable. This is certainly not a strong anti-baronial statement. Given that Vico wrote the work soon after the rebellion, he may simply be reporting the sentiment at the time. His harsh description of the plebs who did join the conspiracy, though, seems to indicate a recognition that the earlier rebellion of Masaniello was a legitimate response to an unjust system.

Vico shares a frustration with the barons in a letter he wrote in 1726 to the French Jesuit Edouard de Vitry.[121] He had spoken highly of the first *New Science* and wrote to Vico asking about the publishing industry in Naples and Sicily. As one might suspect, Vico complains about it. He specifically laments the fact that no one has published an epic account of the War of Spanish Succession, probably because he wanted to write it himself.[122] More broadly, he complains that new ideas are not being published. He lists a variety of disciplines in which progress is not being made. He specifically criticizes the church for promoting the vulgar version of the Bible, which has left the study of Greek and Hebrew to the Protestants. Further, he claims that theological debates sleep, while dogmatic views are accepted. He laments the popularity of the Cartesian method because its followers use its reliance on clear and distinct ideas to write simple books and physicists do not actually do experiments. Because of the general lack of originality, publishing houses try to print books that represent old material or publish books with fancy diagrams with little content.

What is relevant here, however, is that Vico claims that the nobles are not helping the situation. He claims that there are authors in Naples who have the capacity to write new books from their own ideas. This claim, in itself, is interesting because Vico steps outside of himself to pass a positive judgment on his contemporaries. He specifically praises the collection of Giuseppe Valletta for gathering the best editions of important works. The nobility, however, does not support this culture. He writes, "the majority of nobles are numbed by the pleasures of a pleasant life" ("*i nobili la più parte addormentati da' piaceri della vita allegra*"). The less fortunate nobles who have to work either get immersed in the politics of the Neapolitan forum or, he writes, "in order to live life more serenely, they unfortunately practice professions that certainly deaden their faculties if not waste them entirely" ("*per menare più tranquillamente la vita, esercitarsi in occupazioni che, se non gliene dissipano, certamente pur troppo gliene infievoliscono la facoltà*").[123] This implies a criticism that the nobility is failing to break out of tradition and think creatively about new ways of governing and organizing the state.

The third instance comes much later in his life. In 1738, he wrote an oration on the occasion of the wedding of King Charles of Bourbon to the thirteen-year-old Princess Maria Amalia Walburga of Saxony, daughter of the King of Poland.[124] The king had named Vico his court historian, and he had planned to write a history of the Bourbon reconquest of Naples but he did not finish it.[125] This oration is the last one he wrote in Latin for which the text still exists. It may hold special significance because it represents one of his most mature statements about the political situation in Naples. The oration contains much of what one would expect. Vico spends a good deal of time praising the noble birth, the beauty, and the high virtue of the couple.[126] Nevertheless, he also offers some nontraditional idiosyncratic thoughts, including a discussion of Hermes Trismegistus and the Egyptian god Theut to illustrate the problem with the conceit of nations.[127] This is an odd point to introduce given the purpose of the oration.

Nonetheless, Vico includes, as Gian Galeazzo Visconti writes, "a sort of overview [*affresco*] of the social and political life of Naples at the time of the oration."[128] Vico claims that the new monarchs will help lead Naples to its glorious destiny that has been assured by its geographic location, gentile climate, dense population, and many nobles. The citizens will carry the couple on their shoulders and hope they will give birth to a monarch born in Naples who will rule them.[129] From there, he describes how the ostentatious wedding ceremony itself will benefit the city and province.

He claims that the lower classes ("*il popolo minuto*") will enjoy that wedding celebration because it will distract them from the very cold winter and the plague that devastated the livestock. They will see the money spent on this large celebration and enjoy it simply because it is entertaining. The middle class ("*il ceto medio*") will have a more sophisticated understanding of the celebration's importance. For them, this demonstration of wealth will impress the ambassadors and rich guests from other nations. It will show that Naples is developing into a realm that will be at the level of the rest of Europe.[130] This benefits the middle class, at least in part, because it will stimulate trade. Earlier in the oration, Vico praised Charles for encouraging the Neapolitans to engage in commerce, specifically supporting his decision to add a professor of nautical arts to the faculty at the University of Naples. Perhaps to help his audience remember that the liberal arts are important, Vico also celebrates Charles for encouraging the students to study generally and hopes that this will encourage a Neapolitan student to become the next Torquato Tasso.[131]

Vico pushes the nobles far into the margins. He praises the large number of nobles as one of the benefits of the realm, but he never really explains what they contribute nor does he explain what they will get from the marriage ceremony or from the rule of King Charles. He vaguely hints that the nobility is an asset but he does not identify how nobles can improve themselves or the province. He says the nobility will not be jealous of the wealth of the foreign guests of the ceremony or the ceremony itself.[132] This only serves to highlight the noble wealth without indicating how this wealth will help the new nation. Vico identifies the king's creation of a military order dedicated to San Gennaro as a benefit for the nobility.[133] Vico praises the king for recognizing the connection between military virtue and virtue of character. However, he associates the military order and the nobility to the miracle of the liquefaction of the blood of the Saint.[134] This connects the nobility to an old and mythic past instead of the rich future that Naples has before it.

Obviously, Vico had to lavish praise both on the royal couple and the new Neapolitan nation. Nevertheless, the optimism of this document is surprising for those who take a pessimistic reading of the barbarism of reflection. It is certainly a dramatic contrast to the private letter discussed above. That letter, however, was written when it was unclear whether Austrian rule would ever end. In this oration, Vico suggests that the corner has been turned and a new monarch could actually improve the situation. The fact that the barons are almost entirely overlooked implies that they do not have a part to play in this. This invites a reading of the *New Science* as an anti-baronial document. In the next chapter, I will isolate an anti-baronial argument at the origin of Vico's thought.

5
Secret Laws

It is tempting to look at Vico's account of poetic wisdom either as an epistemological formula or as an index of the evolution of political institutions. The first explores mythical thought as a way of knowing the world. The second links Vico's interpretation of Roman myths to his history of natural law.[1] Both approaches are productive, but my goal is to navigate between them. I will take seriously the idea that poetic wisdom and Roman law need to be understood together to recognize the way feudal institutions functioned in the heroic age. This will then shed light not only on the institutions that the barons defend so tenaciously in Vico's Naples but also on the mentality that drives them.

This chapter will be dedicated to a position of Vico's that underlies his entire political philosophy. During the early modern period, advocates of the new modern political paradigm were concerned about a government's ability to use secret laws. The prevailing assumption was that if a government did not promulgate the law, then it could enforce the law arbitrarily, since the public could not know if the law had changed or not. Modern thinkers debated whether the government should have the power to keep laws secret in order to maintain stability or whether that was contrary to the principles of democracy. In an underappreciated argument, Vico points out that this assumes that rule by secret law would allow a government to rule arbitrarily. People living under secret laws, he asserts, would watch the rulers closely to see whether there really were laws at all or whether they were just being arbitrarily invented. Their scrutiny would actually increase the pressure on the rulers to act consistently rather than lessen it. Especially in an aristocracy, rule by secret laws would require rigid obedience among the oligarchs lest the people lose respect for legal authority. This is an important example of a place where Vico starts from a concern of early modern philosophers and then develops an entirely different way of framing the question.

I am going to place this argument at the center of my interpretation of poetic wisdom. Vico presents this argument in the *Study Methods*. In that text, he struggles to explain how the laws could have developed secretly without a premeditated plan by the ruling class. Twenty years later, the discovery of the imaginative universals solves this problem. Poetic characters are both rituals and ideas. They are a way of mimetically expressing a paradigm that has meaning for others. They were spontaneously generated by the first poets without premeditation. Further, the second comers to the asylums could have seen the performance of the poetic characters without knowing what they meant. This would explain the origin of secret laws. The fact that the poverty of language calls for the rigid obedience to the paradigms reinforces the idea that secret laws call for discipline. When Vico claims he worked twenty years to discover the imaginative universals, I see his intellectual journey as framed by the problem of secret laws.

In this chapter, I will work through Vico's texts on this argument. To place it in early modern context, I will discuss how Niccolò Machiavelli and John Locke debated the legitimacy of rule by secret law. I will then show how Vico undercuts this debate by arguing that the first governments were oligarchies. For the nobility, the advantage of secret laws is that they promote self-discipline within the upper class and put the plebeians in awe. These benefits only happen, however, if the nobility is willing to obey their own secret laws strictly. This point, I will argue, contributes to the discovery of poetic wisdom. When one understands the restrictive power of the imaginative universals, it is possible to see how they connect to the strict legal discipline of the nobility. This brings Vico's political philosophy together with his theory of myth. Before I begin this analysis, I will lay some groundwork by speculating on the power of secret laws. For a contemporary thinker living in a democracy, it is frightening to think that the government has secret laws because that would remove any check on its power. This fear is real, but I will present another dimension of secret law that is also readily apparent when one notices it. This will open the way to Vico's alternative argument about secret laws.

The Power of Mute Gestures

I have noticed a custom when being invited to dinner with a group at a restaurant in Italy. The person who arranged the meal occasionally finds a way to pay the bill secretly. The organizer excuses herself or himself on some pretense without drawing any attention and pays before returning.

When everyone gets up to leave, someone asks about the bill and the host just silently motions that it has already been settled. For those raised in the United States like myself, such generosity would elicit boisterous exclamations of appreciation. This is not the appropriate response in Italian culture. A guest is expected to understand that the organizer's generosity stems from a sense of caring, propriety, and decency. It is not to hear shouts of thanks. To respect this, guests should show appreciation in a meaningful but understated way. They can quietly place their hands over their hearts and bow slightly. This mute gesture is sufficient and there is no need for further verbal praise. The physical performance of payment and gratitude is much more powerful than long discussions of who should not have done what and who will pay next time. The power of this mute ritual comes from the fact that both parties share an understanding of its significance. By holding to this subtle but dignified performance, the parties show respect for each other because they know that the others have such a sense of propriety that no explanation is necessary. I do not know if this custom is widespread on the Italian peninsula, and readers of this text should not expect that their meal be paid for. Nevertheless, I have seen how powerful it can be.[2]

Cinema offers many examples of the power of such mute gestures. I will point to one. In Marco Bellocchio's 2019 film *Il Traditore*, there is a depiction of the life of Sicilian mafia leader Tommaso Buscetta and his testimony at the anti-mafia Maxi Trial in Palermo. Long before he turned informant, he had fled to Brazil. He was eventually captured, interrogated, and tortured by the Brazilian government. He was then extradited back to Italy. When his plane landed in Rome, the famous mafia adversary Giovanni Falcone came on board to meet him for the first time. Reporters and others were gathered outside the plane, perhaps hoping to get a picture of the former mafia boss. This film depicts Falcone using a complex set of mute gestures to win the trust of Buscetta.

In the plane, Buscetta stood up and held his arms out to have handcuffs placed on him. The police guard got them ready, but Falcone quietly told him they would not be necessary. He did not need to explain to Buscetta the significance of not using handcuffs. This mute gesture itself indicated to Buscetta that Falcone recognized both his status and his sense of civility. Falcone also showed that he understood that Buscetta was a man of honor and did not require an explanation. By performing this act without explaining it, Falcone showed his dedication to propriety and his recognition of Buscetta's importance. Falcone then reached down and picked up a towel. Without words, his facial expression sent a complex message. He had demonstrated his trust of Buscetta, but the masses outside would not understand this gesture. Non-verbally, he asked Buscetta to trust him and use the towel to hide the lack of handcuffs. This contributed to the bond between the two by keeping a secret from the masses. The two of them understood how decent people treat each other while the uninitiated plebeians did not. The mute gestures reinforced the importance of self-discipline between the two while then maintaining an aura of mystery for the people.

Bellocchio's scene illustrates how powerful mute gestures can demonstrate a shared sense of community founded on strict obedience to rules of propriety. This example is drawn from a fictionalized encounter of a mafia leader with a police detective. Nevertheless, I think it depicts the political and social significance of mute gestures.

Ritualistic mute gestures of this sort are diametrically opposed to philosophical discourse. Obviously, there are highly sophisticated forms of sign language that can communicate complex ideas. The sort of mute gesture I am interested in, however, is focused on demonstrating self-discipline to others in a way that excludes outsiders. As such, it excludes rational critique. Philosophical discourse uses articulate language to formulate arguments for and against a type of behavior. It then endorses a course of action on a rational basis. For the discipline of mute gestures, this need for rational critique is a sign of weakness. Inherent to the mute gesture is recognizing that it does not need expressed justification but rather ought to be already understood as proper behavior. If one needs to be rationally persuaded to follow a code of honor, one does not have honor. Critique is antithetical to the self-discipline of mute gestures. As such, the philosophical attitude and traditions based on mute gestures are at odds with each other.

One philosopher who analyzes this tension is Søren Kierkegaard. While Kierkegaard's interest is very different from Vico's, I introduce his account because he presents an intriguing portrait of the hero that I think is helpful for considering Vico's idea of aristocracy. In *Fear and Trembling*, which Kierkegaard wrote under the pseudonym Johannes de Silentio, he distinguishes two types of people who remain silent without articulating their motives. One is the true knight of faith while the other is the aesthetic hero. In Problema III, he discusses the possible dialectic between the aesthetic and the ethical or between hiddenness and disclosure in order to distinguish both from the real experience of faith. I am interested in his discussion of the persuasive force of mute gestures that philosophical arguments lack. He also describes how they elicit obedience in those who cannot understand their meaning.

The aesthetic hero maintains an aura of mystery by concealing all personal motivation. Kierkegaard describes this hero: "The single individual, qualified as immediate, sensate, and psychical is the hidden."[3] The hero reveals the physicality of the body so as to obscure what lies underneath. Whether the hidden content is psychic trauma or a divine curse, the hero must remain silent to maintain authority over others. Heroes buttress their strength by refusing to reveal what they really are. The ethical, on the other hand, is called to disclose. He writes, "his ethical task is to work himself out of his hiddenness and to become disclosed in the universal."[4] To assume moral responsibility in the face of reason, the ethical hero must reveal all motivations so that they may be submitted to objective reason. The goal of the ethical is to be understood by reason and by the people. The aesthetic and the ethical are driven in two different directions.

The key difference between the two is their source of moral validation. The ethical hero looks outside the self for moral praise or blame. This means that the ethical hero has to reveal her or his character and actions to receive the judgment of others and of reason itself. He writes, "The tragic hero, who is the favorite of ethics, is the purely human; him I can understand and all his undertakings are out in the open." Because everyone can relate to the ethical or tragic hero, everyone gets an opportunity to praise or condemn. This may positively justify what the hero has done. Nevertheless, the hero appears weak for relying on external criteria of judgment. On the contrary, the aesthetic hero needs no external validation. This hero has the confidence to act without concern for moral evaluation. In fact, the hero keeps all intentions hidden so as to block any attempt to pass judgment. This makes the esthetic hero much more awe inspiring than the ethical.

Kierkegaard's account illustrates how the aura of mystery inspires authority. The hero's silence communicates an inner confidence that inspires admiration. When ordinary insecure commoners meet, they feel compelled to share their motivations to demonstrate that they are not a threat to each other. The silent hero intimidates by not partaking in such banter. This exposes the hero to possible threats, but it also shows that the hero has the confidence not to worry about what others might do. The hero projects the aura of authority by communicating primarily through mute gestures. It also means that the hero will neither engage the philosopher in discourse nor alter a code of behavior. Kierkegaard's account focuses on the aesthetic hero as a loner, so he does not describe the way mute gestures form a class as Vico does. Nevertheless, he shows how the common people may be inspired by the mysterious actions of the hero that they do not understand.

Many of the Platonic dialogues are dramatizations of the inability of philosophy to speak to the hero. Meno and other Socratic interlocutors act as heroes. This is not because they have done anything particularly admirable. Rather, it is because they live by the aristocratic code of mute gestures. They live in conformity to the self-disciplinary paradigms they have seen in other heroes. The philosopher Socrates can force them to admit that they do not know why the rituals of noble behavior are what they are. Nevertheless, one does not get the sense that this causes them to abandon the behaviors imposed by traditional mute gestures. Socrates is often accused of being childish, the implication being that adults act in a self-disciplined way that does not require philosophical discussion. In Plato's depiction of Socrates's trial, he defends himself against the charges as they were stated. Everyone there knew, however, that what was at issue was the unwritten aristocratic code and not the charges as stated. His defeat symbolizes the frustration of philosophers to change the attitude of nobles whose behavior is centered on self-disciplinary obedience to tradition rather than rational critique.

Plato and Kierkegaard critique the way heroic mute gestures shut out philosophical discourse while presenting a code of self-discipline that inspires awe in the people. I suggest that Vico's account of the imaginative universals shares this concern. I do not see the *New Science* as a nostalgic call for communities to rediscover their ancient collective myths or reinvent new ones. It is too much of an analysis of class conflict for that. I see the imaginative universals as a form of exclusive communication that binds together an aristocratic class and captivates the masses. Poetic wisdom does not take philosophical reflection seriously. This is not because it does not understand philosophical thought but because the rejection of rational discourse is inherent to its morality. This is the main obstacle to reform in oligarchies such as Naples.

This may also be a concern in contemporary Western society. I will briefly speculate on a personal experience to reveal what I am considering. I have occasionally been invited with other faculty to formal gatherings that include administrators and members of other governing bodies. I have always been treated kindly. My ability to conform appropriately to expectations of the middle class has probably contributed to this. Also, contemporary upper-class morality in the neoliberal West generally calls for the wealthy to appear gracious and not act superior to others. Underneath this veil of congeniality, however, I am not convinced that anything I or my colleagues say really matters to the aristocrats. Professors are invited to these events to display to the donors what they are supporting. The wealthy recognize that those professors do not conform to their upper-class behavioral expectations. From a Vichian perspective, this is because the professors do not know the hidden laws that demonstrate worthiness. While the professors can verbally express sound rational arguments, their inability to perform the proper mute gestures invalidates their credibility. My interpretation of these encounters could be tainted by my sense of social awkwardness, and I am not sure objectively why me and my colleagues do not seem to be taken very seriously. Nevertheless, I cannot help but think that beneath the friendliness of aristocrats there is still a deeply rooted code of behavior that controls their behavior while refusing to engage the ideas of the uninitiated. I introduce this image as a way of inviting the reader to consider the presence of mute gestures in their own experiences of class.

The Problem of Secret Laws in Early Modern Thought

There is a reason why secret laws became a concern during the early modern period. Very broadly speaking, the medieval view held that monarchs ruled by divine right and were tasked with leading their subjects to virtue. If this were the case, then it would be obvious that their inherent superiority would give them the right to keep anything from the people they wanted. Just as parents are charged with withholding ideas and experiences from children so that they may develop in a psychologically healthy way, a king would have a right to withhold from citizens those ideas that would be detrimental to their characters. As modern political philosophy dawned, more thinkers thought of leaders not as inherently superior but as citizens in unique positions of responsibility. This brought to the fore the question of whether secret laws are legitimate. If rulers were equal to the people, then it would seem they should not keep secrets from them. At times, however, secret rules seem expedient and necessary to maintain social order. This becomes a question for early modern political philosophy.

In contemporary thought, this way of framing the problem has become common sense for anyone considering the appropriate limits of governmental power. I do not think people use the term "secret laws." It is much more common to wonder whether a government or board is doing enough to promulgate the laws or whether there is a secret agenda. The fundamental concern is whether the people know enough to be able to stop the government from acting in arbitrary or even corrupt ways that run counter to the best interest of the people. If the government is acting by a set of hidden rules, how can the people know how to vote on what it is doing?

There are two further issues with rule by secret laws. From the perspective of the citizens, it is a great infringement on their freedom.

Since they do not know what the law is, they would have to monitor their actions carefully in hopes that they did not accidentally break it. This would cause them to refrain from actions simply because they would not know if they were illegal. If arrested, they would have Kafkaesque difficulties proving their innocence, since they would not know what law they had broken. From the perspective of the government, rule by secret laws would allow it to act arbitrarily while appearing strong and consistent. Since the people did not know what the law was, the government could change and adapt it while claiming no change has been made. The government would never have to appear weak by changing its mind or going back on a promise. As long as the people did not have access to the laws, the government could then adapt them however necessary.

These two benefits depend on the people believing that there really are secret laws. For the people to be in awe of the government's power, they need to believe that it is obeying a law even if it is not public. If they suspect that the government is just making things up, they will resent the arbitrariness of the leaders and rebel when they have the opportunity. The advantage of secret laws is that they actually give the people a sense of stability. While they do not know what the laws are, they will at least believe that the government does not just invent policies at any given moment. The means that the government has to take care to maintain the aura of legal consistency.

Depending on how strong the memory of the people is, there will be restraints on how quickly the government can change directions. It can strengthen its position by adopting rhetoric that constantly reminds people of the sanctity of the law. It can also obscure historical narratives to disguise legal changes. One can see this practice in contemporary businesses. Managers and companies often do not like to talk about an organization's history. By keeping past decisions and actions concealed, managers have the freedom to change policies while not admitting to previous mistakes. As long as the laws are secret and history is obscured, managers can always appear steadfast to the employees while changing what needs to be changed.[5] If the laws are secret and the historical record is hidden, the people will believe that there is a stable and consistent law although they cannot see it.

For early modern philosophy, it was fairly clear that rule by secret law gave a government an immense amount of power to rule arbitrarily even if it had to maintain an air of consistent authority. The question was whether this power could be justified as necessary for a government's survival or whether it was inherently unjust. To show the two sides of this view, I turn to Machiavelli and Locke.

Although Niccolò Machiavelli wrote well before the early modern period, his ideas were obviously highly influential during that time, and Vico included him among the Epicureans he criticized (1109).[6] He was an extremely complex and multi-dimensional thinker. He is the sort of rich philosopher who can inspire many ideas about political philosophy. I want to focus on just one of his more renowned arguments. It suggests that secret laws are necessary for maintaining the stability of the state. He advocated the "reason of state," which would justify exceptional government responses to threats to stability. In this context, there are specific arguments that bear on the topic of secret laws. This view might appear extreme, but it gains traction when one considers situations in foreign policy or law enforcement. In these cases, the need for flexibility may be paramount.

Machiavelli titles chapter 18 of *The Prince* "How far rulers are to keep their word." This entails asking whether leaders should lie to the citizens and anyone else. The core of the issue, though, is whether the flexibility afforded by deception and breaking promises is justified to maintain social order. This would sacrifice strict rational moral standards in exchange for political stability. In this passage, he thinks so. He writes, "In the end, they [who have not kept their word] have been able to overcome those who have placed store in integrity."[7] The leaders who engage in deception are more successful at preserving their governments, thereby justifying the practice.

He gives two primary reasons for this. First, he holds that political circumstances change quickly, requiring different responses. He constructs an analogy to say that an effective leader must sometimes resemble a lion, who is powerful but not cunning, and other times act like a fox, who is the opposite.[8] Because fate can change situations dramatically and rapidly, rulers need to be able to change their positions as needed.[9] This will eventually entail breaking promises. He writes, "So you see a wise ruler cannot, and should not, keep his word when doing so is to his disadvantage, and when the reasons that led him to promise to do so no longer apply."[10] The next obvious step from here is to claim that leaders should refrain from giving their word when possible. This becomes more explicit in the second justification.

Machiavelli's negative view of human nature creates another reason for rulers to break their word. He writes, "Of course, if all men were good, this advice [to not keep promises] would be bad, but since men are wicked and will not keep faith with you, you need not keep faith with them." While the narrow self-interest of people justifies the ruler in breaking promises, it also explains how the ruler may succeed. He writes,

"You will find that people are so simple-minded and so preoccupied with their immediate concerns, that if you set out to deceive them, you will always find plenty of them who will let themselves be deceived." So, the narrow desire for survival makes people easy to manipulate, which helps the astute ruler maintain order. The leader needs to take advantage of this human tendency to assure the real survival of the state. Machiavelli insists that the ruler has to be careful. He writes, "it is essential to know how to conceal how crafty one is, to know how to be a clever counterfeit and hypocrite."[11] This suggests that keeping the laws secret will aid the ruler.

Social contract theory goes in the opposite direction. It holds that the source of a ruler's authority ought to come from the consent of the citizens. This power is granted through an agreement between the people. Whether the contract is initially tacit or explicit, it can only be legitimate if the parties know to what they are agreeing. Otherwise, it is not a true agreement. As a result, in the *Second Treatise on Government*, Locke asserted, "the legislature or supreme authority cannot give itself a power to rule by sudden, arbitrary decrees. It is bound to dispense justice and decide the rights of the subject by published standing laws and known authorized judges."[12] If the people do not know what laws the government is enforcing, then the people cannot know if they should continue to grant their consent or not. In order to avoid unjust authoritarian rule, the government must promulgate the laws. In Locke's view, if secret or arbitrary laws are in place, except in extreme circumstances, the social contract is broken and the government becomes illegitimate and subject to a just revolution.[13]

There are many ways one could frame this debate between Locke and Machiavelli. I would emphasize that there is a strong connection between it and the central question of whether enlightened self-interest can civilize humanity. Locke holds that if people are allowed relative independence with enough resources, then they will generally be able to recognize what is in their best interest. They will be able to monitor objectively the workings of government and vote accordingly. Machiavelli thinks that people are capricious and can easily be seduced away from what is in their best interest. The government will have to keep many things hidden because popular opinion can easily be manipulated. One can imagine many scenarios in which this debate could play out. For example, one could argue about whether the people could handle full disclosure of the government's intentions during trade negotiations or criminal investigations. It is time, however, to return to Vico.

There are many ways in which Vico would contest the foundations of this debate. The fundamental issue turns on what one thinks or fears a government will be. Locke and Machiavelli are both primarily concerned with abuses that could follow from rule by a monarch. Vico would not deny that in the third age a monarch or tyrant could fall into corruption to the detriment of a civilization. His primary concern, however, is the power of oligarchy, as I have discussed. If the law is maintained by a group of oligarchs rather than a monarch or prince, the entire problem of secret laws changes.

When a government is run by one ruler and close advisers, it is easy to imagine how it could manipulate the law while maintaining its image of consistency. If the secret laws were in the hands of an oligarchy that is distributed over a territory, it would be much harder to alter the law while appearing consistent. If various nobles started enforcing laws differently, the people would suspect that there really was no universal law at all. An oligarchy would have great difficulty using secret rules to rule arbitrarily while maintaining authority in the people. The aristocrats certainly could secretly meet at times to make hidden alterations. Practically speaking, this would be hard for them to do on a regular basis. It would still be in the best interest of an oligarchy to use secret laws. These laws would still have an aura that would instill fear in the people who would be afraid of breaking them accidentally. To get this benefit, however, the nobility would have to enforce the law strictly and consistently.

To visualize this, I imagine a child begging a parent for a cookie. The parent might say "No" and justify it by saying "Because I said so." This straightforwardly asserts the individual parent's authority. It also cuts off any argument from the child since the parent has left no grounds for debate. This becomes problematic as more adults get the right to distribute cookies. The group would want to keep the child in awe of their authority by keeping her or him ignorant of the rules of cookie distribution. As soon as two adults gave cookies at incongruous times, the child would become suspicious. The more arbitrary the distribution appears, the more the child will think there are actually no rules at all. This will encourage the child to demand cookies whenever the urge strikes. The only way for this system to keep the child in line would be for the adults to coordinate when cookies were given so that none of them would violate the law. This would require self-discipline on the part of the parents. This could actually become inconvenient at times. For example, a guest could come over with cookies at a time when adults were not allowed to give them. This would be an exceptional case in which the child should be given a cookie. The adults may be reluctant to do so because it would undermine their system of authority.

This example is oversimplified, but it illustrates how an aristocracy will have to obey the laws carefully to benefit from keeping them secret. To use secret laws to encourage obedience, the aristocrats will not only have to sacrifice the benefit of adapting the law but will also have to obey the law more much more strictly than they would have otherwise. It shows how the problem with secret laws is not that they would be enforced arbitrarily but that they would be enforced too strictly. This is counterintuitive, but it makes sense when one considers how aristocracy would have to function to maintain the aura of mystery that keeps the plebeians in line.

Aristocratic Rule in the Ages of Gods and Heroes

Vico's position on secret laws depends on the point that legal traditions originated out of oligarchies. He presents a substantial argument for this. I think this point has been undervalued by people who have a passing acquaintance with Vico. On one level, it is much easier to think about a binary conflict between rule by one and rule by all than to carve out a theoretical place for rule by a class. Further, popular culture tends to portray the struggles of a royal family between themselves and the people. It is harder to dramatically depict the struggles of an oligarchy than a single monarch. Certainly aristocrats appear in film and literature, but depictions of monarchs are more pervasive. The contemporary predisposition to think of past governments as monarchies obscures Vico's point that the evidence of history dictates that the first governments had to be aristocracies. In this section, I will present his philological and philosophical arguments for this position.

Vico directly addresses the extent to which scholars and philosophers have overestimated the role of monarchies in history, particularly in the history of ancient Rome. Axiom LXXIII reads, "It is a vulgar tradition that the first to govern the world were kings" (251). He attributes this to the conceit of scholars. Since monarchies have become more prevalent in Vico's era, scholars have assumed that ancient kings ruled like modern ones. This has corrupted the modern vision of Roman history. Vico asserts that while ancient Rome was initially ruled by seven kings, he denies that they were monarchs in the modern sense. Instead, he claims that the people identified as kings were the head of councils of aristocrats who had authority in their own territories.

His argument turns on his reading of Livy. He claims that historians assume that the word "people" has always meant what it now means. As a result, "everyone has believed that the Roman kingdom was monarchic and that the liberty instituted by Junius Brutus was popular" (663). In other words, scholars assume that in very ancient Rome there was a king who ruled over the people. They then assume that when Brutus overthrew Tarquinus Superbus, he did so for the Roman people. Vico argues that Brutus actually reasserted the original rights of the nobility. According to the original Roman constitution, the nobility originally had the right to remove a king. When Brutus introduced rule by two annual consuls, he made that process more formal but did not actually change the authority of the king or nobility. The nobility still wielded all the power. Further, the change did not give the plebeians more power either (664). For Vico, then, ancient Rome was in the hands of an aristocracy until the rise of the Caesars.

Whether Vico is correct about Livy, I think this application of the conceit of scholars is instructive. It is easy to look at contemporary popular uprisings against dictators and assume that ancient revolutions worked the same way. This obscures the class divisions and other rigid political stratifications that were in play. For example, one could easily present the American Revolution as a struggle of the people for freedom against a monarch. This popular image is highly problematic. The revolution was orchestrated largely by aristocratic colonists who had economic and political power. The English king responded in conjunction with parliament and the nobility. From this perspective, it was much more a conflict between two aristocratic orders than a revolution by the people against a monarch. This is underlined by the fact that the original United States Constitution allowed only land owners to participate in voting. More importantly, neither side showed substantial interest in expanding political rights to women or slaves. This indicates that the revolution was not actually fought for the people. Vico calls us to recognize that these governments of the past were largely aristocratic. Obviously, there were more popular uprisings such as Masaniello's rebellion of 1647. Nevertheless, Vico's position is that when one looks seriously at history, one recognizes the dominance of aristocracy as a form of government.

Vico has a more theoretical argument for his view about the primacy of aristocracy. This argument is quite important for understanding how he values the civilizing power of the imaginative universals with their mute gestures and secret laws. His argument is that the difficult psychological and physical process of civilizing giants into human form could only happen in close quarters where individual nobles demanded discipline from a small group of followers. In a monarchy, the ruler would be too far away to instill civil behavior. In a democracy, the power would be diffuse to restrain bestial passion. In the close confines of a fief, however, a lord could demand discipline in both the family and the *famuli*.

In defense of this point, Vico argues that the first poets would never organize themselves into a nation under a king. This is a recurring theme throughout the *New Science*, but key aspects of it are revealed in chapter 5 of the section on "Poetic Politics." The argument is grounded on two of his main principles. First, the giants had learned in the wilderness to live in solitude. It would take a long time to break them of this habit. This means that the poets and even the heroes would be reluctant to socialize with others more than necessary. Second, he holds that the strong will work to protect what they have built. This means that they would be reluctant to give up their ritualistic authority to anyone else. These points combine to demonstrate that the lord of each fief would strive to maintain its independence as much as possible. Each would protect his or perhaps her one asylum separately from the others. Each poet would rule as a monarch over a family, which included the *famuli*, without allowing any other ruler to question what they were doing.

Vico reinforces this point by reminding the reader that while these poets understood the importance of protecting their asylums, they would not have developed the ability to think about a larger community. He writes that "the minds of men were preoccupied with particulars and incapable of understanding a common good; they were accustomed never to concern themselves even with the particular affairs of others" (629). Unless there was an immediate threat that could not be handled alone, they would not see the long-term benefits of working together. So individual poets defended their authority over their own fiefs. This conforms to the picture of feudalism in early modern Naples. While the nobles could come together to protect their class authority, as was shown in the story of Conversano, and they did invest their money together to pay for dowries, they generally ruled their fiefs independently and did not try to incorporate them into larger associations to increase profit.

This period of separation was important for the civilizing process that turned the giants into humans. Rather than wandering individually or moving from asylum to asylum, the first people remained in tightly knit communities that were separated from each other. This increased the social pressure that the pagan religion imposed on them. Because they constantly watched each other, the immediate members of the family had to make sure they rigorously obeyed the gods. This then carried over to the second comers of society who did not hear Jove. The *famuli* did not understand the rituals of the nobility but were always under their watchful eye and had to obey. This encouraged the disciplinary training necessary to civilize them. These close associations allowed poetic wisdom to bring the giants back to their human form.

This is a remarkable example of the way divine providence works. He writes, "At their very birth providence causes the commonwealths to spring forth aristocratic in *form*, in conformity with the savage and solitary nature of the first men" (629). The poets founded separate asylums not because they knew it was necessary to teach civil behavior, but because it was part of their bestial condition. Divine providence offered them the opportunity to civilize their vassals even if they did not recognize it as such. Those lords who choose to maintain the self-discipline of poetic wisdom would effectively restrain the passions of everyone on the fief and transform them from giants to humans. They would do this despite not realizing what they were accomplishing.

When the *famuli* finally did rebel, this gave the poets the incentive to band together. The upper class recognized the need to work together to protect what they had created from the plebeians who did not understand their rituals. When they did so, however, they would not look for one king to whom they could turn over their power. Each hero was too accustomed to having authority over their own kingdom for that. They may have selected leaders, but they would not have given them the power to take control of individual fiefs. Authority would have remained in a class of lords rather than the king. Vico writes, "For the family fathers, who owned all the aforesaid rights over their clients, at the time when they banded themselves together in a natural order against the latter, came to confine all the aforesaid properties within their civil orders against the plebs" (631). The tendency of the heroes to protect what they have created thus formed the rigid aristocratic class that then concealed their shared laws from the people.

Vico's argument conforms to the structure of Neapolitan feudalism. If one thinks about the nobility as part of an economic or military structure, then his argument for the primacy of aristocracy is hard to grasp. Both of these conceptions focus on interaction between fiefs either in trade or supplying soldiers. On the other hand, if one thinks of it as a legal structure, then his position makes more sense. In the mountainous terrain of southern Italy, each noble had the separate legal authority to maintain civility among the vassals. While they followed the legal code of the province, it was their individual responsibility to police the people in a way that maintained order. I interpret Vico's account of the civilizing force of aristocracy as rooted in or at least consistent with the structure of the judicial system in the province of Naples.

While this may help make sense of Vico's position, it does open him up to a criticism. If this view is so dependent on his particular perspective on Neapolitan feudalism, could it have wider philosophical application? Does this make his view just a relic produced by a European political backwater? My initial response to this would be to recall from the last chapter that there were many other thinkers who shared the idea that aristocracy was the initial form of government. I would add that this form of feudalism was once much more widespread in Europe. It just lasted longer in Naples than other places. I would also suggest that this ad hominem argument could be turned around against Locke, for example. He was involved with Anthony Ashley Cooper, the Earl of Shaftesbury, who fought for the power of the noble parliament against King Charles II. This association may have blinded him to the dangers of aristocracy and pointed him too narrowly at the dangers represented by the monarchy. Ultimately, the question is going to be whether Vico's interest in aristocracy led him to a valuable account of the relationship between aristocratic thought and systems of power. To see the value in his thought, I now turn to his account of secret laws in the *Study Methods*.

Secret Laws in the *Study Methods*

In the chapter on imaginative universals, I mentioned Vico's claim that the search for poetic wisdom took twenty years and culminated in the 1730 *New Science* (338).[14] He probably was not very concerned about the exact number twenty. As Verene points out, he indicates in the first *New Science* that it took him twenty-five years to discover the poetic characters (NS25 154).[15] So, it appears he was estimating. Nevertheless, this puts the start of his journey roughly at the same time as he produced his two important early works. He delivered a special inaugural oration in 1708. It was part of a special ceremony for Cardinal Vincenzo Grimani, who was one of the first Austrian viceroys and a famous librettist (AU 146). He had to cut the oration down because he did not want to misuse the Cardinal's time, "which is so precious for princes" (AU 147). He published the complete version separately as the *Study Methods* in 1709. In 1710, he published his *Ancient Wisdom of the Italians*. These two works contain his most direct attacks on Descartes's critical method, which earned him the reputation of being an anti-modern thinker. This invites one to see his later discovery of the poetic wisdom as the culmination of his defense of rhetoric and the imagination against the prevailing critical method. When Vico talks about these works in the *Autobiography*, what does he say?

It is important to remember that he wrote the first draft of the *Autobiography* in 1725 just as the first *New Science* was being published. This was, presumably, before he had discovered the imaginative universals. Nevertheless, it should give a picture of what he thought was important from these earlier texts in his intellectual development. I think it is significant that he does not highlight his anti-Cartesian view. Earlier in the text, he laments the dominance of Cartesian thought, and he is frustrated by the way the *Discourse on Method* has caused students to reject the value of rhetoric (AU 122, 130, 137). This criticism is placed at the time of his appointment as professor of rhetoric, but this was about ten years before the *Study Methods* was published. At that time in his life, he may have lamented the way his own students were struggling to learn rhetoric in the prevailing culture of the university. When Vico describes these publications from 1709 and 1710, he does not emphasize their anti-Cartesian arguments.

Vico draws attention to the way the *Ancient Wisdom* introduced ideas that would become important for his later ideas of mythology. He discusses how he followed Plato's lead in looking for wisdom in ancient etymology, but he glosses over most of the arguments where he does so, including the *verum-factum* argument (AU 148). Instead, he focuses on the one spot in the text where he describes ancient thought itself rather than discussing its possible metaphysical insight. He emphasizes a very brief argument in chapter 5 about the way ancient Latin speakers thought everything was powered by an *anima* or soul (AW 85). He proposed that the ancients connected the principle of life to the air, which allowed them to explain how it animated both the blood and nervous system, which was referred to as the *animal spirits* (AW 86). This argument, as summarized in the *Autobiography*, appears in the *New Science* (695–696). Even though he does not name Jove in the *Ancient Wisdom*, he writes that in that work he had developed an idea of Jove as a god that provided an initial inspiration for thought (AU 149). He hoped that his *Study Methods* would be worthy of a place next to the *Novum Organum*, and he claims Bacon's work on myth was the inspiration for his *Ancient Wisdom* (AU 146, 148). He connects his work to other authors while emphasizing the importance of his early ideas about poetic wisdom.

What is most striking is what he says about the *Study Methods*. He identifies its overall purpose as comparing the advantages and disadvantages of ancient and modern methods of study. This is not what he highlights, however. He calls it a first draft of the *Universal Law* (AW 146). This portrays the work as being primarily about jurisprudence rather than rhetoric. He draws attention to chapter 11, which is dedicated to the history of Roman law. It is the longest chapter but comes near the end of the work. He highlights just one argument from it, and it concerns secret laws. He writes, "he [Vico] discussed at length in this dissertation the secrecy of the laws of the ancient Roman jurisprudents and essayed a system of jurisprudence for interpreting even the private laws from the point of view of the constitution of the Roman government" (AW 147). It is entirely possible that he highlighted this topic simply because it garnered attention. He tells us that the Roman antiquarian Vincenzo Vidania noticed and took issue with his claim that all Roman jurisconsults were patricians (AU 147).[16] Nonetheless, it invites one to read this particular argument about jurisprudence as a model for Vico's later ideas about politics. It also encourages the reader to look for a connection between the idea of secret laws and the imaginative universals, since this argument came twenty years before the 1730 *New Science*.

Bergin and Fisch translate the phrase *arcano delli leggi* as "secret laws."[17] This is the same phrase he uses in axiom XCII, which I will discuss later (284). The Italian word *arcano* can certainly mean "secret," and Vico describes the aristocratic laws as both *segrete* and *arcane* (953). So he holds in a literal sense that the aristocrats made sure that the plebeians did not know what the laws were. Nonetheless, the word *arcano* can also mean "mysterious," just as the word "arcane" in English. It implies they were actually awe inspiring, which is what Kierkegaard saw in heroic secrecy.

The *Study Methods*' discussion of jurisprudence has not gone unnoticed in the scholarship. Naddeo sees it as a significant step in the development of a new idea of cosmopolitanism that is developed later in the *Universal Law*.[18] She focuses specifically on the emphasis Vico places on the importance of interpreting the law in a way that promotes the common good. She writes, "With his criticism of contemporary jurisprudence, in other words, Vico both reasserted the centrality of the public welfare to the task of the law and, therewith, affirmed the role of the courts in the good governance of the polity."[19] While this promotes a new cosmopolitan idea of social responsibility that would help the common good, she also recognizes that this argument is a call to reduce the power of the baronial class. Vico's chapter ends with a proposal to give the Sacro Consiglio of Naples more power to restrain the authority of the baronial class. Vico claims that this court has already made rulings that promote the common good in ways that go beyond both the letter of Roman law and the promotion of natural equity. He implies that these decisions often ran contrary to the interests of the barons. He concludes that this practice should be spread to all law courts (SM 70). Naddeo rightly sees this as an attack on baronial prerogative. She writes, "Vico's call was a plea to the judiciary to bring the criteria of the common sense and of the common good to bear upon the (selection and) judgment of cases concerning baronial practices."[20] If more courts acted like the Sacro Consiglio, then vassals and other citizens would have the opportunity to protest the traditional authority of the nobility. Naddeo discusses in detail the workings of the Sacro Consiglio and why it was surprising that Vico put his hopes in that legal body. Nevertheless, the overall point is that Vico calls for the government of Naples to break the power of the nobility and promote justice.

Naddeo's account highlights a very important dimension of Vico's position. I want to expand this point to connect this argument to his account of poetic wisdom. To do this, I need to present some textual context. The *Study Methods* argues that the basic difference between modern and ancient study methods is that the former seeks absolute certain truth while the latter works from probabilities. The modern method is reflected in the fourth rule of the *Discourse on Method*, which says that one should know the whole truth about a topic before moving forward.[21] The ancient method assumed, practically speaking, that people must often choose a course of action before they have time to attain certain knowledge about the situation. Both schools have disadvantages. He writes, "The specialists in topics fall in with falsehood; the philosophical critics disdain any traffic with probability" (SM 19). The ancient method allows the possibility that a wrong assumption could undermine any decision. The demands of modern critique can cause analysis paralysis that would block one's ability to take practical action. To avoid both disadvantages, Vico advocates learning both strategies.

He traces this paradigm through a variety of areas of study. He always finds advantages and disadvantages to both methods. Usually, his emphasis is on defending the contributions of the ancient ones not because they are inherently superior but because the excitement over Enlightenment discoveries in medicine and physics, for example, was eclipsing the benefits of ancient approaches (SM 26–33). When he arrives at jurisprudence, this orientation gets inverted. The transformation is complex. To put it most directly, ancient jurisprudence looks for absolute certainty in the letter of the law, while modern jurisprudence is willing to adapt the law along the lines of probability to different particular cases. Here, Vico defends modern jurisprudence against the ancient. This change is understandable given the context. Broadly speaking, the judicial system in the providence of Naples had not evolved unlike practices in medicine. As a result, he wanted to promote what the modern methods had to offer to change the system. What is his argument?

At stake here is a traditional debate in the philosophy of law: should judges read the law literally or should they interpret laws to enforce the spirit of the law? Vico argues that the ideal response to this question would be to balance the two conflicting concerns. When the law is interpreted literally, it commands strict authority, which promotes stability in the community. He writes, "To demonstrate the inflexibility of justice in a specific case instills in all citizens a deeper reverence for the law" (SM 62). The problem is that there is no way to write the law so that its literal interpretation will always result in a just decision, particularly in private cases. The goal, therefore, should be an application of the law that goes beyond its literal meaning but does not sacrifice its aura in order to maintain the stability and discipline of the community.

To demonstrate this, Vico employs an early version of the strategy that figures so prominently in the *New Science*. He draws an analogy between Roman legal history and the situation in Naples. In the early republic, the Laws of the Twelve Tables were applied in a way that "was uniformly unbending" (SM 52). The only way to handle a situation that the law did not clearly address was by highly exceptional decrees that were difficult to execute. This rigidity helped to stabilize the political culture, but it often led to unfair judgments based on laws that were not written to cover a particular situation. Part of the reason the emperors came to power was because private individuals demanded a fairer judicial system. The first emperors instructed the praetors to go beyond the letter of the law in order to promote justice for private individuals (SM 55). This worked for a long time because the traditional respect for the law retained its power despite the fact that it was interpreted less rigidly. The period of the early empire had the best balance of political stability and justice.

Unfortunately, Rome eventually pushed this too far in the modern direction. A tipping point came when Hadrian published the *Edictum perpetuum*, which replaced the Twelve Tables as the focus of legal study (SM 56). This meant that lawyers would study primarily how to argue for judgments that would promote *aequitas naturalis* or an equal exchange of goods based on their worth. By the time Constantine came to power, the *jus civile*, which was dedicated to the preservation of society, had been forgotten. He writes, "*Aequitas* began to be the controlling factor of all controversies in the courtroom" (SM 57). The courts had become so focused on the fair distribution of practical goods, honors, and punishments that they emphasized private interests over the needs of the state. In Vico's account the *jus civile* that is needed to maintain the stability and virtue of the state goes beyond these practical concerns. When the lawyers stopped studying it, they lost the ability to balance justice with political stability. Once the focus was placed solely on natural equity, decadence creeped in and the empire eventually collapsed. Vico's view of Constantine and the history of the Roman empire changes in the *New Science*, but his theoretical point remains the same.

Even if one is not well versed in ancient Roman law, it is not hard to see the implications of Vico's account. They are summarized by Herman Melville's famous story *Billy Budd*. A sailor accidentally kills the captain of the ship. While the tragedy was clearly unintentional, the letter of the law defines it as mutiny and calls for the death penalty. This leaves the admiral adjudicating the case in a difficult position. It would be clearly unjust to execute Budd, given that the death was obviously unintended. At most, it was manslaughter rather than murder. Nevertheless, if an exception were to be granted in this case, this would loosen the authority of military law. It might encourage other sailors to kill their captains in ways that appear accidental. In early Rome, the strict application of the law made for a highly organized but unjust society. During the early empire, there was an appropriate balance of reverence for the letter of the law and for equal justice. Ultimately, the authority of the law fell as the barbarism of reflection inevitably took hold. Vico's position is that society should try to exist in the balance between the two for as long as possible.

Having presented this summary of Roman legal history, he then asks the reader directly to compare this ancient history to modern Naples. Yet he is quite specific about how he wants that comparison made. He writes, "Let him [the modern jurist] draw a parallel between the Roman Empire and the monarchic system of our age, in order to investigate whether the same beneficial effects spring from both of them" (SM 66). This appears to be a call to the new Austrian monarch and his viceroy to use a more interpretative approach to the law as the early Roman empowers did. When one looks at the analogy closely, one sees that it asks the monarch to curtail noble judicial privilege.

During the time of the republic, Vico writes, "The patricians, then, were the only ones entitled to exercise the profession of law" (SM 52). Just as in modern Naples, the aristocratic class controlled access to the legal system. The emperors changed this by reducing the number of nobles who could serve as judges. They selected aristocrats who were loyal to the state rather than the aristocracy. He writes, "The right of publicly giving decisions having legal force—*jus respondendi*—was granted by the Emperors; however, not indiscriminately, not to any nobleman, but only to individuals of unquestioned devotion" (SM 54). This meant that the judicial system would be driven not by a desire to maintain the rights of the aristocratic class but by a desire to advance the empire as a whole. Further, the emperors gave the praetors the authority to interpret the law to ensure justice for private individuals. The effect of this was "to undermine even this mere semblance of aristocratic power" (SM 54) that came from the fact that the judges were still aristocrats. Even though the nobles were still in positions of authority, they were charged with serving what was in the just interest of the people. This produced the most effective balance between protecting political stability and maintaining justice across a range of classes and private interests. By analogy, the Austrian viceroy should remove or reduce baronial judicial privilege over their fiefs and consolidate that authority in institutions such as the Sacro Consiglio, which would then be populated with educated judges who would work for the good of the state rather than the nobility. Further, the viceroy should encourage a broad interpretation of the law that was suited to the contemporary situation in Naples. This is the thrust of Vico's argument.

What makes this analogy hard to follow is that Vico does not complete it. He connects the early Empire to the Austrian monarchy, but he does not spell out the link between the Roman republic and medieval European feudalism. In my reading, this is a strategic move to deny any sort of value to baronial privilege. Their primary defense is that they need to strictly enforce their traditional and immediate authority over their fiefs to keep social order. Vico claims that this was indeed important for the early Roman republic. Nevertheless, I suspect he does not want to highlight this function of medieval feudal law, since that would only strengthen the position of the barons. So he leaves it to the reader to fill in this connection between the Roman republic and the medieval European law. Vico offers a brief discussion of the way scholars in the medieval period analyzed Roman law. He concludes, however, that they overlooked the fact that laws need to be adapted to the culture that they are intended to govern (SM 65). This leads him to claim that Roman law will need to be adapted to a monarchical form to be applied in Naples. He writes that "the jurist will need a firm grasp of the doctrine of monarchical government" (SM 65). In this way, he draws attention to the idea that the Roman model can offer reform if adapted rather than by taking a conservative view of the importance of tradition. Overall, however, he leaves it to the reader to connect the Roman republic to feudal law.

Vico is careful about making sure his call for reform is not too extreme. He is also concerned that a focus on loosening legal interpretation to benefit private justice could lead to a degradation of political order. As Naddeo rightly emphasizes, he counters this by emphasizing that lawyers always need to remember the ancient principle that the purpose of law is protecting social order. Vico wants to make sure that lawyers remember that only thinking about *aequitas naturalis* could degrade the *jus civile* of a community. Jurists need to remember that. At the same time, however, this does not mean that *aequitas civilis* should not just accept the traditional legal order. Rather, the jurist needs to think about equality in a way that also can encourage people to support the state.

He carefully defines the relationship between *aequitas civilis* and *aequitas naturalis*. The latter is equality defined by the raw value of goods. The former adds to the later what is in the best interest of the community. He writes that the two are the same but *aequitas civilis* "spans a still wider compass, since it is not dependent on the utilitarian motive of the promotion of the interests of private individuals but its major concern is the public weal" (SM 66). He does not make a sharp separation between the two. In the case of Billy Budd, obviously, there was a tragic opposition. Generally, however, Vico holds that the two are not in conflict. *Aequitas naturalis* provides the basis for sound legal interpretation, with *aequitas civilis* providing an important and necessary consideration. If the spirit of the law is understood properly within sound institutions for legal interpretation, then sharp differences between the two should be minimized or eliminated.

Vico gives a long list of examples of instances when the Roman empire promoted equality in ways that also supported the state. In these examples, citizenship is granted to more people, which has the positive effect of making them loyal to the common good. He writes, "Why were all freedmen made Roman citizens? So that all freeborn Romans might have a feeling of greater reverence for the emperor" (SM 67). He adds the rhetorical assertion, "Why were all subjects of the Roman empire granted citizenship? . . . so that all should have equal interest in the preservation of the Roman empire?" (SM 68). Other examples include curtailing noble privilege to prevent the abuse of vassals so that they too will be loyal the central government. This is a basic plea to treat everyone fairly and equally since that will encourage everyone to coexist harmoniously. His underlying point, however, is that this will not happen automatically if lawyers concentrate simply on fair exchange or traditional privileges. The lawyers must consciously consider how these decisions can support the community.

He concludes this chapter by writing, "The modern monarch, therefore, who wishes his realm to prosper, should be well-advised to have Roman laws interpreted according to *aequitas civilis*" (SM 69). The immediate point, although he does not state it directly, is that judges should make decisions for the good of the state rather than the good of the individual or, especially, the good of the noble class. Since *aequitas naturalis* is entailed within *aequitas civilis*, the monarch will encourage judges to issue fair decisions that will promote individual justice. Well-trained lawyers will help this process by defending the particular interests of private citizens. They should realize that the outcome of their efforts should be *aequitas civilis* rather than just *aequitas naturalis*. He writes, "having become experts in civil doctrine, they will bring the political training that they have acquired, to bear on the governance of the state itself" (SM 70). Perhaps Vico's argument is not particularly glamorous. Can one get overly excited about a philosophical call for the importance of lawyers? Nonetheless, when one grasps the context, one sees both a strong assault on the baronial class and a call to rally around the central authority of the viceroy.

Having laid out the general structure of his argument, it is time to look specifically at the role secret laws play in it. When used effectively, secret laws maintain order in the people because they would be afraid to question the legal authority of the rulers. Perhaps more importantly, they maintain order among the aristocratic class because they need to obey the secret laws strictly to defend their own authority. In the *Study Methods*, Vico emphasizes that the Roman republic was great and long lasting because its aristocrats held onto this discipline of secret laws for so long. He maintains this view in the *New Science*, but there he has combined his idea of secret laws with pagan religion and so it is harder to sort through (1101). His account in the *Study Methods* is valuable because it lays out clearly how the secret laws gave authority to the Roman patriarchs.

He writes, "The patricians, however, made use of their knowledge of the law as an *arcanum*, a secret source of power" (SM 50). This aura of mystery instilled a sense of wonder and obedience in the plebeians. As he describes it in the *Study Methods*, this did mean literally that the patricians did not allow the lower classes to read or find out what the law actually was. In the early republic, only aristocratic families could know and teach the law. The texts of the laws were kept hidden and written judgments were abridged before distribution. Further, the laws were given prestige and a powerful aura because "they saw to it that the *formulae* of judicial proceedings should be absolutely fixed and endowed with the utmost solemnity" (SM 51). In other words, ancient Roman courts were conducted with profound and mysterious rituals that baffled and intimidated ignorant audiences. The secrecy of laws compelled people to obey.

In an important paragraph, Vico summarizes the two main reasons why secret laws were so beneficial for the ancient Romans. First, the laws kept the people in order because "the aura of secrecy surrounding justice . . . aroused in the people the greatest reverence for the law" (SM 51). As I have emphasized, because the people were both ignorant of the law and in awe of the silent mystery surrounding it, they would not have risked breaking it. Second, the aristocrats saw that staying in conformity to the secret law would do more long-term good than using it for expediency or personal gain. They realized that they "could accomplish more by the pursuit of strict justice than by acts of injustice and overbearing insolence" (SM 51). In other words, they saw that it was in the long-term interest of their class that they all obey the law consistently in order to maintain the aura of secrecy. Individual nobles certainly could have preyed on the ignorance of particular vassals, but that would have fostered resentment. By acting consistently, however, the noble class was able to defend its position of superiority over the plebeians. This is Vico's clearest statement about the power of secret law and their importance for the early republic.

This now brings into focus the difference between ancient and modern study methods of jurisprudence. It would have been an anathema for the aristocratic Romans to make an exception to the law. Any exception could compromise the aura and authority of the law. Therefore, when jurists argued a case, it would have been useless for them to ask for a loose interpretation of the law. Since they could not get any movement on the definition of the law, their only recourse was to change the facts of the case. He writes, "the jurists resorted to legal fictions and excogitated some formal devices of their own invention so as to avoid amending the law" (SM 52). These legal fictions were not simply falsehoods about the facts of the case. They appear to be situations when a good orator would recount events in a particular way to fit what the law prescribed. It could also involve acting in a way that satisfied the requirements of the law despite not being what the law intended. From Battistini's annotations, the clearest example involves the emancipation of minors. Sons were slaves to their fathers, who had the right of life and death over them. Fathers could also sell their sons three times. The law did not explain, however, how a father could liberate a child. Instead of changing the law, the father would fake three sales of the child, which would be the limit. These fictional sales, which needed to be performed but did not literally sell the son to anyone, would then grant the son his freedom, since the last sale could not be revoked.[22] Basically, instead of trying to reinterpret the law, a good ancient lawyer would redefine the facts of a case or even stage facts to get the necessary result from the law.

This may sound odd, but I believe I have practiced this as I have dealt with contemporary bureaucracies, particularly when there is a gap between old and new computer systems. For example, I often have to fill out a form that asks for my faculty number. This form has not been updated for decades, and most faculty, me included, have not been issued a faculty number. We make one up as a fiction to satisfy the system. Rather than changing the form, which would require committee reviews, administrator input, and votes by a variety of governing bodies, it is easier to plug a number in each time to move things along. When laws or practices become so rigidly entrenched, it becomes simpler to change, invent or redefine the facts of a situation rather than change the law. Vico's point is that ancient study methods actually taught lawyers how to do this. This aspect of legal training, however, has actually become outdated.

In the modern courtroom, the laws are interpreted to fit the situation. He writes, "it was by means of such fictions that the jurists succeeded in adjusting the facts to law. Today, instead, our practice is to adjust the law to the facts" (52). This makes the modern study of *aequitas naturalis* important because it is now the driving principle in the courtroom rather than the letter of the law. He writes, "A further advantage of our system is that our law experts aim more at equity than at strict law and treat the private individuals with greater consideration" (SM 61). As part of this, the law is made public to the people so that they can see what laws are in play. The aura of the secret laws is sacrificed. How, then, does the legal system support the stability of the government?

Vico responds to this question with a surprisingly Cartesian defense of the modern study of law. He writes, "In the courtroom it is indeed sufficient to discover a straightforward presentation of the arguments in equity, based on a close examination of the facts, so that the law may be easily adjusted to such facts by taking into consideration, not its verbal formulation, but its spirit" (SM 60–61). The modern lawyer can use new developments of science to present a much clearer picture of the facts of the case. The legal system now derives its authority from tangible evidence rather than the sanctity of the law. Modern judges can rely more on the spirit of the law because they can point to actual evidence as a basis for decisions. Presumably, in ancient times it was difficult to present evidence, since lawyers would have been dependent on oral testimony. When the facts were vague, it was necessary to turn to the stability of the law to provide the appearance of objectivity. As the facts become more demonstrable, they can be used with the philosophical idea of justice to provide an objective basis that can rightfully persuade an audience. When the word of the law was interpreted slightly differently, a judge could point to hard evidence to justify that decision.

Deploying a Cartesian sensibility, Vico argues that the modern lawyer needs to study the facts of the case rather than learn how to use oratory to obfuscate them. This does not eliminate other positive values of oratory, namely knowing how to connect to an audience. Nevertheless, the value of ancient study methods of jurisprudence is not oratory. Instead, the ancient methods provided two other related benefits. First, the ancient method helped lawyers to understand the importance of *aequitas civilis*. He writes, "our lawyers are deficient in the knowledge of how to set in order and maintain a commonwealth through laws." This, he maintains, is the "source of all jurisprudence" and ought to be taught first (SM 60). As discussed above, however, this means not a return to the strict obedience of the law but a recognition of the connection between justice and civil order. In fact, he is specifically concerned about the way modern jurisprudence is "weaker in its separation from philosophy" (SM 60). To preserve the common good, modern lawyers should be studying not the text of Roman law but rather the underlying metaphysics that guided the creation of those laws and the first societies. That way lawyers could understand the spirit of the law to understand how it contributes to social order. This is an early statement of his call to understand the ideal eternal history to understand the context of the law.

Second, in support of this, the ancient methods help lawyers understand the importance of spectacular ceremonies to give law the aura of authority. He gives a curious and classist example to demonstrate this point. Because modern law is based on factual evidence rather than the aura of ritual, anyone with the right evidence could win a case. He writes, "any peasant, however halting and ineloquent, would be able to obtain justice by demonstrating the equitable points in his plea" (SM 61). Unfortunately, this might undermine the law's authority in the eyes of the people who have only looked at the participants involved and not studied the case. Vico would not want a judge in this case to interpret the law strictly and block justice. Nevertheless, he hopes that lawyers will learn how to perform proper courtroom ceremonies to reinforce the importance of reverence for the law. He might support the way lawyers continue to wear black robes with white tabs in Italian and French courts. This is, perhaps, superficial, but there is something to be said for maintaining an appearance of professionalism in the courts to remind everyone of the importance of protecting the law. In an intriguing way, Vico here supports the image of tradition while modernizing the content.

The conclusion of chapter 11 is that a modern monarch ought to make the laws public. The more lawyers who study the law openly, the better the legal system will enforce the spirit of the law justly. The aristocratic defense of their secret laws is stifling the growth of the province not because it allows them to abuse their power individually but because it allows the barons as a class to maintain a legal system that is designed to protect their interests. In Vico's view, this impedes the development of both commerce and an equitable sense of justice. Vico calls for the Austrian viceroy to encourage the continued study of law and prioritizing the needs of the province over that of the baronial class. As a member of that class who will seek the post of professor of jurisprudence, Vico has a stake in this debate. He appears sincere, however, in arguing that this was the route that led to ancient Rome's success and he thinks this is the path Naples needs to follow.

This chapter has a large problem, however. It fails to explain how the secret laws became secret in the first place. How could the early Roman patriarchs have had the foresight to write the laws and know not to tell them to the plebeians? The explanation he offers in the *Study Methods* is that the Roman nobles separated into three branches. Each one kept hidden a particular type of law: sacral law, public law, and private law (SM 50). Very few patricians knew all of the laws. The rest could use their sect's secret laws to monitor the other nobles, but they had to restrain their own actions so as not to breach the laws of the others. This enabled each group of nobles to keep the others in check and use the culture of mystery to keep the plebeians in awe and obedient (SM 51). One could see how the rivalry between sects could cause them to recognize the importance of keeping the laws secret. This, however, does not really solve the problem. It assumes that someone had recognized the value of dividing the three sets of laws before they were instituted. This is contrary to the axiom that the order of ideas must follow the order of institutions. I suspect he recognized this and worked on this problem until he got to the 1730 *New Science*. I now turn to that text to see how this argument reappears.

Roman Law as Poetry

This argument about secret laws from the *Study Methods* is repeated in the *New Science*.[23] Most dramatically, it appears near the end of the axioms, starting with axiom XCII. Axiom CIX states, "Men of limited ideas take for law what the words expressly say" (319). Then Axiom CXII goes in the opposite direction: "Intelligent men take for law whatever impartial utility dictates in each case" (323). This is consistent with his view in the *Study Methods*. The "men of limited ideas" are the nobles working from ancient jurisprudence. The intelligent monarchs and lawyers go beyond what the rituals and laws of poetic wisdom literally say in order to find equity. Between the 1730 and 1744 edition of the *New Science*, he decided to place more emphasis on this point.

In the later edition, he expands the chapter in book 4 on the three types of reason during the three ages of civilization. He adds a section entitled "Corollary: Fundamental History of Roman Law." This is an updated summary of his argument in the *Study Methods*. I will not rehash his entire restatement. Instead, I want to highlight the way this more mature version of the argument is recast as a critique of Machiavelli. His final statement is Lockean in that he wants the laws to be publicly studied. Nevertheless, he does not prescribe a specific form of government, and he does insert a critique of the idea that the market can instill virtue in the people.

The *New Science* argues against Machiavelli's position on secret laws by placing it in the historical context of the ideal eternal history. Book 4 is dedicated to showing how aspects of civilization manifest themselves differently in the three ages of humanity. The three types of reason are "divine reason, reason of state and natural reason" (947). While divine reason was the poetic wisdom of the earliest poets, he links Machiavelli's notion of reason of state to the nobles of the heroic age. This is intriguing. Ordinarily, one would expect an opponent of Machiavelli to claim that his position grants too much power to a tyrant. Vico, instead, argues that Machiavelli's view would, in practice, pull civilizations back to the heroic age.

As in the *Study Methods*, the *New Science* claims that the laws of the heroic era were known only by a select few experts. He highly praises the early Roman senate for initially denying to the plebs any voice in public affairs and later for only letting them participate when carefully guided (949). He quickly clarifies, however, what the wisdom of the senators entailed. It was based not on magnanimity toward the plebs or even on a sustainable society but on the senator's own self-discipline and strict obedience to the law. He writes, "By this superstitious observance of their words, they made the laws march straight through all the facts, even where the laws turned out to be severe, harsh and cruel, just as reason of state operates today" (950). Just as in the *Study Methods*, strict dedication to the law obliges the heroes to change the facts to meet the law regardless of how much harm that does. At the end of the statement, Vico explicitly ties ancient Roman obedience to the law to the modern Machiavellians who defend the privilege of the barons.

Machiavelli's position is that secret laws are necessary to give the ruler the flexibility to respond to threats to political stability. He addresses *The Prince* to a new ruler who has the opportunity to instill political order through a new government. Theoretically, it would make sense that a new leader would keep the laws secret to have the flexibility necessary to build authority. In practice, however, Vico's position implies that this use of secret laws would not lead to a monarchy. A new prince would have to work with an existing aristocracy or instill discipline through the rigid interpretation of law. Just as in the time of feudalism, the prince would need to use the secret laws in a coordinated and consistent way to maintain authority over the people. The prince could certainly use the secret laws to intimidate the people while at the same time convincing them that their own survival depended on obeying the tyrant. This would represent, however, a retreat into the rigid and inflexible heroic mentality. Vico's point is that philosophers might argue theoretically that rule by secret law would allow a leader the flexibility needed to adapt to the whims of the people, but in practice it would just be a return to a government that used force and intimidation to preserve laws that were actually not adaptable at all (260). For an administration to respond appropriately to the actual needs of the people, it would need to respect them by making the laws public.

Heroic reason becomes outdated in the human age when "free popular states or monarchies develop" (951). Both forms of government are directed toward equality, but the monarchy has a separate prince to look after the public good. In the human age, the people have largely restrained their passions and no longer need to be encumbered by the rigidity of aristocratic rule. They can be trusted with knowledge of the laws because they will use them in an enlightened way to satisfy their practical desire for long-term political stability. They will recognize that fairness is the best road to a well-functioning society. Essentially, Vico suggests that instead of relying on the market to promote enlightened self-interest, the legal system will be able to resolve small disputes while promoting the importance of making fair agreements. As long as the government does not promote excessive luxury and decadence, the court system should be able to keep everyone's private desires in perspective.

This will have at least two further positive effects. First, because the people will be focused on practical concerns, they will not be distracted by abstract and barbaric ideas or ideologies. Rather than falling under the influence of theoretical political movements, they will use tangible evidence to settle disputes in court. They will "attend to the smallest considerations of justice which is called for by cases where the facts are fully specified" (951). This will forestall the barbarism of reflection. Second and more generally, as in the *Study Methods*, he holds that interest in individual welfare will lead to a wider sense of civil responsibility. Private utility produces "the *aequum bonum* considered by the third kind of reason to be discussed here, namely, natural reason which is called *aequitas naturalis* by the jurisconsults" (951). *Aequum bonum* now takes the place of the *aequitas civilis* from the *Study Methods*. His overall point is that by giving the people access to the human law in the third age, they will use it to increase the stability of the community and just distribution of goods and punishments. He admits that the monarch and the government may need to use their prerogative in exceptional circumstances as in Locke's system, but for the most part an extensive legal system should maintain order. He writes, "in monarchies there are needed a few men skilled in statecraft to give counsel according to civil equity on public emergencies in the cabinets, and a great many jurists of private jurisprudence to administer justice to the peoples by professing natural equity" (951). In other words, a well-trained infrastructure of lawyers should be able to resolve particular cases based on the facts to avoid conflicts. In exceptional circumstances the monarch may have to make a dramatic decision, but for the most part the system that resolves individual disputes should keep everyone content.

Importantly, Vico claims that private utility is not solely concerned with property and wealth acquisition. While popular states and monarchies developed from a desire to satisfy private interests, that is not the only factor. He writes, "To this [private and public interest] we must add the natural causes which produced these forms of state (which are quite opposite to those which had produced heroism); namely, as we have shown above, love of ease, tenderness toward children, love of women, and desire of life" (951). As discussed earlier, Vico holds that humans are naturally social and that the period of barbarism drew people away from that. What humans naturally desire most of all is living a relaxed life in the company of a family. While material wealth certainly helps to attain those goals, it is not the final purpose. What should maintain civil institutions of the human age is not the desire for wealth but providing the people with their natural goal. If human government can replace the harsh poetic institutions of religion, marriage, and burial, and fulfill human desire with more rational alternatives, the people should be content (666–678). Hence, to achieve social stability, it is necessary to think beyond just market forces.

Politically, Vico ends up on the side of Locke at least in that he wants the laws to be public in the third age. In the human age, it is important that the government reach an understanding with the people. He concludes that good monarchs "wish the laws administered according to natural equity and consequently in harmony with the understanding of the multitude, and thus makes the powerful and the weak equal before the law, which monarchy alone can do" (952). Obviously, he disagrees with Locke in defending the monarchy as opposed to democracy. I see Vico's position on monarchy more as a response to the situation in Naples than as a universal prescription. It was commonly understood in Naples that it would take a central authority—either a viceroy or King Carlo of Borbone—to undercut the power of the aristocracy. The point, is that the monarch will support the people and be open to them in a way the aristocracy can never be. I see nothing in Vico's account that would preclude the possibility of using a contemporary model for a more sophisticated democratic system, although it would face the same dangers as a monarchy.

Vico does warn of an important danger about public laws in the third age. In the axioms, he summarizes how heroic rule leads to monarchy. The most significant axiom on this point is XCII. It starts, "The weak want laws; the powerful withhold [*ricusano*] them" (283). One could also translate the verb *ricusare* as "refuse" in the sense to refuse to give the plebeians legal recognition. I like Bergin and Fisch's translation because it further emphasizes that the heroes do not even tell the plebeians what the laws are. Vico clarifies this by saying that "the nobles want to keep the laws a secret monopoly of their order, so that they may depend on their choice and that they may administer them with a royal hand [*la mano regia*]" (284). Again, however, this does not imply that the nobles administer the laws arbitrarily. They are enforced harshly but in a consistent way that confirms both their mystery and authority (321).

The axiom continues with this warning: "the ambitious, to win a following, advocate them; princes, to equalize the strong with the weak, protect them" (283). Once the laws are public, unscrupulous people will come to power by offering rights to the multitude that may be impractical or otherwise decadent and disastrous (293). A strong prince will try to protect the laws to prevent this collapse. Despite this, corrupt leaders will emerge who appeal to the baser passions of the people by fulfilling their immediate desires rather than what ensures justice and political stability. This could certainly mean lower taxes or free distribution of goods or entertainments. One could also imagine contemporary promises to protect the dominant ethic group or increase law enforcement. As the leaders do this, they tempt the people away from their natural desire for a life of ease and point them toward wealth acquisition. This eventually leads to destructive conflict. In this case, "in times of peace nothing remains but to struggle for power, not by law but by arms, and use the power to make laws with a view to increase of wealth." This has grave results: "The result is civil wars at home and unjust wars abroad at the same time" (288). To maintain a civilization at the height of the human age, it will be necessary to avoid this temptation. The government and its system of lawyers must remember the role of the law in maintaining social stability by resisting selfish temptation.

One could say that the conclusion of Vico's positive political philosophy is a call to the monarch to use prudence to resist a variety of forces that pull humanity away from its social nature. The tradition of poetic wisdom threatens to pull civilization back into harsh aristocracies. The temptation to use excessive philosophical abstraction pushes civilization toward the barbarism of reflection. The remnant of bestial desires threatens to pull the people into decadence. By staying grounded in empirical evidence and recognizing true human nature, a wise monarch can maintain civilization at the high point of the human age.

Unfortunately, as with any philosopher whose advice is to be prudent, there is not much specific help Vico can offer. His whole point is that the spirit of the law must be interpreted to adapt to particular circumstances. Since he does not know what those circumstances will be, he cannot give specific advice for adjudicating particular disputes or give specific recommendations for constitutional structures. So, his philosophical text focuses on what is universal: the metaphysics of history and the ancient structures of heroic law. It may seem surprising to think of pagan religion or ancient law as universal. Nonetheless, because this law is produced as a spontaneous response to the need for self-discipline and the inevitable political problems connected to class warfare, Vico holds that it has a universal structure (141–142). The *New Science* tries to help the monarch and the people understand the rigid aristocratic mentality it needs to confront and places it in the context of the greater pattern of history.

The *New Science* thus endeavors to analyze pagan religion to answer a question that the *Study Methods* could not: how could secret laws have evolved in the first place? This may seem like a simple question. As one cycles through Vico's presuppositions about early humanity, however, it gets increasingly complex. It culminates in one of his most bizarre claims. He dedicates a section at the end of book 4 to the argument that ancient Roman law was a serious poem (1037). If one reads this out of context, this may seem highly peculiar. Nonetheless, if one understands his account of secret laws and the limitation imposed on poetic wisdom by the poverty of language, one can see that this is a key moment where Vico brings together the history of jurisprudence with his depiction of pagan religion. When one sees this connection, it is possible to see how the problem of the origin of secret laws led to his discovery of the imaginative universals.

In Vico's model, the first poets could not have recognized the benefits of keeping the laws secret before they actually started hiding them. As Hirschman pointed out, human institutions come into existence through the guidance of divine providence, and the people who create them rarely have an awareness of their beneficial effects (238). So, the first poets could not have simply called a meeting where they decided to keep the laws hidden. The natural human tendency to protect what they have created is at the center of the conservative mindset of the aristocracy (261). This would have prevented the poets from sharing the laws with the *famuli*. It does not explain, however, how the laws were spontaneously created such that they were hidden at their origin. How could that have been possible?

The answer to this question, in my interpretation, is what compels Vico to think of poetic wisdom as an epistemological structure. He had to clarify what it was about the early laws that would have been kept secret. In the *Study Methods*, he assumed the laws would have been written down and physically hidden, but that does not make sense particularly because the law would have been developed long before writing was. He needed another answer. If poetic characters were concepts rather than just commands or prayers, it would be possible for the first poets to have spontaneously invented rituals with meanings that the *famuli* could not recognize. The second comers could see the actions and respond appropriately. They could not think their meanings as the poets could. If poetic wisdom was an epistemological structure, then it would be possible for its rituals to be physically performed and secret from the plebeians at the same time.

This resolves the problem of how early laws could be secret. It also explains how the poets could keep meaning hidden even though they lacked the ability to lie. Vico is committed to the idea that the first poets lacked the capacity to reflect and so they could not separate a thought from a bodily expression. They had to either perform or witness a physical action to have an idea of an imaginative universal. Because of this, they had to believe the religion they created was real. He writes, "since the first men of the gentile world had the simplicity of children, who are truthful by nature, the first fables could not feign anything false" (408). At the same time, it means they could not have practiced deliberate deception. The heroic character Ulysses may represent duplicity, but this is more through his selfish behavior and savage mistreatment of the plebeians than premeditated deception. Particularly in the age of gods, the poets could not lie. Nevertheless, if the imaginative universals had a significance that the *famuli* did not grasp, the poets could have kept the meaning from them.

The poets felt the civilizing force of the rituals directly, while the *famuli* did not. The first rituals were performed to channel the poets' emotional energies against themselves and compel them to create rudimentary religious institutions. Those poets who really heard the thunder experienced the terror and shame necessary to motivate such behavior. As they expressed their passions in mute gestures, the other poets empathetically recognized each other's self-discipline. More importantly, they shared the meaning that the images embodied. If the rituals were purely behavioral, then the *famuli* could imitate them or not and they really would not be secret. Because they represented a paradigm that could be remembered and recognized, however, there was something to keep secret. The second comers did not feel the sublimity of the terror in such a profound way. As a result, they did not feel the self-discipline. It also prevented them from recognizing the ideas that the mute gestures represented. This is an explanation of how the poets recognized the significance of the rituals while the second comers did not. Thus it is an explanation of how the first poets were able to keep the laws secret.

Obviously, it is unclear whether this has anything to do with the anthropological origin of humanity. It does, however, seem to conform with the mentality of the barons that dominated the province of Naples. Two important features of poetic wisdom tie it to the account of secret laws. As discussed in chapter 3, a basic principle of poetic wisdom is that "the human mind is naturally impelled to take delight in uniformity" (204). This means that the mind is directed to see identity within a set. This is compounded by the fact that a poetic thinker's inability to reflect means that the thinker cannot distinguish essential from inessential attributes. Therefore, in the mind of a poetic thinker a representation of an imaginative universal either will be identical to the paradigm or will not fit into the paradigm at all. Obviously, however, no two manifestations of Jove or Godfrey could ever be identical in reality. They would only be so in the mind of the poetic thinker, who would latch on to essential characteristics and overlook everything that did not fit. If the resemblance was strong enough, the poetic thinker would cut through all else to see the identity. If there was a key element that did not match, however, the person would not be seen as connected in any way to the paradigm despite the presence of remarkable similarities.

From a contemporary perspective, the poetic thinker is, in effect, changing the facts to fit the ideas. This original feature of poetic wisdom established a lasting tradition of jurisprudence that carried into feudal Naples. The poetic mentality is directed at recognizing the way paradigms repeat. As this evolved into the early study of jurisprudence, lawyers learned to force the law onto situations by changing the facts. The inability of poetic wisdom to make subtle distinctions becomes the practice of altering circumstances to fit the text of the laws.

Moreover, poetic wisdom is restricted by the poverty of its language. The first poets would have created new universals only when compelled by extreme circumstances. It would have been hard for them to invent new words, since the poetic mentality is pointed at finding sameness rather than noticing difference. More ordinarily, they would have found ways to adapt the words they did have to a wider variety of situations. This will explain why the images of the ancient gods were so complex. As they evolved, new institutions were attached to them instead of creating new poetic characters.

This evolved into the noble tendency to avoid changing the law. The Neapolitan barons continued to dominate their fiefs through the rigid framework of their own judicial privilege. They resisted all attempts at legal evolution or innovation in order to maintain their status. They probably could have increased their wealth if they had decided to reform their economic—if not their judicial—practices. Their mentality that restricted the development of new ideas, however, kept them from seeking new opportunities. They kept patching together their outdated system since they could not conceive of radical change. In Vico's view, the struggle against the barons was hard not because they had all the resources, but because they could not see any alternative to their own language for describing the world.

One could certainly object and suggest that Vico is going quite far to explain a simple point. It is obvious that tradition has a strong hold on the world view of the people and, especially, on the world view of those who benefit from those traditions. Is it necessary that Vico develop an epistemological account of pagan religion to explain it? In my reading, however, this is precisely what makes the *New Science* so interesting. If the traditions of aristocracy were maintained simply because of the power of tradition and wealth, then it would be a matter of arbitrary tyranny. In Vico's view, however, there is an epistemological structure to the thought of the nobles that connects directly to the institutions and the self-discipline they promote. As with any early modern philosopher, his lack of evidence may hold back his results, but it indicates that he recognized the need to critique the aristocracy at the level of their mentality. This, I suspect, is the road to give it contemporary relevance.

Before tracing that point in the next chapter, I want to discuss an important passage where Vico ties ancient laws together with poetic wisdom through a discussion of mute gesture. It appears at the very end of book 4 in a section entitled "Final Proofs to Confirm the Course of Nations." The first part of the section is dedicated to showing how the harsh punishments during the heroic age become more compassionate in the human age (1021–1022). The second part is a corollary that endeavors to show that "all ancient Roman law was a serious poem, represented by the Romans in the forum, and ancient jurisprudence was a severe poetry" (1037). This passage is very significant for my reading because it shows how Vico connects the imaginative universals to ancient jurisprudence. It is easy to overlook this section because, as with many parts of the *New Science*, he works on many dimensions of his theory at the same time. Moreover, if one focuses on the creative and imaginative aspects of poetic wisdom, this passage seems incongruous because it emphasizes the harshness and rigidity of the poetic mentality. Nevertheless, it shows how poetic wisdom explains the operation of ancient laws.

He concludes this section with a concise summary of his view of the history of jurisprudence and his practical philosophy. He describes the human condition by saying, "a man is properly only mind, body, and speech, and speech stands as it were midway between mind and body" (1045). Over the course of history, humans move from being ruled by the body to being properly ruled by the mind. Originally, law was certain and grounded in mute gestures. As humans evolved, they developed speech to produce better legal formulas. The culminates in the highest level of human reason. He writes, "it reached its end in the true in the ideas themselves with regard to what is just, as determined by reason from the detailed circumstances of the facts." He writes further that "this truth is a formula devoid of any particular form" (1045). This emphasizes that in the human age lawyers and monarchs are supposed to use prudence to bring together a philosophical idea of justice with the particulars of the situation. There can be no definite statement of how this will appear because the facts will be different in every case. This is his call to interpret the spirit of the law. In this section, he traces this evolution in the change of emphasis from public law to private law. He also discusses the rise of Platonic philosophy. For my reading, what is most important is his account of mute gestures in relation to the certainty of the law.

Vico starts this section with a discussion of ancient property rights. Ownership of slaves, or mancipation, was based on *vera manu*, which was the literal physical force of the hand (1027). Ownership of property, or usucapion, was based on the physical settling of territory that established ownership (1028). Since there were no laws governing private disputes, they were settled by actual physical duels (1029). As civilization evolved, these physical acts of violence were replaced by acts of imitation. Vico gives a detailed explanation of how the laws concerning mancipation and usucapion evolved from physical acts, to mute gestures and ceremonies, to symbols, to finally laws. As the earliest civilizations were organized, the physical force used to control the slaves became symbolic. He writes, "the first peoples, by nature poets, must naturally have imitated the real forces that they had previously employed to preserve their rights and institutions." A mute gesture imitating violence replaced the violence itself but with the same authority. This connects the imaginative universals to the law. Vico does not speak of the thunder here, but he does claim mancipation was symbolized by "a symbolic knot in imitation of the chain whereby Jove had bound the giants to the first unoccupied lands" (1030). These mute gestures and ceremonies evolved into ceremonies that much later became a legal declaration (1031). One can see here how Vico traces back pagan religion to acts of political force and authority through the power of mute gestures.

This becomes more striking when he discusses usucapion. This is the right of property established by remaining physically on the land. This seems simple enough until the owner dies. One of the weaknesses of poetic wisdom is that it cannot recognize a member of a set without identifying two objects together. This means that the poets could struggle to recognize the rightful heir to a property. To convince a lord of a right to property, children would have to wear masks so that they could actually become their fathers through imitation. He writes, "under the person or mask of the father of a family were concealed all his children and servants, and under the name or emblem of a house were concealed all its agnates and gentiles" (1033). Vico underlines that this would be the only way that poetic wisdom could recognize such rights of ownership. He writes, "The childhood of the world could have followed no other path; for children have a powerful faculty for imitating the truth in matters within their capacity, and it is in this that poetry consists, which is nothing but imitation" (1032). This is how the imaginative universals connect to ancient Roman law. He includes an odd etymology of the word *persona*, which he claims comes from a word for the practice of wearing animal skins, as only heroes like Hercules could do. He links this to the Italian word *personaggi*, which means great or important person. As fanciful as this etymology is, it shows how he connects the imaginative universals to noble rule. I will return to this characteristic of poetic wisdom when I discuss the imaginative universal Apollo. Regardless, his point here is very instructive in bringing together his account of secret law and poetic wisdom.

This is what Vico means when he calls ancient Roman law a serious poem. What it codifies are these original mimetic mute gestures that were used to show authority. Its strict interpretation of the law based on the certainty can be traced back to the imaginative universals (1033). He reiterates and strengthens his claim from the *Study Methods* that ancient Roman jurisprudence altered the facts to fit the law. Originally, this was seen when a son would become his father and wear a mask in the forum to demonstrate rightful ownership. Even though the first poets could not commit an act of deception, they maintained their authority through mimetic fictions. He writes, "By its fictions what had happened was taken as not having happened; and what had not happened as having happened." By using the imaginative universals, the poets converted the facts of the situation into a way that would fit the formula. He summarizes his point when he writes, "Thus all the fictions of ancient jurisprudence were truths under masks, and the formula in which the laws were expressed, because of their strict measures of such and so many words—admitting neither addition, subtraction, nor alteration—were called *carmina* or songs, as above we found Livy terming the formula dictating the publishment of Horatius" (1036). Again, because the ancient law needed to derive its authority from the certain, it left no room for legal interpretation.

In an interesting way, Vico underlines how important identity was to poetic wisdom. Ancient tales have a tendency to depict a small group defeating an entire army. He gives the examples of Ajax and Horatius holding a bridge against all of Tuscany and forty Normans defeating an army of Saracens in Palermo. He claims that there were really many more people there, but they were members of the family and the plebeians of the heroes who were thought of as identical to the hero. This indicates the tendency of poetic wisdom to identify different people as the same when they imitate each other. He writes, "The founders of Roman law, at a time when they could not understand intelligible universals, fashioned imaginative universals" (1033). This represents how poetic wisdom could only find perfect identity between objects, and it suggests the pressure that it imposed on those who wanted to imitate the paradigmatic heroes.

Throughout this passage and the *New Science*, Vico emphasizes how the crudeness and strictness of poetic wisdom created an exceptionally harsh basis for political authority. He often invites the analogy from ancient Rome to the returned barbarian times. This, in turns, invites the reader to think about the rigidity and harshness of the Neapolitan barons. When one sees how these ideas in Vico fit together, one sees how a critique of their rule is formed. The barons combine the authority of mute gestures with the strictness of secret laws to maintain an iron-fisted and harsh rule over their fiefs. The crux of Vico's argument is that baronial power is not simply based on tradition or wealth. It is based on a rigid epistemological structure that cannot adapt to change. The only way to overcome it would be to have the plebeians, who never seriously used poetic wisdom as a form of thought, gain control. As that happens, lawyers and monarchs can find the philosophical guidance to rule effectively by open laws.

The advantage of reading the *New Science* this way is that it can explain the pantheon of pagan gods that Vico presents in book 2. My task for the next chapters will be to dig into the specifics of his account to show what it says as a critique of aristocratic rule.

6

The Roman Pantheon

In the 1744 *New Science*, Vico first lists the twelve gods of the greater gentes in axiom CVIII (317). These correspond to the twelve gods ordinarily thought to make up the Roman pantheon. I do not think it is accidental that this comes right before his axiom stating that people of limited ideas must interpret the law in a rigidly literal fashion. These pagan gods, which were unwittingly created by the first poets, represented the certain basis of law, which was strictly followed by the poets and heroes. They prescribed the ritualistic discipline that civilized the theological poets as they lived in separate fiefs that were scattered across the mountains and forests. The poverty of poetic language combined with the social pressure produced by the use of mute gestures compelled the nobles to use these poetic characters to restrain their desire.

In this axiom, Vico criticizes the natural law theory of the Grotius, Selden, and Pufendorf triumvirate. When he discusses these authors, he often chastises them for committing the conceit of scholars and overestimating the capacity of the first humans to agree to any sort of contract. Here, he specifically faults them because "they begin with nations reciprocally related in the society of the entire human race." In other words, they tell their origin stories as if all nations rose up at the same time and in contact with each other. They forget to explain how the first nations separated or, as Vico would have it, developed independently from each other. Specifically, Vico claims that they overlook the fact that separate families would have developed apart from each other. Vico writes, "among all the first nations, as we shall show, the race began in the time of the families, under the gods of the so-called greater gentes" (318). This is consistent with his argument that the civilizing process would have required that there be a large number of distant communities in which individual family leaders instilled monarchical self-control in their families while demanding obedience from the *famuli*. These individual leaders later joined to form the aristocratic class. I interpret the placement of axiom CVIII in the midst of his account of law to highlight that the poetic characters represented early legal institutions and, more importantly, that they were concerned primarily with self-discipline.

Contemporary thinkers have become accustomed to conceiving human evolution as primarily a technological process in which communities develop tools to increase the chances of survival. This tempts the reader to expect the *New Science* to connect poetic wisdom with technological advancement. As the placement of axiom CVIII highlights, however, the imaginative universals are not about fulfilling the practical needs for survival but about tending to the practical needs for maintaining social cohesion. The giants had the strength to keep themselves alive and did not require special tools to do so. They needed a restraining force to bind their passions so that they would remain obedient in communities as they transformed back into humans. His description of the Roman pantheon connects the ancient myths to the evolution of the political institutions needed for this rather than the development of physical survival aids and luxuries. He does not ignore these advancements entirely, but he often draws attention to the way that the myths emphasized the promotion of self-discipline over efficient ways for tending to physical survival. One could, of course, try to weave technological development back into Vico's account. This might explain how mythical thought could develop its own type of physical science as depicted in the Star Trek episode "Darmok." I think this project would obscure an important aspect of Vico's agenda.

I do not read Vico as simply overlooking the historical fact that early civilizations developed tools and other instruments. The *New Science* may not provide the evolutionary account readers expect, but it is not evidence of Vico's eccentricity. In my reading, it is part of his anti-baronial position. He wants to show that the heroic institutions of the nobility had value in the first ages of humanity but are no longer useful in the human age. By showing that poetic wisdom was directed toward the civilizing process rather than tool-making, Vico provides an important reason to explain why it becomes obsolete. Once the giants return to their human form, the civilizing force of poetic wisdom is no longer needed or, at least, it does not need to be as strong as it once was. In the human age, technological development becomes more important and so discursive reason needs to become prominent. From this perspective, the entire depiction of poetic wisdom becomes an attempt to depict it as the foundation of the judicial privileges that the barons had in their own fiefs. Then, by showing how poetic wisdom is focused on the civilizing process, the account reveals why it becomes an impediment for later social and technological advancement.

In this chapter, I will discuss the gods of the greater gentes that were invented before the first plebeian uprisings. In doing so, I will highlight the ways in which Vico's account emphasizes their role in aristocratic self-discipline and de-emphasizes their connection to technological advancement. On the way, I will also offer a suggestion as to why poetic wisdom ultimately becomes untenable in its confrontation with the growth of human reason. While I will discuss ancient Roman law and religion, since Vico puts his account in that context, I will not spend much time questioning whether or not Vico's science is an accurate depiction of this history. My focus will be to show how his account is a reflection of the feudal institutions of Naples. This is consistent with my overall approach of not seriously considering the *New Science* as a story of the origin of civilization. While Vico himself may have been frustrated by my interpretative strategy, I think I am maintaining my connection to Mercer's "getting things right" approach. Given that Vico wrote in a feudal context and tells us he wants to understand modern Europe, it makes sense to assume that he would have recognized his poetic wisdom as connected to Neapolitan feudalism.

As a starting point, I turn to the three principles of the *New Science*: religion, marriage, and burial (333). These principles do not provide the theoretical basis of the science but rather are the first and most essential elements of a civilization. The section dedicated to them focuses on demonstrating their universality across all civilizations. It also emphasizes the need for human agency in the development of civil institutions (335). I maintain that the more fundamental point is that they do not represent technological innovations that are immediately connected to material needs for survival. They do not represent the invention of tools or advancements in building shelters or gathering food. The principles represent practical social developments rather than technological ones.

Religion, generally speaking, compels poets and heroes to prioritize superstition over the fulfillment of bestial desire. Marriage checks the powerful lust for promiscuous sex, which is one of the strongest and most destructive of the animalistic desires (336). More than just putting someone in the ground, the principle of burial centers on the recognition that humans are separate from animals. He writes that before the development of that institution, "Men will go about like swine eating the acorns found amidst the putrefaction of the dead" (337). Once burial is developed, the poets recognize that their rituals make them something other than animals. This instills a fear in them of losing their humanity. This compels them to restrain their desire as they perform the rituals prescribed by the gods. The three principles are primarily ways of civilizing the poets by generating civil passions that can overcome animalistic ones. These principles may be associated with material improvements. The practice of burial in particular would be useful for sanitary conditions in the first settlements. The institution of marriage would encourage parents to care for their children. These benefits would be secondary, however, to the more essential need of promoting self-control.

An underappreciated aspect of the poetic wisdom is that these principles appear in the different gods of the greater gentes. It seems as if religion, marriage, and burial would line up with Jove, Juno, and Diana. This is not the case. Each of these three gods manifest all these principles in different ways. As Vico builds his account, he does not explicitly trace all three principles in each god of the greater gentes, but his descriptions generally touch on them in some way. This is an important point for my hermeneutic approach to poetic wisdom. When one looks for the way the three principles manifest in each poetic character, it becomes possible to contextualize and structure Vico's descriptions.

As an initial example of this, I return to Jove. Most immediately, the thunder creates the first auspices, which were the basis of the first religions. The fear associated with them caused the giants to follow superstitious portents rather than their bestial passions. He writes, "They believed that Jove commanded by signs, that such signs were real words, and that nature was the language of Jove" (379). That is the principle of religion. The rituals of Jove also created a profound fear and guilt that impeded the desire for promiscuous sex. The thunder caused the first poets to feel shame about copulating indiscriminately out in the open This compelled each one to "drag one woman into his cave and would keep her there in perpetual company for the duration of their lives" (504). Entailed in these two is the compulsion to stop wandering and settle which created the impetus for the development of burial. While this involves a material concern, it sparks awareness in the first poets that their dedication to their altars makes them different from the wandering beasts. This is the core of the third principle. The Jovian thunder is the development not just of religion but of all three of the principles. I will discuss later in the chapter how Juno is not simply the imaginative universal of marriage but the tradition of noble lineage, which is connected to all three principles as well. Since each imaginative universal is connected to the principles, which are not based on technological utility, Vico advances his point that the poetic wisdom is primarily about social development.

There is a bigger point to be drawn from these principles. Vico holds that they are necessary throughout human history and not just in the first two ages (332). They transform into philosophical ideas in the human age (1110–1111).[1] For example, burial of the dead leads to the idea of the immortality of the soul (529). This provides a basis for his argument that the desire for material gain will not be sufficient to maintain political cohesion as someone like Mandeville suggests. For Vico, civilization depends on a sense of obedience to the pagan or metaphysical divine. If civilization is to be preserved in the third age, humanity needs to continue to adhere to these principles in their more enlightened form. This means that market forces will not be sufficient to provide the necessary socializing bond. I will return to this point as I build my interpretation of Vico's critique. Before getting to that, I want to explore Vico's pantheon in depth. Having covered Jove, I turn to Apollo and Diana, the fourth and third poetic characters he presents. This will present a road into the complexity of the second poetic character, Juno.

The poetic character Apollo contains the activities of self-beautification that help distinguish the nobles from the animals (538). To develop an interpretation that covers the range of Vico's comments about Apollo, it is important to think about the three principles of the science. Vico's interpretation of this imaginative universal is brief but complex (533).

In the traditional version of the story, Apollo becomes enamored with the nymph Daphne and pursues her. She flees and prays to her father for help. To save her, he turns her into a laurel, thereby associating Apollo with the wreath.[2] Commentators often read this story as a depiction of the male lust for women and an account of what it means to pursue or be pursued.[3] Vico rejects this as a product of the conceit of scholars. He writes, "later, when the language of this austere history had been forgotten, Apollo's pursuit became a libertine's and Daphne's flight a woman's" (533). During the age of gods the theological poets would have been cowed by Jove and the still-wandering giants would continue to be randomly promiscuous. There is no place for romantic seduction or lustful pursuit. That image of Apollo does not fit. So, he offers an alternative.

He starts with the idea that Apollo was "held principally to be the god of divination" (508). Apollo's pursuit of Daphne represents the need to check one's desires in order to obey the superstitions derived from natural signs. The imaginative universal is not about seduction, but about the obligation to obey what the objects of nature command. This is the principle of religion. The principle of marriage is represented by Daphne praying to help from the gods because their auspices were "necessary for solemn nuptials" (533). This is what allowed her to change into a laurel. It is through the ceremony of marriage that the act of divination is connected to natural signs.

Religion and marriage unite in Apollo to compel the poets to demonstrate their superiority to the beasts. Vico writes, "the pursuit of Apollo was the act of a god, and the flight of Daphne that of an animal." Apollo never takes full possession of Daphne as a nymph because that would represent transformation back into an animal. Instead, Daphne is only obtained after she becomes the laurel, which embodies the family tree of the nobles. The ritual of Apollo separates the poets from the animals by compelling them to recognize their unique offspring as a unique family lineage. Vico writes that the laurel is "a plant which is ever green in its certain and acknowledged offspring" (533). By performing the rituals of Apollo, the poet is able to have an actual family that is distinct from the giants, who continue to abandon their children.

This separation from the animals is what makes Apollo "the founding god of humanity and the arts" (537). This connects the ritual of Apollo to riding on horseback. This was not learned in order to facilitate labor or transportation. Horseback riding was a ritual by which the nobles imitated Apollo simply to demonstrate their superiority to the animals, both to the horses themselves and to the giants, who could not ride. This led to the image of Pegasus. Vico then shows how this is associated to burial by writing, "This humanity had its origin in *humare*, to bury" (537). From there, these rituals of separation are then extended to include self-beautification (538). Further, Vico acknowledges that Diana's brother is the "god of civil light" (533). Originally, however, this was not connected to the arts and the humanities because the first people could not have known such refinement. "Civil light" in the age of gods refers only to the control of bestial passion to act in the civilized manner of the poets in that age. This entails performing rituals that did not necessarily have material benefits but brought cohesion to the poetic families.

Obviously, there are many interpretative leaps here. In terms of technological evolution, Vico places the origin of horseback riding at an odd moment. Further, I do not see why he thinks the laurel is particularly suited to be a symbol for a family tree. Nonetheless, if one sees his point that these rituals are about social cohesion among the individual families of the upper class rather than technological advancement to promote survival and luxury, one can see an intriguing claim he makes about the upper class.

Aristocrats traditionally have engaged in rituals of propriety and the material display of wealth. One might attribute this to jealousy and competition. Certainly Jean-Jacques Rousseau attributes it to *amour propre*.[4] He posits that the nobles display wealth in order to show superiority in relation to each other rather than virtue. For Vico, the ritualistic displays of wealth are meant to show self-control in order to maintain a place in the elite. Aristocrats need to perform these mute gestures to signal continually that they are worthy of being in the ruling class. Jealousy could certainly play a part of this, but it would come more from the desire to demonstrate the superiority of one's self-control over another. Jealousy would not motivate an aristocrat to seek more wealth and honor just for the sake of competition. Instead, it would enable to nobles to enjoy stabilizing their places in the upper class by watching another fall out of it. The main point is that the driving fear in the aristocrats is not a need to win but the need to preserve status to avoid being shunned. The need for these rituals was so strong in the first two ages that it echoes among the nobility in the human age. As a result, they continue to perform the traditional rituals despite the fact their civilizing force is no longer necessary and they contradict the true virtue of the human age.

I take this as an invitation to speculate for a moment on our current situation. In contemporary Western neoliberal society and especially in the United States, dress codes are losing their importance. Workers and managers may dress much more casually than they once did. Nevertheless, one still sees the pressure placed on them to conform to established rituals of dress and performance. Although there are exceptions, their manner of dress does not generally help them work better or make them look substantially superior to others. In Vico's view, it is because they still want to show the self-discipline that allows them to maintain their rank in the company. The direction of the rituals of dress may have shifted from formal to casual, but the civilizing principle remains the same. Even if they display that self-control by dressing casually and acting in a gregarious manner, it is still motivated by a desire to maintain their status in the elite. This would then explain why it can still be so difficult to change the direction or the policies of a company. In spite of this casual appearance, managers may not implement new work practices because they might be misinterpreted as a lack of dedication. I am often amazed at how relaxed managers or administrators can appear and yet how serious they can be when they perceive a transgression of subtle norms of behavior. Vico's *New Science* offers an explanation of this phenomenon. When one realizes that customs in the business culture are often still centered on displays of worthiness rather than material gain, one can see why it is so hard to change them. I will build on that point later. I now move to Apollo's sister, Diana.

In mythology, the two siblings are portrayed as hunters. It would appear that this represents a technological need for survival. Vico's text actually goes the other way. He writes, "They [Apollo and Diana] do this [hunting] first in defense of themselves and their families (since they are no longer permitted to save themselves by flight as the vagabonds of the outlaw life had done), and later to provide food" (536). This is precisely the point I am trying to emphasize. The pagan religion compelled the poets to settle and construct altars. Contained in the fear of wandering away from the altar was the fear of losing the altar to outside threats. The initial motivation for hunting was to protect the asylums. Finding food to nourish themselves physically was secondary. I interpret this as a prime example of the way Vico's account of social evolution prioritizes the civilizing process over tending to material concerns.

In popular culture, Diana does not have a clearly defined sphere of influence.[5] Beyond hunting, she is associated with the moon and wild animals. Vico focuses on two tales associated often with her. In the first, she falls in love with the hunter Endymion. She has Zeus put him to sleep so she can always have him. In some variations of the story, it is Selene representing the moon and having many children by the sleeping hunter.[6] Vico uses the more popular variant of the story in which the chaste Diana lies with the sleeping Endymion but does not have intercourse with him (528, 730). The other tale is about another hunter, Actaeon. He accidentally comes across Diana naked in the forest, and she turns him into a stag who is eaten by his own dogs. Francis Bacon read this allegorically as a moral tale about court politics. This is, of course, a product of the conceit of scholars. Others speculate that this myth explains the origin of human sacrifice.[7] Vico's interpretation of these stories comes into focus through the three principles.

The myth of Endymion connects Diana to marriage. He writes that it signifies "the modesty of marriage" and emphasizes Diana's chastity (528). Marriage is not about having children, since the giants would tend to do this anyway. The ritual is about restraining desire.

The other two principles are found in the tale of Actaeon. Vico identifies this as "the fearful religion of the water springs." To make sense of this, it is important to take seriously the idea that when Actaeon sees Diana naked, what he is seeing is "the living spring" (528). When the goddess sprinkles him with water, he becomes the stag. Whereas Jove was the experience of thunder, Diana is the experience of seeing the source of fresh water and hearing the command to not pollute it. I imagine this specifically as a superstitious command to not urinate into it, although Vico does not specify this. Like hunting, this command originates from the fact the poets had now settled in particular asylums and could no longer simply wander to a new source of water. The atrocity of polluting the stream would cause a poet to lose noble status and descend to the level of the animalistic giants as Actaeon became a stag. Having fallen so far, the poet's own conscience would devour him just as the dogs ate Actaeon's flesh (528). Diana thus instills in the poets the fear of losing their humanity by desecrating the water.

The seriousness of this compulsion leads to the discussion of burial, which is the focus of Vico's next paragraphs (529–532). Although Diana drops out of his discussion, I think the connection is apparent. Just as one should not pollute the fresh water, one should not bury the dead in it. Rather than making this explicit, Vico underlines the fact that burial becomes the way in which the nobles establish the territory they need to defend. He evokes the idea that the founders of the cities were the "sons of earth" rather than second comers (531). He actually accuses Livy of stating a "barefaced lie" when he gets this wrong and portrays the plebeians as connected to the land while the nobles are not (532). Vico emphasizes that the upper class is committed to the defense of their territory while it is the *famuli* who can move around. This fits feudal institutions and the way that the Neapolitan barons protect both their castles and their privileges. This strong association of land to the nobility becomes a defining trait of poetic wisdom and the institutions of oligarchical rule. The rituals of Diana certainly entail a sort of material practical utility. There is no serious discussion, however, of the invention of shovels, latrines, or even water pots. The connection of aristocratic authority to the land is primarily oriented around the central necessity, which is social cohesion.

Here, I have not emphasized the mimetic quality of these two imaginative universals. It is not difficult to make this connection at least in broad strokes. A theological poet becomes Apollo when riding a horse in the proper ritualistic way. A poet becomes Diana when carrying a corpse away from the perennial spring. This is always part of my interpretation even if I do not make it fully explicit. Further, the social pressure of mute gestures are also always in play. The poets do not need to explain to their families the importance of burial away from the stream. They should recognize its importance as part of their association with the aristocracy. The mimetic and mute nature of the meaningful performance of the imaginative universals is always underlying the way I imagine this.

These two imaginative universals highlight the gap between poetic wisdom and human reason. Poetic wisdom orients the poets so that they had a greater fear of losing class status than of physical death. From the perspective of human reason, this makes no rational sense. A philosopher looking at this claim would dismiss it as so outlandish that it could not be attributed to even the ignorance of the first humans. Indeed, a philosopher like Thomas Hobbes might build an entire political philosophy on the belief that the first people were profoundly concerned with survival. Vico, in contrast, looks directly at the mentality of the Neapolitan aristocrats. He sees both the way they prioritize class over technological developments and the way they refuse to listen to human reason. Because he takes philology seriously, he diagnoses this attitude and works to explain it epistemologically.

This becomes the basis of his call toward reform. In the *Study Methods*, he makes clear his position that a monarch working with a trained legal class can provide a judicial system that balances the need for justice and equality with the need to maintain civil cohesion and *aequitas civilis*. He does not strongly emphasize this position in *New Science*, but there is enough consistency between the works to invite reading the later work as a continuation of the former. Before moving to the other poetic characters of the gods of the greater gentes, I would like to set some general context for how his section on poetic wisdom could be read as a call for reform. There is no call in the *New Science* for an outright revolution, but on my reading Vico does want to help the monarchy and the middle class continue the process of centralizing power at the expense of baronial judicial privilege. In the next section, I will discuss how one can read his work as providing this advice. In the following section, I will offer a general explanation of how human reason could overcome the pull that draws societies back into heroic institutions. This will provide context for my interpretation of the other gods of the greater gentes.

Sensus Communis and the Possibility of Reform

As I have discussed, in the twentieth century an image came to prominence of Vico as a defender of the value of tradition and myth. On a political level, this presented him as a thinker who wanted to forestall the barbarism of reflection by maintaining ancient traditions. A key text to support this view comes from Vico's invocations of the *sensus communis* or common sense that underlines all civilizations. Axiom XI states, "Human choice, by its nature most uncertain, is made certain and determined by the common sense of men with respect to human needs or utilities" (141). This was read politically as a call for studying poetic wisdom in order to recognize the ancient images on which all civilizations depend. This interpretation concludes that since poetic wisdom is necessary to found civilization, the underlying common sense it creates needs to be politically defended.

Hans-Georg Gadamer has drawn attention to Vico's idea of the *sensus communis*.[8] To my knowledge, he does not ascribe this political defense of tradition to Vico. Nevertheless, his reading of Vico in *Truth and Method* is connected to it. Put very broadly, Gadamer's hermeneutical project is to show the importance of tradition for interpreting texts. Since texts are inherently a call for action, they cannot be understood outside of practical interests. This is at the core of his anti-structuralist view. He presents Vico as an early advocate of the ancient school of rhetoric that took seriously both the importance of tradition and the practical value of speech. He recognized in Vico an acknowledgment of the inherently political function of rhetoric to direct human activity. While Gadamer did not emphasize this point, this connection between tradition and political engagement encouraged a reading of Vico as a defender of tradition.

My interpretation does not deny that Vico is concerned about maintaining the stability of civilizations in the human age. The call for *aequitas civilis* recognizes that lawyers and monarchs need to think about how social order may be maintained. Nevertheless, I do not want this to overshadow his anti-baronial agenda. In my reading, Vico is much more concerned with a possible regression into the heroic age than with a movement toward barbarism. This implies a desire to reform the institutions established by poetic wisdom rather than defend tradition. I have already outlined how my reading goes in a different direction from this other approach. I have no interest here in entering into a detailed critique of Gadamer's interpretation. I introduce it in order to discuss the insights of another commentator who builds his view of Vico through a critique of Gadamer. He offers an alternate way of interpreting Vico's idea of *sensus communis* that contributes to my reading.

While John Schaeffer is well-versed in the philosophical tradition, he comes at Vico primarily through the study of rhetorical theory and natural law. This puts him in a position to recast the tradition Gadamer describes as well as Vico's role in it. He argues that Gadamer rightly sees in Vico an account of the practical use of rhetoric but he wrongfully removes the possibility of critique from Vico's approach. Schaeffer emphasizes that Gadamer investigates Vico's work to understand how to interpret historical texts in a way that is not structuralist. He is not interested in considering how hermeneutics could lead to specific avenues of social change. Schaeffer writes, "Gadamer's idea of community is purely linguistic and cultural, not political."[9] This leaves Gadamer's Vico in an awkward position. His Vico is focused on considering ideas contextually in order to demonstrate practical wisdom. Gadamer does not explain, however, how Vico's idea of rhetoric could ever actually produce social change. As a result, he uses Vico to build a theory of textual interpretation based on practical wisdom in a historical context, but he cannot explain how Vico's position could deploy that wisdom. To summarize Schaeffer's view, Gadamer is too much of an abstract philosopher to recognize the political importance of rhetoric.

Schaeffer argues that Vico should be situated in a rhetorical tradition that emphasizes oral persuasion rather than textual interpretation. What matters here is the ability to persuade people and communities toward virtuous behavior. Schaeffer draws from Habermas's emphasis on the way Vico connects thought to human action.[10] Schaeffer writes, "Because Vico's *sensus communis* takes it for granted that communities are communities of dominance and fear, he can articulate a theory of social change that takes account of the social interaction of language and institutions, something Habermas says Gadamer's hermeneutics cannot do."[11] Schaeffer recognizes how harshly Vico portrays early civilization and the need to use oral persuasion to improve human institutions.

Schaeffer also recognizes that Vico posited a universal value to the three principles of his science. They provide a universal point of origin that gives a universal stability to civilization that is always necessary to sustain political institutions together. Out of this comes the *sensus communis*, which is the *arche* of civilization. Gadamer and other philosophers in the hermeneutic tradition miss this point.[12] As a result, they tend to mistakenly portray Vico as a cultural relativist. Not only did Vico think of the ideal eternal history as universal, he also prescribed a universal natural law to all human institutions that transcend historical context.

Schaeffer develops an important way of framing Vico's practical philosophy. He summarizes his position by writing, "although Vico's idea of *sensus communis* creates the rhetorical 'spaciousness' that makes eloquence possible, it also sets a theoretical limit to the potential range of meanings and praxis."[13] In other words, a good rhetorician ought to understand the *sensus communis* from two perspectives. On an immediate level, it is a product of a particular historical context. From a broader perspective, it is the product of a universal necessity that transcends the immediate situation. The rhetorician ought to persuade the people in a particular nation to goodness while working within the boundaries prescribed by the universal principles of humanity. If rhetoricians can accomplish this, they will fend off the abstract philosophers who could bring about the barbarism of reflection.

In Schaeffer's recent work, *Giambattista Vico on Natural Law*, he gives more substance to his account. He presents a brief but intriguing picture of the way in which the *New Science* depicts the three principles operating across the ideal eternal history. For example, the principle of marriage originally dictated that families ought to stay loyal to their children. This principle then expanded when the *famuli* were brought into the asylums. This was the start of a continual expansion of rights to a greater number of people. Once the human age fully arrives, rights should be extended to everyone in a nation. Throughout this evolution, the principle of marriage always remains essential. The task of the good rhetoricians in the third age is to persuade rulers, aristocrats, and the people to widen this definition of marriage to promote a more just society.[14] There is always a danger that the philosophers of the barbarism of reflection could argue for this on the basis of abstract concepts that are separate from the fabric of human life. This may be avoided if their rhetoric works from the ground of *sensus communis* rather than theory.[15] This picture of reform within the principles of the science helps explain what Vico means by the *aequitas civilis*. It also allows one to see how the *New Science* could serve as a call to change radically the institutions of the heroic aristocracy while remaining within the guidance of divine providence.

This is just a small part of Schaeffer's analysis. I have chosen this aspect of it because it emphasizes two points that are significant for my reading. First, he portrays Vico as an advocate for social change. Vico did not examine poetic wisdom because mythic traditions are necessary for political cohesion. The *sensus communis* is not just a traditional set of religious beliefs that a community ought to defend. A rhetorician ought to improve on the oppressive structures of the past ages and help those principles evolve into human form. Second, Schaffer rightfully emphasizes the way religion, marriage, and burial have significance throughout the ideal eternal history. My reading wants to do justice to this aspect of Vico's thought. I would agree that Schaeffer's reading of the relationship of the *sensus communis* to rhetoric holds up through the 1725 *New Science*. My project builds on Schaffer's insights, but it focuses specifically on the transition from heroic morality into the human age. My work is trying to see how Vico's later discovery of the imaginative universal includes a critique of feudal and aristocratic rule.

Vico refers to *sensus communis* in the section on Method in the *New Science*. He claims that the "common sense of the human race" is the "criterion of our criticism" (348). I read this primarily as part of the *New Science*'s argument for a universal metaphysics of history. As I mentioned earlier, he proposes that his science will be proven if it can efficiently explain all the evidence in a way that shows the harmonious workings of divine providence. The science must effectively align the history of religious and political institutions with its proposed universal structure of history. I highlight this passage to compare it with a point he makes about justice and the Hebrew tradition later in that section.

I have already discussed the way the Hebrew and gentile traditions merge. Here, I am interested in Vico's comments on how the Hebrews maintained their tradition after the flood. The Hebrews did not turn into giants. Whatever one thinks of his reasons for making this separation, it reveals something interesting about his ideas about philosophy and justice. He writes that the Hebrews after the flood practiced actual philosophical justice. He cites as evidence the fact that "the Hebrews, who [were] illuminated by the true God, were by his divine law forbidden to ever have unjust thoughts" (350). The only way the Hebrews could have understood the possibility of having sinful thoughts is if they recognized a separation between thought and action. This means that the Hebrews were not buried in the embodied thought of the pagans. The intriguing point here is that the Hebrews were able to sustain a human civilization that did not need the tradition of the earlier ages. This implies that in the future there once again could be a civilization that frees itself of the need of pagan tradition in order to operate on the basis of philosophical justice. While the three principles of humanity are necessary for a civilization, the embodied thought of poetic wisdom is not.

Obviously, there are all sorts of problems with Vico's separation of the ancient Hebrew tradition from the gentiles. In this context, it actually appears at odds with his metaphysical commitments. If the Hebrews did not need poetic wisdom, how could it be universal? This would raise the question of whether the Hebrews needed poetic wisdom before the flood. Vico himself did not bother with such speculation. I think he reveals his main point when he connects the civilization of the ancient Hebrews to philosophical wisdom. He writes, "This same inner justice [as understood by the Hebrews] was later reasoned out by the philosophers, who did not arise until two thousand years after the nations were founded" (350). The number of years here is consistent with his chronological table. I take this to be a call for modern philosophers to use the same rational justice that the ancient Hebrews understood. This requires a separation from embodied thought in order to achieve a universal perspective. This would entail a philosophical rejection of the tradition of poetic wisdom.

The most curious but most helpful part of this paragraph comes at the end. He claims that his science is a philosophy of authority. He specifies that its focus is examining the poetic conception of authority held by the poets and heroes rather than the ideas of the learned. This is consistent with his overall project, which spends much more time examining poetic wisdom than the philosophical questions of justice in itself. From there, he turns to Hugo Grotius, who argued against the validity of ancient Roman authority. He writes, "Grotius . . . combats the Roman jurisconsults in almost every particular detail of this doctrine." His objective was to show that the heroic jurisprudence of the Roman republic was not a philosophically defensible way of running a government. From Vico's perspective, Grotius attacked the heroic institutions supported by poetic wisdom. These attacks did not have an influence, however, because he did not realize the linguistic and epistemological separation between poetic authority and philosophical justice. He continues, "all his blows fall short, for the jurisconsults established their principles of justice on the certainty of the authority of the human race, not on the authority of the learned" (350). Grotius had fallen into the trap of believing that philosophical argumentation could dismantle the traditions of the aristocrats. He did not realize that they would not or could not listen. This is what he means when he says they do not reach their target ("*i colpi tutti cadono a vuoto*"). Practical utility and philosophical insight are foreign to the aristocratic mentality. So philosophical persuasion does not influence it.

I think this makes even more sense if we replace the Roman jurisconsults with the modern nobility. It does not make much sense to think of Grotius as fighting with (*combatte*) ancient Romans. Grotius did cause quite a stir in Holland, and he did spend time in prison. I take Vico's point to be that *On the Rights of War and Peace* did not have much success in reforming the political situation in Holland because it could not persuade the aristocracy. The *New Science* is trying to understand noble authority to develop a way to critique it. As Schaeffer indicates, this is going to require both persuasive force and a recognition of the importance of the principles of civilization. Given the epistemological gap between the two authors, the path to political reform is difficult.

The main point I want to emphasize about this paragraph is this: Vico claims that without the guidance of philosophy, the nations had to rely on poetic wisdom. He writes, "the nations were governed by the certainty of authority, that is, by the same criterion which is used by our metaphysical criticism; namely the common sense of the human race, on which the consciences of all nations repose" (350). Both poetic authority and philosophical reason are grounded in the *sensus communis* of the people and the three principles. Nevertheless, as I discussed in the last chapter, the fact that heroic authority is grounded in the certain is actually an impediment to just government. When laws are interpreted strictly and literally, the people suffer under the tyranny of tradition. This authority flows from the common sense of a civilization but during a time when class division is ingrained into the mentality of the culture. Philosophy also uses common sense as its criteria, but it does so in order to understand correctly how it functions and how to direct its evolution. It does not try to defend it simply as tradition.

This reading of Vico may surprise those who want to hold onto the idea that Vico was dedicated to the defense of traditional values. Nonetheless, he actually defends this position quite explicitly. The heroic mentality was effective during the height of aristocratic rule because of its context in the evolution of civilization. During the heroic age, the rulers "were naturally strongest" and "the public good was the family monarchies preserved by the fatherland." He writes, "Given such natures, customs, commonwealths, institutions, and laws, the heroism of the first peoples will flourish." In modern times, however, this mentality stops flourishing. He writes, "this heroism is now by civil nature impossible, since its causes, just enumerated, have given place to their contraries" (677). In the human era, the public good is no longer the interests of the families but the private interests of each citizen of the nation. What sustains civilization in this era is a justice system that works to maintain the interests of all people. Heroism, which is directed to cruelly maintaining the authority of the lords, does not contribute any more to this type of legislation. Any attempt in the human age to find a philosophical sense of justice in the aristocratic heroes commits the conceit of scholars.

The idea that the hero could care about equality is entirely antithetical to the foundation of the aristocratic worldview. The romantic image of the lord who is honestly concerned with the people is a dream. Vico writes, with Bergin and Fisch's addition, "we must conclude that such a hero [as devotes himself to justice and the welfare of mankind] is desired by afflicted peoples, conceived by philosophers, and imagined by poets, but is not included among the benefits afforded by civil nature as covered by our axiom" (677). I read this in the context of Naples. While the barons want to assure their vassals that their privileges are in the best interest of the people, Vico claims that it is entirely contrary to the upper-class mentality that they could care about the people. Obviously, individual nobles could show concern and work for a more just system. Paolo Mattia Doria, who was from a famous noble family, took such an approach. Vico's point, however, is that it is a fundamental contradiction to defend baronial privilege on the grounds that it is useful and helpful for all the people.

In my reading, when entering Vico's account of the Roman pantheon, his agenda is to show that the stories of the gods reveal a mentality that was oriented toward oppression and could not conceive of the justice. Because the poetic wisdom was founded to instill civility in beasts, it would lose its purpose once humanity had returned to its natural social status. He needs to show that the violence necessary to maintain civil order was expressed through profound cruelty that would no longer be needed in modern Naples. His exploration of the ancient myths is not to find how they provide a common ground of communication but to show how they had a specific purpose for a specific stage in humanity's development that is no longer needed. These are the rituals on which he focuses.

Overinclusion

So far, I have emphasized the point that it will be difficult for a philosopher to persuade the nobility to relinquish their judicial privileges. It may be worth speculating on how human reason ever gets the foothold it needs to start promoting reform. I suspect that there is a mechanism within poetic wisdom itself that opens up the possibility for taking power from the oligarchy. I offer one possibility that Vico does not address explicitly but that is close enough to his argument that one could suspect he would recognize it. Further, it would actually explain why he presents the poetic characters in the way he does.

When I described poetic wisdom in chapter 3, I centered my account on how it was a product of the poverty of language. This term does not refer simply to a shortage of vocabulary. It is a reference to the fact that the non-reflective poetic mind is resistant to inventing new words. In the 1725 *New Science*, Vico connects the poverty of language directly to the "harsh jurisprudence of the ancients" (NS25 202). He emphasizes that "when men are superstitious and of limited ingenuity they observe the words used in pacts, laws and, especially, legal oaths, with extreme care." He emphasizes that this would have been the case, "above all in times when nations are either short of words, or use them in their literal meanings, because they have not as yet an abundance of metaphors" (NS25 202). This connects the poverty of language to the use of secret laws in the first two ages of humanity. Both drive the poetic mind to change what one sees rather than change the laws. They ground the authority of poetic laws on the certainty of its own ritualistic traditions rather than philosophical investigation. The strict interpretation of law, at the expense of the particulars of a case, reinforces in both the nobility and the plebeians the importance of conforming to its commands. Thus the poverty of language blocks the heroes from adapting the law to meet changes that stem both from increases in technology and in the social stability of the people.

In the earlier edition, he focuses on how the poverty of language would have been a major factor for drafting treaties (NS25 202). He is particularly concerned with the way the precise language of treaties of surrender could be abused to further damage the losing party. He also uses Agamemnon's sacrifice of Iphigenia as evidence of how the literal use of language could cause great harm. He does not discuss it here, but one can see how this could also lead to mistreatment of the lower classes. It suggests a typical image of bullying. The strong person with authority waits for the weaker party to misspeak. As soon as that happens, the bully uses it as a pretext to injure or exploit the victim. Vico's point is that the aristocracy will not simply injure arbitrarily. Instead, the heroes will use their special knowledge of the laws and their imaginative ability to reimagine the facts to assert their dominance over others.

Nonetheless, the vocabulary of poetic wisdom does expand. When something noticeably dramatic did happen, poetic thinkers would be inspired to invent a new god. More typically, they must have expanded the image of an existing poetic character to cover the new situation. Over time, the images of the gods became remarkably complex, and the connections between the stories and symbols became obscured. This would explain why the ancient myths appear so confused and distorted.

He makes this hermeneutic point most clearly in the 1725 *New Science*. In a passage I discussed earlier, he presents seven principles to explain "the obscurity of fables." In the 1744 edition, he alludes to them and claims they can still be found in book 2, which implies that he still finds them relevant (814). The third principle is the one most relevant here. It states explicitly that the poverty of language causes poets to gradually graft new ideas onto existing images, producing tangled variations of the stories. He writes, "This confusion is born of minds that are limited, slow and impoverished in words, as a result of which, with only the most miserable ability to explain themselves, men will unite things wholesale" (NS25 273). Because of their limited vocabulary and reluctance to create new words, the poets were forced to subsume ideas into images with which they had little substantial connection. In their desperate effort to express new ideas, they greatly distorted existing ones in a way that is hard to grasp from a modern perspective.

He uses the tale of Cadmus as an example of this. He connects this hero to two different legends. It is generally claimed that Cadmus was a Phoenician who wrote histories (NS25 491). There is also a legend that he slayed a great serpent and sowed its teeth. From the fields came warriors who fought each other (NS25 335). Vico takes this to mean that Cadmus was originally the poetic character of the aristocrats who raised soldiers to defend the confines. To this name was later added the idea that he also wrote histories of the combat of the warriors (NS25 273). In this way, two different activities were both attributed to Cadmus. This is an example of how the poverty of language can fuse together two activities in a single character despite the fact that those activities appear disconnected to an abstract thinker.

The 1744 *New Science* holds onto the point that Cadmus reveals how the imaginative universals change over time. He writes, "the fable of Cadmus contained several centuries of poetic history, and is a grand example of the inarticulateness with which the still infant world labored to express itself" (679). This new version, however, changes the interpretation to focus on the aristocratic tendency to frame their world on the basis of class differences. In the later edition, he now explicitly denies that the soldiers born from the teeth of the dragon fought each other. He writes, "From the furrows armed men spring forth . . . and unite in arms against the plebs, and they fight not among themselves but with the clients that have revolted against them." The goal of the soldiers is attributed no longer to a desire for fame but to the need to protect aristocratic authority to maintain cohesion in the territory. He writes, "the furrows [in which Cadmus planted the teeth] signifying the orders in which they unite and thereby give form and stability to the first cities on the basis of arms" (679). In later versions of the story, Cadmus became the serpent itself and this now represents the formation of the aristocratic senates that brought the heroes together to protect their traditions. The story of Cadmus changes over time, but those changes come from developments in the way the heroes imposed their harsh authority over the plebeians.

In the later work, Vico addresses the legend that Cadmus, more than just writing history, invented the act of writing with letters and gave them to all the nations. If this were true, then it would contradict the conceit of nations and close off one of Vico's main sources of evidence. He disputes this legend on chronological grounds as well as by pointing out that Greek and Phoenician letters do not look the same (66). He actually ridicules Erasmus for holding that Cadmus could have invented letters for all the other Mediterranean civilizations (679). In doing so, he makes an obscure point that becomes clearer when placed in the context of a political agenda. He says that the Greek legend of Cadmus kept hidden the fact that the vulgar invented letters in many nations. This legend was created "in order to keep hidden from the vulgar such a great invention of vulgar wisdom that from the vulgar these letters received the name of vulgar letters!" (679).[16] Vulgar wisdom, as opposed to poetic wisdom, is the practical wisdom of the plebeians that leads to the philosophy of the human age (37, 414). Vico here suggests that the plebeians created letters to replace the symbolic hieroglyphs of the heroes since the letters were more practical (935). The heroes did not want to admit that this beneficial invention was the idea of the masses. So they absorbed the invention of letters into the poetic character of Cadmus to make it appear to be a heroic invention rather than a plebeian one. This is a classic example of the workers developing a great idea that the boss takes credit for. Should one accept Erasmus's interpretation, then one would promote the idea that poetic wisdom and heroic rule are responsible for such innovations. Vico argues that they are incapable of such advancement. Thus, the imaginative universal Cadmus is a way for Vico to illustrate how odd ideas can get merged into a single divine image. It also alludes to his anti-baronial position that wants to demonstrate the inefficiency of poetic wisdom in the human age.

At this point, I believe that the *New Science* invites the reader to consider that poetic wisdom would have to become progressively more mentally taxing over time. As the heroic age continued, it would have taken considerably more effort to remember the details of the rituals as the images expanded and the original connections of the symbols were forgotten. As discussed in chapter 3, because poetic wisdom demands the exact imitation of paradigms, it would have been vital to remember the precise details of the symbols and rituals associated with them in order to follow them meticulously. Their ability to remember may have been more powerful given that they were not preoccupied with discursive thought. Vico does suggest this (211). Nonetheless, the complexity of the poetic characters must have demanded a substantial amount of mental effort that would be placed on top of the creative demands imposed by the poverty of language and the need to keep laws secret. One can envision how the nobility would have spent their time studying the rituals of aristocratic behavior rather than tending to the problems arising on their own fiefs. They would be so concerned with the demands of tradition that they simply would not have time to innovate or reframe their worldview. This would ultimately open the door to discursive reason. Once the need to civilize humanity had largely passed, its efficient way of adapting language to fit the evidence of the world would be able to rise to dominance.

Remo Bodei's philosophical investigation of the logic of delusion gives helpful insight into this picture of the development of poetic wisdom.[17] Vico was not interested in showing why pagan superstition is false because that was obvious. His strategy was to understand the epistemological structure that underlies the human world that was created by the barons. Bodei contextualizes his project in a similar fashion. He laments the fact that modern philosophy has tried to use the rationality of the mathematical and physical sciences to advance modern society without seriously considering the reality of human thought and development. In so doing it has "adopted a model that is strictly inappropriate to the human world" and has written off most of civil life without seriously investigating it. Referring to Lévi-Strauss, he writes that contemporary thought has failed to investigate the *"vie sauvage,"* which he defines as "that whole area of human experience—including our passions, fantasies, beliefs, and delusions, that is left to the mercy of the 'irrational.' "[18] Bodei's project, like Vico's, then strives to find the logic within the delusional. He works to uncover the way in which delusion organizes the world of perceptions and beliefs even if they "do not conform to the criteria of argumentation and expression a determinate society shares."[19] Where Bodei comes closest to my reading of Vico's poetic wisdom is when he examines the delusional logic of overinclusion.

According to Bodei, the idea of overinclusion was discovered by Norman Cameron in 1944 in reference to schizophrenia. Bodei writes that overinclusion "consists in the inability to choose the elements belonging to a concept, eliminating those less relevant or completely unrelated."[20] In other words, when one overincludes, one places objects into a category that a non-delusional person would find irrelevant. Christopher Frith argues that overinclusion occurs because schizophrenics become hyperaware of their surroundings. They see things so clearly that they struggle to distinguish important information from background noise and end up organizing their world by putting objects into categories where they do not belong. Bodei emphasizes that schizophrenics have filters that do direct how they shape their world. Because of the excess information, those filters often direct the mind in a way that a non-delusional person would not follow.[21] This does not match poetic wisdom exactly, in that the heroes would not have been inundated by data in the way that a schizophrenic in contemporary society might be. Nonetheless, the result appears to be similar. Both have filters with which they try to organize information coming toward them. Because those filters are inadequate to the task, they end up expanding their concepts in ways that appear confused and distorted to someone outside that worldview. Whereas the poetic thinker and the schizophrenic establish fundamental connections between certain ideas, there does not appear to be any substantial connection from the perspective of the outsider. As a result, they dwell in a lifeworld constructed out of complex concepts that are filled with connections that do not contribute to organizing practical tasks.

Bodei points to the fact that overinclusion can bring cultural or religious elements into areas in which they are not related. An undeluded mind would see such associations as irrelevant and ignore them, but they are seen as vital from the perspective of the logic of delusion. This strikes me as comparable to the way in which Vico's heroes connect the need to maintain class status to such a wide range of poetic characters. It also explains how they would attribute civil institutions to their own authority when they actually came from the ingenuity of the plebeians. Bodei's point is that the associations made in overinclusion are not simply arbitrary but are the product of a complex way of creating meaning the far exceeds what the evidence ordinarily suggests. In a passage that could echo what Vico says about poetic wisdom, Bodei writes, "The deluded individuals are in this respect highly metaphorical, for by means of analogical and subjective intentions they cross-pollinate and hybridize ideas and images that are remote from one another, sometimes inadvertently producing poetic effects, but more often producing associations that are strange and absurd."[22] This appears akin to the way in which the imaginative universals expand in poetic wisdom.

I do not want to push this comparison too far. Bodei is describing a logic of delusion within the complexity of the contemporary world, and he warns about problems in comparing this logic to certain characterizations of primitive thought.[23] Nevertheless, I think Bodei's brief essay helps orient my approach to the imaginative universals. For Bodei, delusion occurs because of conflicts between past structures of thought and present realities. This produces an absurd worldview, but one that nevertheless reinforces itself with an internal rational consistency. For Vico, the driving force of poetic wisdom is its desire to protect itself and defend the authority of the nobility. As such, it grows into a confounding logic of images that are difficult for an outsider to untangle because its support is internally consistent rather than a response to material concerns. This is what I think he is trying to portray in his account of the imaginative universals. With this in mind, I return to early gods of the greater gentes.

Juno, Goddess of Familial Judicial Authority

Juno is the second imaginative universal Vico discusses. I have saved it until now because it is exceptionally complex. I think the earlier discussion of Diana and Apollo along with the principles of the science and overinclusion will help give direction for interpreting Vico's account. As I have mentioned, the rituals of Juno are not exactly centered on marriage. The goddess is famous for representing marriage through her association with Jove. Vico certainly acknowledges this, but his account spins off in many different directions and contains all three principles. In my reading, this imaginative universal extends beyond marital fidelity to a range of activities that involve the work of the family. Juno contains authoritarian rituals by which the theological poets ordered their families to care for the asylum.

To understand this, it is helpful to remember how the Neapolitan barons managed their fiefs. These families were not contemporary emotional support networks or the hives of intrigue that one sees in fictional descriptions of monarchy. The fiefs were political structures dedicated to managing people and resources carefully and with precision to maintain financial stability and protect a place in the aristocracy. A baronial family had to control reproductive practices and use judicial authority to manage production. This is certainly present in Apollo's dedication to noble lineage. The rituals of Juno more broadly include the control of reproductive practices, family economics, and, most importantly, judicial baronial privileges.

The primary function of Juno is to check lustful desire in order to restrict procreation to the noble class. Jove had compelled the poets to select one woman to mate for life. Juno now motivates them to select that wife from the ruling class to avoid losing the status of human. In the first asylums, which were distant from each other, this would have meant incest. Indeed, Vico claims that Juno was originally the sister and wife of Jove because the first weddings must have been between siblings. The significance of this is that "legitimate marriages" were kept strictly in the immediate family to the exclusion of others (511). In order to maintain this exclusivity, modesty was needed to discourage promiscuous sex. The fear of Juno compels the early poets not to seduce anyone but their partners. He emphasizes that Juno was fully clothed as part of the moral discipline required to keep marriages strictly between appropriate couples. Whereas the shame inspired by Jove forced the first poets to copulate with just one other person out of the view of the sky, the fear of Juno provokes a fear that causes the poets to restrain any sort of seduction. Given the problem with incest, it is hard to believe Vico's account is literally correct here. If one wanted, one could say that the families were originally small herds, but I am not sure this is significant. What I find interesting is the way Juno describes the ideology of the later modern Neapolitan barons who were focused on controlling birth practices.

At its core, marriage was not just a belief in fidelity but a behavioral conception of marriage as way to keep an altar within one's kinfolk. Inherent in their thoughts and actions concerning marriage is the compulsion to exclude outsiders. When one turns to the modern Neapolitan barons, one sees their preoccupation with controlling marital and reproductive practices. Vico suggests that this is not merely an efficient or strategic way of maintaining wealth. Instead, exclusivity is inherent to their identity as upper class. Obviously, the barons no longer consciously imitate Juno, but their practices are still based on an ideology that shapes the noble worldview around class division. For them, the separation between family and all others is a feature that is inherent to the world and that they cannot seriously question. It thus blocks any notion of just rule for all.

When the *famuli* later arrive, the rituals of Juno turn toward separating noble offspring from the others. Vico writes, "She is also known as Lucina, who brings the offspring into the light; not natural light, for that is shared by the offspring of slaves, but the civil light by reason of which the nobles are called illustrious" (513). Further, she was politically jealous, which kept marriage out of the hands of the lower classes. Because of these rituals, "the Romans down to the 309th year of Rome excluded the plebs from *connubium*, or lawful marriage" (513). The marriage rituals of Juno were secret laws that the plebeians were not allowed to understand, reinforcing marriage as an instrument of class separation.

The Neapolitan family was about much more than just marriage and reproduction, however. It was at the center of judicial authority. As I discussed in chapter 4, the feudal lords wielded judicial authority over their fiefs. This is at the center of Juno's rituals. Vico connects the goddess to family inheritance through a fanciful etymology of the Greek name Hera as the root of the word *hereditas*. The content of these inheritances was not primarily wealth but power. The main element of the inheritance was "a despotic sovereignty." He quotes a Latin fragment of the Twelve Tables, which Bergin and Fisch translate "As the family father has disposed concerning his property and the guardianship of his estate, so shall it be binding." This signifies that the judicial authority of the family leader was absolute over the fief. From this he asserts that it "proves only too conclusively the monarchic power that the fathers had over their families in the state of nature" (513). This is consistent with his tendency to identify the first ages of humanity as the state of nature rather than the time of the giants. His point is that from the very start of civilization individual fathers were the arbiters of law over their families and, later, the *famuli* who became slaves of the nobles. Juno is thus the mechanism by which noble families established and maintained the judicial privilege that they would demonstrate in Vico's Naples.

Vico makes explicit the connection between the judicial authority represented by Juno and aristocratic authority in the human age. He assures us that this absolute judicial power was retained by the lords in the heroic age. He offers as proof the way the aristocracy holds onto this power later in the human age. He writes, "These [heroic cities] must in origin have been aristocratic, that is, commonwealths of lords, for the fathers still retained their power even in the popular commonwealths" (513). This is probably a direct reference to the Roman empire, but it could also refer to the Neapolitan barons. If nothing else, it signals to the reader that one ought to consider aristocratic judicial privilege in the human age to understand what he is saying about Juno in the first age. For one who thinks of feudalism primarily as an economic system, I suspect this aspect of Juno is difficult to untangle. When one considers feudalism as primarily a legal system, his comments about inheritance and domination fall into place.

While the feudal lords were responsible for overseeing the production of resources in the fiefs, it was secondary to their judicial power. Vico connects the production of resources to Juno, but he does so through Hercules in a way that suggests its secondary status. Juno gives Hercules the twelve labors, which were "for the nourishment of the families" (540). Vico's specific analysis of these labors is complex. The slaying of the Hydra was the ritual of digging irrigation, and the slaying of the Nemean lion was plowing the fields. He discusses the dragon that protected the golden apples in the garden of the Hesperides. He does not clarify exactly what this represents, but one could assume it is related to the harvest, since Hercules steals the apples. He claims, "All these beasts vomit forth fire, which is the fire set to the forest by Hercules" (540). This connects Hercules to the plowing of the fields. Hercules's labors only work, however, because they are commanded by Juno, who restrains the passions of the aristocrats. Juno oversees the work of the other members of the family but only because of her ability to command their loyalty to the aristocratic class.

Whereas a contemporary reader might expect to find a discussion of technological development in relation to Juno, Vico does not provide that. Instead, the rituals of Juno and Hercules continue the process of civilizing bestial passions. He writes of the twelve labors, "This signifies that piety and marriage form the school wherein are learned the first rudiments of all the great virtues" (514). Resource management is more of a way of inspiring moral behavior than actually supplying food to the family. Presumably, the giants could feed themselves before the altars were raised. Because they were now establishing permanent settlements, this created new difficulties. Nonetheless, the primary function of managing resources was to civilize the nobility.

This now introduces an interesting contrast with traditional early modern theories of capitalism and the invisible hand. The position of Mandeville and others is that practical needs civilized the first people, and from there the market can continue to steer human sentiment toward enlightened self-interest. Vico's view suggests that managing resources was primarily a way of instilling civility and only secondarily a way of surviving. This means that the civilizing force of gathering resources was measured not by how much was gathered but by how virtuous the people became. From a theoretical perspective on capitalism, this looks very strange. Nevertheless, when one thinks about the situation in modern Naples, it makes sense. The nobility were not trying to improve conditions or make lives better. Their focus was on maintaining consistency to ensure that the social order did not fall into chaos. They were unaware of how out-of-date their infrastructure had become, since their objective was keeping everyone in line rather than striving for luxury. Their view of the world was so centered on maintaining emotional discipline that they could not see that the rituals had grown far removed from the technological developments that could help humanity live better.

Speculatively, one can understand this by making a comparison to contemporary attitudes toward work in Western capitalism. Parents often encourage their children get jobs in high school. The point is not that the jobs improve the financial status of the children of the family. It is often unclear whether the jobs contribute anything to the well-being of the community. The goal is that teenagers develop their character and virtue by learning discipline at the job even if the labor and salary do not amount to much. I think this is what the fundamental role of Juno and Hercules expresses. At its origin, work is about not survival but moral discipline. As a result, work may promote an ordered society, but that work may not contribute to the betterment of humanity.

The underlying issue, as Hirschman's book addressed, is whether the market can instill virtue. In Mandeville's view, it is possible to encourage the development of moral virtue through capitalism by connecting survival to the market. He holds that the market can provide the infrastructure to channel the desire to fulfill basic needs toward civil behavior. Vico suggests that the problem with this is that historically labor is already connected to survival through the aristocracy. The barons have convinced the plebeians that their best chance for survival is to act as the baron dictates. The aristocracy always has the potential to retake that power. Whether Vico could have envisioned exactly how this would happen or not, he tells us that he is concerned that humanity would fall back into the heroic age. If society were to do as Mandeville suggests, a new group of aristocrats would figure out how to establish new types of fiefs that would reconnect labor to the civilizing process through demands of loyalty to them. The aristocracy will once again instill discipline at the expense of justice. This is why a greater sensibility than simply the market will be needed to maintain a government proper to the human age.

Returning to Juno, Vico emphasizes that she had nothing to do with romance and that she was not originally effeminate. These attributions were the result of corruptions of the myths by later authors. In his reading, Juno was not an adulteress but, instead, was a paragon of poetic virtue. He describes at length an image of a bound Juno whose feet were held down with rocks. Later interpreters saw this as an unfair punishment from Jove. Vico, on the other hand, says it had to be a symbol of marriage and the violence associated with the first families (NS 514). He then criticizes Plato for finding metaphysical meaning in the fable of Juno (NS 515). This stresses the point that the myths of Juno do not provide wisdom into how the modern family or government should function, but instead they provide the ground for the aristocratic institutions of discipline that resist just rule in the human age.

Finding Settlements and Agriculture

I close this chapter with a brief discussion of an exceptionally curious point that Vico makes at the opening of the section on poetic economy. Vico offers an explanation of how the first poets came to choose where to build the altars. He concludes that they thought that vultures were auspices of Jove. The poets followed them to mountaintops, where they found easy access to perennial springs and decided to settle (525). He uses this to conclude that the first settlements were all on the tops of mountains. One could attribute this conclusion to the fact that Vico spent his lifetime looking at castles in southern Italy but had never traveled beyond the Italian peninsula. When one considers the range of environments in the world, this claim is obviously not correct. This whole account is one of the many passages in the *New Science* that one would be tempted to write off as either eccentric or simply dated.

When one understands the objectives of the science, however, this passage makes a good deal of sense. At least it is consistent with the idea that the focus of poetic wisdom is not technological development but the use of superstition to tame bestial desire. I turn to this passage not because it will, in itself, make the *New Science* more philosophically defensible; I do it as an example of how my reading of the work illuminates a broad range of its obscure passages. I also present it because it is another area where Vico seems to praise the wisdom of the theological poets. On closer examination, it actually reveals another problematic element of the aristocratic world view and provides further reason to reform the tradition of poetic wisdom.

In a key phrase, he makes a positive statement about the first poets. He writes, "In the very birth of [domestic] economy, they fulfilled it in its best idea, which is that the fathers by labor and industry should leave a patrimony to their sons." Not only does he present the poets as hard working, but he also claims their efforts make practical and useful improvements for the lives of their families for generations to come. He claims the poets did their work "so that they may have an easy and comfortable and secure subsistence, even if foreign commerce should fail, or even all the fruits of civil life, or even the cities themselves, so that in such last emergencies the families at least may be preserved, from which there is hope that the nations may rise again" (525). One could say this shows concern about the development of trade and a free market. One could see it as a call to protect the traditions of a community to protect it against coming change. It looks like a defense of the value of poetic wisdom. In context, however, I think it says something quite different.

Any early modern philosopher trying to shape an account of the transition from the wilderness to civil society might address the question of where the first people would settle. This seemingly simple point raises a difficult question. Returning to the problem of human sociability, if the first humans struggled to recognize the benefits of civil society, how could they have identified a good place to settle? If they did not fully understand the benefit of a settlement, how could they recognize where they should settle? In the second *Discourse*, Rousseau understands this difficulty and presents a straightforward solution to this problem. He holds that over a long period of time, the first humans would have recognized the practical benefits afforded by one territory over another. He writes, "Soon they ceased to fall asleep under the first tree or to retreat into caves, and found various types of hatchets made of hard, sharp stones, which served to cut wood, dig up the soil, and make huts from branches they later found it useful to cover with clay and mud."[24] He is careful because he assures the reader that this could only happen after a long period of time, since it would take a long time for their minds to recognize the benefits of staying in one place and constructing huts. They slowly formed habits based on available resources that encouraged them to remain in the same place. The exceptionally slow evolution of practical sense allowed them to recognize good places to stay which led to intermingling and then communities. Vico is not satisfied with this.

Instead of attributing settling down to practical utility, Vico explains it by the mechanisms of divine providence. This metaphysical power somehow shaped natural circumstances to help the first poets find good settlements. He reminds us that divine providence does not force humans to act but guides them. He writes, "Such were the institutions that providence established for the state of the families, not like a tyrant laying down laws but like the queen it is of human affairs working through customs" (525). As discussed earlier, this is Vico's way of arguing that human society is not the result of either random chance or determinant necessity but came from an active choice to follow the advice of providence. Generally, the poets did not understand what they were doing when they spontaneously followed divine guidance. Nevertheless, they at least had to demonstrate a certain amount of determination and ingenuity to move forward. In this view, there is value in human agency because it is needed to move civilization forward. Here it is possible to see fully the benefits of Vico's metaphysical position.

Vico is suggesting that divine providence orchestrated a connection between a natural sign and a good place to settle. He praises the theological poets for following the signs, but that praise is not connected to their practical ability. After all, they were acting on superstition rather than a practical sense of where to live. Vico praises the poets who could restrain their passions enough to civilize themselves. He does not discuss this, but one can imagine other poets who did not find good places to settle. Their asylums would have faded away. There would have been two causes for this. In some cases, the auspices witnessed by the poets would not direct them to a good spot. These poets would have obeyed the auspices but been unlucky. In other cases, the poets would not have had the discipline to obey the auspices. Their settlements would fail not because they did not find a good spot but really because they lacked discipline. Conversely, those who succeeded did so because of a combination of self-discipline and luck, but not practical wisdom.

Vico opens this section with a reminder of how difficult it must have been for the giants to civilize themselves. It was not just a mental transformation but a physical one (524). Furthermore, it required individual heads of families to impart the superstitious religion to the rest of the clan. He writes, "they must also have been the kings who had the duty of carrying the laws from the gods to their own families" (521). This again speaks to the fact that feudal authority was originally judicial. It was originally thought of as religious law before civil or criminal law, but these three were collapsed together at this early point in the civilizing process. The basic responsibility of the head of a family was to educate the family by making sure they obeyed the law. This presumably happened by communicating passions that would encourage others to imitate rituals. The effect was that the family leaders could turn the passions of the others in on themselves through powerful rituals.

He clarifies that while each head of a household had monarchical authority, there was no one monarch that ruled over all the families. He reminds us that the idea that one monarch civilized all the people was a product of the conceit of scholars. He writes, "in the natural equality of a state in which each of the fathers was sovereign in his own family, one cannot conceive of either fraud or violence by which one man could subject all others to a civil monarchy" (522). This becomes a restatement of his argument about the importance of small and individual fiefs for civilizing small groups of people. The work of civilizing humanity would have been not to develop technology but, instead, to civilize bestial passions. In finding the proper places to settle, then, the poets displayed commendable discipline but not a capacity to find a place that would provide material resources even fresh water.

In this context, the idea that the first poets followed the birds to their settlements makes sense. Presumably, they looked at Jove in the sky and saw the birds flying close to him. These vultures, which became transformed into eagles in later traditions, nest in the mountains near sources of water. When the poets followed them, they found the perfect places to settle with the needed perennial springs (525). Obviously, it is impossible to accept the idea that birds were specifically what led all poets to their settlements, just as there is no reason to accept the universal significance of Jovian thunder. Nonetheless, I do not think Vico's position relies specifically on birds as the relevant auspices. I think his larger point is that superstition often gives good guidance in spite of itself. As a common example many have already considered, it is regarded as unlucky to walk under a ladder. In fact, it is a bad idea to walk under a ladder whether one is superstitious or not. The unfounded belief reinforces a practice that should be followed anyway. I propose that this is the general mechanism to which Vico refers. His point is that the first poets could not have practically developed the sense to find the right place to settle. It must have been through superstition. Given how few good places to settle there were, the fact that the poets were guided to one suggests the divine guidance that his science hopes to metaphysically demonstrate.

Vico advances this argument when he praises the poets for finding settlements that would provide security for their decedents. His point is that the settlements would protect the families when Rome collapsed during the barbarism. He writes, "But in the recourse of barbarism which destroyed cities everywhere, it was in just this way that the families were preserved and whence sprang the new nations of Europe" (525). When he talks about the end of trade, he is not criticizing trade in general but referring to the breakdown of infrastructure during the returned barbarism. There is no way that practical evolution could have caused the first poets to recognize that their castles were ideally suited to survive the barbarism of reflection, yet divine providence orchestrated things that way. This lends support to the idea that barbarism and divine providence are a safety net that will keep humanity alive regardless of negative decisions that get made.

This passage of the *New Science* would be easy to ridicule if one wanted to claim that Vico's philosophy was just an odd sort of mysticism. I think I have shown that it actually fits his project, even if the specific details of his account do not work. Furthermore, there may be a deeper point. One might try to defend feudalism and noble privilege by arguing that they were the original families that made the best choices necessary to set up the fiefdoms in the first place. The reason to keep the barons in control would be that they had always known how to rule effectively. Vico's point is that while the barons may have originally set up the first fiefs, this was not because they fully understood what they were doing. They succeeded in spite of themselves. Thus, arguments in support of them based on their history of effective rule are problematic. Vico is undercutting the assumption that the nobles are the nobles because they are superior in some way. He is suggesting that the first nobles were able to restrain their passion, which is commendable, but practically speaking they got lucky. This suggests that he is suspicious of anyone who has a position of power based solely on tradition.

The last gods created before the *famuli* arrive were the gods of agriculture: Vulcan, Saturn, and Cybele or Vesta. Vulcan includes the ritual of using fire to clear the fields. This would later come to include the rituals of the forge (564). Saturn represents the sown fields themselves (73). Vico does not say much about these two poetic characters. He does not even try to clarify the overlap between them and Hercules. It seems as if both Vulcan and Hercules used fire to clear the field. Since Vico does not say much about them here, I will pass over them. They take on more relevance once the *famuli* arrive.

I will discuss his interpretation of Cybele. His presentation of this god is brief but instructive because it displays the process of overinclusion described above. He only dedicates one long passage to her. Nonetheless, I think it is a good example of how Vico uses the evidence he has to show the haphazard way in which imaginative universals grow.

Like Diana, who protected the perennial springs, Cybele protects the plowed fields and the harvested grain from anyone who might want to trespass or soil them in some way. Vico writes, "Among the Romans, she was called Vesta, goddess of divine ceremonies, for the lands ploughed at the time were the first altars of the world" (549). Presumably, Vesta or Cybele would severely punish any member of the family who might try to damage the fields or stored food. In Vico's view, the main challenge for the early communities was not protection from the forces of nature or the need to develop technology. The challenge was always how to prevent the families from losing control of their emotions and damaging the work they have done. Vesta meets this challenge. Because the fields were so vital to the permanent settlements, it was imperative that her rituals be powerful imperatives to protect these resources. Because of this central importance, many other things get attached to her.

From one direction, because the fields became essential for the family's survival, Cybele was associated with permanence. She is shown riding a lion to show that she is the mother of all gods, and she was associated with the pine since it was "a sign of the stability of the founders of peoples." On top of that, however, she becomes the "goddess of divine ceremonies" because the act of plowing the fields was one of the most important ceremonies. This combination of stability and plowing connects her with the clearing of the fields, the tending of the fields and harvesting. So her rituals come to include fire, water, and spelt, which was the first grain. From her central association with the land comes a nexus of ceremonies that invoke the importance of stability and the harvest.

The growing concern, however, is her ability to protect the fields. Vico indicates the severity with which her rituals would have dealt with trespassers. He writes, "On these first lands Vesta sacrificed to Jove the impious practicers of the infamous promiscuity [of women and things], who violated the altars (the first fields of grain)." Anyone who violated the principle of marriage or burial by defiling the sacred altar of Vespa were considered enemies of the city and the human race as a whole. He ties these ideas together by saying, "among the Romans it remained the custom to cover with spelt the brow and the horns of sacrificial victims" (549). The fire represented in these rituals comes to connect her to the myth of Prometheus who steals it. His sacrifice is a representation of the ritual of killing those who violated the cultivated fields.

This passage is, no doubt, confusing. Nonetheless, when one understands that Vico's primary concern is discipline rather than technological development, one can see how these various stories and images come together in rituals of discipline. Moreover, I see his account as a way of showing how hard and how inefficient it must have been to think poetically. Remember that poetic thought would demand perfect imitation to be recognized. As the imaginative universals expanded in arbitrary ways, it must have been difficult for the priests and barons to remember all of these elements as they struggled to keep their meaning hidden from the plebeians. Their effort must have gone to keeping these rituals straight rather than legitimately improving society. It reminds me of how administrators and managers become so focused on keeping straight traditional practices that they overlook obvious possibilities for improvement.

Up to this point in Vico's chronology, the poetic characters have been rituals kept within the families of the theological poets. The animals still wandering the forest are excluded from their asylums. Indeed, the poets defend their territory from them by performing the rituals of Apollo and Diana. Eventually, the second comers arrive to constitute the *famuli*. This is when politics begins in earnest.

7

Poetic Wisdom and Class Conflict

The class struggle is a significant topic of the *New Science*. Much of book 2 is dedicated to explaining the way the plebeians got access to the secret laws of the nobility. Metaphysically speaking, this conflict is important because it is a mechanism that divine providence offers to encourage civilizations to advance toward the human age. Peasant uprisings cause the nobles to make decisions that they think will provide short-term stability. They grant the peasants various forms of legal recognition as a means of appeasing them while keeping them under their authority. Over the long term, this has the opposite effect of expanding the road the peasants can use to achieve greater equality. If the participants in this struggle play out their roles properly, as did the ancient Romans, then this will put a civilization in a position to enter the human age.

When commentators have examined the *New Science*'s depiction of the class struggle, they have tended to bypass Vico's account of poetic wisdom as a distinct epistemological structure. They have examined Vico's portrayal of the pagan gods as primarily a description of steps in the evolution of political institutions.[1] While this can lead to a productive reading, it obscures a remarkable portrayal of how noble authority functions and ultimately stimulates revolution. By holding Vico's theory of poetic wisdom together with his political theory, my reading paints the class struggle in the *New Science* as an epistemological conflict. The plebeians need to find a way into the secret laws of the aristocrats. This means learning how to think like the nobles and ultimately open up lines of communication. This is needed to reform heroic institutions and earn political recognition.

The challenge for the plebeians is that noble authority is based on a profound sense of self-discipline that is integral to poetic thought. Their rituals dictate that they demand obedience from the lower class. They obey those rituals more to demonstrate their piety than to manage the labor of the plebeians. The nobles do not rule to expand their power, wealth, or even opportunities for pleasure. They command the plebeians because their pagan religion compels them. For the plebeians to gain equality, their struggle will not be a practical matter of securing resources. Rather, the plebeians need to move the civilization away from its dependence on poetic thought.

To introduce how unique Vico's account is, I will contrast it with a more typical picture of ancient authority offered by contemporary theorists of biopower. They generally hold that ancient sovereignty flowed from the top to the bottom, with rulers giving direct commands to the people. They emphasize that ancient monarchs had the direct power of life and death over subjects. This is in contrast to contemporary authority that permeates throughout society and controls life from a variety of directions.[2] While modern systems of authority engage in surveillance and punishment by turning the population against itself, ancient leaders directly commanded their subjects to obey or face a penalty. This is an oversimplification of their portrayal, but it helps to illuminate the contrast.

Vico's position is that ancient sovereignty was not as simple as just command from above. As I discussed in the chapter on secret laws, the primary channel of power was directed by the upper class inwardly against themselves through shared rituals of self-discipline. Nobles constantly watched each other to make sure no one was breaking ranks. Control of the plebeians was a function of this self-discipline and was conducted according to the dictates of pagan rituals. Rather than being an arbitrary way of barking orders, noble authority over the plebeians was inherent to the strict adherence to the demands of pagan religion and then heroic law. The nobles had all the power in the first two ages. Vico stressed that the oligarchs had the right of life and death over the lower class (582). He even refers to it as a "sovereign right" (991). Nevertheless, the nobles still had to conform to the system of rituals that were dictated by the tradition of their pagan religion. Rather than being simply top-down and arbitrary, ancient authority was a system in which ancient rituals dictated to the nobility that they control the plebeians in a traditional way.

To understand Vico's characterization of the nobility, it is important to look at axiom LXXXVI. He draws a passage from Aristotle that states, "the nobles [i nobili] swore to be eternal enemies of the plebs" (271). One reason this passage is significant is because it refers to the upper class as nobles. While this could be a reference to the class division in Aristotle, I think it also points to the fact that Vico considered the poets and heroes of the first two ages to be aristocratic nobility. This strengthens the link between Vico's account of poetic wisdom and the Neapolitan barons.

More significantly, I take his claim that the nobles "swore to be eternal enemies of the plebs" as a reference back to two aspects of poetic wisdom. First, the use of the term "swore" indicates that this is an aspect of aristocratic self-discipline that was instilled by pagan religion. The nobles did not regard the plebeians simply as annoying workers that needed to be managed effectively. It was their sacred duty to treat the plebeians as the enemy. Second, I take the term "eternal" to refer to the fact that it is inherent to poetic wisdom to see an absolute distinction between the human nobles and the animalistic plebeians. The class division is not an accidental attribute based on who happens to be wealthy. Rather, poetic wisdom considered the two classes to be on two different levels of being. As long as aristocrats think along the traditional lines founded by pagan religion, they will frame their worldview around this conception.

Vico's brief commentary illuminates the axiom. He claims that this oath "explains the cause of the haughty, avaricious, and cruel practices of the nobles toward the plebeians" (272). He then points to the fact that the nobles drove the plebeians into debt by making them pay for war and then used their fiscal obligations to further exploit them. This appears to be a fairly straightforward description of aristocratic power. It actually emphasizes the way the noble worldview steadfastly refuses to acknowledge the humanity of the plebeians.

Vico's comment is a reference to his discussion of the census instituted by Servius Tullius, the sixth King of Rome. Vico tells us that this census raised a difficult issue for his science (25). It gave legal recognition to the plebeians by registering their names with the government. While it made it easier to tax them, it also meant that the government had to recognize them as individuals. Traditionally, the implementation of the census was thought to indicate that some aristocrats had come to recognize the humanity of the plebeians and sought to treat them better. Servius Tullius is praised as a defender of the rights of the lower class. If this interpretation were correct, it would contradict Vico's position. It would deny that the oppressive cruelty of the nobles was inherent to their worldview. If Servius Tullius did grant the plebeians this right out of a sense of benevolence, then the aristocratic worldview could not have been as severe as Vico suggests.

Vico defends his position by saying that all the census tax did was transfer the money raised privately by the nobles to a central pool administered by whoever was leading the noble class (107, 111). This was actually meant to strengthen the position of the aristocracy against the growing number of plebeians. As such, it was never intended to make life better for the plebeians but instead was meant to protect the nobles from possible uprisings. The institution of the census did open the door for greater legal recognition of the plebeians eventually with the later development of the Publilian laws, but that was never the original intent (619). Vico's interpretation turns the census into another instance of the mechanism of divine providence by which the aristocrats inadvertently create more rights for the plebeians. More importantly, it allows Vico to maintain that it was impossible for an aristocrat to recognize the equality of the plebeians from within the framework of poetic wisdom. With this background, one can see how axiom LXXXVI is not merely a reference to a sense of animosity, inconvenience, or even fear that the nobles felt toward the lower classes. The nobles' oath of animosity is a fundamental aspect of aristocratic self-discipline that is inherent to the epistemological structure of poetic wisdom.

This axiom also denies the possibility that aristocratic cruelty was arbitrary. In the view that ancient authority floated from the top to the bottom, it is easy to imagine how nobles could treat the lower class as slaves. This would involve wealthy aristocrats arbitrarily demanding that their servants attend to their whims. In Vico's view, the nobles followed rigid patterns of behavior that were certainly cruel but were not based on capriciousness. They were based on strict laws and rituals. The census represented a shift from private law to public law, but the taxes were always collected according to a strictly interpreted secret law and enforced by the judicial authority of each noble. The census tax standardized the practice across different fiefs, and this may have altered the content of the law but it kept its enforcement within strict legal prescriptions. The plebeians suffered greatly under this system, since the taxes would have been excessive and the nobles did use them to pay for their wars that they made the plebeians fight. They were never arbitrary, however. This conforms with Vico's insistence that in the first two ages the lower classes were not slaves. The idea of ownership of a person only develops later when the heroes start taking captives from other fiefs (958). Noble authority was cruel but stayed within the parameters defined by the secret laws, which held the plebeians in an ignorant and subservient position.

Vico connects his discussion of the census to the returned barbarism in Europe. He ends the section by mentioning that medieval fiefs in France came to pay a tax to a central monarch through a similar census (622). In Naples, the money would have been sent to the viceroy or King Carlo, but they were largely subservient to the aristocracy. The point is that the goal for the plebeians was not stopping the excessive brutality of a few sadistic lords. Their opponent was an entire administrative system designed to withhold legal rights from them. The vassals in Naples did not have to change the minds of a few nobles; they had to reform an entire system.

Vico does claim explicitly that a long class struggle was valuable for the proper development of a stable civilization. Since the physical and mental transformation from giant to human was so difficult, it was necessary that nations prolong their time in the first two ages to develop an appropriate amount of civility. If the chains of poetic wisdom were broken too early, a civilization would not last in the human age because it would descend rapidly into decadence. When a civilization like Rome shows the discipline to pass through this evolution slowly, it can produce a just and fair legal system in the third age. Vico writes in axiom XCI, "The contests waged by the orders in the cities for equality of rights are the most powerful means of making the commonwealths great" (280). He admires both the plebeians for wanting to have civil rights and the nobles for protecting them. This produces the greatest chance for a stable human culture that does not collapse directly into selfishness and greed.

Ultimately, the outcome of the class struggle should be equality for the plebeians enforced along the lines of philosophical justice. Axiom XCV states, "At first men desire to be free of subjection and attain equality; witness the plebs in the aristocratic commonwealths, which finally turn popular" (292). To avoid corruption, a system of equality must be administered by the rule of law interpreted in the interest of justice and social stability rather than literally. In the *New Science*, he writes that the class struggle produces lawyers who have "the wisdom of the jurisconsults in interpreting the laws and extending their utility little by little as new cases demanded adjudication" (281). The resolution of the class struggle, then, does not occur when the plebeians overthrow the nobility. It also does not occur when material wealth is somehow redistributed. It ends when everyone has truly equal and legally protected rights. This can only happen when there is a knowledgeable and intellectually sophisticated legal class that can ensure that everyone is treated fairly. At the end of the chapter I will discuss how he uses the images of Ulpian and Solon as examples of politicians who were able to extend the legal rights of the people.

Within this context, I will now try to give substance to Vico's idea of the class struggle by discussing the remaining five gods of the greater gentes. I will not outline every aspect of Vico's interpretation of the evolution of Roman law and its connection to the development of feudal institutions. Instead, I will highlight aspects that seem to be influenced by the context provided by the Neapolitan barons. I think this will illustrate how the *New Science* offers a diagnosis of political injustice that is within the early modern paradigm and yet radically different than his contemporaries. I also hope it invites reflection on the behavior of the aristocracy in contemporary neoliberalism. I will speculate on this more in the conclusion.

Mars, God of Defense

Axiom LXXXI presents the fundamental motivation of the nobles throughout the class struggle of the heroic age. It is found among those axioms dedicated to feudalism. It states, "It is a mark of the strong not to lose by sloth what they have gained by valor. Rather do they yield, from necessity or from utility, as little as they can bit by bit" (261).

In accord with this, the imaginative universal Mars does not contain bold expeditions of conquest. Instead, Mars contains rituals for defending the religious and political institutions that the nobles had invented. Vico acknowledges that Mars is connected with glory in battle, but they are defensive battles that respond to a present danger. He writes that the poetic character represents "properly fighting for their altars and hearths" (562). The paradigms of Apollo and Diana also originated as acts of protecting the asylums. The rituals of Mars are different because they are linked specifically to the defense of religious institutions.

Mars was not inspired by the rebellious *famuli*, since they were so subservient they could not imagine rebelling. The class conflict begins in earnest when the plebeians inspire the heroes to create Minerva. Mars was inspired by the fact that the theological poets had begun to outline their territory. Because different poets could settle near the same perennial spring, there would be outbreaks of violence as they fought over where the boundaries would be. He describes these conflicts by writing, "it cannot be understood save as taking place among men of extreme wildness, observing a frightful religion which had fixed and circumscribed them within certain lands, and whose bloody ceremonies had consecrated their first walls" (550). The important point is that the conflict was not over land and resources but rather religion. It was not because they wanted to grow more food that the poets wanted to defend their territory. Their burial grounds and altars were sacred. They would not tolerate another poet imposing on their sacred space. Hence, Mars was not the god of conquering more land to augment living space. Mars was the god of protecting the sacred religion from the encroachment of others.

A Hobbesian would expect Vico's account to discuss the need for the first poets to protect their food and water to ensure their survival. This is not what the *New Science* gives us. Instead, he emphasizes that the rituals were invented specifically to defend their religion. He writes, "This sort of fighting was always heroic, for it was fighting for their own religion, to which mankind takes recourse when all natural help is despaired of" (562). As with Jove and the thunder, it would require strong stimuli to evoke the internal restraining force necessary to check their bestial passions. Since the poets retained their gigantic strength, a physical threat to their bodies would not offer enough motivation. The greatest fear would be evoked by a threat to the divine religion. The poets already felt a profound need to obey the ritualistic demands of self-discipline. Moreover, they would already sense that those rituals were under constant threat, given the superstitious belief that any flawed performance could incur the wrath of god. The self-disciplinary rituals of Mars would thus be inspired by a threat to the altars rather than a threat to their bodies. It would be a sign of a conceited scholar to assume that the first people would have primarily thought about defending their resources rather than their pagan traditions.

As evidence of this, he points to the fact that wars during the heroic era were fought primarily over religion and not land. He writes, "the heroic wars were all wars of religion, and the heralds, in delivering a declaration of war, called forth the gods from the enemy city, and consecrated the enemy to the gods" (958). Vico's specific example here is from the history of ancient Rome. Nonetheless, it invites reflection on the modern world. In the abstract, it makes sense to assume that conflict would be motivated by a need for resources. Historically speaking, however, as civilizations have done a better job of attending to the practical needs of the people, the amount of warfare has not gone down. The soldiers fighting those wars have often been motivated by religious symbols or nationalistic images. While the aristocracy may profit from these wars, their rhetoric often centers around the need for self-discipline in defending their position and their nation. Obviously, war is an exceptionally complicated issue. Recognized and unrecognized environmental factors play a large part in motivating nations to fight. My point here is that Vico does have a case against Hobbes. Commentators are so familiar with framing the early modern debate about the origin of civilization in terms of questions about resources that Vico's position here may seem strange. When one does what Vico asks and looks at the history of civilization, his case becomes stronger.

Relics did play a major role in the politics of early modern Naples. In *Church and State in Spanish Italy: Rituals and Legitimacy in the Kingdom of Naples*, Céline Dauverd discusses the role that spiritual relics played in rituals during the time of the Spanish viceroys. For example, she discusses the rituals surrounding the blood of San Gennaro and the importance of the miracle of its liquefaction.[3] She also discusses the political significance of the rituals of the Corpus Domini celebration in which the body of Christ was venerated.[4] Her thesis is that the Spanish viceroys maintained their authority in part because of their ability to insert themselves into these rituals and displace the nobility who traditionally controlled them. This supports the point that religious artifacts were central to the channels of power in government and were necessary to demonstrate legitimate authority. It is easy to imagine that Vico considered this or something similar as he thought about Mars as a defender of religion instead of resources.

Vico reinforces this historical argument with a psychological one. Within the discussion of Mars, he claims that when people feel physically threatened, their fear drives them to seek refuge in the spiritual. As evidence, he suggests that atheists on their deathbeds turn to religion. He writes, "Libertines, too, as they grow older, turn to religion, for they feel nature failing them" (562, also 339). As the value of the atheist's material possessions diminish, the fear drives that person to care for the spiritual, since that is the only thing that can still offer protection and reassurance. When people can no longer protect the material, only the supernatural can give them solace. Vico's point is that even for the atheist, protecting a connection to the divine is more fundamental than protecting physical possessions. When they are passing from this world, they do not just give in as their bodies deteriorate; instead, they defend their previously hidden religious commitments. Given this human trait, the first poets would have been most strongly motivated by the desire to protect their religion rather than their body or their possessions. When poets faced hazardous physical conditions, they would either live or die depending on their physical strength. True terror would drive them to protect their religion and sacrifice their physical self if necessary. That extreme fear would inspire the invention of Mars.

Vico's portrayal of Mars adds to his anti-baronial position. Since the barons are concerned with protecting their traditions and not their land, they probably are ill-equipped to defend their land in the most effective way possible. If nothing else, because they are trying to defend their noble status and privilege, they will sacrifice land, resources, and even the lives of the plebeians to retain it. Poetic wisdom is ill-suited for warfare not only because it struggles to use technology but also because it has a misguided idea of the objective of warfare. The underlying poetic mentality of the aristocracy will ultimately be ineffective for maintaining a modern army.[5]

More philosophically, his portrayal of Mars coheres with his suspicion about the role that material forces have in the development of civilization. An Epicurean such as Hobbes would want to understand war in terms of material stimuli. This explanation would be easiest to make on the basis of natural resources. Contrary to this, Vico argues that the desire for physical sustenance would never provide enough motivation to instill the self-discipline necessary to create complex civil institutions. A poet might live or die, but without the compulsion to protect a religion the fief could never develop real social order. This point carries through all ages of history. A nation's progress depends on people recognizing the importance of divine religion. This motivation becomes more sophisticated as civilization progresses through the three ages, but it is always necessary that the rulers of a society value something beyond the material to move forward. Mars embodies this particularly in the divine age before the rise of the lower class.

In this context, it is possible to make sense of the most curious aspect of his account. He discusses how the first poets used pointed wooden spears and leather-covered shields to protect the asylums. This shows that he does not entirely deny the practical aspects of protecting the land (562, 564). His emphasis, however, is on a much different point. He writes, "The first shield in the world was the ground of the field where dead were buried" (563). This implies that in the minds of the first poets the sacred ground protected the religion rather than the religion protecting the territory. He spends a good deal of time on this point as he connects the colors of the land to the heraldry of the nobles. This is a moment in the *New Science* that would be easy to write off as eccentric. I argue that it is consistent with the idea that the defensive rituals of Mars were about protecting religion rather than resources.

To grasp this point, it is important to remember a fundamental characteristic of poetic wisdom. Its conceptual structure struggles to separate the essential from the accidental. Because the poetic mind thinks in terms of complete conceptual paradigms, it does not separate out what is of practical significance for a ritual from what is not. Given that the rituals of Mars were focused on defending the religion itself, one can see how in the minds of the poets the burial ground would have served as a part of the defensive ritual like any other weapon. While the ground did not literally serve as an actual bulwark, the sacred space of the dead would have had the superstitious value necessary to inspire its defense and would be sensed as an essential part of the activity of protecting the religion. Although from a contemporary perspective the land would be the thing to protect, the poets thought of it as an accessory to the defense of the religion.

There is a temptation to find in Vico an environmental reading of myth that unveils a spiritual connection between pagan religion and the natural world. The discussion of Mars could be a place to find this. Consistent with my approach, I do not want to deter readers who find this environmental dimension in the *New Science*. Nevertheless, I think this reading would conceal this important critique of the oligarchy. The barons are the true sons of the earth who are tied to their sacred land. It is they and not the plebeians who recognize its spiritual value and are reluctant to leave it. The barons value the land as a symbol of their own authority and self-discipline. Their noble world view always prioritizes religion and tradition over practical benefits, and so they would not possess a deep understanding of how the land produces food or a deep connection to the activity of working the land. From a modern perspective, this explains why the nobles see wealth as a means to protect their tradition rather than an end in itself. It helps explain why the Neapolitan barons use their wealth to maintain their positions rather than invest it to become even more wealthy.

Vico dedicates a lengthy passage to illustrating how the colors of the land became the colors found on heraldry shields (563). This explicitly links control of land to a symbolic expression of authority. He connects the color black to the burning of the fields, green to the leaves of the plants, gold to the plants during the harvest, blue to the sky, and red to the blood of the thieves whom the heroes slayed. He then claims that these colors appear on coats of arms as a sown field. It is very unlikely that this is historically correct. Philosophically, however, it further develops the idea that at the core of the aristocratic mentality is the idea that land is a symbol of power. This implies that aristocrats want to acquire land not primarily to increase wealth but instead to expand their symbols of their own self-discipline. For the class struggle, this means that from the aristocrat's perspective, class warfare is not primarily over ownership of land. They regard land as a symbol of a much deeper connection to religion and tradition. If the plebeians are going to gain legal recognition, the defense of tradition will need to be undermined rather than simply finding a way to gain land.

Vico discusses the way the connection between land, defense, and symbols of authority reappeared in the returned barbarism. This invites the reader to think about how this power dynamic exists in the mentality of the Neapolitan barons. He claims explicitly that during the returned barbarism in Europe, medieval coats of arms display lions with the same colors as ancient heraldry. He also discusses the way that the first defensive weapons were also farm implements. This furthers the idea that the cultivated fields served in the poetic mind as the defenses rather than the thing defended. He also claims that it explains why European heraldry often has farm equipment. He concludes, "agriculture was the first foundation of nobility not only in the first barbarian times, as we ascertain from the Romans, but also in the second" (563). In the heroic age of the Romans and the returned barbarism, agriculture served primarily as a way to demonstrate the authority of the nobility rather than as a utilitarian means of providing sustenance.

He continues that "Mars fought on truly real fields and behind truly real shields." He then connects this to the medieval period through a fanciful etymology of the Latin word *cluer*. He then extends this point by connecting the medieval word for defense to pasture, "just as from the time of the returned barbarism pastures [*pascoli*] and enclosed woods [*selve chiuse*] have been called defense [*difese*]" (562). Battistini provides a reference to du Cange's glossary of medieval Latin to show an example of how the Latin word *difese* would be used in this way.[6] This etymological connection between the words for "pasture" and "defense" furthers Vico's call to think about the way the barons thought of the land as a symbolic way to defend their tradition.

He builds on this point as he goes deeper into the discussion of heraldry and coats of arms. "The science of blazonry" is one of his favorite topics, and it is one of the three main points that he carries over from the 1725 *New Science* (28). Anyone who has visited prominent historic buildings in Italy has seen how prevalent these symbols were. Vico's science tries to explain how they were generated originally out of the imagination of poetic wisdom. The designs of the coats of arms were imitations of the rituals and auspices of the noble religion (484). As the poetic wisdom began to incorporate the class distinction more prominently into its rituals, the heraldry became a way to demonstrate noble authority and ownership. It became a lasting symbol of noble power when they could not be physically present. As with the defensive use of the land, the *New Science* invites the reader to think about the power of coats of arms in modern Europe. After the fall of Western Rome, very few people were literate. This necessitated a return to the using the coats of arms to indicate noble superiority (485). This is such a prevalent aspect of the noble mentality that these symbols were placed everywhere. He writes, "we do not find a single wall in ancient houses without some emblem carved upon it" (486). As the heroic age transitioned into the human one, these symbols became the basis for writing (930–931).

I will go into more detail about the connection of pagan ritual, heraldry, and ownership when I discuss Mercury. What is important here is that Vico explicitly argues that these coats of arms were originally about religion rather than warfare. One might expect that heraldry was originally developed to identify military forces and distinguish them from one another. After all, the coats of arms were put on shields and weapons. He argues, instead, that the symbols were originally religious and only later became military. As evidence for this, he discusses the way in which birds feature so prominently in heraldry. As I discussed, he proposed that birds, as auspices of Jove, led the first poets to their first hilltop settlements. The religious significance of these birds encouraged many ancient civilizations, including the Egyptians, Etruscans, Romans, and English, to use the eagle as their symbol. It primarily represents the auspices of Jove. Only much later did the eagle become a symbol of warfare. He writes, "Later they became public ensigns in time of peace, and from these were derived the medals, which, with the introduction of warfare, were found suitable for military insignia" (487). This is another situation where the use of evidence is no longer sustainable. Nonetheless, what is really at stake here is the consistent reinforcement of the noble mentality as primarily defensive and protective of religious traditions more than physical security. Their military symbols were initially religious and only later developed into symbols of authority rather than the other way around.

Before concluding this section, I want to mention one more reason why Mars was about defensive warfare rather than conquest. Axiom LXXXVII states, "The aristocratic commonwealths are most cautious about going to war lest they make warriors of the multitude of the plebeians" (273). Particularly at an early stage, nobles would be reluctant to try to arm the *famuli* because that would mean strengthening their most immediate enemy. So, the nobles would have avoided warfare in order to avoid turning their *famuli* into a fighting force.

The historical evidence from ancient Greece and Rome dictates that offensive wars did happen in the ancient world. Vico acknowledges this point, but he argues that those wars would have happened much later in human development (634–661). Based on a variety of myths about characters abducted by sea, he portrays those wars as primarily acts of piracy and corsair raiding (634). Land raids then developed later (645). One could speculate that later technological advancements such as ships would have made it easier to do quick raids, which would allow the heroes to attack other fiefdoms and return before a plebeian uprising could get going. Vico does not make this point, however. He emphasizes that what made these raids possible was that the heroes regarded all aliens as enemies (639). He does offer an explanation of how the Romans were actually to acquire territory and how other alliances were made (640, 643). I would argue that his picture of war was heavily influenced by the practice of banditry in Naples. As discussed earlier, barons would employ bandits to raid other fiefs or to rob travelers passing through the territory. This is what Vico seems to be describing in this section.

As the number of raids increased, another type of warfare also grew. These were defensive wars fought by the nobles against the rebellious plebeians. Vico claims that the majority of the wars during the heroic era were of this type. He goes to great lengths to show how many ancient myths about warfare were in some way descended from class conflicts (81). Sometimes this makes more sense than others. His interpretation of the tale of Penelope and the suitors as a description of plebeian uprising seems possible (654). It is harder to accept his claim that Dido left to found Carthage because she lost a heroic contest (78). He does not clarify whether she lost to her brother-in-law, who represents the plebeians, or to some other noble. Regardless of this detail, it is time to discuss the development of the *famuli* and how it led them to a position to start the heroic contests.

The Basis of the Class Division

Vico's clearest statement about the difference between the two classes comes in a section of the "Poetic Economy" when he describes the moment the *famuli* entered the asylums. Here, he praises the theological poets for their ability to invent the poetic characters. He emphasizes that they were motivated by a noble reverence for religion and procreation, which "thus gave a beginning to noble and lordly friendship" (555). Conversely, he portrays the lower classes negatively because of their focus on tangible and practical concerns. He writes, "The second comers, since they came out of a necessity of saving their lives, gave a beginning to society in the proper sense, with a view principally to utility, and consequently base and servile" (555). They did not feel the passions necessary to develop the pagan rituals needed to civilize them. They entered the asylums because they needed physical protection. Unlike the poets who fought to protect their religion, the *famuli* desired simply to feed themselves. This is consistent with Vico's overall view of the lower classes. For him, there is always the possibility that the plebeian's desire for wealth will lead to destructive selfishness. If this is unchecked, civilization will become undone. Hence, while the human age offers justice to all, it still has a legal system to ensure political stability. Looking at this passage alone, one might think that Vico would support the nobility rather than critique it. Indeed, he certainly praises the poets and heroes for inventing the religion necessary to civilize humanity in the first two ages. Nevertheless, as one gets into the details of his account of the early relationship of the two classes, one can see how Vico lays a foundation that explains how the aristocracy becomes problematic for the human age.

At the end of the introduction to book 2, Vico makes a remarkable claim that I think has been overlooked in the scholarship. He restates the division of humanity after the flood into the Hebrews and giants. He then divides the giants before the thunder into two types. This means that the giants were not an indistinct mass of animals. The difference between the classes already existed in the physique or the emotional fortitude of two types of giants. He writes, "Of the giants, there were in turn two kinds: the first, the sons of Earth, or nobles, from whom, as being giants in the full sense of the term, the age of giants took its name, as we have said (and it is these whom sacred history defines as 'strong, famous and powerful men of the age'); the second, less properly so called, those other giants who were subjugated [*altri giganti signoreggiati*]" (372). It is important to remember Vico's emphasis on free will, so it could not be the case that one set of giants were simply programmed to create Jove. Those giants still had to think creatively to invent that ritual. It does imply that the other class of giants could not do it.

Earlier in this section, Vico gives a fanciful etymology of the Latin word *indigenae*, which could be translated as "native" or "indigenous." He connects it to the word *nobili* and writes, "For nobles alone . . . composed the first cities, in which the plebeians were slaves or precursors of slaves" (370).[7] This reinforces the idea that the class distinction was not produced by societal influences. The idea of nobility refers to an original sense of strength and freedom that connected the noble giants to the land. The other giants did not have this.

The prevailing image of the time of the giants in the scholarship emphasizes the passage earlier in this section that describes the indiscriminate mixing of the giants (369). Roberto Esposito uses this passage to build a reading of Vico that has civilization rising out of a primordial mass of proto-humanity.[8] These later passages in this section suggest that Vico did not see the time of the giants as so amorphous. Rather, he recognized the philosophical need to address the question of what caused the original class distinction. For unspecified physiological reasons, one type of giant could hear the call of Jove while the other did not. While this answer is not fully satisfying, it represents an attempt to resolve an internal difficulty of the science.

Vico does not defend this answer outside of providing a few etymologies. With this lack of support, it is difficult to know how much emphasis to place on it. It is important to remember that Vico's science is an attempt to explain the historical fact that civilizations have demonstrated a class distinction. This natural separation would explain this origin, but it does not endorse it. The normative project of the science argues that humanity ought to move into the human age in which the courts protect the rights of everyone with justice and equality. So despite the fact that the class separation originates before the thunder, Vico would not claim that this distinction should be maintained in the future. Indeed, Vico recognizes that there is not a strong material distinction between the two classes. While this separation led one type of giant to hear Jove while the other did not, it becomes a challenge for the nobles to keep the *famuli* aware of their superiority. Even though Vico posits this difference during the age of the giants, his science suggests that this difference loses value as history progresses.

I choose to interpret this claim as underlining how Vico's system portrays a strict division between the two classes within poetic wisdom. Regardless of whether one chooses to ignore this claim of Vico or not, the science itself emphasizes that the structure of aristocratic thought makes it extraordinarily difficult to bring justice and equality to all humans. If philosophers could convincingly argue that the distinction was based on an illusion, it would be easy enough to promote social reform. The fact that history has demonstrated how difficult this task is in practice shows that philosophers and humanity in general need to work much harder to uproot this distinction from the aristocratic mentality.

I think the main takeaway from this passage really is not so much what it says about the division within the giants but what it says about the nobility. This passage characterizes the noble giants as "sons of Earth" ("figliuoli della terra") rather than the *famuli* or plebeians (370). As I mentioned earlier, he faults Livy for thinking that the plebeians had a special connection to the land (532). As indicated by the rituals of Mars, it is really the nobles who are dedicated to using the land to defend their tradition. This connection stretches back before the invention of Jove and presumably encourages the poets to settle down while the other giants ignore the divine auspices. Since my project is actually not overly concerned with Vico's early modern project of divining the origin of civilization, it is easy enough to ignore this claim about the age of giants. Nevertheless, I do take Vico seriously as he talks about the way the class divide presents a serious obstacle to reform, and his portrayal of the nobility as tied to the land rather than the peasants.

I now turn to another philosophical problem. Vico is committed to the idea that the first poets did not go out and capture the other giants. This would have made the initial relationship between the classes that of master and slave. As I discussed earlier, Vico does not accept this. He portrays the initial relationship between the classes as one in which the theological poets offer protection to the second comers, which then leads to the relationship of lord and vassal. He states this explicitly when he turns to Tacitus's account of the Germanic tribes for evidence. He faults Tacitus for mistakenly calling the *famuli* slaves, but he accepts the way Tacitus paints their original relationship. He reports that they were given fields with the task of providing the heroes what they required. He further reports that the *famuli* had to defend the land. Vico writes, "If we look for a legal name to define such relationships, we shall clearly see that there is none that fits them better than our term feudalism" (608). He occasionally states that the *famuli* lived in a state of slavery, but when he does he qualifies it by indicating that technically they were only the precursors of slaves (556). I take these moments to refer only to the distinction between the free nobility and the unfree serfs. I take the class relationship to be generally characterized by the general progress from *famuli* as worker to the sharecropping relationship of feudalism. The important point here is that the *famuli* came to the asylums rather than the poets going out and taking them for labor. This opens up the question of why the *famuli* would ever enter the asylums to be subjugated.

In *The Occasions of Community: Giambattista Vico and the Concept of Society*, Timothy D. Harfield raises this question.[9] Earlier, I discussed the problem of human sociability, which wonders why humans who were surviving in an animalistic state would ever enter civil society. Since they could not recognize the benefits of human society, why would it ever occur to them to invent it? The poets heard the thunder and spontaneously imagined their religion. Why would the other giants who could not hear the thunder ever recognize the benefit of wandering into the asylums, given their physical strength?

I think Harfield rightfully points out that there is a difference between establishing a civilization out of nothing and recognizing the benefits of an already existing institution. The poets needed an extra motivating force to invent something that they had never seen before. The second comers, on the other hand, could see the asylums and then chose to enter them. This would have been a practical choice suited to the mentality of those giants who had not heard the call of Jove. Vico offers an analogy that supports this point. He compares this second type of giant to "Grotius's simpletons and Pufendorf's abandoned men" and claims that they entered the asylums to escape "Hobbes' violent men" (553). Interestingly, Vico implies that the early modern philosophical debate about the state of nature was incorrect because it did not recognize the distinction between the two types of giants. The other authors debate over whether all proto-humans were naturally violent or nonviolent because they do not realize there were two types of them. I cannot find Vico ever making this point directly, but it explains why he raises the distinction between these two early modern views. Regardless, the analogy Vico offers is that the second type of giant enters the asylums "as beasts driven by intense cold will sometimes seek salvation in inhabited places" (553). This implies that the second comers did not really understand what they were entering but had a sense that it would be safer. Like animals, they vaguely wandered into the space while seeking protection wherever they could find it. This explains how they could have entered subjugation without an awareness of what they were doing.

Up to this point, Harfield's initial analysis conforms to my reading. After that, however, he follows a different path. He draws heavily on the *Universal Law* and the 1725 *New Science* to portray the nobles as educating the second comers out of a sense of piety. Whereas the poets used their superstition to discipline themselves, he writes, "The *famuli* arrived at the same [civil] state, acquiring language and reason, through education."[10] He suggests that the poets allowed the *famuli* to enter the asylum because it was their religious obligation. He writes, "Their [the first rulers'] piety and generosity eventually compelled them to admit the *famuli*."[11] This emphasizes the nobility as having a fatherly role and tending to the character of everyone inside the fief. From this perspective, the *famuli* then appear quite ungrateful when they use their practical ability to turn against their educators.

Harfield's reading may be correct on the basis of these earlier works, but I hold that Vico's attitude toward the nobility became harsher as he developed the idea of poetic wisdom. In the later *New Science*, the poets instilled discipline in *famuli*, but it was not because the poets were somehow magnanimous. The epistemological structure of poetic wisdom would never have allowed the poets to see the *famuli* as equal to their own family. Further, not only did the poets feel an obligation to keep their laws secret, the rigid enforcement of these secret laws forced their sense of discipline to be cruel. Since they did not have a real sense of philosophical justice, they enforced their laws strictly according to their letter. This meant that punishments always had to be cruel with no exceptions, since that was the only idea of equity the poets could muster. He writes, "if, as a consequence of this [civil] equity, the laws turned out in a given case to be not only harsh but actually cruel, they naturally bore it because they thought their law was naturally such" (38). Vico often discusses the cruelty of heroic law. For example, he writes, "These people [the heroic Lacedaemonians], in order to teach their sons to fear neither pain nor death, would beat them within an inch of their lives in the temple of Diana, so that they often fell dead in agonies of pain beneath their fathers' blows" (671). Within this picture, it is hard to imagine the poets or heroes deciding to teach the *famuli* out of a sense of moral obligation. On the contrary, their duty would have been not to teach them in order to keep the ranks of the aristocracy separate. The harsh discipline of the nobility only trains the second comers as a secondary effect of their own rituals of self-discipline. This also implies that the plebeians would have been justified in rebelling given the way they were treated.

According to the 1744 *New Science*, then, why did the second comers enter the asylums? To answer this question, it is necessary to start by clarifying why the second comers sought shelter in the first place. Before Jove, there was no institution of marriage, so there was no fighting over women. After Jove, women were no longer held in common and poets would fight over them to find a mate (553). The institution of marriage would help stabilize the early asylums, but it would not stop the conflicts entirely (554). Poets and wandering giants would lose these fights and need to seek protection. They saw the advantage of seeking shelter in the asylums of the powerful poets.

Vico's description becomes curious when he explains how the theological poets reacted when these losers arrived at their asylum. He writes, "the strong, with a fierceness born of their union in the society of families, slew the violent who had violated their lands, and took under their protection the miserable creatures who had fled from them" (553). The poets assessed whether the newcomers were threats to their authority or animals willing to submit to their rule. They slew the threatening intruders and subdued the others. This conforms to the defensive posture of the poets, as was discussed in Diana and Apollo. It also emphasizes the cruelty of the poets, who executed whomever they saw enter who was a threat. He praises specifically the ancient Roman nobles above all other civilizations for having the strength to execute the strong and retain the weak. There is no sense of magnanimity in the theological poets in this account. The poets responded strongly and cruelly. This initial act of judgment is the foundation for their judicial authority over their asylums.

The underlying point, however, is that this initial act of judgment defines the initial relationship between the lords and the *famuli*. The second comers who survive recognize both the authority and the mercy of the poets. They feel thankful for being spared by the owners of the fief. This makes them thankful for being allowed to exist under the supreme authority of the poets. They feel as if their rulers are being wise and kind. Of course, the rulers are nothing of the sort, since they are just following the commands of their pagan religion. Nevertheless, the *famuli* come to feel that their survival depends on their leader. I am putting this in a straightforward manner to make a philosophical point. If I were to imagine this in terms of the epistemology of poetic wisdom and primitive passion, I would express this more in terms of an emotional dynamic created by fear. The point, though, is that the barons can use their judicial authority to elicit the adulation of the vassals even when imposing their law in a cruel manner.

At this point, the poets now realize what they are gaining from this relationship: fame. They did not realize they wanted this, but when they started to receive it from the second comers, they came to desire more of it. This is an underappreciated element of Vico's account. In some ways, it is the inverse of Mandeville's account. Mandeville had suggested that the rulers used praise and honor to keep the lower classes in order. In Vico's account, the praise the *famuli* give the poets feeds their desire for self-discipline. Their subservient adulation feeds the poets even more motivation to obey the superstitious commands of their secret pagan gods. Obviously, there is no reason to think that Vico is responding directly to Mandeville. This comparison does highlight the negative attitude Vico displays toward the nobility.

Vico spends a good deal of time developing his view that the poets accepted the second comers to receive their praise. He speculates that there would have been little to distinguish the *famuli* from the poets. The two groups would have lived together closely with no substantial difference in wealth, possessions, or clothing to distinguish them. He writes, "To distinguish the sons of the heroes from those of the *famuli*, the former were called *liberi*, free. But it was a distinction without a difference" (556). He clarifies what he means by referring back to Tacitus, who claimed the rulers in the Germanic tribes were not more refined than the rest, showing that there was little physical or behavioral difference between the two classes. Even with the nobles holding the power of life and death over the *famuli*, the nobility would have felt pressure to make sure that they were recognized as distinct from the others. This meant the *famuli* were expected to praise the superiority of the nobles.

He provides a good deal of evidence for his claim. Citing Vergil, he writes, "whence on the battlefield before Troy, fame flies amid the ranks of the Greek heroes and not amid the masses of their plebeians" (555). This refers to the way the epic poems of Homer only discuss the acts of the heroes. It is left to the reader to assume that the armies of common soldiers are actually doing the fighting. The exclusion of the soldiers indicates their obligation to give all of the praise and honor to their leaders. He also mentions that for a long time in medieval feudalism the peasants were not allowed to have a last name (581). Only the nobility had last names, to emphasize their fame and superiority. These examples support an image of the barons as being primarily interested in receiving praise from their servants, with the products of their labor being secondary.

His primary description of the *famuli* emphasizes the way they give fame to the aristocrats. He writes, "the *famuli* were called *clientes*, originally *cluentes*, from the ancient verb *cluere*, to shine in the light of arms . . . for they reflected the light of the arms born by their respective heroes" (556). He makes a similar claim about the *socii* who came into existence along with the *famuli*. They were a type of *famuli* who served as subordinate leaders in the defense of territories. Based on the examples he gives (Antonius, who served Ulysses, and Misenus, who served Aeneas), they appear to have been commanders among the soldiers of the heroes but were not nobles themselves. Vico emphasizes that they had to fight for the heroes, who had the right of life and death over them (558). The important point is that they worked to increase the fame of the heroes. He writes, "The *socii* shared only the labors of the heroes, not their winnings and still less their glory" (559). The lower class existed in the fiefs to provide a contrast that revealed the superiority of the heroes.

In a key passage of this discussion, he calls the reader to make a comparison to modern Naples. Citing Tacitus again, he writes, "the principal oath of these *famuli* or clients or vassals was to guard and defend each his own prince and to assign to his prince's glory his own deeds of valor; which is one of the most impressive [*più risentite*] characteristics of our own feudalism" (559).[12] He then gives examples of histories from both ancient Europe and the medieval period in which individual heroes performed deeds and won battles that they could not have possibly done alone. These stories were told in this way because the feudal mindset attributed all glory to the hero and none to those who did the work. More importantly, he cites the ancient Roman practice of putting a bust of an ancestor in a courtyard to give fame to the noble at the expense of all others. He connects this to the modern practice of placing *medaglioni* or circular portraits of ancestors in the courtyards of modern buildings. This invites the reader to think about the noble heraldry on buildings in modern Naples and consider the extent to which the modern aristocracy was still motivated by fame.

This argument expresses a fairly common concern about the aristocracy. One can see situations in which the upper class take credit for the work of the middle and lower classes. Certainly, on an early modern fief, the lord would have been the symbol of everyone's work regardless of how much he did for the fief or if he even spent time there. In the contemporary world, owners of companies take credit for their good management decisions when often it is the labor of the workers that make a business succeed. Part of what it means to adapt to the culture of a business is to learn how to make sure the bosses are given credit for new ideas. Whether or not this is widespread in contemporary business and governmental culture, Vico places it at the center of the relationship between the aristocracy and the lower class. He suggests that the noble desire for fame is not simply a side effect of their ownership of a territory and control of resources. The noble desire for fame is actually their primary motivation with regard to the lower class and any practical developments are secondary to the goal of garnishing more praise. This is at the core of his anti-baronial portrayal.

There are two other ways that the nobles epistemologically frame their separation from the plebeians. The first is via the distinction between citizen and foreigner. The plebeians did not have access to the rites of pagan superstition and so they did not have citizenship. As per the inherent structure of poetic wisdom, the nobles did not allow the foreigners to have access to their rituals. Although the plebeians lived in the asylums with the nobles, they were considered foreigners and so were enemies of the state who needed to be constantly controlled (610). The second is that between citizen and *hostis*. The term *hostis* can mean both "guest" and "enemy." Vico cites a variety of ancient texts in which guests are treated as enemies to show how common it was for guests to be treated with suspicion (611). The point of this passage is to illustrate how the class division was inherent to the noble mentality. This put the plebeians into an exceptionally difficult position.

Perhaps, then, the most important passage where Vico draws the distinction between the nobles and the plebeians is this: he writes that "the plebeians always want to change the form of government" while "the nobles always want to keep it as it is" (609). The structure of the poetic mentality makes that inevitable. Since the superiority of the nobles is not based on a substantial difference, they have to keep the plebeians repressed. It is inherent to their rituals and the way they understand their world. The plebeians are in a difficult position because they are shut out of the noble power structure entirely. They have to rebel, but they initially have no way of doing so that the nobility can recognize. Whereas they may have resources and practical ability to assert themselves, they need to enter into the poetic mentality in order to cut into the unjust institutions of the nobles. Vico has an intriguing way to explain how this happened.

Naked Venus

While Masaniello's revolt in 1641 was the most celebrated revolution during the Spanish period in Naples, a significant event initiated an earlier uprising in 1585. The council of Naples had allowed the export of an unusually large quantity of grain to their colonial rulers in Spain. They then authorized an increase in the price of bread at home. Rosario Villari notes that this was not that unusual in itself. Nonetheless, at that time inflation was causing a growing separation between the price of goods and wages earned.[13] This led to a general uprising and the Neapolitan nobility had to flee to their castles for protection. The most notable moment was the lynching of Giovan Vincenzo Starace. He was the people's representative on the city council but was generally disliked because of his loyalty to the upper class.[14] The details of his execution are helpful for understanding the rise of the plebeians in the *New Science*.

Villari argues that the mob did not kill Starace in a random and disorganized manner. Instead, it was a deliberate attempt to imitate and invert the rituals of the nobility. As per tradition, Starace had arrived in a sedan chair at the church of Santa Maria la Nova to meet the captains of the districts. An unexpectedly large crowd was waiting for him. They captured him, removed his hat and carried him on his chair in a procession backwards through the streets. This was calculated. By forcing Starace to perform the opposite of a triumphal march, the plebeians communicated through their own inverted ritual that they were striking out against upper class authority. Taking off his hat put him in the position of the lower classes while elevating the mob. Villari writes, "To stand bare-headed before certain persons implied, beyond all possibility of misinterpretation, recognition of the superiority of the class to which they belong."[15] The act did not simply humiliate Starace as an individual. The peasant appropriation of the traditional rituals signaled a general rejection of noble authority.

After Starace was killed, they mutilated his body and dragged it through the streets. The path went through the working-class districts to build popular support and finished at the viceroy's house. There were rumors that the plebeians would go so far as to imitate Christian symbolism by engaging in cannibalism. The peasants sacked Starace's house, but, understanding the significance of noble symbols of authority, they did not simply steal his furniture for material gain but distributed it to monasteries.[16] This signaled that the plebeians recognized that their goal was discrediting the rituals of the nobility rather than gathering wealth. Certainly, the revolt included looting. Nonetheless, the symbolic act of distributing Starace's furniture suggested an inversion of noble rituals. Whereas the nobility use their possessions to maintain their power, now the plebeians distribute their possessions to take away their power. This plebeian ritual imitates noble authority in a way that turns control over to them.

Villari claims that by imitating and inverting the aristocratic rituals, the plebeians were able to communicate their intentions in a way everyone understood. The nobles recognized that the rebellion was not about the price of grain but that the plebeians were signaling an attempt to overturn the social order and establish their own authority. Villari writes, "Contemporaries were not blind to the meaning of these gestures. More than in the killing of the representative, they saw in them the precise implications of the rebellion, namely, the loss of respect and reverence for social superiors, a cause for fear and anguish among the rich."[17] The mass of plebeians, recognizing the inverted noble rituals, joined together as a class to engage in the revolution. The rebels did not know all the rituals of the nobility and so they could not mock all of them. They focused on the rituals they had witnessed. Specifically,

Villari claims, they used the rituals of punishment. He writes, "On what occasions had the people learned to understand the meaning of this ritual? The most basic experience—aside from certain elements of very ancient origin—without doubt came from the procedures for administering capital punishment, procedures which varied according to the social position of the condemned."[18] As Vico emphasizes, the nobles controlled the right of life and death over their subjects. The plebeians had often witnessed the rites by which their members were executed. This put them in a special position to imitate them when they executed Starace. They used their own experiences to invent their own version of the ritual. This served as both a rallying call for the plebeians and a warning that the nobility could understand.

By mocking the noble rituals, the plebeians also asserted that they did not depend on tradition. This is, perhaps, part of what terrified the nobility so much. The poetic character Mars prioritizes the defense of tradition over all else. The barons connect the protection of their privilege to the survival of civilization. They do not want to face the possibility that the practical mentality of the plebeians could allow them to maintain a society without them. The plebeians do not need the social pressure of secret laws to develop their sense of virtue. As they get on with the practical work of running the estates of the barons, they can build social and political relationships without depending on ritualistic displays of power. By inverting the rituals, the plebeians force the nobles to recognize that they can function without the trappings of poetic wisdom. This inspired a strong response from the nobility, who were able to put down the rebellion. Villari discusses where this event appears in the writings of seventeenth-century Naples.[19] Given his knowledge of history, Vico would have known about it, although I do not believe he refers to it. I raise this incident because it serves as a vivid illustration of an important topic in Vico's science: the plebeian invention of their own religion, which is an imitation of the noble religion. Regardless of whether Vico's depiction of the naked poetic characters was directly inspired by the execution of Starace, it gives a vivid image that illuminates Vico's account.

The challenge for the plebeians in the class struggle is based primarily on an epistemological separation rather than a lack of resources. Poetic wisdom compels the nobles to keep the plebeians ignorant and to deny them legal recognition. For the plebeians to make any progress, they need to find a way communicate in a language they do not fully grasp. Vico's science holds that when people are ignorant, they imitate the unknown using what they can understand (211). While the plebeians cannot understand the noble rituals fully, they can learn to imitate what they see of them. In the uprising against Starace, this meant inverting the noble procession in the opposite direction and then recreating the rituals of execution, since those were the rituals they had witnessed. For the plebeians in the asylums, it meant imitating the noble rituals to create naked versions of the poetic characters. The *New Science* includes references to naked Mars, Mercury, and Vulcan as well as many other mythical figures (560, 579, 589, 604). The plebeian rituals did not have the full meaning of the noble ones, but they were physical imitations of the gestures of the rituals that the nobles could not hide. The plebeian poetic characters had the same names as the noble paradigms because of the poverty of poetic language. Rather than invent their own names for gods, they used the names that were in circulation (581).

One could say that the ceremonies of the plebeian gods were naked because they involved the raw physical performance of the paradigm without the trappings of meaning. This is not what Vico emphasizes, however. He stresses that the plebeian characters were naked as a way of signifying that the nobility considered them to have less dignity. Since they were created by animals rather than humans, the nobles did not think of them as actual demonstrations of piety to the gods. They lacked the compulsion to self-discipline. As a result, the nobles thought of them as naked because they lacked noble dignity and actually encouraged licentious behavior.

These plebeian rituals were not initially acts of rebellion. The *famuli* were in such a subservient position that they could not have conceived of themselves as seizing power. They regarded the naked poetic characters as private rituals rather than demonstrations of authority. The plebeians used "private or minor auspices" (568). The plebeian gods were a way of organizing their private world around the model provided by the nobility. This gave them certain practical benefits but no political power.

The ridicule that the nobles unleash on the plebeians becomes a major interpretative point for Vico. He claims that the nobles actively mocked the false plebeian religion for its inability to encourage pious behavior. This affords him another reason to explain why many myths tell degenerate stories of the Greek and Roman gods. The stories that have been preserved are not the original noble paradigms but the noble mockeries of the plebeian religion. For example, he claims the famous story of Vulcan rigging his bed with a net to catch his wife Venus cheating on him with Mars is an example of the nobles distorting the plebeian religion to illustrate that it did not properly civilize the passions (579). While this hermeneutic approach is highly problematic, it represents another way in which Vico's attitude toward the nobles deteriorated. In the 1725 edition, he attributed the licentious images to the slackening of the heroic morality. Now he attributes them to the animosity that the nobility had for the plebeians. Rather than lamenting the erosion of the heroic age, he blames the immoral tales on the noble compulsion to abuse the lower classes.

The invention of the plebeian religion raises a question in political philosophy that is more engaging than this hermeneutic point. If the noble mentality is so directed against recognizing the value of the plebeians, why would the naked poetic characters ever open up lines of communication between the two classes? If the nobles ridiculed the pagan religion, how could a common ground open?

Vico speaks to this point in his interpretation of the imaginative universal Venus. The *New Science* does not generally devote much space to the naked poetic characters, but Vico discusses the noble and naked Venuses at some length. On one level, this is because naked Venus is the first poetic character of the *famuli* and so calls for some explanation. On another level, there are many tales of a licentious Venus. This affords Vico the opportunity to use his hermeneutic principle to explain how these stories are the product of the noble abuse of the lower class. There is also a philosophical reason why the naked Venus warrants so much attention. The rituals of the noble imaginative universal are centered on demonstrating their superiority to the *famuli*. Whereas the rituals of Apollo also exhibited noble superiority, the noble Venus is created with the *famuli* living in the asylums. It was inspired by the increased pressure on the nobility created by living in close proximity to the *famuli*. In a sense, Venus was the poetic character that symbolized the importance of not intermingling with the lower class. The noble Venus thus reinforces the class separation established by earlier rituals. The invention of the naked Venus affords Vico an opportunity to speculate on how the communication gap closed.

The noble Venus represented the rituals of beauty but only civil beauty. Vico grounds this claim on the difference between discursive thought and poetic wisdom. He specifies that Venus could not represent natural beauty because that can only be recognized by "those men of perception and comprehension who know how to discern the parts and grasp their harmony in the body as a whole" (565). To see natural beauty, therefore, requires the reflective ability to understand the relationship between parts and wholes. Poetic wisdom cannot grasp this distinction and so only recognizes entire paradigms. As a result, poetic thinkers cannot recognize natural aesthetic beauty because they cannot recognize a harmonious relationship between distinct elements. Further, the poets cannot recognize the beauty of virtue because it "is understood only by philosophers" (565). This emphasizes that the theological poets do not have a rational or human idea of moral character or obligation. They only have the harsh paradigms of self-discipline by which to measure each other. The only type of beauty left for the noble Venus is civil beauty, which is the beauty that comes with loyalty to the pagan religion and its laws and rituals.

The key difference between Venus and Apollo is that the second comers are now present in the asylums. He writes, "The idea of civil beauty must have been engendered in the minds of the theological poets when they saw that the impious creatures who had taken refuge in their lands were men in aspect but brute beasts in their habits" (566). The fact that the *famuli* were expected to give praise to the poets worked to maintain the class separation. Venus, however, was imagined to deal with a new and specific concern. While the need to keep the classes separate connects Venus to religion and burial, its main impetus derives from the principle of marriage. The paradigm of Jove demanded that couples mate for life, and Apollo compelled the poets to maintain a strict family lineage. Maintaining monogamy becomes more difficult with the *famuli* living among them. While Vico does not say this explicitly, his account suggests that the proximity of the lower class meant that there was an increased chance of lust or arousal. It would have been unthinkable for a noble to marry one of the animals living in the asylums. Nonetheless, a member of the *famuli* could tempt the sexual interest of a noble. Venus represents stronger rituals of sexual restraint to prevent such behavior. Venus is thus referred to as the "patron goddess of solemn marriage" (512). Whereas the earlier imaginative universals commanded that sex occur only between married partners, Venus specifies that they both be nobles. As part of his analysis, he makes the point that in the rare case where a noble and plebeian would produce an offspring, the child would have been considered a "natural monster" (566). By extension, I take Venus to include any of the rituals that would bar the *famuli* from enjoying the benefits of either pagan religion or legal citizenship.

The paradigm of Venus is consistent with the idea that the initial civil worth of the nobility was based on their ownership of rituals and judicial privilege rather than their material wealth. When the nobles would exclude the *famuli* in some demonstrable way, it would not be by withholding resources. Instead, they would exclude them from the rites of the nobility like marriage. One can recognize this aristocratic tendency in modern and contemporary contexts. While wealth might be a necessary condition to enter into the upper class, even in today's world it is not sufficient. Boards or clubs could block entry to rich individuals who desire to rise in status. They can withhold from them the ceremony that would allow them entry. In Vico's Naples, it was possible for non-nobles to raise enough money to buy a fief. This may get them judicial privileges on the fief but it did not automatically grant them access to the political authority of the baronial class. Inherent to the noble worldview is the idea that people can have a place in the upper class only if they display the self-discipline that nobility entails. I suggest Vico's depiction of the noble Venus is an attempt to explain how self-discipline becomes more important for attaining aristocratic privilege than wealth. In this way, the noble Venus becomes the embodiment of the exclusion of the *famuli* from noble authority.

In response to this exclusion, the *famuli* invent the naked Venus as a way to formalize private relationships in their households. He discusses a variety of differences between the two Venuses. For example, eagles symbolized the noble Venus; the plebeian one was symbolized by doves (568). His focal point, however, is a claim of Horace and Livy that the plebeians "practiced marriages like those of wild animals" (567). This could be interpreted to say that the nobles could marry the plebeians. He assures the reader that this could not have been possible. He argues that the term *more ferarum* is a general slur against all the lower class. So the phrase *agitabant connubia more ferarum* indicates that the plebeians conducted private marriages among themselves rather than marriages with the nobility.

Vico does not directly explain why the plebeians started conducting their own weddings, but some reasons are implied. First, marriage is a principle of civilization. As the plebeians worked to create their own subculture amid the commands of noble poetic authority, they would model the principles that were the basis of noble society. Second, it is practically useful to have marriages, since they can allow families to recognize offspring. The plebeians might not show the reverence for lineage that the nobles did when they performed the rituals of Apollo. Nevertheless, they would probably recognize the value of knowing whose child belongs to whom. This would be the value of creating private marriage ceremonies based on what they could see of noble practices.

The nobles, of course, would not be able to understand any of this. For them, marriage is a foundational component of the civil world. They marry out of superstitious obedience to the gods and to demonstrate their self-discipline to fellow nobles. Since the plebeians did not follow the paradigm of noble Venus exactly, they would not recognize the rituals of naked Venus as legitimate. They continued to regard the plebeians as a mass of animals distinguished by their feudal lords and not their own families. Vico writes, "with reference to this uncertainty [about identifying the father of a child] the plebeians were said to have intercourse with their mothers and daughters as beasts do" (567). This is a prime example of the way in which the poetic wisdom of the nobles prevents them from comprehending what the plebeians were doing or even recognizing them as people. Noble religion dictates that the literal law be performed exactly for a ritual to count. Since the naked Venus did not conform to the exact ritual, it did not count at all. Nonetheless, the plebeians had developed their own version of Venus.

The two Venuses represent both the commonality and the separation of the two classes. Because the naked Venus is an imitation of the noble one, there is a similarity that could open up the possibility of real agreements between the two classes. Unfortunately, the noble Venus prevents the heroes from acknowledging that similarity. This reinforces the class divide. How could the creation of the plebeian Venus ever lead to any sort of legal agreements between the two classes? How could it lay a foundation that could ultimately lead to the more sophisticated agreement of bonitary ownership which gave individual plebeians the lasting right to work the fields in exchange for giving part of the harvest to the noble lord (597)? Eventually the aristocrats recognized the rituals of the plebeian Venus enough to recognize the ability of children to inherit bonitary ownership from their fathers (598). How could such sophisticated agreements ever be possible given that the self-discipline of the nobility would never allow for such an agreement?

Vico gives a remarkably inventive answer to this question at the end of the second section of the "Poetic Economy." After he introduces the plebeian Venus, he offers a long paragraph about different types of binding and non-binding agreements (569). This passage initially seems incongruous because he does not make clear the connection between this topic and the plebeian marriages. When one recognizes that Vico is trying to explain the different ways the two classes make agreements, the passage becomes quite important.

The solemn marriages of the noble Venus are public. As with all noble rituals, their authority depends on their proper public performance and the participation of the other aristocrats to verify that all the relevant superstitions are followed properly. Noble weddings depend on the recognition of others within the bounds of religious and legal rules. Private plebeian marriages did not have such public validation. There was little or no social pressure from the other plebeians on the couple to follow the proper marriage rituals. Moreover, there were no laws that bound the couple to stay in the marriage. The only thing holding a plebeian marriage together was the mutual trust of the couple making the agreement. The plebeian Venus taught them how to form agreements without needing the external support and guarantees provided by public recognition and pressure.

This leads Vico to posit another reason why the plebeian Venus was naked. He writes, "For that [nakedness] was later taken as an incentive to lust which in truth had been invented to signify the natural modesty or the punctuality of good faith with which natural obligations were fulfilled among the plebeians" (569). He corrects those interpreters who assumed that the plebeian Venus was naked because they could not control their passions. The idea that the plebeian Venus encouraged indiscretion was a corruption stemming from noble mockery. He praises the plebeians because they learned to demonstrate a sense of common decency and marital fidelity without the need for strict rituals of beautification. Their marriages were based on simple obligations that encouraged them to stay loyal on the basis of a mutual agreement without the guarantees provided by public recognition. This is substantial praise for the sensibility of the plebeians because it praises their ability to build authentic trust. At the same time, it implies criticism of the nobles, who need to rely on the social infrastructure of ritual because they have not learned how to treat each other with decency outside of it. It suggests a picture in which the nobles live trapped within the obligations of custom and tradition while the plebeians are free to develop human relationships.

Vico then enters into the details of feudal law to show that the plebeian marriages led to other types of agreements. He writes, "Hence to Venus were attributed the Graces, likewise nude; and among the Latins *caussa* and *gratia* meant the same thing, so that the Graces must have signified to the poets the *pacta nuda*, or simple agreements which only involve natural obligation" (569). The plebeians learned to make more agreements even if they had no contractual guarantees or, as Vico calls them, stipulations. They could make other agreements between themselves simply on the basis of trust. Their natural sensibility led them to recognize the practical benefits of such agreements and so they entered into them despite the possibility they could occasionally be betrayed.

This is important because it meant that the plebeians would be naturally willing to enter into agreements with the nobles even if there were no contractual or legal assurances. The self-discipline of poetic wisdom would prevent the nobles from entering into a legally binding agreement with the plebeians. They could, however, enter into one-sided agreements in which they would have all the control since they had all of the power. The plebeians, having no options, could at least get the nobles to agree to some lasting agreements even if they knew there was nothing binding the nobility to them. The plebeians wanted recognition from the nobility that they had the right to farm certain tracts of land. This would not have been binding on the nobles but at least it would clarify among the plebeians who had the right to work what farms. This would reduce disputes among the lower class even if the upper class did not recognize the promises.

This lays important groundwork in the *New Science* for explaining the later development of bonitary ownership. In terms of modern feudal society, it explains how the peasants got themselves into a position of living under the judicial authority of the barons with few assurances of protection. As the central government of Naples gained more authority, the peasants were afforded more opportunities to appeal unjust treatment and there was more oversight over abusive lords. Overall, however, the feudal agreements were heavily one-sided in favor of the baron. Vico's explanation for this is epistemological. The noble mentality with its emphasis on self-discipline prevented the nobles from recognizing more beneficial agreements. The practical mentality of the vassals did allow them to see how contracts could help their situation, but they had little opportunity to formalize them given their subservient position. This epistemological gap, reinforced by the disparity of resources, kept the vassals on the fiefs with few rights.

In the 1730 edition, Vico's account of natural contracts ends here (NS30 216). In the 1744 edition, he expanded this discussion by adding an entire section entitled "Corollaries concerning Contracts Sealed by Simple Consent." When one recognizes the importance the science places on agreements that do not have legal guarantees, it makes sense that Vico would want to expand his account. This addition is still quite technical, but it affords Vico the opportunity to underline how unjust the noble laws were and to introduce the idea that philosophical justice had its origin in the natural agreements of the plebeians.

The addition starts by presenting a fundamental principle: "They [the nobles] were extremely crude and therefore suspicious, for crudeness is born of ignorance and it is a property of human nature that he who does not know is ever doubtful" (570). This seems reasonable. To build a relationship of trust, one would have to base it on some knowledge or experience that would indicate that another person could be relied upon to act as they said they would. No one would enter into a contract of "simple consent" with someone they did not know. If someone had not ever had the opportunity to form such relationships with anyone, that person would never enter into such a contract. Since the first nobles lived in separate fiefs, they would have never had an opportunity to develop this trust. This explains why they would not form together into a monarchy. Vico writes, "Partnerships were unknown, by that cyclopean custom whereby each family father cared only for his own affairs and did not trouble himself with those of others" (576). This rejects the possibility that the nobles could have formed a unified government based on social contract theory. It also denies the possibility of founding a civil society based on enlightened self-interest, since there would have been no initial moments of trust on which to build systems of exchange. The important point here is that it would also keep the nobles from entering into contracts of simple consent with the *famuli*.

In accord with their bodily nature, the early nobles would have only agreed to contracts that were based on a physical exchange. He writes, "they [the nobles] made sure of all obligations by a real or fictitious physical transfer" (570). This would mean bartering the physical right to use land with the physical produce from that land (571). I take the phrase "fictious physical transfer" to refer back to the idea of the legal fictions by which the early jurisconsults adjusted facts to fit the letter of the law or, in this case, the agreement. If a vassal was supposed to turn over a certain amount of spelt, for example, but instead gave another type of produce, the noble might agree to call the other produce spelt. The main point is that there would be no guarantees on the part of the noble that any allowances would be made for crop failure or other disasters. Any client who could not pay rent would be subject to eviction from the land. The technical term for this arrangement was *emphyteusis* (573).

By expanding his account of the origin of feudal contracts, Vico opens up an opportunity to emphasize how those agreements were so unjust. He does this by making reference to the Roman jurist Ulpian, who wrote around AD 220.[20] He does not appear in the 1730 edition.[21] Vico claims that Ulpian initiated a "revolutionary change" (578). The right of *emphyteusis* had been considered to be "*de iure heroico romanorum*" or an aspect of heroic Roman law. Ulpian revised this right to bring it in line with the "*ius naturale gentium humanarum*" or "the natural law of the human gentes" (575).[22] Vico assures us that Ulpian's revision did not target the law of foreigners but the heroic age of Roman law. What this change did, quite simply, was make it so that all contracts would happen with legal stipulations or assurances. In other words, all contracts would be made with the understanding that if any party broke an agreement, the other would have legal right to compensation. This meant that contracts based on emphyteusis would no longer be valid and the law would protect equally any citizen who made an agreement rather than just the nobility.

The addition of Ulpian to the 1744 edition suggests a good deal about the practical dimension of the *New Science*. Ulpian represents a model of what the modern lawyer ought to be doing. Ulpian was able to use his position in the Roman government to persuade it to expand the rights of the citizens. He evidently paid with his life in an upheaval of the government, but nonetheless he was able to use his powers of persuasion and philosophical insights to help Rome move closer toward a stable and fair judicial system. I will provide more discussion of this as the class struggle evolves with the invention of Minerva.

Before moving forward, I want to make one more observation about the plebeian religion and the naked poetic characters. I have already discussed how Vico calls the aristocrats the "sons of earth." This draws attention to the connection that ties noble authority to the land to maintain their class status. The plebeians may go out into the fields and do the farming, but they have the opportunity to leave one fief and go to another one.[23] Since the plebeians were not slaves, they had the right to change feudal lords even if it was difficult at times to do this in practice depending on the prevailing economy. So it was really the nobles and not the peasants who had a connection to the land.

Following this point, one might assume that myth and poetic wisdom would be primarily in the hands of the peasants. Romantically, it is the vassals with their simple lives and honest work who seem to have the true pagan religion. The wealthy aristocrats appear as too sophisticated for such superstition. With the discussion of the naked poetic characters, Vico turns this around. The legacy of pagan ritual is in the heroic laws of the aristocrats. It rests in the continued self-discipline of the nobility that refuses to acknowledge the equality and humanity of the plebeians. The practically minded peasants have their own imitation of the noble religion, but it just serves to help them take care of their own material concerns. It is the noble superstition that is problematic for political evolution. They created their religion to instill self-discipline. Once that has been achieved, that tradition of rigorous and closed-minded self-control is no longer needed. The plebeian material and technological sensibility is.

This is a challenging position for Vico. Even in the early modern period, it was recognized that the peasants in the southern Italian countryside were practicing a religion that was quite distant from Roman Catholicism. Indeed, the church actually sent Jesuit missionaries into the territory to convert them from paganism.[24] The traditions that Carlo Levi witnessed when he was exiled to Basilicata in the 1930s had a history that stretched back well before Vico. So when his science suggests that the nobles rather than the vassals were the true pagans, it would have been a difficult point to sell.

Nevertheless, this opens up a new way to frame Vico's description of the noble mockery of the peasant religion. By suggesting that the traditions of the countryside are unsophisticated and backwards, the nobility give themselves a foundation for arguing that the problems in Naples are caused by the peasants. It allows them to reinforce the idea that the nobility is necessary to protect the poor peasants who cannot sustain themselves. Moreover, it allows the nobles to distract attention away from themselves. By claiming that the peasant religion is primitive, they call people to focus on their beliefs rather than to analyze critically the aristocratic traditions of the baronial class. Vico may not have wanted to make this argument explicit because it might shine too bright a light on his claims about the way paganism combined with Catholicism after the fall of the Roman empire. His depiction of the naked plebeian gods, however, not only serves as a way to explain the source of rural peasant religions, but also invites the reader to see it in the shadow of the aristocratic religion that is the actual impediment to political reform.

It is important to value peasant traditions and to preserve the folklore it produces. This anthropological point is indisputable. As I have been saying throughout this study, however, I do not see the *New Science* as primarily an attempt to find poetic wisdom in the peasantry. By discussing the naked poetic characters as an offshoot of the noble rituals, Vico frames the peasant religion as a product of noble oppression. One might think that the way to support the peasants is to defend the value of their own religion. There is inherent value in taking this position, but I do not read this as Vico's point. He defends the plebeians by praising their practical resourcefulness and honesty in opposition to the nobility. Taken in this light, the *New Science* is not a call to return to the innocence of myth but a call to support the practical reason of the lower class. Of course, there is a limit to this, and the lower class always presents the danger of a fall into decadence. Nevertheless, their challenge to noble religion is important and needs to be supported in opposition to the rigidity and injustice of noble authority.

Minerva and Solon

Vico's account of class warfare does not present a convenient narrative. After all, the history of ancient Roman law does not provide a simple thread. There are the basic categories of kingdom (which for him was not really a kingdom), republic, and empire. In his view, these broad categories only conceal the circuitous route that the plebeians took to legal equality. This path starts in earnest from the institution of the Twelve Tables around 450 BC and culminates with the rule of Constantine from AD 306 to 337 (1001). This legal history contains many steps forward and backward as laws are proposed for the plebeians and nobles rescind them. Further, popular leaders like Julius Caesar arrive who interrupt the flow of progress by unjustly manipulating the will of the plebeians for personal gain. Vico's presentation of Roman history does not try to explain every particular misstep but tries to show the general structure by which Rome arrived at the human age.

While the rise of Julius Caesar and the ensuing wars were significant, the rise of the plebeians was not primarily military. The class struggle does not culminate in some triumphant revolution. It ends when those running the legal system finally use reason to reform the laws and to administer them in a just way. The clearest summary of the class struggle is found in a chapter entitled "The Guarding of the Laws" at the end of book 4. It restates in more detail the tension between the literal and figurative interpretation of the laws that was presented in the *Study Methods*. It describes how the ancient Roman law was initially kept secret as a part of the noble religion (1000). This changed when the Law of the Twelve Tables was enacted because it made the law public and introduced the importance of equity. This led to a struggle between the plebeians, who tried to expand the number of laws to find just resolution in more cases, and the nobles, who tried to restrict them. Since the nobles still had the power, the strict application of law still dominated. As an example, Vico writes, "it took all Cicero's eloquence to prevent Sextus Aebutius from keeping a farm of Aulus Caecina's because of the omission of a 'd' from the formula" (1001). Centuries later, the Emperor Constantine finally eliminated such antiquated and strict formulas so that "every particular motive of equity prevailed over laws" (1001). This represents the summit of the human age in which the law is not interpreted literally but rather is applied with regard for impartial utility, as recommended in axiom CXII (323). Violence does not lead to the culmination of the human age, because that does not necessarily change people's minds of how law should be enforced. The summit is reached when enough citizens start thinking rationally enough to understand the true function of law.

Vico describes Constantine's legacy by writing, "a point was reached under the monarchy where the emperors did nothing but grant privileges, than which, if proportioned to merit, there is nothing more in harmony with natural equity" (1001). This may seem alarming because it puts a great deal of power in the hands of the monarch/emperor with no mechanism for oversight. I take his specific point here to be that it is better to have an intelligent person interpret the laws fairly than to retain a traditional oligarchy that interprets the law in a literal but oppressive way. I do not see the need to assume that Vico proposes a totalitarian regime as ideal. As described in the *Study Methods*, he thinks of a monarch not as isolated but as informed by an educated class of lawyers who were dedicated to placing the laws into the service of impartial utility. Their administration would balance the need for traditional stability with a philosophical understanding of fairness. From a contemporary perspective, it makes more sense to achieve this in the context of a democratic system. Given Vico's context in which the monarch was seen as the strongest alternative to the nobility, it makes sense that he would have used his science to promote the interests of the king, but I think the spirit of his proposal is promoting the use of sound jurisprudence to balance social stability with justice.

In this final section of the chapter, I will continue examining the two themes I have been developing. From the perspective of the nobles, Minerva and Mercury are extensions of Mars in that they expand the defensive posture of the aristocracy. They involve rituals that consolidate the power of the nobles and demonstrate their authority to the rebellious plebeians. These rituals provide the political stability that allows them to invent the last poetic character, Neptune, and to start wars with each other. These conflicts would always be waged within certain limits since the nobles would never jeopardize their authority over the fiefdoms. From the perspective of the plebeians, it is necessary to continue to develop their own religion. Their decisive step forward will be the development of their own poetic characters based on ideas of equality. These paradigms ultimately allow the plebeians to reform the judicial privileges of the nobility.

Minerva represented the rituals of lords from different fiefdoms joining together to resist the growing attacks of the rebellious plebeians. This is symbolized by Vulcan splitting open the head of Jove, allowing Minerva to appear in full armor. He writes, "By this they meant to signify that the multitude of *famuli* practicing servile arts (which came under the poetic genus of the plebeian Vulcan) broke (in the sense of weaking or diminishing) the rule of Jove" (589). This echoes the way rebellions worked in modern Naples. The barons did have permanent ruling councils, but they only really seemed to work in close tandem when a plebeian rebellion required them to pool their resources. In Vico's science, the invention of Minerva represents the birth of the city state.

Minerva is associated with the owl and the night. Vico assures the reader this is not because Minerva was philosophically wise, since the early heroes could not have been wise in this sense. Instead, her rituals are associated with the secret knowledge of the laws, which was guarded by the nobles. Her association with the night is "to signify that the heroic senates that composed the cities conceived their laws in secret" (590). This alliance of the nobles was possible since all those who heard Jove had sworn that the plebeians were their enemies. While each noble desired isolation, protecting their authority from rebellion was more important.

Vico does not outline the structure of the councils that were organized to defend noble privileges. Instead, he focuses on the point that these councils were strictly aristocratic and were designed not only to exclude the plebeians but also to punish any noble who might break ranks. The nobles recognized the threat that some among them would learn to think philosophically and would try to help the plebeians. He cites a story in which these noble councils hanged king Agis because he introduced a law to wipe out the debts of the people and allow for inheritances to go beyond the ranks of the nobles (592).[25] He discusses the Gracchi and other Roman citizens who suffered similarly for trying to support the rights of the plebeians. Other rebellious nobles would be less enlightened and try to use the rebels to advance their own political agenda. He cites stories from Homer in which Minerva wounds Mars with a stone and conspires against Jove. These represent examples of "the manner of aristocracies, in which the lords by secret counsels overthrow their chiefs when the latter affect tyranny" (596). While the plebeians were certainly a threat, the poetic character Minerva was invented to punish any noble who questioned their own superior nature, in a way similar to the rituals of Diana, who punished nobles for defiling the perennial streams. These stories highlight the cruelty of the heroic age. They also emphasize the way in which poetic wisdom demanded conformity among the elite.

Vico goes into some detail as to how the plebeians combined their numerical superiority with their ability to imitate the noble religion in order to gain concessions. Per the wisdom of divine providence, the nobility tries to appease the plebeians to solidify their power, but this opens the possibility for the plebeians to get more legal recognition. The most important example of this, although it comes later chronologically, is the development of the census of Servius Tullius, which I discussed earlier (619). Vico works through many specific aspects of the evolution of feudal law. Rather than exploring these details, I will conclude my discussion of the gods of the greater gentes by examining the birth of Mercury.

As class tensions grew over the original highly unjust feudal right of emphyteusis, the nobles were forced to develop new ways of communicating with the plebeians that when beyond the natural pacts associated with Venus. Mercury contains the rituals of communicating the laws to the *famuli*. These rituals were a demonstration of noble force to show the plebeians that they still had control of the laws. He writes, "It is he who carries the law to the mutinous *famuli* in his divine rod (a real word for the auspices). The same rod with which, as Vergil tells, he brings back souls from Orcus" (604). This signified the way that the intimidation of Mercury was able to bring the *famuli* back into order. Although he was a noble poetic character, he was portrayed as naked because he communicated messages from the nobles to the lower class. Vico develops a lengthy interpretation of the caduceus to identify various dimensions of the communication between the classes. The auspices and the divine rituals belonged to the nobility, and the plebeians were expected to obey without the hope of political participation. While Venus represented rituals that expressed superiority among the nobility, Mercury is the means by which the nobles menace the plebeians directly.

In the poetic mind of the aristocrats, the poetic character Mars represented an inversion of the relationship between land and religion. Rather than using the rituals to defend the land, the land was considered the shield that would be used to defend the more important religion. The land itself became the basis of the coats of arms with which the nobles identified their families and their religion. Mercury completes this process by using that heraldry to show the plebeians that they own the land. The idea of ownership and property is produced as a response to the unruliness of the plebeians rather than out of material need or utility.

Vico proposes another fanciful etymology to explain his view: the name *Mercury* comes from the verb *mercare*, which means to mark. Hence, the poetic character came from the need of the nobles to identify what was theirs. This later expanded into the terms *merchandise* and *commerce* (483). Specifically, it originated with the exchange of the land and produce of the land, since this was all they could comprehend at that time (606). The point is that what one now considers commerce is actually a derivation of the need to display power. Invisible hand theorists often justify the market as a way of instilling morality on the basis of the idea that exchange is fundamental. Vico's position is that given the epistemological structure of poetic wisdom, they must have first been displays of power inspired by the continued need to express the distinction between noble and plebeian.

I close my reading of the noble poetic characters here because I believe I have reached the farthest distance from the canonical early modern position. The typical view is that commerce was created through acts of bartering to fulfill practical needs. Locke suggests that individuals acquired property when they mixed their bodily labor with something they found in nature. Because they could not let things go to waste, if they had an excess they were obliged to barter.[26] Vico does not deny the possibility that early nobles bartered. Indeed, he never denies that early civilizations took care of material needs. His position, however, centers on the point that the creation of civilization depended on the need for self-discipline rather than satisfying practical necessity. This self-control occurred in the context of a strong class divide. It follows that land would be initially thought of as a symbol of power rather than an object of trade. In Vico's view, the amassing of natural resources through trade would not lead to power. Rather, commerce develops within the context of a pre-established noble authority. This explains why the aristocracy in modern Europe rules on the basis of tradition rather than by effective trade. This also explains why the Neapolitan barons, who do not usually have a good business sense, can still maintain their authority.

This pushes Vico's anti-capitalist position farther. He already holds that the free market does not have the strength to instill moral discipline. His portrayal of Mercury suggests that what appear to be acts of philanthropy may actually be products of an enduring aristocratic tradition that calls on the wealthy to demonstrate their authority. In the heroic age that Vico describes, the heroes use their heraldry to show the plebeians that they still have ownership of the secret laws. In early modern Naples, the barons used their heraldry to maintain their control of their judicial privileges and dominate their fiefs. By extension, in the contemporary world the wealthy continue to name buildings to legitimize their right to decide how communities are developed. Although many philanthropists may make charitable contributions in good faith for the betterment of all, the donations are still based on the idea that the wealthy get to decide which charitable agencies, cultural institutions, sports teams, and university buildings get to be constructed. By putting their name on buildings and agencies, the wealthy remind the lower classes to regard this generosity as a positive demonstration of the willingness of the upper class to care for them and protect them. This obscures the fact that the lower classes do not get substantial input into community decisions.

After one reads the *New Science* in my fashion, this seems like a legacy of feudalism. It is a powerful remnant of noble authority that free market capitalism has not removed and is not sure how to face.

There is a traditional modern justification for the way communities rely on philanthropy. The free market view of morality holds that the rich earn their profits. Through competition, those who most effectively supply the public demand are rewarded with wealth to reinvest in those private and public institutions that will help humanity the most. Andrew Carnegie took this view to its logical conclusion, arguing that economic social Darwinism puts the wisest people in charge and manages resources in a way that is ultimately best for even the poorest. Underneath this argument, there is a deep assumption about the connection between wealth acquisition and self-discipline. While navigating the stock market is important, it is generally thought that business success also depends on a person's ability to restrain their passions and behave appropriately. Wealth comes to those who work the hardest, resist the temptation to waste money, and comport themselves in a professional manner. As a corollary, it is assumed that poverty comes to those who lack moral discipline. When one sheds light on this dimension of the position, one recognizes its moral dimension. The wealthy get to determine what cultural institutions exist because they have superior moral characters. The names that adorn university campuses and concert programs in the United States should not be thought of simply as people with good business sense. Instead, they should be admired for their superior ability to control desire and behave properly in the highest and most important levels of society. Their names should make the rest of us feel glad to have their protection as the vassals enjoyed the protection of their barons.

Many will attack this argument by questioning whether wealth has any real connection to market success. Its moral dimension is harder to contest. Even if many wealthy individuals succeed in business because of familial connections or financial support, it is argued, they still need to display self-discipline to hold onto their money and use their connections wisely. While they may not be self-made, they still have displayed strong character in the face of temptation and so deserve to have their names chiseled into the brickwork of whatever building strikes their fancy. Yet in recent decades, some prominent members of Western aristocracies have shown that one can be a rich philanthropist while wasting colossal amounts of money on a range of licentious indulgences. Looking at the example of the extreme behavior of some Roman emperors, the *New Science* does discuss the way wealthy leaders can indulge in the basest morality of the masses (243, 1407). The larger point is that the

New Science calls into question the practice of wealthy philanthropy by denying the value of aristocratic morality entirely.

Vico's view of poetic wisdom argues that the self-discipline of the nobility is not based on a philosophical understanding of justice and virtue. It is a self-discipline that maintains its elitism for its own sake. The rich are compelled to demonstrate restraint as they navigate the increasingly complex world of proper social behavior as it plays out in board rooms and country clubs. Those behaviors, however, are only empty symbolic gestures designed primarily to make sure the elite are distinguished from the poor. The behaviors do not promote practical utility, particularly in a capitalist environment. Further, the inherent noble assumption about the superiority of the rich prevents them from understanding the concept of justice philosophically. Moreover, the *New Science* suggests that the main motivation of the nobility is not betterment of the community but conforming to aristocratic expectations. In this sense, Vico shares the concern of Rousseau and others that the wealthy only give to demonstrate their worthiness to their class rather than to better the world. He suggests that the wealthy continue to perform the traditions of Mercury to maintain their class position. This has the effect of showing the rest of us the inherent superiority of their class and encouraging us not to question it.

I should emphasize that I am speaking entirely theoretically here. I have not examined enough empirical evidence about the motivations for philanthropy in Western nations well enough to form a case for or against Vico's presentation. I could share personal opinions about some of the great things I have seen philanthropists accomplish and perhaps some questionable things, but I am not sure how useful it would be. I am most interested here in bringing Vico into conversation with his early modern contemporaries. On a theoretical level, the free market position assumes that supply and demand will satisfy most societal wants and desires. For any needs that exist outside of that sphere, the government uses taxation to fulfill them. Philanthropy is merely a luxury added to the more important realms of the public and private sphere. The *New Science* calls this into question in at least two ways. First, it points to the long history of feudalism that dominated Europe for centuries. It suggests that one cannot so easily disconnect demonstrations of philanthropy from the history of oligarchical power that nobles used to retain privileges over their estates. This questions what this giving really represents. Second, it encourages one to consider the extent to which philanthropy actually directs the way nations and communities develop. The wealthy drive many decisions about research, culture, education, religion, health care, and entertainment. Far from being an added luxury, many of the entities that depend on donations of the wealthy to survive are vital institutions. Through donations and grants, the aristocracy has a good deal of control over how individual citizens live their daily lives. Vico calls us to question whether this is too much influence and to question the effectiveness of those mechanisms designed to limit the power the wealthy has over these institutions.

In the traditional capitalist view, taxation is discouraged because it takes resources away from the free market and gives it to the central government. When one frames the issue of taxation in a feudal context, the problem appears quite different. In Naples, the central government was seen as the institution that could counter the power of the aristocracy. Obviously, in other feudal societies like eighteenth-century France, a strong central government only served to aid the nobility. The intellectuals of Naples hoped the king could cut into the feudal privilege of the nobility. Specifically, they hoped that a centralized police and court system could limit the judicial privileges that the nobles had over their fiefs. They saw the central government as a place the vassals could go to resist the oppression of a noble. As gentrification continues to grow in the West and with the growth of private security firms, one wonders if the central government should be seen more as a way of checking the power of the aristocracy rather than a way of impeding the function of the free market.

In this context, Vico's practical solution comes into focus. If he is correct and the free market cannot give people a voice in practical decision making, then perhaps the courts can. If the legal class can hold onto the importance of a philosophical sense of justice then perhaps it can oversee a centralized legal system that can treat people fairly while maintaining internal stability. I will discuss this more in the conclusion. I will conclude this chapter by addressing one other addition he made to the 1744 *New Science* as he was considering the practical dimension of his work. I have already discussed the way in which he added Ulpian as a plebeian model for someone who helps revise the judicial system to move it toward equity. He makes another addition to the 1744 *New Science* that expands this point.

In the section on "Poetic Logic," there is a chapter entitled "Corollaries concerning Speech by Poetic Characters among the First Nations" (412). In the 1730 edition, this passage connected his theory of imaginative universals to ancient Roman law. It reminded the reader that while his account of poetic logic emphasized ancient myths, this was done in service to his interpretation of Roman law. He connected the laws of social classes to Romulus and the census to Servus Tullius. These passages remain in the later edition (417, 420). Nevertheless, he greatly revises and expands his discussion of Solon and Aesop.[27] They become plebeian poetic characters who contain the seeds of later philosophical insight. They become paradigms invented by the plebeians to serve the interests of justice rather than to imitate the model of the nobility. In the 1744 edition, the separation of two religions becomes a vital movement in the development of the human age.

In the 1730 edition, Vico presents a brief comparison of Lycurgus of Sparta, who may have lived around 800 BC, and Solon of Athens, who may have lived around 600 BC. His brief account shows how their legal arguments actually demonstrate the prevailing power of the aristocrats in the city states. Lycurgus is thought to have inspired Sparta to a communal militarism, and Solon to have encouraged Athens to democracy. Vico claims that while this may have been the case, the fact that the laws did not substantially change until much later illustrates that these figures were aberrations and that aristocratic rule continued for some time. This conforms with the other corollaries that tie poetic wisdom to aristocratic rule.

In the 1744 edition, Lycurgus drops out and the vulgar wisdom of Solon is celebrated. Vico writes, "Solon must have been a sage of vulgar wisdom, party leader of the plebs in the first times of the aristocratic commonwealth at Athens" (414). He asserts that Solon must have been a poetic character because the plebeians attach a range of political reforms to his image that go far beyond what one man could have done. This plebeian poetic character becomes the core of "all the institutions and laws that shape a democratic commonwealth" (416). Solon was a universal model for the plebeian jurist who wants to push reforms that will take judicial power away from the aristocrats.

The basic message of Solon was straightforward. The character was formulated at a time when the aristocrats thought of the plebeians as "men without gods and hence without auspices." They gave them "only the uses of natural liberty." Solon rejected this inequality. Vico writes, "Solon, however, had admonished the plebeians to reflect upon themselves and to realize that they were of like human nature with the nobles and should therefore be made equal with them in civil rights" (414). The plebeian poetic character also appeared in Rome although the particular name is not identified. Through this plebeian imaginative universal, the Romans realized that Jove was equal to all rather than just the nobility. Through this poetic character, the Roman plebeians came to realize that "*Iupiter omnibus aequus.*" As a result, "By this reflection the

Roman plebeians began to achieve equality with the patricians in civil liberty, until they entirely changed the Roman commonwealth from an aristocratic to a popular form" (415). The insights of the poetic character Solon in its Greek and Roman manifestations were instrumental for the plebeians in their work of dismantling aristocratic rule.

Vico speculates that Solon's call to the plebeians to recognize their equality is the reason why the phrase "know thyself" is attributed to him (416). Ordinarily, when a philosophical insight is connected to a poetic character, Vico writes this off as an example of the conceit of scholars. He does not emphasize that here. Instead, he talks about how the meaning of the phrase evolves from the original desire for equality to its metaphysical level. He writes, "Later the learned preferred to regard it as having been intended for what in fact it is, a great counsel respecting metaphysical and moral things" (416). This leaves open a fairly direct line from the poetic character Solon's original political insight about Jove to a much broader understanding of the value of metaphysical truth. I read this as suggesting that the practical wisdom of the plebeians represents the beginning of the road to philosophy rather than the fear inspired by Jove's thunder.

The passage on Aesop in the 1730 edition is just one brief line claiming that he wrote the *Fables* (NS30 159). The 1744 edition expands this dramatically. He identifies Aesop directly as a "poetic character of the *socii* or *famuli* of the heroes" (425). He was considered a slave, since he represented the *famuli*, and ugly because he did not participate in the civil beauty of the noble Venus. Nevertheless, Vico writes, "Such counsels, then, dictated by natural reason as useful to free civil life, must have been sentiments cherished by the plebs of the heroic cities" (426). Just as the law of equality was attributed to Solon, human morality was attributed to Aesop. This too was a form of the conceit of scholars but in this case the moral insights of Aesop did ultimately contribute to a philosophical understanding of morality.

The most intriguing comment Vico makes about Aesop comes at the beginning of the passage. He uses this opportunity to show the weakness of noble poetic wisdom. Aesop's morality, like all poetic wisdom, was taught on the basis of comparing one paradigm to another. Vico implies that Aesop's comparisons, which come long after the birth of poetic wisdom, are what starts the movement toward philosophy. The original poets had to use similarities to express themselves. Vico writes, "the order of human ideas is to observe the similarities of things first to express oneself and later for purposes of proof." It is when talking about the plebeian poetic character that he explains how reason ascends out of poetic wisdom. He continues, "Proof, in turn, is first by example, for which a single likeness suffices, and finally by induction, for which more are required" (424). The journey that starts from Aesop leads to Socrates and Aristotle as they develop the syllogism that allows the mind to connect particulars to philosophical universals.

Aesop himself still had to use metaphorical comparisons to persuade the plebeians to develop their moral character. Vico does not make this leap, but it seems as if he is attributing to Aesop the role Gravina attributed to Homer. The difference is that the heroic poetry of Homer instilled a heroic morality into the minds of the nobles. This had no future use for philosophical morality. Aesop, who spoke to the practical wisdom of the plebeians, instilled moral messages that did have useful value for future philosophical investigation. Read this way, the message is that the poetic wisdom of the nobles, which uses its paradigms to incorporate class into its structure, does not have value in the human age. The poetic wisdom of the plebeians is based not on class and exclusivity but on practical wisdom and natural pacts and associations. Such insights need to evolve in order to reveal their philosophical merit. Nonetheless, it is the plebeian natural mentality with its direct access to the principles of civilization through natural law that serve as the basis for philosophy.

It is a mystery to me why Vico inserted Ulpian, Solon, and Aesop into the text where he did. If he had put these points more strongly in the axioms or the conclusion, maybe the practical message of his masterwork would have been clearer. Of course, I also cannot say if this is the meaning Vico intended in any case. Nonetheless, by taking the "getting things right" approach and taking seriously the political situation in early modern Naples, one can see why Vico would have wanted to resist the nobility. Given the growth of the legal class, one could see why he would want to present Ulpian, Solon, and Aesop to law students as models for human philosophical morality. The fact that they were put in the text, I hold, completes my reading of the *New Science* as a work about the epistemology and politics of class consciousness. Ultimately, the work is still primarily a work about the metaphysics of history. It is a metaphysics that is not ruled by fate or chance. It is a metaphysics ruled by strong humans making choices to move forward in accordance with the advice of divine providence. Given where civilization was in early modern Naples and where it perhaps still is today, Ulpian, Solon, and Aesop give us models to help us continually strive for the sort of just government that humans are capable of in the human age.

8

Is Vico Right?

Axiom XL is one of those curious passages that might cause a reader to doubt the sincerity of the *New Science*. It reads, "Witches, who are full of frightful superstitions, are also exceedingly savage and cruel. Indeed, if it is necessary for the solemnizing of their witchcraft, they do not shrink from killing and dismembering tender innocent children" (190). As Battistini reports, he made a similar if less colorful claim in the 1725 *New Science* (SN25 196). If one hopes to find in the *New Science* a positive view of the power of myth and the imagination, it is hard to know what to do with this passage. It is moments like this, however, that inspired me to search for a different way of thinking about the value that Vico places on the imagination. I have no reason to think that Vico's claim bears any historical merit. Nonetheless, my reading provides an explanation of what he is trying to illustrate.

As an Enlightenment thinker, Vico was concerned about the power of superstition. His primary worry, however, was not that superstition was false, because pagan religion obviously did not portray metaphysical or scientific reality. His concern was that the hold of superstition was so strong that the aristocracy would never let it go. Poetic wisdom was produced by a need to civilize the wild passions of the early humans and also to start humanity on the path to rational thought. In Vico's view, it succeeded because it combined these two needs. As an epistemological structure, it represents the smallest intellectual leap from pure passion to imaginative conceptualization. This structure was constrained by the requirements for physical imitation, the poverty of poetic speech, over-inclusion, and the inability to distinguish essence from accident. These very limitations, however, compelled the strongest giants, the "sons of earth," to act with rigid self-discipline and tame their passions. In Vico's view, poetic wisdom played an essential and beneficial role in human development. Indeed, he holds it is impossible to have a civilization that does not start with religion. The problem is that this form of thought has three crucial downsides that become exacerbated as civilization evolves.

First, poetic wisdom relies on a strong distinction between nobles and animals to instill discipline. As humanity develops, this transforms into a class distinction that becomes chiseled into the aristocratic worldview. Even as the original sources of the imaginative universals fade, the barons continue to organize their behavior around the need to maintain the separation between classes. Second, poetic wisdom was never closely tied to fulfilling material human needs. Since its purpose was instilling discipline in the nobility, it emphasized rituals that demonstrated power and only tangentially fulfilled a desire for physical comfort. The majority of the technological advancements came from the practically minded *famuli* and plebeians rather than the aristocrats. As humanity moves toward more advanced forms of commerce and technology, poetic wisdom becomes an obstacle. Third, poetic wisdom is designed to resist change and adaptation. The imaginative universals were strict paradigms that needed to be reproduced precisely. These evolved into the secret heroic laws but in such a way that they continued to be interpreted literally. The poetic foundation of the heroic mind maintained the connection between self-discipline and a strict obedience to the laws and rituals as they were precisely written. Thus, the heroic mentality is structured to resist the reforms necessary for moving civilization into the human age.

Vico offers axiom XL as an example of the rigidity of poetic wisdom. Dismembering young children is obviously horrifying. For the poetic mind, however, if this is what the pagan religion calls for—"if it is necessary for the solemnizing of their witchcraft"—then the witches will perform such sacrifices. He reinforces this point in the commentary where he writes, "For all this [ritualistic sacrifice] was necessary to tame the sons of the cyclopes and reduce them to the humanity of an Aristides, a Socrates, a Laelius, and a Scipio Africanus" (191). Strict obedience to the secret paradigms and laws of pagan religion was essential for the development of philosophical reasoning and just rule. There comes a point, however, when this stringent discipline to the literal interpretation of the law becomes an severe obstacle to the development of just political institutions. By analyzing the structure of poetic morality, the *New Science* provides help for lawyers and legislatures who are working to pull the nobility away from its rigid adherence to traditional superstition and create a judicial system that will provide philosophical justice and political stability for all.

This study began from Giarrizzo's insight that the *New Science* is much more about early modern Naples than ancient Rome. I have used Christina Mercer's "getting things right" approach to look at Vico's account of the Roman Pantheon through the lens of European feudalism. I have highlighted the fact that those barons had judicial privileges over their fiefs. Their tenacious defense of these rights represented a major obstacle to the development of Charles of Bourbon's kingdom. This goes a long way to explaining why Vico's discussion of poetic wisdom looks the way it does. In this conclusion, I want to move beyond this analysis to speculate about the relevance of the *New Science* for contemporary society. I hope I have shown how the *New Science* provides an alternate paradigm within early modern thought because it is a response to oligarchy rather than monarchy. If this paradigm is going to be something other than a historical oddity, it needs to have contemporary practical value. Throughout this work, I have tried to highlight some key places where Vico's ideas appear relevant. In this conclusion, I want to consider more directly the way that Vico's paradigm may be significant for developing our contemporary ideas of early modern thought and for advancing political philosophy.

To read early modern philosophers profitably, it is important to ask whether the problems they diagnose still exist in the contemporary world. For reading Locke, one should ask whether there is still a need to design a government that protects private property from a monarch. For reading Rousseau, one should ask whether there is a need to propose an idea of general will that mitigates against the impositions that government places on free will. When one reads Vico, the question is whether the self-discipline of neoliberal aristocrats holds onto a strict classist morality that refuses to adapt.

With the development of the free market and commerce, there have been remarkable technological advancements. Nevertheless, one could argue that those developments have been hampered by the need for the aristocracy to maintain a class distinction. As an example, one can point to the climate crisis. For quite some time, science has known that it would become extremely dangerous to pollute the environment in the way to which industrialized nations have become accustomed. This became a major point for the student revolutions of the 1960s. In response, the aristocracy has systematically resisted the development of alternative energy, preferring instead to defend their control over their corporations. They have done this in spite of overwhelming evidence to suggest that this is leading to the ruin of humanity. The wealthy have occasionally conceded on tangential issues such as encouraging the protection of dolphins from tuna fishing. They have strongly resisted, however, any institutional change that could threaten their positions within the aristocracy. Despite the existence of consumers in industrialized nations that would readily purchase alternative energy, the aristocrats have been unwilling to provide it because they prioritize their self-discipline and their class status.

As a related example, it has become clear that one of the prime ways in which the environment could be helped would be by changing to a meatless diet. Despite the fact that there is a growing market for vegan options, restaurants in the post-industrial West have been reluctant to promote them. From a Vichian perspective, this is because consuming meat is a traditional sign of aristocratic authority. The rise of veganism is perceived as a threat coming from the plebeians to that authority. As a result, the aristocrats continue to consume meat and generally avoid those restaurants that cater to vegans. As the vegan movement has evolved, there have been attempts to make a vegan diet a symbol of aristocratic power. This has meant offering vegan options in restaurants that cost the same or even more than meat products. By making vegan food more expensive than meat, it is hoped that it will be valued by the wealthy as a status symbol despite the fact that vegan food is generally much less expensive to prepare. In Western countries, this has the effect of taking vegan cuisine from the hands of the people who most want it. From a free market perspective, none of this makes any sense. The conversion to a vegan diet is being blocked by aristocratic self-discipline despite the obvious benefits to health, the environment and ultimately the economy.

Perhaps the most dramatic example would be that despite a neo-liberal ideology that claims otherwise, it still remains extremely difficult for women and non-whites to advance in class in the West. Although the market and technology could grow much more quickly if everyone had the opportunity to participate in Western business and government, the aristocratic self-disciplinary need to exclude much of the population has largely remained in place. I am obviously oversimplifying here and there are many more factors involved in all of these examples. I am merely trying to show how the *New Science* might highlight the classist dimension of some of these issues.

The current prevailing picture of early modern philosophy coming out of Hobbes, Spinoza, Locke, and Rousseau does not take feudal relationships seriously. Speaking broadly, they are interested in developing a government that can provide the maximum amount of security and protection while placing the minimal amount of restriction on individual liberty. They acknowledge the need to reform radically existing political institutions. In particular, Spinoza dedicates his *Ethics* discussing how superstition can be broken and replaced with a strong sense of personal self-interest in order to sever traditional ways in which people associate themselves with religious and political leaders. As far as I can tell, these authors do not consider seriously the particular relationships between vassal and lord and the way in which those connections might undermine attempts to bring political reform.

In my reading, the primary goal of the *New Science* is about uncovering these feudal relationships. It encourages the reader to wonder to what extent contemporary institutions continue to hold onto these feudal connections. The aristocracy now resides in boardrooms of companies and non-profit institutions of various sizes. They demand obedience and loyalty from the hierarchies of managers and employees underneath them. Wealth is a necessary condition to live among the ranks of these leaders, but it is not sufficient. The true requirement to live among this class is recognition and acceptance by its other members. The social network of aristocrats defends a powerful behavioral code that determines who can enter and who is excluded. As in feudalism, this code demands that the aristocrats show self-discipline by demonstrating their authority to the workers. This means using private jets on the company budget while blocking all attempts for the workers to unionize. As executive salaries continue to grow at an exceptionally decadent rate while worker salaries do not move, it is becoming more and more apparent that the salaries exist to display noble self-discipline rather than to reward hard work. These salaries are the contemporary equivalent of the Apollonian ritual of horseback riding to illustrate the distinction between human and animal.

The institutions of the free market do mitigate against such feudal authority. If a worker can learn a skill that is in demand, then it is up to management to make jobs more attractive. Further, when a manager fires an employee, it is possible for that person to find another job. However, this was also a feature of Italian feudalism. A vassal could leave a fief for another feudal lord. After a plague hit and vassals were in demand, lords had to work to attract them. So these features of a free market economy are not really advancements over feudalism. Further, one could think about the way the aristocracy in contemporary neoliberalism manipulates demand for workers. In the United States, many students go into nursing and computer programming because starting salaries are so high. The problem is that these salaries are high because of employee turnover. Companies save money by dismissing higher-paid and more experienced nurses and programmers and hiring ones fresh from college. Despite the high starting salaries and terminating those employees who have become highly skilled, the boards still make money for their institutions. More significantly, the boards can control who rises in their ranks and who does not. Certainly, there is more class mobility now than there has ever been. This does not mean, however, that executives are no longer using feudal authority to control the lives of the workers beneath them.

One could argue that because early modern philosophy overlooked the prominence of this feudal relationship, the political institutions that rose during the eighteenth and nineteenth centuries did not do enough to remove those relations. There have been strong advances in democratic institutions. For many in Western neoliberal capitalisms, however, democratically elected governments have little direct influence on everyday life. This is because executives still demand company loyalty and obedience from their employees—a dedication that is not reciprocated. Like a feudal baron, an executive shows authority by retaining the power to not be loyal to the employees. The daily life of workers is thus controlled by the directives of the lords, while the workers have little effect on higher level decisions. Regardless of the workers' political parties, their behavior is largely regulated by their bosses.

What's more, in the first two decades of the twenty-first century, certain business executives have risen to such political prominence that they have been able to use their power to defy the social norms of the aristocracy. I think the *New Science* warns us of that danger. During the twentieth century, with the rise of technology and mass collectivization, scholars pointed to the barbarism of reflection as the primary danger foretold by the *New Science*. I suggest throughout this work that the real danger has been falling back into feudalism without ever reaching the human age. If the aristocracy loses its sense of self-discipline before civilization has time to establish a sound and just judicial system, then it will break apart. These decadent executives could be a sign of this. Ancient Rome survived Caligula and Nero long before the human age arrived with Constantine. I think the *New Science* should challenge contemporary readers to consider how far there is to go before civilization arrives in the human age. In my reading of the *New Science*, Western neoliberalism will not come undone because of the barbarism of reflection. It will come undone because poetic wisdom will have lost its strength before the human age could fully arise.

For most of its existence, the *New Science* has been excluded from mainstream ideas about early modern political philosophy. In my reading this is not at all surprising. Since the mainstream has overlooked the question of feudalism, it makes sense that it would not know how to confront a work dedicated to feudalism as a philosophical problem. If feudalism were not a problem for contemporary neoliberalism, then perhaps the *New Science* would not have political relevance. The suggestions I have offered in the opening of the chapter are to suggest that perhaps feudalism is indeed still a major concern. While it is certainly not the only concern, the more I have come to understand the structure of Neapolitan feudalism, the more it seems to resemble the relationships that I see between my associates and their places of work. I have thought for quite some time that many business decisions appear to be much more about demonstrations of power than about sound business strategy. The *New Science* brings this intuition into focus.

Specifically, the discussion of poetic wisdom suggests a powerful connection between the aristocratic worldview and the demands of self-discipline. I am not sure to what extent it might be possible to associate specific poetic characters with contemporary executive behavior. Nevertheless, the presentation of poetic wisdom makes an important argument. It argues that aristocratic self-discipline is based on the class distinction itself rather than practical value. As a result, the need for aristocratic self-discipline can be removed if it can be replaced with better institutions for maintaining social order that effectively improve living conditions. These institutions would distribute justice on the basis of real human equality rather than the class distinction. This is the challenge of the *New Science*.

In the next two sections, I will speak more directly about what Vico offers as a political solution. Rather than relying on the free market, he proposes an enlightened judicial system that will balance the need for political order and philosophical justice. Is this solution worthy of consideration alongside the more prominent ideas of early modern thought?

Vico and Early Modern Thought

The prevailing view to come out of the early modern period is that the market can encourage a sense of enlightened self-interest that can transform selfish desire into a force that betters civilization as a whole. This view is so deep in Western neoliberalism that many do not recognize it. In the United States, the value of self-interest has led to the rampant promotion of self-esteem and personal happiness.[1] This view is so ubiquitous that it is hard to take seriously Vico's call for an enlightened legal class. After all, lawyers are stereotypically portrayed as parasites on the free market rather than making a positive contribution. How can one take Vico's idea seriously?

In the *Study Methods*, he emphasizes that the legal distinction between public and private property needs to be clarified (SM 58, 69). In feudalism, fiefdoms represented an odd midway point between public and private. Since the barons administered the law in their territory, they were essentially running public institutions on private lands. Vico wants to put the law clearly in the hands of the government. This would remove the public dimension of baronial fiefdoms. The castles would become private property that would be subject to the public laws administered by the central government. At the time this was a radical proposition. The barons did not trust the central government to enforce the law. They held that it was beneficial to have an immediate and traditional authority present in a territory to maintain civil order. They did not think that a distant king in Naples could do this.

Vico's advice is that there needs to be a system of lawyers and courts who could resolve private disputes. This would be an improvement over the feudal courts because the lawyers would be more objective than the barons, who would manage the courts to the benefit of their families. At the same time, a network of lawyers could be spread out over the territory to interpret the law in order to provide justice in different cultures and environments. Because the lawyers would be educated and professionally trained, they would have the best chance of finding rational solutions to private disputes. Vico does not give a good deal of substance to his answer, since the *New Science* focused on critiquing the baronial courts instead of proposing a new system. Nevertheless, one can deduce from his principles some ideas about how this would work.

Vico's legal system would be guided by philosophical ideas of justice. It would do so in a way that would provide civility and stability. This means that lawyers would have to work closely with their clients. Lawyers would be charged with effectively explaining to their clients why decisions would be made. Since the laws would no longer be secret, the lawyers could use them to defuse the anger and resentment that clients might feel. The lawyers could also inspire the clients to accept decisions on the basis of solid character and civic responsibility. This would be challenging, since the clients would be disposed to see the dispute from their own perspectives and would be understandably angry when the court ruled differently. Nonetheless, the lawyers could work to build lines of communication that would help preserve the fabric of society. One of the advantages of secret laws is that they could not be disputed by the plebeians. Once the laws are public, this opens the possibility of frustration and resentment. The lawyers, however, could work to minimize the unrest that this would cause.

The lawyers I have spoken to and worked with in the United States (which is not that many) recognize that part of their job is helping clients understand the greater legal system. Particularly in civil law, they understand that their goal is to get the fairest result for their clients. If a contract has not been fulfilled or harm has been done, the objective is generally not to punish the wrongdoer but to get a settlement that provides fair compensation. Beyond that, the lawyer frames both the context of the decision and the law itself for their clients so that they can be satisfied with the settlement. In this way, lawyers, judges, and the court system as a whole resolve quite serious and emotional disputes in a way that allows everyone to return more or less contentedly to their lives. Not only will the dispute itself be handled in a fair and transparent way, the clients will understand how this has happened. Obviously, this would not work in every case, but the courts could make it work often enough to provide stability.

In many ways, the legal system in Europe and the United States already tries to offer what Vico suggests. Unfortunately, it seems to go largely unrecognized. The problem is that so few people have access to the legal system that its influence is not as widespread as he would want. Early modern Naples had a ridiculous number of lawyers per capita, a number that was still growing in Vico's lifetime. In these circumstances, his solution seems practical. In contemporary neoliberal capitalisms, lawyers are not as prevalent, and they are extraordinarily expensive. Despite many lawyers who advocate for lower- and middle-class clients, the court system is largely a tool of the aristocracy. Most citizens only encounter lawyers in rare and dire circumstances. As a result, many are unaware of the pedagogical function of attorneys and, instead, form an image of them based on television portrayals and billboards for personal injury attorneys. Particularly in the United States, this is not helped by an increasing number of incidents coming to light that suggest that issues of race and gender impede the fair prosecution of the law. This keeps many citizens in Western democracies from recognizing the stability that the legal system does provide.

The practical message of the *New Science* is a call to expand the pedagogical function of the legal profession. I do not know exactly what this would look like. It could mean more lawyers, more legal assistance, more on-line access to solutions to legal questions, or even artificial intelligence. The point is that if more people could have access to the law, there would be less resentment in the community toward the state and toward the democratic process. Lawyers and court officials could explain legal rights and procedures in such a way that a broader range of settlements between employers and employees or between sellers and consumers could be resolved amicably. This would help make sure that the exchange of work for resources would be just. This would then provide a foundation for a civilization in which citizens were rewarded fairly for their efforts and appreciated the civil institutions that provide the infrastructure on which the community is built. This would become a strong incentive for moral behavior. As I said from the outset, the key question driving early modern philosophy is the question of how a civilization can inspire virtue in its citizens without relying on religion. Vico suggests that if there was a legal system in place that ensured that citizens would be fairly rewarded for their work, they would do that work and not turn to crime or other unjust methods for getting by.

This vision of a legal system would be well suited to prevent the rise of an oligarchy. The rule of an arbitrary and selfish dictator would be horrible. There is no disputing that. For Vico, however, the real threat is of a return to feudal relationships. I do not mean this literally in the sense that there would be an actual return of fiefdoms in which land was worked and the harvest was given to the landlord as rent. I do suggest, however, that the owners of companies could use their power to make sure that employees were not fully rewarded for their work. More significantly, owners could manipulate the law to serve their own interests just as the barons used their judicial privileges in their fiefdoms. If there were strong communities of lawyers who did not have a special financial connection to the aristocracy, then they could make sure the law was not written and enforced in a way that would benefit the rich at the expense of the poor. This strong legal class would make sure all the citizens knew their rights such that they would not be abused by the aristocracy. In this way, the legal system would create a social infrastructure based on fairness rather than aristocratic authority. To prevent a dictator, one would hope that a civilization would have a strong enough central democratic government to prevent one person from taking the reins in an unfair way. To prevent a return to oligarchy spread across a civilization, it will take a culture dedicated to keeping the law out in the open such that everyone would know their rights and prevent private abuse.

Put in these terms, Vico's legal model appears to have advantages over the more traditional idea of a free market and the promotion of enlightened self-interest. In the traditional view, the government will interfere as little as possible with free market competition and expect the culture of business to instill proper social behavior. Vico's problem is that once a group of people have acquired wealth, they will look to preserve it. This means they will look to take control of the law and gather judicial privileges. While they may claim they want to stop government interference to allow the growth of the free market, what they will really be doing is taking control of judicial authority over their own businesses. This would give owners authoritarian control over their workers. This would not instill civil behavior in the workers. Instead, it would subject them to feudal authority with its reliance on secret laws.

Instead of relying on the free market, Vico's position is that the legal system and its team of lawyers can educate people how to live properly. By informing all the classes of the law and allowing them to participate in its workings, the people will learn their civic responsibility. They will also learn the benefits of civil behavior since that will be important for all court proceedings. After all, Vico does want the lawyers to maintain the pageantry of the courts so that all will recognize their authority. This will have a better chance of promoting civil behavior in everyone than a competitive market that will inevitably produce rich winners and disenfranchised losers. Vico does not write anything to suggest that he is opposed to the development of commerce, as far as I can tell. His point is that a solid legal system run by dedicated and well-educated professionals would do a much better job of instilling morality than the free market.

At this point, I am still quite a long way from making a fully convincing case for Vico. Much more theoretical and empirical evidence would be needed to do this. Further, as Remo Bodei told me at the first Society of Italian Philosophy conference, Vico alone will not resolve all the problems of the contemporary world. Nonetheless, one of the goals of this study has been to put Vico into contemporary conversations about early modern philosophy. I feel like this is a debate between Vico and his colleagues that is worthy of further discussion and would be accessible and relevant to students in the classroom as well as scholars. I hope I have said enough to indicate a starting point for this debate.

In that spirit, I would suggest the fundamental issue between the positions is this. The traditional early modern view prioritizes liberty and wants to limit government restrictions on freedom. When they think about good government, the question is about how much liberty the government allows. In my reading of Vico, the question is justice and equality. He holds that the aristocracy is always a threat to take back judicial authority in some way. This could be by using wealth to control their companies or by using it to control the government itself. The question he thinks should be asked is whether people are being justly rewarded for their work. That is how a government ought to be measured. He never says anything to suggest he would be in favor of an absolute redistribution of wealth. Such a claim would be beside the point. What he wants to prevent is the aristocracy, whether they be lords or executives, from exploiting their people without giving them fair appeal.

Again speaking generally, I would suggest that the United States government in the early twentieth century made a decision to support the rights of workers and consumers. The government took seriously its role of making sure people were not exploited by their bosses. This legal infrastructure was instrumental for allowing a rise of the middle class. It also made the European American male citizens of the United States feel relatively secure that the government would protect them against corporate abuse. This sense of security, however, has masked two things. First, it masked the fact that there were and continue to be great legal injustices done against large populations in the United States. While the European Americans felt good about the way their rights were protected, many of them did not notice how deeply unfair the legal system really was. Second, it masked the fact that the nobility in the United States have been finding ways to take back their judicial authority. There are many examples of this. I will point to banks. After the stock market crash in 1929, banks were regulated so that they would not fail. Further, they were regulated such that they would provide ways for all citizens to manage their money and seek opportunities. In the past few decades, this has changed. Regulations were restructured to define banks more as profit-making entities than as institutions for helping the community. This has contributed to the growth of student loan debt, which has thrown a generation of Americans into indebted servitude. The promotion of the free market has resulted in many Americans losing their rights. This is a complicated issue, but I raise it to show the different paradigms. Many are excited about the rollback of government legislation because it makes business freer. Those business are using that freedom to create more debt so that they can control consumers. In this way, they gain back legal authority over their workers. I think this is the core of the debate between Vico and his contemporaries. I think that it is worth looking more closely at the Neapolitan Enlightenment rather than the Scottish one to see a view of early modern philosophy that prioritizes law over mercantilism.

Vico and Contemporary Italian Thought

Vincenzo Cuoco and others connected Vico's writings to the Risorgimento. In the *Study Methods*, he had made comments about the superiority of Italian philosophy to French philosophy that made him suitable to take the role of the national Italian early modern thinker (SM 39–41).[2] This was part of what gave him a lasting place in Italian philosophical thought. From being a philosopher of history, he became a historical figure within a national tradition.

The investigation of the essence and value of tradition has become a major topic in contemporary Italian and French philosophy. Mass migration and the global economic crisis has problematized the modern idea of a nation-state. In order to develop an idea of justice in this changing environment, philosophers have sought ways of undermining the relationship between historical tradition and national identity. Given the emphasis Vico placed on the ideal eternal history and the tradition of mythical thought, it appears that his writings could be put in the service of a typical defense of tradition. As Timothy Brennan has argued, however, there is another way of reading his metaphysics.[3] Because his method was cross-cultural, it sought to take Europe and European traditions out of the center of the science. His search for a universal pattern of history meant that no one culture had an exclusive understanding of the truth. While perhaps certain nations could pass through the pattern of history more effectively than others, the truth itself was not limited to any one nation. In this sense, Vico prioritized the metaphysical over the tradition. This reading puts Vico into the camp of modern philosophers who tacitly rejected European colonization.

My reading of Vico emphasizes a different way in which the *New Science* speaks to the philosophical problem of tradition. As I have argued, I do not see him as a defender of tradition at all. Despite the fact that poetic wisdom was a product of great human ingenuity, it needs to be superseded by philosophical reasoning. He advocates for the reform of the aristocratic judicial system. At the same time, however, this reform cannot be a complete rejection of history. This is not because traditional institutions need to be defended but because they have served a psychological need to civilize bestial passions. For Vico, human beings are naturally social, but they can only be fully human once their corrupt bestial desires have been subdued. It is important that any sort of political reform understand this psychological purpose.

In my reading, the *New Science* suggests that this psychological function of the imaginative universal would be important for understanding the rise of contemporary nationalist movements. There is a great deal of work being done on this topic, and I do not want to be reductionistic. I think Vico would emphasize that one should not overlook the way in which the fear of one's own bestial passion can drive a person to seek a community that will separate the self from the beasts. That group will institute defensive rituals on the basis of an "us versus them" mentality to help its members feel secure that they are superior and in control of their lives. Such a group would engage in a contemporary recreation of the poetic character of Mars in which the heroes demonstrated their willingness to defend their religion to demonstrate self-discipline. Vico would argue that this aspect of poetic wisdom once served a real human need in the civilizing process. This needs to be understood if it is going to be overcome and replaced by a just system of government. To enter the third age fully, humanity must overcome this dimension of human thought. To do so, however, it cannot deny that it happened. If nothing else, when a lawyer tries to represent a client in civil or criminal court who is a member of such a nationalist organization, the lawyer should use an understanding of poetic wisdom or at least this sort of imaginative paradigm to understand why the client frames the world in terms of the defense of tradition.

In this way, I think that Vico is suggesting that the psychological and social nature of human beings makes the denial of history impossible. The movement to the third age requires that the laws of poetic wisdom be buried. After all, the innovations that led to philosophical reflection came not from the nobility but from the natural pacts of the plebeians. It is the practical wisdom of the plebeians that help to understand the true nature of justice. This means lawyers and philosophers in the third age are called to continue the work of the plebeians in removing the judicial authority of the nobility. This cannot be done by ignoring the history of poetic wisdom.

To help explain my reading, I want to contrast it with the interpretation of Vico that Roberto Esposito presents in his discussion of Italian philosophy, *Living Thought*.[4] His work is important for understanding how Vico values the importance of knowing history. He writes, "Nothing is more deadly, for Vico, than the typically modern idea that we can sever the knot that binds history to its nonhistorical beginning, unraveling it through a process that fully temporalizes life."[5] I think this expresses well Vico's anti-modern position, to the extent that he is anti-modern. Further, Esposito has helped me understand the extent to which Vico portrays history as an intermingling of elements and the ensuing conflict. He emphasizes that while Vico divides history into three ages and into secular and sacred, these elements are not presented as out of touch from each other. Most importantly, he shows how Vico separates but intermingles metaphysical and empirical history to produce his science. This is an important aspect of the brilliance of the *New Science*. The work may be frustrating for those looking for clear demarcation lines between categories. Vico had the intellectual capacity to produce such a work, but he did not because he wanted to make a point about the relationship of theory to the world and the relationship of historical epochs to each other.

My reading of Vico takes a different path from Esposito in the discussion of poetic wisdom. Esposito recognizes the basic features of poetic wisdom, but he rarely addresses Vico's account of the gods of the greater gentes. Esposito grasps the imaginative and mimetic structure of the imaginative universals, but he does not look at the specific roles they play in the construction of civil institutions. As a result, he does not emphasize the role poetic wisdom has in civilizing humanity. Alongside that, he does not address the critique of poetic wisdom as a structure of feudalism.

Esposito uses the split between sacred and secular history to locate Vico's unique position. He rightly points out that Western philosophy has vacillated between subsuming history into the sacred, which was the path of Augustine, and subsuming the sacred into history, which is the general path of modern philosophy.[6] Esposito claims that Vico avoids these two extremes by separating sacred history from secular history. He writes, "Now, the disruptive and even disconcerting character of Vico's theory lies precisely in its protrusion outside both these interpretative schemes. For him, sacred history neither subsumes profane history nor is resolved in it. There remains an unbridgeable gap between the two that simultaneously incites and curbs historical development."[7] The important conclusion that follows from this is that it allows Vico to put the origin of civilization into sacred time rather than secular time. As such, the language of secular time cannot express the origin of humanity. He writes, "the origin itself, on which the entire spectrum of difference depends, is opaque to our gaze, since it is impenetrable to all historically formed knowledges, and, even more so, to the logical/systematic and deductive one that has taken the upper hand in modernity."[8] This allows him to find in Vico the idea that civilization arises out of an indistinct chaos that continues to underlie human institutions.

The problem I have with this is that the gap is not unbridgeable for Vico. As I have discussed, over the course of the later Roman Empire, the Judeo-Christians, who had held onto their tradition since before the flood, mingled with the Romans, who took the secular path through divine and heroic ages. Specifically, I would say that the ascension of Constantine to Emperor and the conversion of the Empire to Christianity is the instant they both merged. Probably not coincidentally, this is also the moment that the Roman Empire fully entered the human age. Regardless of how inaccurate this historical point may be, I would underline that book 5 of the *New Science* is dedicated to showing how the Christian religion takes on the forms of poetic wisdom and feudalism during the middle ages. When one overlooks this point, it becomes impossible to see the *New Science* as a critique of modern Naples. It severs the work from its own historical position and turns it into a work of theory.

The difference between our readings about Vico's view of origin becomes clearer on the topic of the giants. Esposito sets up giants and humans as radical opposites. Humans have been formed by civil society and are intelligible. The giants, living in the wilderness, do not have such form and so are unintelligible. Esposito suggests that Vico has little to say about the giants precisely because they are beyond human comprehension. Since they are outside our understanding, all that Vico can attribute to them is excess. Esposito writes, "The decisive element in this account is the excessiveness that precludes form. Their life is certainly characterized by their body, but by a body that resists any form: it is formless, unformed, deformed."[9] This excess leads Esposito to describe the giants in the forest as joined into an undifferentiated collective. He connects the lack of identifiable families in the forest as a sign of this lack of identity and separation. He writes, "Nothing conveys the world of the forest better than 'confusion.' It confuses—fuses together—the elements that compose it, thus depriving them of their proper differential status."[10] He fits this into his philosophical schema by claiming that the heroic families were a *civitas* or *societas*. The giants, because of the "confusion of human seeds," engaged in a basic form of *communitas*. He writes, "It is here—in this 'disbelonging' of each with respect to the all, in this lack of distinction that causes bodies to be confused with one another and humors to be mixed—that life has its beginnings, expressing its expansive potency to the maximum."[11] In this way, Esposito links the giants to the philosophical importance of *communitas* as an idea of human association that is not based on tradition but springs organically out of the relationship between individuals. I have a good deal of sympathy for Esposito's vision of *communitas* but, again, I think his reading overshadows another dimension of Vico's thought.

Vico does indicate that there are differences between the giants in the forest. The "sons of earth" have much more powerful emotions.

This gives them the strength to imagine the poetic characters that then instill an intense self-discipline into them. It allows them to create the myths that become the cornerstones of noble authority. The other giants do not have such powerful emotions, and they are chased into the asylums of the poets. The self-discipline imposed by poetic wisdom on the nobles creates a culture that civilizes the *famuli* by not giving them the opportunity to learn how to think. The road for the lower classes is long and difficult because they first have to learn how to imitate poetic wisdom and then develop the ingenuity to steer that into philosophical reflection. They must do this under the watchful eye of the "sons of earth," who do everything in their power to make sure that they do not get access to their secret laws and rituals. In *Living Thought*, Esposito recognizes the separation of heroes and plebeians as the origin of biopower in the "exchange between protection and salvation."[12] Yet he does not emphasize this class struggle.

The major difference in our readings on this point, however, is this. For Esposito, the movement to the human age represents a return to the forest. Since, in his reading, the giants were equal, a government in which people were treated equally would bear certain resemblances to it. He writes, "The 'multitude' mentioned earlier—heir to the Roman plebs in their resistance to the order of the optimates and the new subject of the popular republics—bears its imprint not only in its collective conformation but also in a corporeality rooted in the animal."[13] In my reading, since the giants were unequal, the human age represents an evolution to a natural state of equality that transcends the differences of the forest. I emphasize that the time of giants was a time of corruption that perverted what humanity is and should be. The work of history is that of curing the damage caused by the fall so that civilization can ascend to the proper human form. With the proper civil institutions, humans can become the philosophical beings that they ought to be who respect the equality and value of all.

I would underline that Vico does not see divine providence as a force that pushes humanity unwillingly through history. Instead, providence offers civilizations a path toward the age of humanity. Only the greatest civilizations succeed. It is difficult to remember this point when reading the *New Science*, since Vico sticks so closely to his ancient Roman model. Nevertheless, I encourage the reader to keep in mind that Rome was the unique civilization Vico identifies that made it all the way to the human age. Many other civilizations tried and fell backward into feudalism or were conquered. The *New Science* is an attempt to help civilization reach the summit of history. Vico calls on civilization to move forward boldly knowing that the safety net of the barbarism of reflection will be on the other side. My concern with Esposito's reading is that it would obscure Vico's powerful message about the need to work for justice.

For a final thought on Vico and contemporary Italian philosophy, I return to Remo Bodei. As I mentioned, his idea of overinclusion was essential for my understanding the growth of poetic wisdom. He has another idea about delusion that has helped shape my general reading of Vico. Drawing on Freud and other psychologists, Bodei suggests that human development occurs through a series of stages. When one moves from one stage to another, the psychological language of the new stage has to incorporate the experiences of the earlier stage. When one experiences a trauma, however, the new stage struggles to put it into the new language. Since the earlier stage could not effectively face and incorporate the trauma, the later stage cannot either. As one continues to grow, there remain experiences in the psyche that continue to have a detrimental effect but cannot be rooted out easily. Bodei writes, "Everyone's biography is in this way studded by areas of darkness, covered with secret wounds that have never been completely closed, its temporal structure a complex curve, broken at various points, full of revisions and second thoughts."[14] This means that we tend to be psychologically divided against ourselves. We hold onto a traumatic element of the past despite the fact that the rest of us has moved forward. This tension forces us into delusion where we have to adjust the facts of our lives in order to create a consistent identity out of our divided parts.

I wonder if this describes the way poetic wisdom exists in Western civilization. In many ways, the West has made great strides to develop civil institutions based on justice and ideas of equality. Many of the poetic characters that were necessary at one stage of development are no longer needed because we have civilized those passions. For example, I did not speak much about the heroic raids of Neptune because it seems like Western Europe, after a period of horrible colonialism, has largely outgrown the need to go on such raids. The United States may not be over this, but other Western nations are. Other poetic characters have not been dealt with in this way. People still cast themselves in the image of Mars to defend their traditions. Despite the fact that the aristocracy does not identify itself according to class, it still performs the rituals of Apollo. The psychological question Vico raises is how do we undo the trauma of those poetic characters so that we can have a just society. He would call on us to study the history, psychology, and epistemological structure of those traumas more so that we can use rhetoric to persuade others to move past them.

The Consolation of Philosophy

Vico scholars have long wrestled with the question of whether Vico was religious. He certainly ends the *New Science* with a religious message: "it is to be finally concluded that this Science carries inseparably with it the study of piety, and that he who is not pious cannot be truly wise" (1112). I have no idea whether not he really was Roman Catholic or writing for the censors. Nevertheless, this passage fits what I have been saying throughout this work.

For Vico, the goal of divine providence is not to create a civilization in which material goods provide happiness. Its goal is to satisfy the psychological needs of humans so that a civilization can achieve a point at which people are treated equally. Divine providence points to a civil society in which justice is seen as more important than material pleasure. The task of the philosopher and the just lawyer in the human age is to privilege the philosophical good defined rationally and objectively over the fulfillment of personal desire. If enough people in a civilization work to keep it pointed toward the good, the civilization will be fair.

Overall, I do not read Vico as saying that the requirements of justice must always sacrifice worldly pleasure. There is nothing in his science precluding the value of luxury up to the point where it becomes decadent. Nevertheless, there will be moments when the educated lawyer in the human age will be given the opportunity to materially benefit from acting unjustly. There will also be moments where lingering unjust elements of society will treat the lawyer in an unjust way. This happened to Vico when he was denied the position of the chair of law. I think when Vico calls the scientist to be pious in order to be wise, I take him to mean that when one is treated unjustly or sacrifices luxury to do the noble thing, one must have faith in divine providence. After all, had Vico gotten the position, he would not have written the *New Science*. This may not be completely satisfying, but Vico is not alone here. Any philosopher who sacrifices utilitarian ends in favor of a higher truth risks sacrificing happiness. At least by embedding his metaphysics in his empirical evidence, he has developed a way of saying that even if the efforts of one individual or one civilization fails, divine providence will see to it that others will rise to take another shot. That idea can at least offer some consolation when the poetic authority of the aristocrats blocks the growth of equality and justice.

Notes

Chapter 1

1. John Robertson has produced an exhaustive study that compares the colonial rule in the Neapolitan and Scottish Enlightenment. This study has been very important for me as I have framed my idea of the power of the Neapolitan Barons. John Robertson, *The Case for Enlightenment: Scotland and Naples 1680–1760* (Cambridge: Cambridge University Press, 2005).

2. Giuseppe Giarrizzo, *Vico: la politica e la storia* (Naples: Guida Editori, 1981), 102.

3. Giarrizzo, 102. Translation mine.

4. For a discussion of this debate, see Kathleen Davis, "Sovereign Subjects, Feudal Law, and the Writing of History," *Journal of Medieval and Early Modern Studies* 36, no. 2 (2006): 223–261. For a broader account of the philosophical debate about feudalism that relied on historical evidence see J. G. A. Pocock, *The Ancient Constitution and Feudal Law: A Study of English Historical Thought in the Seventeenth Century: A Reissue with a Retrospect* (Cambridge: Cambridge University Press, 1987). This work has provided much helpful context for my study.

5. Giarrizzo, 121.

6. Giarrizzo, 117.

7. Bergin and Fisch rightly translate *ragione de' benefizi* as "feudal system" here. Vico does an etymology of the Latin word *beneficia* that connects it to fiefs. He alludes to this in axiom LXXXI but he says it more directly when he talks about the returned feudal institutions (262, 1063).

8. Einer Elhauge, "How Italian Colors Guts Private Antitrust Enforcement by Replacing it with Ineffective Forms of Arbitration," *Fordham International Law Journal* 38, no. 3 (2015): 771–778. I thank Jennifer Murray for drawing this issue and this case to my attention.

9. Battistini looks into the dates Vico gives us (1550). In the first *New Science*, Vico claims that he searched for the poetic characters for twenty-five years, which would be from 1700 to 1725 (NS25, 261). In the 1730 *New Science* and again in the 1744 *New Science* he claims it was 20 years, putting it from

1710 to 1730 (NS30 126; NS44 334). I agree with Battistini that the exact date here is not that significant. The point is that he was thinking about this problem as he was delivering his inaugural orations, the seventh of which he published as the *Study Methods* in 1709. He gave his first inaugural oration to the University of Naples in 1699 when he was thirty-one years old.

10. *Oro* comes from the Latin word *aurum*. According to etymologeek.com, *aurum* comes from a proto-Indo-European word for dawn: etymologeek.com/lat/aurum.

11. Timothy Brennan makes a good case for reading this point of Vico's as a decentralizing of Europe. He puts Vico into a chain of European intellectuals who prioritized taking a global approach to truth rather than a strictly European one. Timothy Brennan, *Borrowed Light: Vico, Hegel and the Colonies* (Stanford, CA: Stanford University Press, 2014): 17–44.

12. Francis Bacon, *Bacon's Essays and Wisdom of the Ancients* (Boston: Little, Brown and Co., 1884), 351–352.

13. I agree with the emphasis Verene places on the fact that Vico's early use of the "true is the made principle" gets intertwined with his later idea that the "true is grounded in the certain" or the *verum/certum* principle. I follow Verene's convention of using *verum-factum* and *verum/certum* to illustrate the difference that the first set of terms are convertible while the second set of terms are connectible. Verene, *Philosophy of the Imagination*, 57. For a discussion of how Vico's idea relates to later philosophical traditions, I have looked specifically at Karl Löwith, "'Verum et factum convertuntur': le premesse teologiche del principio di Vico e le lore consequenze secolari," trans. Anna Lucia Künkler Giavotto, in *Omaggio a Vico*, ed. Pietro Piovani (Naples: A Morano, 1968), 73–112. For the classic account of the traditions that led to the development of the principle, see Rodolfo Mondolfo, *Il 'verum-factum' prima di Vico* (Naples: Guida, 1969).

14. Bergin and Fisch's translation of the last sentence of 384 is problematic. Vico writes, "Onde, come si è incominciato quinci a fare da Giove, si truoveranno tanto importune tutti i sensi mistici d'altissima filosofia dati dai dotti alle greche favole ed a' geroglifici egizi, quanto naturali usciranno i sensi storici che quelle e questi naturalmente dovevano contenere." Bergin and Fisch read "tanto . . . quanto" as if both the mystical meanings and the historical meanings (*sensi storici*) are incorrect. I read it that so much as the mystic meanings are incorrect (*importune*), so the historical meanings are natural and correct. Battistini seems to support this. He clarifies that "I significati dei miti risultano la trasposizione fantastica di vicende storiche, relative alla politica, alla società e all'economia dei popoli primitive" (Battistini, 1564). That is, that the historic meanings relate to the affairs in history of the first peoples as connected to their politics, society, and economy. I thank Emanuela Pecchioli for her help understanding this passage.

15. For a summary of this discovery see Michael Coe, *Breaking the Maya Code* (London: Thames and Hudson, 2012).

16. As further evidence that Vico took this research seriously, one could compare the 1730 edition with the 1744 edition. In the 1730 edition, Vico

makes reference to the Jesuit missionary Joseph-François Lafitau (1681–1746). Lafitau was one of the most important sources of anthropological evidence coming from the Americas. He reports that Lafitau held that the people living in Canada were similar to those living in Asia (NS30 369). Lafitau claims this shows that people in North America came from Asia He asserts that this could not be the case because it would violate the conceit of nations. Vico deletes this passage in the 1744 edition and replaces it with the basic claim that civilizations in the Americas would pass through the ideal eternal history if they were not interrupted by the Europeans (1095). This strikes me as a realization on Vico's part that he does not have enough evidence to dispute Lafitau. In the 1730 edition, all he does is use his science to refute Lafitau's claims but offers no further support. So it does not help his case, and he removes it. This is speculation on my part, and perhaps we do not know the whole story. Nevertheless, I think it illustrates that Vico thought about his evidence seriously. I thank Professor Andreas Motsch for alerting me to the importance of Lafitau.

17. David Hume, *The Natural History of Religion*, ed. H. E. Root (Stanford, CA: Stanford University Press, 1957).

18. Samuel Pufendorf, *On the Duty of Man and Citizen*, trans. Michael Silverthorne (Cambridge: Cambridge University Press, 1991). For his account of the natural state of humans, see 115–119.

19. François Hotman, *Franco-Gallia: or, an Account of the Ancient Free State of France, and Most Other Parts of Europe Before the Loss of Their Liberties*, trans. Robert Molesworth, 2nd edition (London: Edward Valentine, 1721). For additional context, see Donald R. Kelley, *François Hotman: A Revolutionary's Ordeal* (Princeton, NJ: Princeton University Press, 1973).

20. Gianvincenzo Gravina, *Del governo civile di Roma* (Napoli: Stamperia Francese, 1828). This manuscript was not published during Gravina's lifetime. I consulted the original manuscript at the Biblioteca Casanatense MS. 343.

21. Parker Tyler made the link between myth, psychoanalysis, and film popular in the 1940s. Parker Tyler, *Magic and Myth of the Movies* (New York: Simon and Schuster, 1970). For information about him, see David Bordwell, *The Rhapsodes: How 1940s Critics Changed American Film Culture* (Chicago: University of Chicago Press, 2016). Joseph Campbell increased the interest in this. Joseph Campbell, *The Power of Myth* (New York: Anchor Books, 1991).

22. Brennan, 14.

23. Quite some time ago, I had encountered the term *mana* in the works of Ernst Cassirer and Lucien Levy-Bruhl. I was inspired to return to this concept by The Dice Tower podcast episode 574, in which Geoff Engelstein did a historical review of why so many board games and video games use the term *mana* to represent the amount of magical strength a character has. This encouraged me to review the history and philosophical implications of this concept.

24. Robert Henry Codrington, *The Melanesians: Studies in their Anthropology and Folk-lore* (Oxford: Clarendon Press, 1891), 191.

25. Cassirer dedicates a chapter on "The Successive Phases of Religious Thought" to locating the origin of myth in the taboo-mana formula. He writes,

"Since Codrington's early discoveries, the science of ethnology has proceeded to trace the diffusion of these concepts all over the earth." Ernst Cassirer, *Language and Myth*, trans. Susanne K. Langer (New York: Harper and Brothers, 1946), 63.

26. Ernst Cassirer, *The Myth of the State* (New Haven, CT: Yale University Press, 1974).

27. "There is no strong evidence that mana was regularly expressed in this speech community, nor does it appear to have been particularly ambiguous in its application to certain kinds of objects (things, persons, actions)." Alexander Mawyer, "The State of Mana, the Mana of the State," in *New Mana: Transformations of a Classic Concept in Pacific Languages and Cultures*, ed. Matt Tomlinson and Ty P. Kawika Tengan (Canberra: ANU Press, 2016), 203–236.

28. Battistini, 1562.

29. Aratus of Soli, *The Phaenomena*, trans. G. R. Mair, in *Callimachus, Hymns and Epigrams, Lycophron, Aratus*, Loeb Classical Library, vol. 129 (London: William Heinemann, 1921).

30. Carlo Levi, *Christ Stopped at Eboli: The Story of a Year*, trans. Frances Frenaye (New York: Picador, 2020).

31. Vico intentionally misreported his birth year in the opening of his autobiography. There he claims he was born in 1670, although as Verene has demonstrated, his baptismal records clearly state it was 1668. This does signal that the work cannot be fully trusted. For interpretations of this point, see Donald Phillip Verene, *The New Art of Autobiography: An Essay on the Life of Giambattista Vico Written by Himself* (Oxford: Clarendon Press, 1991), 165, and Giuseppe Mazzotta, *The New Map of the World: The Poetic Philosophy of Giambattista Vico* (Princeton: Princeton University Press, 1999), 23.

32. For more discussion of this, I would turn to Badaloni's account of Gli Investiganti. He depicts the history of this academy in terms of the debate over Aristotle and Descartes. Nicola Badaloni, *Introduzione a G. B. Vico* (Milan: Feltrinelli, 1961), 79–164. It is particularly helpful to look at his account of G. A. Borelli's intellectual evolution and his critique of Descartes (89–92). It is also helpful to look at his discussion of Francesco D'Andrea (Vico's teacher) and how he rejected Aristotle in favor of Descartes (149–162).

33. Martina Piperno, *Rebuilding Post-Revolutionary Italy: Leopardi and Vico's 'New Science,'* Oxford University Studies in the Enlightenment (Oxford: Voltaire Foundation, 2018).

34. B. A. Haddock, "Vico's 'Discovery of the True Homer': A Case-Study in Historical Reconstruction," *Journal of the History of Ideas* 40, no. 4 (1979): 583–602.

35. For an account of the influence of Vico on Coleridge see, George Whalley, "Coleridge and Vico," in *Giambattista Vico: An International Symposium*, ed. Giorgio Tagliacozzo and Hayden V. White (Baltimore: Johns Hopkins University Press, 1969), 225–244.

36. For background on the inquisition, see Gustavo Costa, "Vico e l'inquisizione," *Nouvelles de la république des lettres*, no. 2 (1999): 93–124.

37. Damiano Romano, *L'origine della giurisprudenza romana contro alla moderna opinione del Signor D. Gio:Battista Vico* (Naples: Domenic Roselli, 1744).

38. Koen Stapelbroek, *Love, Self-Deceit and Money: Commerce and Morality in the Early Neapolitan Enlightenment* (Toronto: University of Toronto Press, 2008), 172–177.

39. The original title of this work is *Apologia del genere umano accusato d'essere stato una volta una bestia, in cui si dimostra la falsità dello stato ferino degli antichi uomini colla Sacra Scrittura. Operetta che può servire di appendice ai libri De Princip. Jur. Nat. er Gen. del Sig. G. F. Finetti* (Venice: Vincenzo Radici, 1768). As part of his attempt to highlight the church's adversarial stance toward Vico, Croce republished this work. G. F. Finetti, *Difesa dell'autorità della Sacra Scittura contro Giambattista Vico*, ed. Benedetto Croce (Bari: Laterza, 1936). I consulted Croce's edition.

40. Girolamo Imbruglia, "Enlightenment in Eighteenth-Century Naples," in *Naples in the Eighteenth Century: The Birth and Death of a Nation State*, ed. Girolamo Imbruglia (Cambridge: Cambridge University Press, 2000), 74.

41. Tommaso Astarita, *Between Salt Water and Holy Water: A History of Southern Italy* (New York: W. W. Norton, 2005), 215.

42. Barbara Ann Naddeo, "A Cosmopolitan in the Provinces: G. M. Galanti, Geography, and Enlightenment Europe," *Modern Intellectual History* 30, no. 1 (2013): 1–26.

43. For a contemporary discussion of the impact that archeological findings had on the intellectual culture in early modern Naples and, specifically, Vico, see Giovanna Ceserani, *Italy's Lost Greece: Magna Graecia and the Making of Modern Archaeology* (Oxford: Oxford Univ. Press, 2012), 41–49.

44. Christina Mercer, "The Contextualist Revolution in Early Modern Philosophy," *Journal of the History of Philosophy* 57, no. 3 (2019): 529–548.

45. Vittorio Hösle emphasizes this point. Vittorio Hösle, *Vico's New Science of the Intersubjective World*, trans. Francis Russell Hittinger IV (Notre Dame: University of Notre Dame Press, 2016), 14.

46. Mercer, 530.

47. My thoughts on this are deeply influenced by Jean-Luc Nancy. In his essay "Myth Interrupted," he criticizes the Romantics and others who tried to use myth to found new traditions and bring about community. He argues that because the human mind is no longer at a point of origin, it can no longer use myth to function in this way. He briefly suggests that Vico could be seen as a starting point of this tradition. I have never found that Vico calls for myth to be used to found or refound communities. So, I am going to remove Vico from the view that Nancy criticizes in a way that ends up putting him more in line with what Nancy calls for. Jean-Luc Nancy, "Myth Interrupted," trans. Peter Connor, in *The Inoperative Community* (Minneapolis: University of Minnesota Press, 1991), 43–70.

48. Hannah Arendt, *Between Past and Future* (New York: Viking Press, 1961), 57–58. See also Hannah Arendt, *The Human Condition*, 2nd ed. (Chicago: University of Chicago Press, 1998), 298.

49. Joseph Cardinal Ratzinger, *Introduction to Christianity*, trans. J. R. Foster (San Francisco: Ignatius Press, 1990), 31–33. Ratzinger would, of course, later become Pope Benedict XVI. I thank Prof. Robert St. Hilaire for bringing this citation to my attention.

50. Mercer, 541.

51. Mercer, 543.

52. For more information on the Academy of the Investigators, see Max Harold Fisch, "The Academy of the Investigators," in *Science, Medicine and History: Essays on the Evolution of Scientific Thought and Medical Practice Written in Honour of Charles Singer*, ed. E. Ashworth Underwood (London: Oxford University Press, 1953), 521–563.

53. Badaloni.

54. Paolo Rossi, "Chi sono i contemporanei di Vico?" *Rivista di filosofia* 72 (1981): 51–82.

55. Andrea Battistini, *Vico tra antichi e moderni* (Bologna: il Mulino, 2004), 19–39.

56. Paolo Fabiani, *La filosofia dell'immaginazione in Vico e Malebranche* (Florence: Firenze University Press, 2002), 244.

57. Fabiani, 255.

58. Fabiani, 243.

59. Fabiani, 284.

60. Barbara Ann Naddeo, *Vico and Naples: The Urban Origins of Modern Social Theory* (Ithaca, NY: Cornell University Press, 2011), 4.

61. Naddeo, *Vico and Naples*, 33–34.

62. Naddeo, *Vico and Naples*, 142.

63. Naddeo, *Vico and Naples*, 160.

64. Naddeo, *Vico and Naples*, 185.

65. Naddeo, *Vico and Naples*, 186.

66. Battistini confirms that this phrase is taken from the title of one of Bacon's works (1524). Francis Bacon, "Cogitata et visa de interpretatione naturae," in *The Works of Francis Bacon*, vol. 3, ed. James Spedding, Robert Leslie Ellis, Douglas, and Denon Heath (Cambridge: Cambridge University Press, 2011), 588–620.

67. René Descartes, *Discourse on Method and Meditations on First Philosophy*, trans. Donald A. Cress, 4th ed. (Indianapolis: Hackett, 1998), 11.

68. For an important essay that distinguishes Vico from Hegel's dialectic, see Pietro Piovani, "Vico senza Hegel," in *Omaggio a Vico*, ed. Pietro Piovani (Naples: A Morano, 1968), 553–586.

69. Giarrizzo, 102.

70. Croce is most responsible for inventing this picture of Vico. He writes, "Political life rolled past over his head, like the sky and its stars, and he never wasted his strength in a vain attempt to reach it. Political and social controversy, like religious, was outside the sphere of his activity. He was indeed a non-political person." My speculation is that this was part of a general agenda on Croce's part to make early modern Naples appear to be an innocent victim amidst the greater

swirl of politics in the period. Benedetto Croce, *The Philosophy of Giambattista Vico*, trans. R. G. Collingwood (New Brunswick, NJ: Transaction Publishers, 2002), 250.

71. Jennifer A. Herdt, *Putting on Virtue: The Legacy of the Splendid Vices* (Chicago: University of Chicago Press, 2008).

72. Herdt, 222.
73. Herdt, 232.
74. Herdt, 234.
75. Herdt, 255.
76. Herdt, 252.

77. Enrico Nuzzo, *Tra religione e prudenza: la 'filosofia practica' di Giambattista Vico* (Roma: Edizioni di Storia e Letteratura, 2007). For further context on this discussion in Naples, see John Robertson, "Sacred History and Political Thought: Neapolitan Responses to the Problem of Sociability after Hobbes" *Historical Journal* 56, no. 1 (2013): 1–29.

78. Nuzzo, 43–44.
79. Nuzzo, 64–65.
80. Nuzzo, 69–70.
81. Nuzzo, 93–95.

82. Norberto Bobbio, "Vico e la teoria delle forme di governo," *Bollettino del Centro di Studi Vichiani* 8 (1978): 5–27.

83. Riccardo Caporali, *Heroes gentium: sapienza e politica in Vico* (Bologna: Il Mulino, 1992), 244.

84. Caporali, 245.

Chapter 2

1. Giambattista Vico, "Vico's Reply to the False Book Notice: The *Vici Vindiciae*," trans. and commentary by Donald Phillip Verene, *New Vico Studies* 24 (2006): 129–175.

2. Verene discusses the possibility of who wrote this commentary. Vico, "Vico's Reply," 132–136.

3. Isaiah Berlin, *Vico and Herder: Two Studies in the History of Ideas* (New York: Viking Press, 1976), 7.

4. Paola Bertucci, "The Architecture of Knowledge: Science, Collecting and Display in Eighteenth-Century Naples," in *New Approaches to Naples c.1500–c.1800: The Power of Place*, ed. Melissa Calaresu and Helen Hills (Surrey: Ashgate, 2013), 149–174. The text of the quote comes from Placido Troyli, *Istoria generale del reame di Napoli* (Naples, 1752).

5. Recent research has investigated Vico's influence on eighteenth-century art. See Christopher Drew Armstrong. "Myth and the New Science: Vico, Tiepolo, and the Language of the Optimates." *The Art Bulletin* 87, no. 4 (2005): 643-663. Malcolm Bull, *Inventing Falsehood, Making Truth: Vico and Neapolitan Painting* (Princeton, NJ: Princeton University Press, 2013).

6. Croce, 253, 263.

7. For a discussion of Vico's use of irony, see Brennan, 32–36.

8. Gustavo Costa has a helpful essay that questions why Vico published the 1730 edition of the *New Science* if it was not ready. As part of this discussion, he also talks about the general atmosphere of censorship. Gustavo Costa, "Perchè Vico pubblicò un Capolavoro incompiuto? Considerazioni in margine a 'La Scienza Nuova' 1730," *Italica* 82, no. 3/4 (2005): 560–579.

9. Barbara Ann Naddeo has a good account of the history of this text and makes a good case for the way in which his work on this text formed his philosophical outlook. The Spanish Viceroy commissioned this history probably to discredit the rebels. It was decided that Vico's history was in some way too offensive to the nobility so it was not published. Naddeo speculates that he does not mention this in his *Autobiography* because it was too pro-Spanish and would make him look bad before the ruling Austrian Viceroy. Naddeo, *Vico and Naples*, 29–38.

10. Paolo Mattia Doria, *La vita civile di Paolo Mattia Doria con un trattato della educazione del principe*, 3rd ed. (Naples: Angelo Vocola a Fontana Medina, 1729), 459.

11. Doria, 492.

12. Gianvincezo Gravina, *Della Ragione Poetica* (Rome: Francesco Gonzaga, 1708).

13. Giambattista Vico, "Giambattista Vico's 'Reprehension of the Metaphysics of René Descartes, Benedict Spinoza, and John Locke': An Addition to the *New Science*," trans. and commentary by Donald Phillip Verene, *New Vico Studies* 8 (1990): 2–18.

14. Battistini gives a good contextual picture of how the debate about the ancients and moderns that was going on in Northern Europe influenced the Neapolitan intellectual scene. Battistini, *Vico tra antichi e moderni*, 23–26.

15. Larry F. Norman, *The Shock of the Ancient: Literature and History in Early Modern France* (Chicago: University of Chicago Press, 2011), 30–31.

16. At the Northeastern Modern Language Association meeting in Boston 2020, Maurice Lee gave a remarkable address entitled "The Office of Literature" where he gave a persuasive plea for the humanities and sciences to work together. He shares these ideas in Maurice Lee, *Overwhelmed: Literature, Aesthetics and the Nineteenth-Century Information Revolution* (Princeton: Princeton University Press, 2019).

17. Berlin, 67.

18. Berlin, 67.

19. Berlin, 38–39.

20. Joseph Mali, *The Legacy of Vico in Modern Cultural History: From Jules Michelet to Isaiah Berlin* (Cambridge: Cambridge University Press, 2012), 231.

21. Mali, *The Legacy of Vico*, 241.

22. Berlin, 140.

23. Berlin, 26.

24. Giovanni Pico della Mirandola, *On the Dignity of Man*, trans. Charles Glenn Wallis (Indianapolis: Hackett, 1998), 4–5.

25. Berlin, 35.
26. Berlin, 14.
27. Berlin, 111.
28. Berlin, 27.
29. Berlin, 23.

30. For a recent analysis of Vico's metaphysical commitments connected to his theory of myth that works against this point of Berlin, see John Shotter, "Vico, (Particular) Imaginative Universals, Divine Providence, and the Imaginative Work Needed in Relating Oneself to Others," in *Giambattista Vico and the New Psychological Science*, ed. Luca Tateo (New Brunswick: Transaction Publishers, 2017), 113–150.

31. Samuel Beckett, "Dante... Bruno. Vico.. Joyce," in *Our Exagmination Round His Factification for Incamination of Work in Progress* (Norfolk, CT: New Directions, 1939), 1–22.

32. Beckett, 4.
33. Beckett, 10.
34. Beckett, 12–13.
35. Beckett, 6.
36. Beckett, 7.

37. Paolo Rossi places Vico's historical account in the context of the natural science and biblical theology of the early modern period. He also emphasizes the way in which Hobbes took a historical approach. He discusses the similarities of the way Hobbes and Vico worked to separate their common ideas of humans in the state of nature with the story of Adam. Paolo Rossi, *The Dark Abyss of Time: The History of the Earth and the History of Nations from Hooke to Vico*, trans. Lydia G. Cochrane (Chicago: University of Chicago Press, 1984), 250.

38. Mark Morford, Robert J. Lenardon, and Michael Sham, *Classical Mythology*, 10th ed. (Oxford: Oxford University Press, 2014), 84–88.

39. Vico, *Opere*, ed. Battistini, 1525.

40. Costa, "Vico's *Salti Nitri* and the Origins of Pagan Civilization: The Alchemical Dimention of the New Science," *Rivista di studi italiani* 10 (1992): 1–11.

41. Bergin and Fisch's translation of *immane* as "cruel" is fine. It is worth mentioning, though, that *immane* also has the connotation of "enormous." This implies the first poets retained some of their giant stature and used it to terrify the *famuli* who lived under them.

42. For quite some time, scholars have suggested that Vico rejects the modern view of the independent self in favor of a view that sees humans as naturally social and communicative. I would point specifically to Hösle's book *Vico's New Science of the Intersubjective World*, which was an introduction to his translation of Vico but has since been published separately in Italian and English. I appreciate his work because it takes seriously the value of the poetic characters in his thought and their role in class conflict. Hösle, 97–102.

43. For a full discussion of this, see Donald Phillip Verene, "Vico's 'Ignota Latebat,'" *New Vico Studies* 5 (1987): 77–98.

44. Jean-Jacques Rousseau, *Discourse on the Origin of Inequality*, in *The Basic Political Writings*, 2nd ed., trans. Donald A. Cress (Indianapolis: Hackett, 2011), 49.

45. Rousseau, 48.

46. Rousseau, 66–67.

47. Rousseau, 54. See also 66.

48. Rousseau, 71.

49. Rousseau, 74.

50. Rousseau, 75.

51. Rousseau, 88–90. I would point out that Rousseau even contrasts the original state of nature and the state of nature after the collapse of civilization in much the same way Vico discusses the barbarism of sense and the barbarism of reflection.

52. For quite some time, Amartya Sen has been demonstrating that Smith himself did not think of the theory as an ethical one, and has turned to Smith's *Theory of Moral Sentiments* as a source of real insight. See Amartya Sen, "Does Business Ethics Make Economic Sense?" *Business Ethics Quarterly* 3, no. 1 (1993): 45–54. For an example of how he places Smith's theory in the context of early modern thought, see Amartya Sen, *The Idea of Justice* (Cambridge: Harvard University Press, 2009), 44–51.

53. As an example, I would point to Villani's analysis over the debate about whether Neapolitan barons had the right to reclaim territory that they had lost. Part of the argument to defend this right centered on the idea that if the nobility lost power, the province would fall into chaos. These authors could not envision life without the stability of feudalism. Pasquale Villani, "Il dibattito sulla feudalità nel regno di Napoli dal Genovesi al Canosa," *Saggi e richerche sul settecento* (1968): 252–331.

54. Ellen Meiskins Wood, *The Origin of Capitalism: A Longer View* (London: Verso, 2002).

55. Albert O. Hirschman, *The Passions and the Interests: Political Arguments for Capitalism before Its Triumph* (Princeton: Princeton University Press, 2013).

56. For an extensive discussion of how this debate played out specifically in early modern Naples, see Stapelbroek, *Love, Self-Deceit and Money*. His work focuses on Ferdinando Galiani's *Della moneta* from 1751 as a defense of the moralizing power of commerce. He dedicates a chapter to showing how Vico and Doria represent the religious opposition to Galiani's view.

57. Hirschman, 17, 26–27.

58. Hirschman, 56–66.

59. Hirschman, 16–17.

60. Hirschman, 16.

61. Bernard Mandeville, *The Fable of the Bees and Other Writings*, ed. E. J. Hundert (Indianapolis: Hackett, 1997).

62. Bergin and Fisch allude to the possibility that Vico considered Mandeville in their introduction to his translation (F6).

63. Mandeville, 27.
64. Mandeville, 30.
65. Mandeville, 21.
66. Mandeville, 36.
67. Mandeville, 41.
68. Mandeville, 40.
69. Hume, *The Natural History of Religion*.
70. Mandeville, 43–44.
71. Rousseau, 63.
72. Rousseau, 64.
73. Rudolf Otto, *The Idea of the Holy: An Inquiry into the Non-Rational Factor in the Idea of the Divine and Its Relation to the Rational*, trans. John W. Harvey (Oxford: Oxford University Press, 1958).
74. As I was preparing this manuscript, I heard a presentation by Giulio Goria on this topic entitled "Vico, Poetic Logic, and Metaphor," which was organized by Theorizing Italy: A CNYHC Working Group. His talk and the ensuing discussion helped me find a better way of expressing these ideas.
75. Baruch Spinoza, *Ethics*, in *The Essential Spinoza: Ethics and Related Writings*, ed. Michael L. Morgan, trans. Samuel Shirley (Indianapolis: Hackett, 2006), part 3, P1–2.
76. Luigi Pareyson, "La dottrina vichiana dell'ingegno," in *L'esperienza artistica: saggi di storia dell'estetica* (Milan: Marozati, 1974), 39–75.
77. Cantelli emphasizes the way in which poetic wisdom is a form of communication. He also emphasizes how this language is understood and expressed by recognizing the divine in nature and other poets. Verene emphasizes the difference between the intelligible universal and the imaginative universal. He emphasizes the way in which the imaginative universals are immediate metaphors that work mimetically. I am drawing heavily on these two works throughout my study. Gianfranco Cantelli, *Mente corpo linguaggio: saggio sull'interpretazione vichiana del mito* (Florence: Sanzoni, 1986), 53, 58–59; Verene, *Vico's Science of Imagination*, 79–84.

Chapter 3

1. Verene, *Vico's Science of Imagination*, 67.
2. Verene, *Vico's Science of Imagination*, 67.
3. Verene, *Vico's Science of Imagination*, 67.
4. Cantelli, 215.
5. Cantelli writes, "Fra questi due estremi [un immagine creata dalla fantasia o un concetto stabilito dalla ragione] si colloca ogni cosa che l'uomo ha prodotto: gli dèi, le instituzioni, gli strumenti, le opere delle arti e delle techniche, tutto un mondo di umane cose che si è storicamente venuto a formare e che nella sua realtà, l'unica conoscibile dall'uomo, incorpora i sensi e i significati che la mente umana vi ha posto." Cantelli, 289.

6. Jacques Chabot, *Giambattista Vico: la raison du mythe* (Aix-en-Provence: Sarl Edisud, 2005), 233–234.

7. Chabot writes, "La raison mythologique est donc tout à fait 'raisonnable' dans le sens le plus commun, comme quand on dit de quelqu'un, d'un homme en chair et en os, 'qu'il est bien raisonnable,' ou à un enfant turbulent et indiscipliné : 'Sois raisonnable.' Cela signifie : vivre en conformité avec des usages communément reconnus comme utiles à la vie sociale, autrement dit à la morale publique." Chabot, 234–235.

8. Marcel Danesi, *Vico, Metaphor, and the Origin of Language* (Bloomington: Indiana University Press, 1993), 143–147.

9. See Piperno, 136–137, for example.

10. Piperno, 96–97.

11. Verene, *Vico's Science of Imagination*, 220.

12. Battistini, *Vico tra antichi e moderni*, 61–62.

13. Paolo Cristofolini, *Vico pagano e barbaro* (Pisa: Edizioni ETS 2001), 89–92.

14. David L. Marshall, *Vico and the Transformation of Rhetoric in Early Modern Europe* (Cambridge: Cambridge University Press, 2010), 139.

15. Marshall, 187.

16. Marshall, 186.

17. Marshall, 186–187.

18. Marshall, 194.

19. Esposito maintains this view throughout his works on Vico. For an early example see Roberto Esposito, *La politica e la storia: Machiavelli e Vico* (Naples: Liguori, 1980), 274.

20. There are many other works that look at Vico and the imagination that have been helpful for developing my understanding of Vico and my philosophical thought in general. I point to these that have been particularly significant: Michael Mooney, *Vico in the Tradition of Rhetoric* (Princeton, NJ: Princeton University Press, 1984). James Robert Goetsch Jr., *Vico's Axioms: The Geometry of the Human World* (New Haven: Yale University Press, 1995). Jürgen Trabant, *Vico's New Science of Ancient Signs: A Study of Sematology* translated by Sean Ward (London: Routledge, 2004). Nancy du Bois Marcus, *Vico and Plato* (New York: Peter Lang, 2011). Luca Tateo, "Giambattista Vico and the Psychological Imagination" *Culture and Psychology* 41, no. 2 (2015): 1–15.

21. Bergin and Fisch add the phrase "mixed commonwealths" to the title of this section. They make this clear by putting it in brackets. However, I do not think it is necessary. Vico writes, "Altre pruove prese dal temperamento delle repubbliche, fatto degli stati delle seconde coi governi delle primiere." This could be rendered "Other proofs drawn from the temperament of republics that are made from both newer states and previous administrations." This would emphasize Vico's claim that mixed governments do not really exist but that the older echo in the former.

22. In the phrase before this, Vico writes, "The oak tree that is consecrated to Jove proves that he was the oldest of all the gods, for it caused the men who

ate its acorns to stay on the lands" (NS25 413). I have no evidence to suspect that this is a reference to Locke's famous use of the acorn in his argument about property in the *Second Treatise on Government* par. 28. I draw attention to it because it makes an interesting point of comparison. For Locke, the gathering of the acorn is simply a sign of human labor and the taking possession of property. For Vico, the acorn is connected to the ownership of land but only through Jove's spiritual divinity. In the 1744 *New Science*, Vico drops the connection between Jove and acorns. He replaces it with a curious etymology connecting oak trees to the original source of law (240).

23. Gianvincezo Gravina, *Delle antiche favole* (Rome: Antonio de Rossi, 1696). Gianvincezo Gravina, *Della ragion poetica*, 2 vols. (Rome: Francesco Gonzaga, 1713).

24. For a discussion of his influence on early modern Italian thought, see Carla San Mauro, *Gianvincenzo Gravina giurista e politico* (Milan: Franco Angeli, 2006).

25. Gravina, 30.

26. Gravina, 20.

27. Gravina, *Della ragion poetica*, 64–74.

28. This does represent a problem for Vico because he claims that since poetic thinkers could not think abstractly, they could not lie. It is hard to say how Ulysses could be duplicitous. Vico tries to address this in the 1725 *New Science*. He writes, "The model of this heroic jurisprudence of ancient barbaric times whom Homer presents to the Greek peoples is Ulysses, who always tells his stories and makes his promises and solemn oaths with such art that, while he preserves the propriety of his words, he obtains the utilities he has proposed for himself" (NS25 203). The idea is that he could not lie but he could take advantage of the literal reading of laws to adjust the facts to his advantage. This is consistent with what he says about how ancient jurisprudence works, which I will address later.

29. Carla San Mauro discusses Gravina's frustration in his work at the Sapienza Università di Roma. He lamented that the administrators made decisions for prestige and profit rather than listening to the faculty about ways to improve student education. He writes that the administrators, "come il fuoco dentro l'aveario, ove non per altro Dimora che per consumare oziosamente tutto il mele e tutto l'opere e fatiche delle api industriose." San Mauro, 44.

30. Schaeffer discusses the tradition of student violence at the University of Naples. The *Prammatica di Lemnos* was published in 1616 as a set of rules for the university, which included curtailing student violence, which was rampant in the sixteenth and early seventeenth centuries. As evidence of this violence, Schaeffer relates, "before the *Prammatica*, in 1557, a regulation appears in the university records prohibiting students from bringing weapons to class. In 1558 another regulation appears, this one prohibiting students from being accompanied to class by *servants* carrying weapons." John D. Schaeffer, *Sensus communis: Vico, Rhetoric, and the Limits of Relativism* (Durham, NC: Duke University Press, 1990), 38.

31. Battistini, *Vico tra antichi e moderni*, 175–199.

32. Battistini, *Vico tra antichi e moderni*, 183.

33. Battistini writes, "Vossius, quindi, invece di scorgere nelle dodici fatiche di Ercole la storia ingenuamente mitizzata delle dure lotte per l'esistenza sostenute dai primitive, vi ritrova un sublime ed elegante esempio di sapienza riposte, consistente nella riflesse trasposizione allegorica dei dodici segni zodiacali." Battistini, *Vico tra antichi e moderni*, 185.

34. Battistini, *Vico tra antichi e moderni*, 183.

35. Bergin and Fisch point out that Vico attributes a position of Voss's to Jesuit theologian Denis Petau and critiques it. But he does not mention Voss's name (388).

36. This also appears in the *Study Methods*, 13–15. For a fuller discussion of Vico on memory, see Verene, *Vico's Science of Imagination*, 96–126.

37. Descartes, 68.

38. The influence of Tasso on Italian culture is well known. For a specific lens into how his texts appeared in Vico's Naples, see Vincenzo Trombetta, "Torquato Tasso nell'editoria napolitana dal seicento all'ottocento," *Tricontre: teoria testo traduzione* 11 (May 2019): 175–201.

39. In the 1730 edition, this is axiom XLV (NS30 103–104). The earlier part of the axiom is largely the same. There is an interesting change to the axiom itself. In the 1744 edition, it reads "La mente umana è naturalmente portata a dilettarsi dell'uniforme" (204). The words *a dilettarsi* are not present in the 1730 edition. When Vico adds this phrase, it becomes stronger. It is not just that the human mind is inclined to see uniformity but the mind actually enjoys finding uniformity. This leads to the point that it is difficult to break the mind from seeing the world in terms of this uniformity.

40. Axioms XLVII and XLVIII in the 1730 edition appear as axioms L and LIII in the 1744 edition. They are unchanged (NS30 105). Axiom LI of the 1744 edition contains Vico's claim that "he who is not a poet by nature can never become one by art" (213). He draws the conclusion that the first poets were poets by nature and not by art. This could reinforce the idea that the jump to poetic wisdom was a small cognitive jump.

41. "Darmok," *Star Trek: The Next Generation*, season 5, episode 2, aired September 30, 1991. This episode was written by Joe Menosky and Philip Lazbnik. Menosky also co-wrote with Hilary Bader the episode "Hero Worship" in which the NAR-18834 Vico was featured as a starship. The episode "Darmok" is analyzed by Ian Bogost in the essay "Shaka, When the Walls Fell" for *The Atlantic*, June 2014, www.theatlantic.com/entertainment/archive/2014/06/star-trek-tng-and-the-limits-of-language-shaka-when-the-walls-fell/372107/.

42. Erin C. Tarver, *The I in Team: Sports Fandom and the Reproduction of Identity* (Chicago: University of Chicago Press, 2017).

43. Tarver, 41.

44. Tarver, 44.

45. Tarver, 44.

46. Tarver, 43.

47. Tarver, 46–47.
48. Tarver, 74–78.
49. Tarver, 99.
50. Tarver, 90.
51. Tarver, 99.
52. I am not sure why Bergin and Fisch leave out the "the" here.
53. Rousseau famously does this in the *Second Discourse* (58–60). For another example, Catherine L. Hobbs does a remarkable job of comparing Vico to Condillac on this point. Given the limited experiences of the first people, Condillac connects the origin of language to the encounter with nature. Catherline L. Hobbs, *Rhetoric on the Margins of Philosophy: Vico, Condillac, Monboddo* (Carbondale: Southern Illinois University Press, 2002), 104–110.
54. Bergin and Fisch use "languages." Leon Pompa translates "povertà di parlari convenuti" as "A poverty of words of settled meaning" (NS25 97). The idea of translating *parlari* as "words" also seems problematic. He translates *parlari* as "words" in the title to chapter 14 of book 3. But then Vico gives three examples of words, and he uses the term *voci* (NS25 277).
55. I would mention that Vico unfortunately compares the proper arrangement of objects and the addition of emotion to the work of women and children. Unfortunately, Vico holds onto this notion as his thought develops (457).
56. Here Vico compares this to a modern tendency in women and the feeble-minded, as he did in his earlier work.

Chapter 4

1. Descartes, 24.
2. Doria, 86. Translation mine.
3. Doria, 86–87.
4. Finetti, 44–45.
5. Finetti, 36–37.
6. This is from Croce's introduction, in which he argues that Finetti's work is a sign of the general Roman Catholic rejection of Vico. Finetti, xii.
7. Jennifer D. Selwyn, *A Paradise Inhabited by Devils: The Jesuits' Civilizing Mission in Early Modern Naples* (London: Routledge, 2004), 8–9. See also Tommaso Astarita, *The Continuity of Feudal Power: The Caracciolo di Brienza in Spanish Naples* (Cambridge: Cambridge University Press, 1992), 2.
8. There are many accounts of the course of the research. One good summary of the recent work is Aurilio Musi, "The Kingdom of Naples in the Spanish Imperial System," trans. Lydia G. Cochrane, in *Spain in Italy: Politics, Society, and Religion 1500–1700*, edited by Thomas J. Dandelet and John Marino (Leiden: BRILL, 2007), 73–99.
9. A good summary of the historiography of 1500–1800 Naples as one of missed opportunities is Anna Maria Rao, "'Missed Opportunities' in the History

of Naples," in *New Approaches to Naples c. 1500–1800: The Power of Place* ed. Melissa Calaresu and Helen Hills (Surrey: Ashgate, 2013): 203–224.

10. For a remarkable study of life among the civil customs of early modern Naples, see John A. Marino, *Becoming Neapolitan: Citizen Culture in Baroque Naples* (Baltimore: Johns Hopkins University Press, 2011). See also, Maria Antonietta Visceglia, *Identità sociali: la nobiltà napolitana nella prima età moderna* (Milan: Edizioni Unicopli, 1998).

11. John Quiggin, "John Locke's Road to Serfdom," *Jacobin*, December 17, 2021, www.jacobinmag.com/2015/10/locke-classical-liberalism-treatise-nozick-constitution/.

12. Nicolini, "Il Vico nella vita domestica," in Giambattista Vico, *Opere*, edited by Fausto Nicolini (Milan: Ricciardi, 1953), 131.

13. For an excellent overview of how the feudal question continued to influence intellectuals and dominate the economic system after Carlo VII took power, see Anna Maria Rao, "The Feudal Question, Judicial Systems and the Enlightenment," in *Naples in the Eighteenth Century: The Birth and Death of a Nation State*, ed. Girolamo Imbruglia (Cambridge: Cambridge University Press, 2000), 95–117; see especially 100.

14. Anna Maria Vargas-Machuca married the Marchese Francesco Vatolla. When the Rocca line did not produce descendants, the fiefdom and castle went to the Vargas-Machuca family. Nicolini's edited volume on the *Autobiography* with commentary includes a photograph of what is now Via Giambattista Vico in Vatolla but not a picture of the castle, which is rather imposing. Fausto Nicolini, "I Rocca e la imora del Vico a Vatolla," in *Autobiografia di Giambattista Vico*, ed. Fausto Nicolini (Napoli: Istituto Italiano per gli Studi Storici, 1992), 197–208. This is a republication of a work published by the Casa Editrice Valentino Bompiani in Milan in 1947.

15. Nicolini, "I Rocca e la imora del Vico a Vatolla," 202.

16. Nicolini, "I Rocca e la imora del Vico a Vatolla," 205.

17. Antonio Calabria, *The Cost of Empire: The Finances of the Kingdom of Naples in the Time of Spanish Rule* (Cambridge: Cambridge University Press, 1991), 4–5.

18. Calabria, 130–131.

19. Astarita, *Between Salt Water and Holy Water*, 118.

20. Astarita, *The Continuity of Feudal Power*, 155.

21. Rosario Villari, *The Revolt of Naples*, trans. James Newell and John A. Marino (Cambridge: Polity Press, 1993), 1–2.

22. Eric Cochrane, "Southern Italy in the Age of the Spanish Viceroys: Some Recent Titles," *Journal of Modern History* 58, no. 1 (1986): 194–217.

23. John A. Marino, "The Rural World in Italy under Spanish Rule," in *Spain in Italy: Politics, Society, and Religion 1500–1700*, ed. Thomas J. Dandelet and John Marino (Leiden: Brill, 2007), 406–407.

24. Rao, "The Feudal Question," 98–99.

25. Villari, 75. His citation comes from the *Consulte della Sommaria*, XLI, 1637, which he referenced at the Archivio di Stato, Naples.

26. Rao, "The Feudal Question," 98–99.
27. Villari, 109–110.
28. Villari, 80–83.
29. Villari, 98.
30. Villari, 102.
31. Villari, 109.
32. Rao, "Missed Opportunities," 205.
33. Villari, 8.
34. Villari, 10.
35. For a recent discussion of this, see Davis, "Sovereign Subjects."
36. Villari, 2.
37. Susan Reynolds, *Fiefs and Vassals: The Medieval Evidence Reinterpreted* (Oxford: Oxford University Press, 2006), 248.
38. Renolds, 245.
39. Reynolds, 246. Traditionally, the idea of military obligation was thought to be the core of Neapolitan feudal obligation. Reynolds suggests that this derives from the original custom of defense. Astarita, *Between Salt Water and Holy Water*, 38.
40. Reynolds, 248.
41. Reynolds, 71.
42. Astarita, *Between Salt Water and Holy Water*, 36.
43. Astarita, *Between Salt Water and Holy Water*, 49.
44. Astarita, *Between Salt Water and Holy Water*, 52.
45. Astarita, *Between Salt Water and Holy Water*, 67–68.
46. Astarita, *Between Salt Water and Holy Water*, 68.
47. Astarita, *Between Salt Water and Holy Water*, 67.
48. Astarita, *Between Salt Water and Holy Water*, 70.
49. Astarita, *Between Salt Water and Holy Water*, 70.
50. Astarita, *The Continuity of Feudal Power*, 37.
51. Astarita, *The Continuity of Feudal Power*, 38.
52. Astarita, *The Continuity of Feudal Power*, 39.
53. Astarita, *The Continuity of Feudal Power*, 39. See also 74.
54. Astarita, *The Continuity of Feudal Power*, 40. See also 80.
55. Astarita, *The Continuity of Feudal Power*, 40.
56. Astarita, *The Continuity of Feudal Power*, 41.
57. Astarita, *The Continuity of Feudal Power*, 20.
58. Astarita, *The Continuity of Feudal Power*, 235.
59. Astarita. *The Continuity of Feudal Power*, 124. He comments that when the Caracciolo family were in their castle in Brienza, they had no opportunity for socialization and there were no other aristocrats nearby.
60. Astarita, *The Continuity of Feudal Power*, 70. His citation is to Aurelio Lepre, *Storia del mezzogiorno in Italia* (Naples: Liguori, 1986), vol. 1, 241–247.
61. Astarita, *The Continuity of Feudal Power*, 69.
62. Astarita, *The Continuity of Feudal Power*, 119–121.

63. Astarita, *The Continuity of Feudal Power*, 47–49. J. Nicholas Napoli's study of the Certosa di San Martino in Naples gives interesting perspective on this point. He discusses the European tradition of identifying munificence as a virtue, and then discusses how this manifested in charterhouses across Europe. While the charterhouse in Naples was certainly opulent, it did not have the same noble support as others in Europe. He identifies a boom in building in Naples in the late sixteenth century along with an influx of foreign artists. The revenue for this came mainly from the viceroys and religious orders, who wanted to establish their authority and control. While the barons certainly participated in this, they were not the driving force. J. Nicholas Napoli, *The Ethics of Ornament in Early Modern Naples: Fashioning the Certosa di San Martino* (London: Routledge, 2015), 60–62.

64. Astarita, *The Continuity of Feudal Power*, 87.
65. Astarita, *The Continuity of Feudal Power*, 82.
66. Astarita, *The Continuity of Feudal Power*, 84.
67. Astarita, *The Continuity of Feudal Power*, 92–94.
68. Astarita, *The Continuity of Feudal Power*, 95.
69. Astarita, *The Continuity of Feudal Power*, 95.
70. Astarita, *The Continuity of Feudal Power*, 47.
71. Astarita, *The Continuity of Feudal Power*, 162–164.
72. Astarita, *The Continuity of Feudal Power*, 166–171.
73. Astarita, *The Continuity of Feudal Power*, 186–187.
74. Astarita, *The Continuity of Feudal Power*, 140.
75. Villari, 153–170.
76. Astarita, *The Continuity of Feudal Power*, 130–131.
77. Astarita, *The Continuity of Feudal Power*, 155.
78. Villari, 136–137.
79. Villiari, 140.
80. Villiari, 137.
81. Villiari, 128.
82. Villiari, 129.
83. Villiari, 49–55.
84. Villiari, 140–144.
85. Rao, "The Feudal Question," 101.
86. Astarita, *The Continuity of Feudal Power*, 152–153.
87. Astarita, *The Continuity of Feudal Power*, 154–155.
88. Rao, "The Feudal Question," 97–98.
89. Rao, "The Feudal Question," 96.
90. Astarita, *Between Salt Water and Holy Water*, 93.
91. Rao, "The Feudal Question," 96; Astarita, *Between Salt Water and Holy Water*, 94.
92. Rao, "The Feudal Question," 101.
93. Rao, "The Feudal Question," 104–105.
94. Astarita, *Between Salt Water and Holy Water*, 196–198.

95. Lino Marini, *Pietro Giannone e il giannonismo a Napoli nel settecento: lo svolgimento della coscienza politica del ceto intellettuale del regno* (Bari: Gius. Laterza e Figli, 1950), 48.
96. Marini, 32–34.
97. Villani, "Il dibattito," 252–331.
98. Naddeo, "A Cosmopolitan in the Provinces."
99. Michelangelo Schipa, *Il Regno di Napoli descritto nel 1713 da P. M. Doria* (Napoli: Presso Luigi Pierro, 1899).
100. Schipa, *Il Regno di Napoli*, 35.
101. Schipa, *Il Regno di Napoli*, 35.
102. Schipa, *Il Regno di Napoli*, 36–37. Translation mine.
103. Schipa, *Il Regno di Napoli*, 40. "Venute nuove nazioni [francese ed austriaca], ad occupare il Regno, sparsero coll'esempio i propri costumi, senza creare nuove massime corrispondenti. Il Regno ne è divenuto un caos di sentimenti e di azioni in lotta, per cui non si ha virtù intera soddisfazione."
104. Schipa, *Il Regno di Napoli*, 42–43.
105. "Lo schivano con qualche sottigliezza della scienza cavalleresca." Schipa, *Il Regno di Napoli*, 42.
106. Schipa, *Il Regno di Napoli*, 42.
107. Schipa, *Il Regno di Napoli*, 43.
108. Schipa, *Il Regno di Napoli*, 44.
109. Schipa, *Il Regno di Napoli*, 45.
110. Badaloni, 149–163.
111. Francesco D'Andrea, *Avvertimenti ai nipoti*, ed. Imma Ascione (Jovene: Napoli, 1990).
112. Salvo Mastellone, *Francesco d'Andrea: politico e giurista (1648–1698): l'ascesa del ceto civile* (Florence: Casa Editrice Leo S. Olschki, 1969), 62.
113. Francesco D'Andrea, "Discorso politico intorno alla futura successione della Monarchia di Spagna composto dal regio consigliero Francesco d'Andrea," in Salvo Mastellone, *Francesco d'Andrea: politico e giurista (1648–1698): l'ascesa del ceto civile* (Firenze: Casa Editrice Leo S. Olschki, 1969), 183–199.
114. Mastellone, 12.
115. Mastellone, 13.
116. Villani, 281–286.
117. Villani, 260–263. Villani contrasts Genovesi's later writings with Montesquieu's *The Spirit of the Laws* to show how far he is willing to go. Genovesi is willing to say all the land must be gathered under the king but he does not actually attack the barons.
118. Marini, 38–43.
119. Giambatista Vico, *The Conspiracy of the Prince of Macchia and G.B. Vico*, trans. Giorgio Pinton (Amsterdam: Rodopi, 2013), 79.
120. Vico, *The Conspiracy*, 81. Naddeo goes into much more depth about the distinction Vico makes between the vile plebs and the others. Naddeo, 31.

121. Giambattista Vico, "Al padre de Vitry," in *Opere*, ed. Andrea Battistini (Milan: Mondadori, 1990), vol. 1, 326–329.

122. He had written about it in the *Conspiracy of the Prince of Macchia* but also more recently in the Oration on the death of Anna d'Aspermont. Giambattista Vico, "La guerra di successione di Spagna (dall'orazione in morte di Anna d'Aspermont, 1724)," in *Opere*, ed. Fausto Nicolini (Milan: Riccardo Ricciardi Editore, 1953), 987–993.

123. Vico, "Al padre de Vitry," 328.

124. Giambattista Vico, "Allocuzione per le nozze regali di Carlo di Borbone," trans. and ed. Gian Galeazzo Visconti, *Bollettino del Centro di Studi Vichiani* 16 (1986): 243–292. Visconti translates the oration into Italian. My translations are from Italian into English.

125. Andrea Battistini, "Cronologia," in Giambattista Vico, *Opere*, ed. Battistini, vol. 1, XLIX.

126. Vico, "Allocuzione," 275.

127. Vico, "Allocuzione," 267.

128. Vico, "Allocuzione," 247. My translation.

129. Vico, "Allocuzione," 281.

130. Vico, "Allocuzione," 281–283.

131. Vico, "Allocuzione," 279–281.

132. Vico, "Allocuzione," 283.

133. Vico, "Allocuzione," 275. The Royal Bourbon line descending from King Charles still exists, as does this military order, which still has a leader. The official website is realcasadiborbone.it/ordine-di-san-gennaro/.

134. The liquefication of the blood of San Gennaro became famous in 1631 when it coincided with lava from an erupting Vesuvius stopping outside of the city limits. The celebration of this liquefaction is still performed twice a year. Astarita, *Between Salt Water and Holy Water*, 145–147.

Chapter 5

1. Riccardo Caporali's *Heroes gentium* has been extremely influential on my thinking. His work is primarily a discussion of the evolution of ideas of law in Vico's works. He presents an important account of the way that the imaginative universals of the 1744 *New Science* depict the class struggle between the heroes and the plebeians. With good government, this should erupt into philosophic rule in the human age. He writes, "La sapienza dei filosofi sorge sulle ceneri del mito" (Caporali, 193). I am building on some of these ideas by connecting them to an epistemology of poetic wisdom.

2. My thinking about the relationship between morality and mute gestures originates in the thought of David W. Black, whose discussion influences this account. David W. Black, *Vico and Moral Perception* (New York: Peter Lang, 1997), 48–51, 63–68.

3. Søren Kierkegaard, *Fear and Trembling and Repetition*, trans. Howard V. Hong and Edna H. Hong (Princeton, NJ: Princeton University Press, 1983), 82.

4. Kierkegaard, 82.

5. This is discussed at length in Robert Jackall's classic study of ethics in the corporate world. His work has been very useful for my project because he describes the way in which business culture hides laws so that managers can have more control and flexibility over what happens. This use of secret law, though, creates a very oppressive hierarchical culture. It becomes very important that managers know how to control information and share ideas and evidence with just the right people. Many report that the reason they got promoted is not necessarily because of better results but because of their ability to play this corporate game. Robert Jackall, *Moral Mazes: The World of Corporate Managers*, updated ed. (Oxford: Oxford University Press, 2009).

6. Giuseppe Mazzotta argues that including Machiavelli with those who think history moves by fate represents a dramatic break from his position. Giuseppe Mazzotta, "Machiavelli and Vico," in *Machiavelli and the Discourse of Literature*, ed. Victoria Ann Kahn and Albert Russell Ascoli (Ithaca, NY: Cornell University Press, 1993), 259–274.

7. Niccolò Machiavelli, *The Prince*, in *Selected Political Writings*, trans. David Wootton (Indianapolis: Hackett, 1994), 53.

8. In a recent essay, it has been suggested that Machiavelli's images prefigure the way Vico relates symbols to power. It focuses on Machiavelli' image of the centaur but relates to other images in Machiavelli as well. Gennaro Maria Barbuto, "Vico e Machiavelli: il 'centauro' e il 'tuono,'" *Storia del pensiero politico* 2 (2013): 233–258.

9. Roberto Esposito's work focuses heavily on the relationship of fate in Machiavelli to divine providence in Vico. See Esposito, *La politica e la storia*.

10. Machiavelli, 54.

11. Machiavelli, 54.

12. John Locke, *Second Treatise on Government*, ed. C. B. Macpherson (Indianapolis: Hackett, 1980), par 136.

13. For additional background of the relationship between Vico and Locke, see Gustavo Costa, "Vico e Locke" *Giornale critic della filosofia italiana* 49 (1970): 344–361.

14. This is also in the 1730 *New Science* (NS30 126).

15. Verene, *Vico's Science of Imagination*, 64–65.

16. Naddeo discusses that Vidania still had positive things to write about Vico after this dispute and discusses further the effect the *Study Methods* had on his reputation. Naddeo, 89.

17. Vico, *Opere*, ed. Battistini, 37.

18. Naddeo, *Vico and Naples*, 88.

19. Naddeo, *Vico and Naples*, 84.

20. Naddeo, *Vico and Naples*, 87.

21. Descartes, 11.

22. Vico, *Opere*, ed. Battistini, vol. 2, 1351.

23. Caporali's *Heroes gentium* offers a very helpful discussion of how this idea flows through the evolution of Vico's thought. His work shows how Vico relates binary legal terms such as "public" and "private" to build his legal theory. He pays careful attention to the way it is demonstrated in Vico's biography of Antonio Carafa. His analysis of the *Universal Law* is particularly helpful. He argues that this work highlights the liberating power of the law. He shows how Vico both finds the ancient laws problematic and offers ways for philosophical understanding of metaphysics to transform them. He emphasizes throughout the work that the highest law for Vico is not one that is abstractly and literally defined but grounded in particular circumstances. Caporali, 140–143.

Chapter 6

1. Vico makes this point most explicitly in the unpublished "Practic of the *New Science*" (1406).

2. Barry B. Powell, *Classical Myth*, 8th ed. (New York: Pearson, 2015), 192. The most famous account of this story is found in Ovid's *Metamorphoses*, book 1, 438–567.

3. Lisa Maurizio, *Classical Mythology in Context* (Oxford: Oxford University Press, 2016), 379–381.

4. Rousseau broadly introduces this idea in the *First Discourse*, Rousseau, 7–10. He discusses this idea more specifically in the other two discourses; Rousseau, 62–63, 117.

5. For an overview of classical portrayals of Artemis/Diana, see Monford et al., 228–250.

6. Powell, 104.

7. Powell, 244. This myth may also found in Ovid's *Metamorphoses*, book 3, 138–241.

8. Hans-Georg Gadamer, *Truth and Method*, trans. Joel Weinsheimer and Donald G. Marshall (New York: Bloomsbury, 2004), 18–23.

9. Schaeffer, *Sensus Communis*, 120.

10. For example, Jürgen Habermas, *Knowledge and Human Interests*, trans. Jeremy J. Shapiro (Boston: Beacon Press, 1971), 148–149.

11. Schaeffer, *Sensus Communis*, 120.

12. Schaeffer, *Sensus Communis*, 125. On this point, see also Peter Carravetta's point about the myth's existence before method. Peter Carravetta, *The Elusive Hermes: Method, Discourse, Interpreting* (Aurora, CO: Davies Group, 2012), 72–87.

13. Schaeffer, *Sensus Communis*, 160.

14. John Schaeffer, *Giambattista Vico on Natural Law: Religion, Rhetoric, and Sensus Communis* (London: Routledge, 2019), 101.

15. Schaeffer, *Giambattista Vico on Natural Law*, 110–113.

16. Bergin and Fisch's translation seems legitimate and Vico does repeat the term *vulgar* to emphasize that the vulgar invented what are now called vulgar letters. In Italian, he writes, "Così la chiarissima istoria d'un tanto benefizio d'aver ritruovato le lettere alle nazioni, che per se stessa doveva esser romorosissima, Cadmo nasconde al gener'umano di Grecia dentro l'inviluppo di cotal favola, ch'è stata oscura fin a' tempi di Erasmo, per tener arcano al volgo uno sì grande ritruovato di volgare Sapienza, che da esso 'volgo' tali lettere furono dette 'volgari.'"

17. Remo Bodei, "Logics of Delusion," trans. David Webb and Brian Schroeder. In *Contemporary Italian Philosophy: Crossing the Borders of Ethics, Politics and Religion*, ed. Silvia Benso and Brian Schroeder (Albany: State University of New York Press, 2007), 199–209.

18. Bodei, 201.
19. Bodei, 200.
20. Bodei, 206.
21. Bodei, 207.
22. Bodei, 207.
23. Bodei, 208.
24. Rousseau, 71.

Chapter 7

1. Mark Lilla is an example of an author who lines up the gods of the greater gentes with political institutions without spending much time on poetic wisdom. Mark Lilla, *G. B. Vico: The Making of an Anti-Modern* (Cambridge, MA: Harvard University Press, 1993), 167, 183. Going the other way, while Max Horkheimer did not develop an extended account of Vico's poetic wisdom, he did recognize the connection between his theory of myth and the class struggle. I thank John Abromeit for helping me understand his account. Max Horkheimer, "Vico and Mythology," trans. Fred Dallmayr, *New Vico Studies* 5 (1987): 63–75. See John Abromeit, *Max Horkheimer and the Foundations of the Frankfurt School* (Cambridge: Cambridge University Press, 2013).

2. The classic statement of this is found in the dramatic opening of Foucault's *Discipline and Punish* where he contrasts the execution of a regicide to the modern prison. I am drawing on that as well as Roberto Esposito's discussion of the distinction in *Bíos*. Michel Foucault, *Discipline and Punish: The Birth of the Prison*, trans. Alan Sheridan (New York: Vintage Books, 1995); Roberto Esposito, *Bíos: Biopolitics and Philosophy*, trans. Timothy Campbell (Minneapolis: University of Minnesota Press, 2008), 27–35.

3. Céline Dauverd, *Church and State in Spanish Italy: Rituals and Legitimacy in the Kingdom of Naples* (Cambridge: Cambridge University Press, 2020), 103–107.

4. Dauverd, 185–189.

5. My inspiration for this point comes from Vico's fifth inaugural oration. He argues that his students should take the liberal arts seriously because it will make them more effective in war. Giambattista Vico, *On Humanistic Education (Six Inaugural Orations, 1699–1707)*, trans. Giorgio A. Pinton and Arthur W. Shippee (Ithaca: Cornell University Press, 1993), 108–122.

6. Battistini, 1631.

7. Battistini suggests that when Vico writes "as we have said" in paragraph 372 it refers back to this passage in paragraph 370. I read his description of the plebeians as slaves to emphasize the sharp distinction between the two classes. He catches himself, though, and adds "or precursors of slaves" because the plebeians could not have been slaves as I discussed earlier.

8. Roberto Esposito, *Living Thought: The Origins and Actuality of Italian Philosophy*, trans. Zakiya Hanafi (Stanford, CA: Stanford University Press, 2012), 76.

9. Timothy D. Harfield, *The Occasions of Community: Giambatttista Vico and the Concept of Society* (Eugene, OR: Wipf and Stock, 2017), 112. He actually cites paragraph 555, which I discussed in the opening of this section.

10. Harfield, 113.

11. Harfield, 115.

12. I take issue with Bergin and Fisch's translation of *più risentite* as "most impressive." The term "impressive" generally has a positive connotation, which I do not think the text implies. I suggest *risentite* here just means "notable or recorded characteristic" in the sense of most well-known trait of feudalism.

13. Villari, 22.

14. Astarita, *Between Salt Water and Holy Water*, 103.

15. Villari, 25.

16. Villari, 24.

17. Villari, 24.

18. Villari, 25.

19. VIllari, 216–218.

20. For information on the life of Ulpian, see Tony Honoré, *Ulpian: Pioneer of Human Rights*, 2nd ed. (Oxford: Oxford University Press, 2002).

21. He even adds a reference to Ulpian in paragraph 569 before the new section. This reference is not in the 1730 edition (216). According to the list of ancient sources in that work, Ulpian does not appear (654).

22. Battistini reports that while Ulpian does refer to naked pacts, he does not actually make this claim about human laws, though this may have been attributed to him during Vico's time. Vico's inaccuracy here I do not think really has an effect on my point.

23. As evidence of this, I point to a debate about feudalism in Tuscany. There is a discussion about how oppressive feudalism was for the peasants in that region. Given how few rebellions there were, it is thought it could not have been that bad. Part of the evidence for this is the ability of peasants to change lords. They discuss the way plagues created a labor shortage. Feudalism lasted much longer in Naples, so I think it was probably harsher there. But the

discussion in Tuscany shows the general point that the vassals could move while the nobles did not. Francesco Galassi, "Tuscans and Their Farms: The Economics of Share Tenancy in Fifteenth Century Florence," *Rivista di storia economica*, 9 (1992): 77–94; S. R. Epstein, "S.R. Epstein and Francesco L. Galassi: A Debate on Tuscans and Their Farms," *Rivista di storia economica* 12 (1994): 111–137; Gregory Hanlon, *Human Nature in Rural Tuscany: An Early Modern History* (New York: Palgrave Macmillan, 2007): 39–52.

24. Selwyn, *A Paradise Inhabited by Devils*.

25. As I discussed early, the issue of noble privilege over inheritances was a major issue in eighteenth-century Naples.

26. Locke, 20–21.

27. Robert Miner recognizes the significance of this discussion of Solon and Aesop. He sees how they are plebeian appropriations of poetic thought. He also emphasizes how they exist on the way to Socrates. Robert C. Miner, *Vico, Geneaologist of Modernity* (Notre Dame, IN: Notre Dame Press, 2002), 121–125.

Chapter 8

1. There are many discussions of this phenomenon in the United States. For example, Barbara Ehrenreich, *Bright-Sided: How the Relentless Promotion of Positive Thinking Has Undermined America* (New York: Metropolitan Books, 2009).

2. For an account of the influence of this idea on later readings of Vico, see Piperno, 27–36.

3. Brennan, 36–45.

4. Esposito has been working on Vico for a long time. For the origin of his though on this, see Roberto Esposito, *Vico e Rousseau e il moderno Stato borghese* (Bari: De Donato, 1976). His writing has been heavily influence by the work of Carillo who has helped me to understand his approach. Gennaro Carillo, *Vico: origine e geneaologia dell'ordine* (Naples: Editoriale Scientifica, 2000). De Simone's study on the subject has also helped me understand the influence of Vico on contemporary Italian thought. Antonio De Simone, *Il soggetto e la sovranità: la contingenza del vivente tra Vico e Agamben* (Napoli: Liguori Editore, 2012).

5. Esposito, *Living Thought*, 27.
6. Esposito, *Living Thought*, 72.
7. Esposito, *Living Thought*, 72.
8. Esposito, *Living Thought*, 73.
9. Esposito, *Living Thought*, 77.
10. Esposito, *Living Thought*, 77.
11. Esposito, *Living Thought*, 78.
12. Esposito, *Living Thought*, 80.
13. Esposito, *Living Thought*, 83.
14. Bodei, "Logics of Delusion," 202.

Bibliography

Abromeit, John. *Max Horkheimer and the Foundations of the Frankfurt School.* Cambridge: Cambridge University Press, 2013.
Aratus of Soli. *The Phaenomena.* Translated by G. R. Mair. In *Callimachus, Hymns and Epigrams, Lycophron, Aratus.* Loeb Classical Library, vol. 129. London: William Heinemann, 1921.
Arendt, Hannah. *Between Past and Future.* New York: Viking Press, 1961.
———. *The Human Condition.* 2nd ed. Chicago: University of Chicago Press, 1998.
Armstrong, Christopher Drew. "Myth and the New Science: Vico, Tiepolo, and the Language of the Optimates." *The Art Bulletin* 87, no. 4 (2005): 643–663.
Astarita, Tommaso. *Between Salt Water and Holy Water: A History of Southern Italy.* New York: W. W. Norton, 2005. Kindle edition.
———. *The Continuity of Feudal Power: The Caracciolo di Brienza in Spanish Naples.* Cambridge: Cambridge University Press, 1992.
Bacon, Francis. *Bacon's Essays and Wisdom of the Ancients.* Boston: Little, Brown and Company, 1884. Accessed on Google Books.
———. "Cogitata et visa de interpretatione naturae." In *The Works of Francis Bacon*, vol. 3, edited by James Spedding, Robert Leslie Ellis, Douglas, and Denon Heath, 588–620. Cambridge: Cambridge University Press, 2011.
Badaloni, Nicola. *Introduzione a G. B. Vico.* Milan: Feltrinelli, 1961.
Barbuto, Gennaro Maria. "Vico e Machiavelli: il 'centauro' e il 'tuono.'" *Storia del pensiero politico* 2 (2013): 233–258.
Battistini, Andrea. *Vico tra antichi e moderni.* Bologna: Il Mulino, 2004.
Beckett, Samuel. "Dante... Bruno. Vico.. Joyce." In *Our Exagmination Round His Factification for Incamination of Work in Progress*, edited by Samuel Beckett et al., 1–22. Norfolk, CT: New Directions, 1939.
Berlin, Isaiah. *Vico and Herder: Two Studies in the History of Ideas.* New York: Viking Press, 1976.
Bertucci, Paola. "The Architecture of Knowledge: Science, Collecting and Display in Eighteenth-Century Naples." In *New Approaches to Naples c.1500–c.1800: The Power of Place*, edited by Melissa Calaresu and Helen Hills, 149–174. Surrey: Ashgate, 2013.

Black, David W. *Vico and Moral Perception*. New York: Peter Lang, 1997.
Bobbio, Norberto. "Vico e la teoria delle forme di governo." *Bolletino del Centro di Studi Vichiani* 8 (1978): 5–27.
Bodei, Remo. "Logics of Delusion." Translated by David Webb and Brian Schroeder. In *Contemporary Italian Philosophy: Crossing the Borders of Ethics, Politics and Religion*, edited by Silvia Benso and Schroeder, 199–209. Albany: State University of New York Press, 2007.
Bordwell, David. *The Rhapsodes: How 1940s Critics Changed American Film Culture*. Chicago: University of Chicago Press, 2016.
Brennan, Timothy. *Borrowed Light: Vico, Hegel and the Colonies*. Stanford, CA: Stanford University Press, 2014.
Bull, Malcolm. *Inventing Falsehood, Making Truth: Vico and Neapolitan Painting*. Princeton, NJ: Princeton University Press, 2013.
Calabria, Antonio. *The Cost of Empire: The Finances of the Kingdom of Naples in the Time of Spanish Rule*. Cambridge: Cambridge University Press, 2002.
Campbell, Joseph. *The Power of Myth*. New York: Anchor Books, 1991.
Cantelli, Gianfranco. *Mente corpo linguaggio: saggio sull'interpretazione vichiana del mito*. Florence: Sanzoni, 1986.
Caporali, Riccardo. *Heroes gentium: sapienta e politica in Vico*. Bologna: Il Mulino, 1992.
Carillo, Gennaro. *Vico: origine e geneaologia dell'ordine*. Naples: Editoriale Scientifica, 2000.
Carravetta, Peter. *The Elusive Hermes: Method, Discourse, Interpreting*. Aurora, CO: The Davies Group, 2012.
Cassirer, Ernst. *Language and Myth*. Translated by Susanne K. Langer. New York: Harper and Brothers, 1946.
———. *The Myth of the State*. New Haven, CT: Yale University Press, 1974.
Ceserani, Giovanna. *Italy's Lost Greece: Magna Graecia and the Making of Modern Archaeology*. Oxford: Oxford University Press, 2012.
Chabot, Jacques. *Giambattista Vico: la raison du mythe*. Aix-en-Provence: Sarl Edisud, 2005.
Cochrane, Eric. "Southern Italy in the Age of the Spanish Viceroys: Some Recent Titles." *Journal of Modern History* 58, no. 1 (1986): 194–217.
Codrington, Robert Henry. *The Melanesians: Studies in their Anthropology and Folk-lore*. Oxford: Clarendon Press, 1891. Accessed on Google Books.
Coe, Michael. *Breaking the Maya Code*. London: Thames and Hudson, 2012.
Costa, Gustavo. "Perchè Vico pubblicò un capolavoro incompiuto? Considerazioni in margine a 'La Scienza Nuova' 1730." *Italica* 82, no. 3/4 (2005): 560–580.
———. "Vico e l'inquisizione." *Nouvelles de la république des lettres*, no. 2 (1999): 93–124.
———. "Vico e Locke." *Giornale critico della filosofia italiana* 49, no. July.Sep (1970): 344–361.
———. "Vico's *Salti Nitri* and the Origins of Pagan Civilization: The Alchemical Dimention of the New Science." *Rivista di studi italiani* 10 (1992): 1–11.

Cristofolini, Paolo. *Vico pagano e barbaro*. Pisa: Edizioni ETS, 2001.
Croce, Benedetto. *The Philosophy of Giambattista Vico*. Translated by R. G. Collingwood. New Brunswick, NJ: Transaction Publishers, 2002.
D'Andrea, Francesco. *Avvertimenti ai nipoti*. Edited by Imma Ascione. Jovene: Napoli, 1990.
———. "Discorso politico intorno alla futura successione della Monarchia di Spagna composto dal regio consigliero Francesco D'Andrea." In Salvo Mastellone, *Francesco D'Andrea: politico e giurista (1648–1698): l'ascesa del ceto civile*, 183–199. Firenze: Casa Editrice Leo S. Olschki, 1969.
Danesi, Marcel. *Vico, Metaphor, and the Origin of Language*. Bloomington: Indiana University Press, 1993.
Dauverd, Céline. *Church and State in Spanish Italy: Rituals and Legitimacy in the Kingdom of Naples*. Cambridge: Cambridge University Press, 2020.
Davis, Kathleen. "Sovereign Subjects, Feudal Law, and the Writing of History." *Journal of Medieval and Early Modern Studies* 36, no. 2 (2006): 223–261.
Descartes, René. *Discourse on Method and Meditations on First Philosophy*. Translated by Donald A. Cress. 4th ed. Indianapolis: Hackett, 1998.
De Simone, Antonio. *Il soggetto e la sovranità: la contingenza del vivente tra Vico e Agamben*. Napoli: Liguori Editore, 2012.
Doria, Paolo Mattia. *La vita civile di Paolo Mattia Doria con un trattato della educazione del principe*. 3rd ed. Naples: Angelo Vocola a Fontana Medina, 1729. Accessed on Google Books.
Ehrenreich, Barbara. *Bright-Sided: How the Relentless Promotion of Positive Thinking Has Undermined America*. New York: Metropolitan Books, 2009.
Elhauge, Einer. "How Italian Colors Guts Private Antitrust Enforcement by Replacing It with Ineffective Forms of Arbitration." *Fordham International Law Journal* 38, no. 3 (2015): 771–778.
Epstein, S. R. "S. R. Epstein and Francesco L. Galassi: A Debate on Tuscans and Their Farms." *Rivista di storia economica*, 12 (1994): 111–137.
Esposito, Roberto. *Bíos: Biopolitics and Philosophy*. Translated by Timothy Campbell. Minneapolis: University of Minnesota Press, 2008.
———. *Living Thought: The Origins and Actuality of Italian Philosophy*. Translated by Zakiya Hanafi. Stanford, CA: Stanford University Press, 2012. Kindle edition.
———. *La politica e la storia: Machiavelli e Vico*. Naples: Liguori, 1980.
———. *Vico e Rousseau e il moderno Stato borghese*. Bari: De Donato, 1976.
Fabiani, Paolo. *La filosofia dell'immaginazione in Vico e Malebranche*. Florence: Firenze University Press, 2002.
Finetti, G. F. *Difesa dell'autorità della Sacra Scittura contro Giambattista Vico*. Edited by Benedetto Croce. Bari: Laterza, 1936.
Fisch, Max Harold. "The Academy of the Investigators." In *Science, Medicine and History: Essays on the Evolution of Scientific Thought and Medical Practice Written in Honour of Charles Singer*, edited by E. Ashworth Underwood, 521–563. London: Oxford University Press, 1953.

Foucault, Michel. *Discipline and Punish: The Birth of the Prison*. Translated by Alan Sheridan. New York: Vintage Books, 1995.
Gadamer, Hans-Georg. *Truth and Method*. Translated by Joel Weinsheimer and Donald G. Marshall. New York: Bloomsbury, 2004.
Galassi, Francesco. "Tuscans and Their Farms: The Economics of Share Tenancy in Fifteenth Century Florence." *Rivista di storia economica* 9 (1992): 77–94.
Giarrizzo, Giuseppe. *Vico: la politica e la storia*. Naples: Guida Editori, 1981.
Goetsch, James Robert Jr. *Vico's Axioms: The Geometry of the Human World*. New Haven: Yale University Press, 1995.
Gravina, Gianvincenzo. *Del governo civile di Roma*. Napoli: Stamperia Francese, 1828. Accessed on Google Books; I also consulted the original manuscript at the Biblioteca Casanatense MS. 343.
———. *Della ragion poetica*. Rome: Francesco Gonzaga, 1708. Accessed on Google Books.
———. *Delle antiche favole*. Rome: Antonio de Rossi, 1696. Accessed on Google Books.
Habermas, Jürgen. *Knowledge and Human Interests*. Translated by Jeremy J. Shapiro. Boston: Beacon Press, 1971.
Haddock, B. A. "Vico's 'Discovery of the True Homer': A Case-Study in Historical Reconstruction." *Journal of the History of Ideas* 40, no. 4 (1979): 583–602.
Hanlon, Gregory. *Human Nature in Rural Tuscany: An Early Modern History*. New York: Palgrave Macmillan, 2007.
Harfield, Timothy D. *The Occasions of Community: Giambattista Vico and the Concept of Society*. Eugene, OR: Wipf and Stock, 2017.
Herdt, Jennifer A. *Putting on Virtue: The Legacy of the Splendid Vices*. Chicago: University of Chicago Press, 2008.
Hirschman, Albert O. *The Passions and the Interests: Political Arguments for Capitalism before Its Triumph*. Princeton, NJ: Princeton University Press, 2013. Kindle edition.
Hobbs, Catherine L. *Rhetoric on the Margins of Modernity: Vico, Condillac, Monboddo*. Carbondale: Southern Illinois University Press, 2002.
Horkheimer, Max. "Vico and Mythology." Translated by Fred Dallmayr. *New Vico Studies* 5 (1987): 63–75.
Honoré, Tony. *Ulpian: Pioneer of Human Rights*. 2nd ed. Oxford: Oxford University Press, 2002.
Hösle, Vittorio. *Vico's New Science of the Intersubjective World*. Translated by Francis R. Hittinger IV. Notre Dame, IN: University of Notre Dame Press, 2016.
Hotman, François. *Franco-Gallia: or, an Account of the Ancient Free State of France, and Most Other Parts of Europe Before the Loss of Their Liberties*. Translated by Robert Molesworth. 2nd ed. London: Edward Valentine, 1721. Accessed on Project Gutenberg.
Hume, David. *The Natural History of Religion*. Edited by H. E. Root. Stanford, CA: Stanford University Press, 1957.

Imbruglia, Girolamo. "Enlightenment in Eighteenth-Century Naples." In *Naples in the Eighteenth Century: The Birth and Death of a Nation State*, edited by Girolamo Imbruglia, 70–94. Cambridge: Cambridge University Press, 2000.
Jackall, Robert. *Moral Mazes: The World of Corporate Managers*. Updated ed. Oxford: Oxford University Press, 2009.
Kelley, Donald R. *François Hotman: A Revolutionary's Ordeal*. Princeton, NJ: Princeton University Press, 1973.
Kierkegaard, Søren. *Fear and Trembling and Repetition*. Translated by Howard V. Hong and Edna H. Hong. Princeton, NJ: Princeton University Press, 1983.
Lee, Maurice. *Overwhelmed: Literature Aesthetics and the Nineteenth-Century Information Revolution*. Princeton, NJ: Princeton University Press, 2019.
Lepre, Aurelio. *Storia del mezzogiorno in Italia*. 2 vols. Naples: Liguori, 1986.
Levi, Carlo. *Christ Stopped at Eboli: The Story of a Year*. Translated by Frances Frenaye. New York: Picador, 2020.
Lilla, Mark. *G. B. Vico: The Making of an Anti-Modern*. Cambridge, MA: Harvard University Press, 1993.
Locke, John. *Second Treatise on Government*. Edited by C. B. Macpherson. Indianapolis: Hackett, 1980.
Löwith, Karl. "'Verum et factum convertuntur': le premesse teologiche del principio di Vico e le lore consequenze secolari." Translated by Anna Lucia Künkler Giavotto. In *Omaggio a Vico*, edited by Pietro Piovani, 73–112. Naples: A Morano, 1968.
Machiavelli, Niccolò. *The Prince*. In *Selected Political Writings*, translated by David Wootton. Indianapolis: Hackett, 1994.
Mali, Joseph. *The Legacy of Vico in Modern Cultural History: From Jules Michelet to Isaiah Berlin*. Cambridge: Cambridge University Press, 2012.
Mandeville, Bernard. *The Fable of the Bees and Other Writings*. Edited by E. J. Hundert. Indianapolis: Hackett, 1997.
Marcus, Nancy du Bois. *Vico and Plato*. New York: Peter Lang, 2011.
Marini, Lino. *Pietro Giannone e il giannonismo a Napoli nel settecento: lo svolgimento della coscienza politica del ceto intellettuale del regno*. Bari: Gius. Laterza e Figli, 1950.
Marino, John A. *Becoming Neapolitan: Citizen Culture in Baroque Naples*. Baltimore: Johns Hopkins University Press, 2011.
———. "The Rural World in Italy under Spanish Rule." In *Spain in Italy: Politics, Society, and Religion 1500–1700*, edited by Thomas J. Dandelet and John Marino, 405–429. Leiden: Brill, 2007.
Marshall, David L. *Vico and the Transformation of Rhetoric in Early Modern Europe*. Cambridge: Cambridge University Press, 2010.
Mastellone, Salvo. *Francesco d'Andrea: politico e giurista (1648–1698): l'ascesa del ceto civile*. Florence: Casa Editrice Leo S. Olschki, 1969.
Maurizio, Lisa. *Classical Mythology in Context*. Oxford: Oxford University Press, 2016.

Mawyer, Alexander. "The State of Mana, the Mana of the State." In *New Mana: Transformations of a Classic Concept in Pacific Languages and Cultures*, edited by Matt Tomlinson and Ty P. Kawika Tengan, 203–236. Canberra: ANU Press, 2016.

Mazzotta, Giuseppe. "Machiavelli and Vico." In *Machiavelli and the Discourse of Literature*. Edited by Victoria Ann Kahn and Albert Russell Ascoli, 259–274. Ithaca, NY: Cornell University Press, 1993.

———. *The New Map of the World: The Poetic Philosophy of Giambattista Vico*. Princeton, NJ: Princeton University Press, 1999.

Mercer, Christina. "The Contextualist Revolution in Early Modern Philosophy." *Journal of the History of Philosophy* 57, no. 3 (2019): 529–548.

Miner, Robert C. *Vico, Genealogist of Modernity*. Notre Dame, IN: Notre Dame Press, 2002.

Mondolfo, Rodolfo. *Il 'verum-factum' prima di Vico*. Naples: Guida, 1969.

Mooney, Michael. *Vico in the Tradition of Rhetoric*. Princeton, NJ: Princeton University Press, 1984.

Morford, Mark, Robert J. Lenardon, and Michael Sham. *Classical Mythology*. 10th ed. Oxford: Oxford University Press, 2014.

Musi, Aurilio. "The Kingdom of Naples in the Spanish Imperial System." Translated by Lydia G. Cochrane. In *Spain in Italy: Politics, Society, and Religion 1500–1700*, edited by Thomas J. Dandelet and John Marino, 73–99. Leiden: BRILL, 2007.

Naddeo, Barbara Ann. "A Cosmopolitan in the Provinces: G. M. Galanti, Geography, and Enlightenment Europe." *Modern Intellectual History* 30, no. 1 (2013): 1–26.

———. *Vico and Naples: The Urban Origins of Modern Social Theory*. Ithaca, NY: Cornell University Press, 2011.

Nancy, Jean-Luc. "Myth Interrupted." Translated by Peter Connor. In *The Inoperative Community*, 43–70. Minneapolis: University of Minnesota Press, 1991.

Napoli, J. Nicholas. *The Ethics of Ornament in Early Modern Europe: Fashioning the Certosa di San Martino*. London: Routledge, 2015.

Nicolini, Fausto, "I Rocca e la dimora del Vico a Vatolla." In *Autobiografia di Giambattista Vico*, edited by Fausto Nicolini, 197–208. Napoli: Istituto Italiano per gli Studi Storici, 1992.

———. "Il Vico nella vita domestica." In Giambattista Vico, *Opere*, edited by Fausto Nicolini, 94–106. Milan: Ricciardi, 1953.

Norman, Larry F. *The Shock of the Ancient: Literature and History in Early Modern France*. Chicago: University of Chicago Press, 2011.

Nuzzo, Enrico. *Tra religione e prudenza: la 'filosofia practica' di Giambattista Vico*. Rome: Edizioni di Storia e Letteratura, 2007.

Otto, Rudolf. *The Idea of the Holy: An Inquiry into the Non-Rational Factor in the Idea of the Divine and Its Relation to the Rational*. Translated by John W. Harvey. Oxford: Oxford University Press, 1958.

Pareyson, Luigi. *L'esperienza artistica: saggi di storia dell'estetica*. Milan: Marzorati, 1974.

Pico della Mirandola, Giovanni. *On the Dignity of Man*. Translated by Charles Glenn Wallis. Indianapolis: Hackett, 1998.
Piovani, Pietro. "Vico senza Hegel." In *Omaggio a Vico*, edited by Pietro Piovani, 553–586. Napoli: A Morano, 1968.
Piperno, Martina. *Rebuilding Post-Revolutionary Italy: Leopardi and Vico's 'New Science.'* Oxford University Studies in the Enlightenment. Oxford: Voltaire Foundation, 2018.
Pocock, J. G. A. *The Ancient Constitution and Feudal Law: A Study of English Historical Thought in the Seventeenth Century: A Reissue with a Retrospect.* Cambridge: Cambridge University Press, 1987.
Powell, Barry B. *Classical Myth*. 8th ed. New York: Pearson, 2015.
Pufendorf, Samuel. *On the Duty of Man and Citizen*. Translated by Michael Silverthorne. Cambridge: Cambridge University Press, 1991.
Quiggin, John. "John Locke's Road to Serfdom." *Jacobin*, December 17, 2021, www.jacobinmag.com/2015/10/locke-classical-liberalism-treatise-nozick-constitution/.
Rao, Anna Maria. "The Feudal Question, Judicial Systems and the Enlightenment." In *Naples in the Eighteenth Century: The Birth and Death of a Nation State*, edited by Girolamo Imbruglia, 95–118. Cambridge, Cambridge University Press, 2000.
———. "'Missed Opportunities' in the History of Naples." In *New Approaches to Naples c. 1500–1800: The Power of Place*, ed. Melissa Calaresu and Helen Hills, 203–224. Surrey: Ashgate, 2013.
Ratzinger, Joseph, Cardinal. *Introduction to Christianity*. Translated by J. R. Foster. San Francisco: Ignatius Press, 1990.
Reynolds, Susan. *Fiefs and Vassals: The Medieval Evidence Reinterpreted*. Oxford: Oxford University Press, 2006.
Robertson, John. *The Case for the Enlightenment: Scotland and Naples 1680–1760*. Cambridge: Cambridge University Press, 2005.
———. "Sacred History and Political Thought: Neapolitan Responses to the Problem of Sociability after Hobbes." *Historical Journal* 56, no. 1 (2013): 1–29.
Romano, Damiano. *L'origine della giurisprudenza romana contro alla moderna opinione del Signor D. Gio:Battista Vico*. Naples: Domenic Roselli, 1744. Accessed on Google Books.
Rossi, Paolo. "Chi sono i contemporanei di Vico?" *Rivista di filosofia* 72 (1981): 51–82.
———. *The Dark Abyss of Time: The History of the Earth and the History of Nations from Hooke to Vico*. Translated by Lydia G. Cochrane. Chicago: University of Chicago Press, 1984.
Rousseau, Jean-Jacques. *The Basic Political Writings*. 2nd ed. Translated by Donald A. Cress. Indianapolis: Hackett, 2011.
San Mauro, Carla. *Gianvincenzo Gravina giurista e politico*. Milan: Franco Angeli, 2006.
Schaeffer, John D. *Giambattista Vico on Natural Law: Religion, Rhetoric, and Sensus Communis*. London: Routledge, 2019.

———. *Sensus Communis: Vico, Rhetoric, and the Limits of Relativism*. Durham, NC: Duke University Press, 1990.
Schipa, Michelangelo. *Il Regno di Napoli descritto nel 1713 da P. M. Doria*. Napoli: Presso Luigi Pierro, 1899.
Selwyn, Jennifer D. *A Paradise Inhabited by Devils: The Jesuits' Civilizing Mission in Early Modern Naples*. London: Routledge, 2004.
Sen, Amartya. "Does Business Ethics Make Economic Sense?" *Business Ethics Quarterly* 3, no. 1 (1993): 45–54.
———. *The Idea of Justice*. Cambridge: Harvard University Press, 2009.
Shotter, John. "Vico, (Particular) Imaginative Universals, Divine Providence, and the Imaginative Work Needed in Relating Oneself to Others." In *Giambattista Vico and the New Psychological Science*, edited by Luca Tateo, 113–150. New Brunswick, NJ: Transaction Publishers, 2017.
Spinoza, Baruch. *The Essential Spinoza: Ethics and Related Writings*. Edited by Michael L. Morgan, translated by Samuel Shirley. Indianapolis: Hackett, 2006.
Stapelbroek, Koen. *Love, Self-Deceit and Money: Commerce and Morality in the Early Neapolitan Enlightenment*. Toronto: University of Toronto Press, 2008.
Tarver, Erin C. *The I in Team: Sports Fandom and the Reproduction of Identity*. Chicago: University of Chicago Press, 2017.
Tateo, Luca. "Giambattista Vico and the Psychological Imagination." *Culture & Psychology* 41, no. 2 (2015): 1–15.
Trabant, Jürgen. *Vico's New Science of Ancient Signs: A Study of Sematology*. Translated by Sean Ward. London: Routledge, 2004.
Trombetta, Vincenzo. "Torquato Tasso nell'editoria napolitana dal seicento all'ottocento." *Tricontre: teoria testo traduzione* 11 (May 2019): 175–201.
Tyler, Parker. *Magic and Myth of the Movies*. New York: Simon and Schuster, 1970.
Verene, Donald Phillip. *The New Art of Autobiography: An Essay on the Life of Giambattista Vico Written by Himself*. Oxford: Clarendon Press, 1991.
———. "Vico's 'Ignota Latebat.'" *New Vico Studies* 5 (1987): 77–98.
———. *Vico's Science of Imagination*. Ithaca, NY: Cornell University Press, 1981.
Vico, Giambattista. "Allocuzione per le nozze regali di Carlo di Borbone." Translated and edited by Gian Galeazzo Visconti. *Bollettino del Centro di Studi Vichiani* 16 (1986): 243–292.
———. *Autobiografia*. Edited by Fausto Nicolini. Bologna: Società Editrice Il Mulino, 1992.
———. *The Autobiography of Giambattista Vico*. Translated by Max Harold Fisch and Thomas Goddard Bergin. Ithaca, NY: Cornell University Press, 1983.
———. *The Conspiracy of the Prince of Macchia and G. B. Vico*. Translated by Giorgio A. Pinton. Amsterdam: Rodopi, 2013.
———. "The Discovery of the True Dante." Translated by Christina M. Mazzoni. In *Critical Essays on Dante*, edited by Giuseppe Mazzotta, 258–260. Boston: G. K. Hall, 1991.
———. "Dissertations [from the *Universal Law*]." Translated by John D. Schaeffer. *New Vico Studies* 24 (2006): 1–80.

———. *The First New Science*. Edited and translated by Leon Pompa. Cambridge: Cambridge University Press, 2002.

———. "Giambattista Vico's 'Reprehension of the Metaphysics of René Descartes, Benedict Spinoza, and John Locke': An Addition to the *New Science*." Translation and commentary by Donald Phillip Verene. *New Vico Studies* 8 (1990): 2–18.

———. *The New Science of Giambattista Vico: Unabridged Translation of the Third Edition (1744) with the addition of the "Practice of the New Science."* Translated by Max Harold Fisch and Thomas Goddard Bergin. Ithaca, NY: Cornell University Press, 1986.

———. *On Humanistic Education (Six Inaugural Orations 1699–1707): From the Definitive Latin Text, Introduction and Notes of Gian Galeazzo Visconti*. Translated by Giorgio A. Pinton and Arthur W. Shippee. Ithaca, NY: Cornell University Press, 1993.

———. "On the Constancy of the Jurisprudent (including *Notae*)." Translated by John D. Schaeffer. *New Vico Studies* 23 (2005).

———. "On the Heroic Mind." Translated by Elizabeth Sewell and Anthony C. Sirignano. In *Vico and Contemporary Thought*, edited by Giorgio Tagliacozzo, Michael Mooney, and Donald Phillip Verene, 228–245. Atlantic Highlands, NJ: Humanities Press, 1976.

———. *On the Most Ancient Wisdom of the Italians Unearthed from the Origins of the Ancient Language Including the Disputation with the "Giornale de' letterati d'Italia."* Translated by L. M. Palmer. Ithaca, NY: Cornell University Press, 1988.

———. "On the One Principle and One End of Universal Law." Translated by John D. Schaeffer. *New Vico Studies* 21 (2003).

———. *On the Study Methods of Our Time*. Translated by Elio Gianturco. Ithaca, NY: Cornell University Press, 1990.

———. *Opere*. Edited by Fausto Nicolini. Milan: Riccardo Ricciardi Editore, 1953.

———. *Opere*. 2 volumes. Edited by Andrea Battistini. Milan: Arnaldo Mondadori, 1990.

———. *Opere giuridiche*. Edited by Paolo Cristofolini. Florence: C. Sansoni, 1974.

———. *La scienza nuova 1730*. Edited by Paolo Cristofolini and Manuela Sanna. Naples: Alfredo Guida Editore, 2004.

———. "Vico's Reply to the False Book Notice: The *Vici Vindiciae*." Translation and commentary by Donald Phillip Verene. *New Vico Studies* 24 (2006): 129–175.

Villani, Pasquale. "Il dibattito sulla feudalità nel regno di Napoli dal Genovesi al Canosa." *Saggi e ricerche sul settecento* (1968): 252–331.

———. *Feudalità, riforme, capitalismo agrario: panorama di storia sociale italiana tra sette e ottocento*. Bari: Editori Laterza, 1968.

Villari, Rosario. *The Revolt of Naples*. Translated by James Newell and John A. Marino. Cambridge: Polity Press, 1993.

Visceglia, Maria Antonietta. *Identità sociali: la nobiltà napolitana nella prima età moderna*. Milan: Edizioni Unicopli, 1998.

Whalley, George. "Coleridge and Vico." In *Giambattista Vico: An International Symposium*. Edited by Giorgio Tagliacozzo and Hayden V. White, 225–244. Baltimore: Johns Hopkins University Press, 1969.

Wood, Ellen Meiksins. *The Origins of Capitalism: A Longer View*. London: Verso, 2002. Kindle edition.

Index

Achilles: example of heroic morality, 32, 91–94; example of imaginative universal, 100–102
aequitas civilis: definition, 175; replaced by *aequum bonum* 183; Roman Republic 175–83; value for reform, 202–205
aequitas naturalis: definition, 172; Roman Empire 175–83
Aesop: plebeian imaginative universal, 269–71
Agamemnon: example of heroic morality, 91–94; sacrifice of Iphigenia, 210
American Express Co. v Italian Colors Restaurant, 7
Antonomasia, 95–99
Apollo: imaginative universal of noble superiority, 197–201, 252–54, 277, 290
Arendt, Hannah, 22–23
Astarita, Tommaso: Baronial judicial privileges, 133–35; Caracciolo di Brienza, 135–38; defensive orientation of the barons, 135–38; history of Neapolitan feudalism, 131–34
Austrian administration of Naples, 126, 143–49, 168–69, 173–74
Avatar, 13
Autobiography: portrayal of *Ancient Wisdom* and *Study Methods*, 168–70; Vico and Neapolitan intellectual culture, 43–47; Vico's birth year, 19n31; *see also* Vatolla

Bacon, Francis: inductive method, 27–28, 48; myth of Actaeon, 9–10; *Novum Organum*, 169
Badaloni, Nicola: intellectual culture of Naples, 24
banditry, 141, 145–46, 239
barbarism after fall of Roman Empire, 120–22
barbarism of reflection: danger, 204–205, 278; forestalling, 183–85; safety net for civilization, 38–39, 57, 289–90
baronial authority: analogy to Roman republic, 173–75; banditry, 141, 145–46, 239; connected to imaginative universals, 215–23; control of reproduction, 138; defensive posture, 232–39; judicial privileges, 132–35; reluctance to innovate, 135–37, 188–89; right of life and death, 228
Battistini, Andrea: intellectual debates in Nales, 24; legal fiction, 177; Vergil, 84; Voss, 93–100
Beckett, Samuel: essay on Vico, 51–53
Berlin, Isaiah: portrayal of Vico as anti-Enlightenment, 47–48;

Berlin, Isaiah *(continued)*
  portrayal of Vico as isolated,
  42–43; Renaissance idea of
  microcosm, 49–51
Berlusconi, Silvio: privatization of
  highway system, 6
blazonry: *see* coats of arms
Bobbio, Norberto: forms of
  government in Vico 38, 86–87
Bodei, Remo: overinclusion, 213–15;
  stages of maturity, 290
Bodin, Jean: primacy of monarchy,
  124
Brennan, Timothy: interpretative
  approach, 14; cross-cultural reading
  of Vico, 285

Cadmus: overinclusion, 210–13
Calabria, Antonio, 125–26
Caloprese, Gregorio: Friend of Vico,
  44
Campbell, Joseph, 13
Cantelli, Gianfranco: imaginative
  universals, 77, 83
Caporali, Riccardo: on barbarism of
  reflection, 38–39, 57
Caracciolo di Brienza, 135–38
Cassirer, Ernst: on mana, 14–15
Chabot, Jacques, 83
Charles of Bourbon, King of Naples:
  appoints Vico historiographer, 42;
  becomes king, 126; relation to
  barons, 143, 184, 230–31, 275;
  wedding, 151–52
Christ Stoped at Eboli: 18, 259–60
coats of arms: 1725 *New Science*,
  88; connection to land, 236–39;
  connection to Mercury, 264–65
Conversano, Count, 140–41, 166
class distinction: difference in
  contracts, 255–58; giants, 240–42;
  see *famuli*
Codrington, Robert Henry: on mana,
  14–15

conceit of nations, 9, 12n16, 30–31,
  34, 211–12
conceit of scholars: definition,
  9; heroism, 90–91, 208–209;
  misunderstanding of monarchy,
  164–65, 222; problem for
  interpreting myth, 10–15, 51, 200,
  270; state of nature, 193–94
Conspiracy of the Prince of Macchia:
  critique of nobility, 149–50
Costa, Gustavo: nitrous salts, 54
Cristofolini, Paolo, 84
Croce, Benedetto, 43, 120, 123
Cybele, imaginative universal of
  protecting the fields, 224–25

Danesi, Marcel, 83–84
d'Andrea, Francesco: critic of
  Baronial rule, 147–48
d'Ausilio, Domenico: friend of Vico, 44
Descartes, René: method, 28–29,
  171; method applied to theoretical
  world, 119; opponent of Vico, 22,
  169; reference in *New Science*, 45;
  reference in 'Reprehension,' 46;
  sensation as judgment 100
Diana: Actaeon, 9–10, 200–201;
  imaginative universal for protecting
  springs, 200–202, 224–25, 263
Divine Providence: class conflict,
  264–65; definition, 33; directing
  first settlements, 221–23;
  mechanism of history, 64–65;
  purpose, 291; relation to human
  agency, 33–39
Doria, Paolo Mattia: critic of Spanish
  rule, 144–46; Friend of Vico, 44;
  La Vita Civilie, 46; separation of
  Hebrew and pagan tradition, 119

Egyptian hieroglyphs, 10–11
Enlightenment thinker, 20; member
  of the *luminosi*, 24; personal
  relationship to Vico, 44–45

Epicureans: critiqued by Vico, 46, 58
Esposito, Roberto: ages of history, 85; divide between pagans and Hebrews, 287–88; giants, 241, 288–90
euhemerism, 97–99

Fabiani, Paolo: Malebranche's influence on Vico, 25–26
famuli: definition, 31, 111, 124; ignorant of noble imaginative universals, 186–88; invention of naked imaginative universals, 252–58; motive for entering asylums, 242–47; tamed in the asylums, 165–67, 193; not slaves, 242; not sons of earth, 201; rebellion, 262–64; separation from noble families, 216–17
feudalism: definition, 129–30; development in Naples, 129–35; independent fiefs, 166–68; independence of vassals, 277–79; natural state of humanity, 6, 56–57; Neapolitan debate, 20–21, 143–48; persistence in eighteenth-century Naples, 125–27; origin of feudal contracts, 258–60; *see* baronial judicial authority
Finetti, G. F.: critic of Vico, 20, 119–20
Flood of Noah: barbarism, 30, 120; creation of Jove, 69; Pico della Mirandola, 50; separation of traditions, 119, 206, 240, 287

Gadamer, Hans-Georg: *sensus communis*, 203–209
Getting things right constraint: Interpretative Strategy of Christina Mercer, 21–24, 41, 48, 53, 195, 271, 275
giants: corrupt state of humanity, 36, 55–57; problem of human sociability, 68–69; tamed by thunder, 72–74; two types, 240–42; Vico's evidence, 54–55
Giarrizzo, Giuseppe: age of heroes, 32; Vico's and Naples, 2–4, 12–13, 122
Giannone, Pietro: critic of Church, 143–44, 148; relation to Vico 44–45
Godfrey; imaginative universal, 103–105
Gravina, Gianvincenzo: *Del Governo civile di Roma*, 12; *Della Ragion Poetica*, 46, 89–94, 115
Grotius, Hugo: natural law theory 35, 193, 243; legal reform 207

Harfield, Timothy D.: *The Occasions of Community*, 242–45
Hebrew tradition: Esposito's interpretation, 287–89; separation from pagans, 54–55, 119–22, 206–207
Hercules: executor of Juno, 216–20; imaginative universal, 94–97; Vulcan, 224
Herdt, Jennifer A: providence in modern philosophy, 34–35
Hirschman, Albert O.: modern debate about capitalism, 63; providence in Vico, 64–65, 75, 186
Hobbes, Thomas: defense of territory, 233; epicurean, 58
Homer: Vico's discovery of the True Homer, 19–20; depiction of heroic morality, 32, 90–94, 117–18, in Gravina, 89–91
Hotman, François: *Franco-Gallia*, 12; natural law tradition, 47
Hume, David: defense of capitalism, 63; origin of pagan religion, 67

ideal eternal history: definition, 30–31; and human agency, 32–39;

ideal eternal history *(coontinued)* starting point, 55; Roman model, 120–22

Il traditore: 155–56

imaginative universals: definition, 98–100; Vico's discovery, 11–12, 82; response to problem of human sociability, 76–77; as means of communication 77–78; as precise paradigm, 101–108, 187–88; Godfrey example, 103–105; as practice of self-discipline, 108–12; poverty of speech, 112–18, 188; connection to Roman law, 186–92; expansion, 209–15; naked, 250–51; harsh portrayal, 273–75; *see also* individual deities and heroes

Jove: as omnipresent, 15–17; as thunder, 54; as response to problem of human sociability, 69–79; as basis for class conflict, 86–88; connection to three principles, 195–96

judgment of Paris, 97–99

Jung, Carl: collective unconscious, 13

Juno: imaginative universal of familial judicial authority, 215–19

Kierkegaard, Søren: ethical and tragic hero, 156–59

Lafitau, Joseph-François: conceit of nations, 12n16

Livy: Roman law, 26, 191; Roman kings, 164–65; on plebeian connection to the land, 201, 242, 254

legal profession: dominance in modern Naples, 142–43; history of ancient Rome, 172–74; instrument of reform, 147–49, 172–80, 279–84; legal fictions, 177–78, 191, 258

Locke, John: mentioned in 'Reprehension,' 46; support of aristocracy, 123–24; on secret laws, 162–63, 184

Machiavelli, Niccolò: in *New Science*, 46; on secret laws, 161–62, 181–82

Malebranche, Nicholas, 25–26

Mali, Joseph: commentary on Berlin, 49

mana: 14–15

Mandeville, Bernard: defender of capitalism, 63; 'Origin of Moral Virtue,' 66–67; fame in early society, 245

Mars: imaginative universal to defend religion, 232–42; naked Mars, 251; wounded by Minerva, 262–64

Marshall, David L: importance of poetic wisdom, 85

Masaniello's Revolt, 135, 139

Mawyer, Alexander: 14

Mayan glyphs, 11

Melville, Herman: *Billy Budd*, 173–75

Menosky, Joe: 'Darmok' author, 105–106

Mercer, Christina: 21–24, 41, 48, 53

Mercury: imaginative universal giving laws to plebeians, 264–68

Minerva: inscription, 42–43; imaginative universal of class conflict, 260–63

monarchy: superiority to oligarchy, 4, 56–57, 86, 148–49, 174, 182–84, 202; developed after oligarchy, 124, 164–66; instability of early monarchies, 132; early Roman Kings, 164–65; Constantine as paradigm, 261–62; potential for corruption, 261, 278

Monty Python, 94

myth, Vico's interpretation: not esoteric language, 8; sources of textual corruption, 8–9; against the Romantic interpretation, 12–16

Naddeo, Barbara Ann: Vico on class and urbanization, 26–27; call for reform in *Study Methods*, 170–71
Naples: intellectual culture, 18–21, 35–36, 46–47; Spanish rule, 125–29, 144–48; history of feudalism, 130–38; rise of legal class, 142–44; Vico's portrayal, 2–4, 122, 149–52, 274–54; Vico's ideas for reform, 174–77, 268–70, 278–81; *see also* baronial authority, Charles of Bourbon, Masaniello's Revolt, Starce, Giovan Vincenzo
Neptune: imaginative universal of heroic raids, 290
New Science (1725): poetic characters, 88–90; depiction of heroic morality, 90–92; poverty of speech, 116–18, 209–11; depiction of Cadmus, 210–12
New Science (1730): evidence of conceit of nations, 12n16; omission of Godfrey, 103–104; short discussion of natural contracts, 257–58
New Science (1744): practical agenda, 33–39, 64–66, 86–88, 231, 280–84; method of proof, 27–29; frontispiece, 57–58; three principles, 195–97; depiction of Cadmus, 211–13; Contracts sealed by consent, 257–59; *see also* imaginative universals
New Science in Negative Form, 45–47
Nicole, Pierre: on grace, 35–36; referenced by Doria, 46
Norman, Larry F., 47–48
Nuzzo, Enrico: influence of *saggezza moderna* in Naples, 35–36

oligarchy: first form of government, 6, 164–68; animosity to plebs, 228–29; *see* baronial authority

Oration for the wedding of King Charles of Bourbon, 151–52
overinclusion: Bodei's discussion, 213–15; example of Cadmus, 210–13; example of Cybele, 224–25

Palazzo Tarsia: Vico's inscription, 42–43
Parasite: as representation of class in myth, 17–18
Pareyson, Luigi, 76–77, 83
philanthropy, 267–68
Pico della Mirandola, 19, 50
Piperno, Martina: *Rebuilding Post-Revolutionary Italy*, 19; on poetic wisdom, 84
Plato: interpretation of myth, 9–10, 15, 169, 219; source for Vico, 23, 44, 48; confrontation with heroic mentality, 157–58
principles of *New Science*: religion, marriage and burial, 195–96; *see also* particular deities
problem of human sociability: definition, 65–66; *famuli* entering asylums, 242–47; first settlements, 220–21; Mandeville's response, 67; Rousseau's response, 67–68; Vico's use of thunder as response, 69–79

Ratzinger, Cardinal Joseph, 22–23
Renzi, Matteo: privatization of Italian Post Office, 6
Reynolds, Susan: early history of feudalism, 130–31
Romano, Damiano: critic of Vico, 20, 43, 46
Roman Civilization: greatest in history, 37–38; originally aristocracy, 164–68; rule of Constantine, 120, 262–63
Roman law: census of Servius Tullius, 229–30; connection to poetic wisdom, 268–70; history, 172–73,

Roman law *(continued)*
  260–62; legal fictions, 177–78;
  Publilian Law, 86–87, 229–30;
  origin in poetry, 189–92
Rossi, Paolo: "Chi sono i
  contemporanei di Vico?," 24
Rousseau, Jean-Jacques: *amour
  propre*, 198–99; class distinction,
  267, 275–76; problem of human
  sociability, 67–68, 221; state of
  nature, 58–60

Saturn: imaginative universal of sown
  fields, 224
Schaeffer, John: discussion of *sensus
  communis*, 202–209
Solon: plebeian imaginative
  universal, 269–71
Spanish administration of Naples,
  124–29, 139–49
Spinoza, Baruch: *conatus*, 74–75;
  mentioned in 'Reprehension,' 46;
  self-interest, 276–77
stoic, 58
Stapelboeck, Koen: Neapolitan
  debate on commerce, 20
Star Trek: The Next Generation
  'Darmok': imaginative universal,
  105–108, 194
Starce, Giovan Vincenzo, 248–50
state of nature: Vico's idea, 55–61;
  Rousseau's idea, 58–60
Study Methods: importance of ancient
  methods, 28, 48, 82–83; Italian
  philosophy, 285; legal reform,
  202, 261–62; public and private
  property, 280; secret laws, 168–86
Stoics: critiqued by Vico, 46, 58

Tarver, Erin C.: fandom and self-
  discipline, 108–102
Tasso, Torquato, 103–104
togati: legal class in Naples, 142–44

Thrice-Great Hermes; imaginative
  universal, 101–102
Tyler, Parker, 13

Ulpian: plebeian imaginative
  universal, 258–59, 271
Ulysses: heroic morality, 91–93, 187,
  246; poetic character, 100–102
Universal Law: ideal eternal history,
  30–31, poverty of speech, 115–16,
  praised by Giannone, 44

Vatolla: Vico's stay, 43–44, 125
Venus: naked imaginative universal
  of plebeian marriage, 254–56;
  noble imaginative universal of civil
  beauty, 252–54
Verene, Donald Phillip; on
  frontispiece, 57–58, on imaginative
  universals, 77, 81–82, 84, 168–
  69
Vergil: Homeric battles 246; Jove,
  15–16, 70; myth of Rome, 84
Vesta: *see* Cybele
Voss, Gerhard Johann: imaginative
  universals, 93–100
verum-factum principle: *Autobiography*,
  169; evidence of Vico's historicism,
  22–23; idea of human as
  microcosm, 49–51; interpretation
  of language, 10
Villari, Rosario; Spanish
  administration, 126–30, 139–41;
  Giovan Vincenzo Starce, 248–50
Vulcan, imaginative universal of
  clearing the fields, 224

Walburga of Saxony, Maria Amalia:
  wedding to Charles of Bourbon,
  151–52
witches, 273–74
Wood, Ellen Meiksins; *The Origin of
  Capitalism*, 63

www.ingramcontent.com/pod-product-compliance
Lightning Source LLC
Chambersburg PA
CBHW031704230426
43668CB00006B/106